STUDIES IN BRETHREN

Bible and Theology
in the Brethren

Cover Key

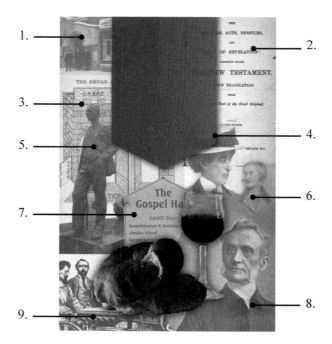

1. The British and Foreign Bible Society offices in Latvia during the Soviet era, from 'Bicentenary of The Bible Society in Latvia', <http://www.bibelesbiedriba.lv/en/Blog?id=7>, accessed 1 Nov. 2018.

2. The title page of J. N. Darby's *New Translation* (^{1}1868; ^{4}1904).

3. 'The Broad and Narrow Way', in Hy Pickering, *How to Make and Show 100 Object Lessons* (London, [1922]), 11.

4. 'The Lady of Luanza' [i.e. Grace Crawford, née Tilsley], in Dan Crawford, *Back to the Long Grass: My Link with Livingstone* (London, [1922]), facing p.130.

5. 'Victor Danielsen' by Hans Pauli Olsen (2008), Fuglafjørður, Eysturoy, Faeroe Islands (photograph, Neil Dickson, Dec. 2012).

6. Agnes ('Nan') Ramage (1918–2005), *c.*1932, member of Balmore Road Gospel Hall, Glasgow, private collection.

7. Notice board, Gospel Hall, Dingwall, Ross and Cromarty (photograph, Neil Dickson, July 2011).

8. George Müller, in G. Fred Bergin (ed.), *Autobiography of George Müller* (London, 1905), frontispiece.

9. George Lawrence (on the right), and his printing press, Caldes, Barcelona, 1877, in *The Quarterly Record of the Trinitarian Bible Society*, No. 68 (Jan. 1877), 3.

STUDIES IN BRETHREN HISTORY

Bible and Theology in the Brethren

Edited by
Neil Dickson
T. J. Marinello

2018

Copyright © Neil T. R. Dickson, T. J. Marinello, and the Contributors 2018

First published 2018 by Brethren Archivists and Historians Network

Brethren Archivists and Historians Network
1/1 99 Wilton Street, Glasgow G20 6RD

23 22 21 20 19 18   8 7 6 5 4 3 2 1

The right of Neil Dickson and T. J. Marinello to be identified as the Editors of this Work has been asserted by them in accordance with the Copyright, Designs and Patents Act 1988.

All rights reserved. No part of this publication may be reproduced, stored in a retrieval system, or transmitted, in any form or by any means, electronic, mechanical, photocopying, recording or otherwise, without the prior permission of the publisher or a license permitting restricted copying. In the UK such licenses are issued by the Copyright Licensing Agency, 90 Tottenham Court Road, London W1P 9HE.

British Library Cataloguing in Publication Data
A catalogue record for this book is available from the British Library

ISBN 978-0-9570177-9-5

Printed by Bell & Bain Ltd, Glasgow

STUDIES IN BRETHREN HISTORY

Series Editors

Neil Dickson   Convener, Brethren Archivists and Historians Network

Tim Grass   Senior Research Fellow, Spurgeon's College, London

T. J. Marinello   Professor of Systematic and Historical Theology,
                   Tyndale Theological Seminary, the Netherlands.

Series Preface

Brethren are a small but significant component of evangelical Christianity. Having their origins in Britain and Ireland in the 1830s, there are now congregations of Open Brethren in at least 155 countries in the world, a tribute to the missionary zeal of the movement. No exact statistics are available, but probably today there are at least 30,800 congregations worldwide, attended on any Sunday by about 2.12 million people. Their influence on evangelicalism has been significant through their ecclesiology, distinctive eschatological interpretations, their principle that Christian workers can and should 'live by faith', and the significant influence that individuals nurtured in the Brethren have had in other groupings and in parachurch bodies.

From the beginning, the Brethren had a strong strain of academic scholarship and this flourished again in the decades following the Second World War. The Brethren Archivists and Historians Network (BAHN) is heir to this. Its main manifestations are an annual publication (*Brethren Historical Review*) and a biennial International Brethren History Conference (IBHC). Studies in Brethren History aims to make readily accessible the product of the conferences, as well as other scholarly works on subjects related to the movement's history, practice, and thought. Volumes are published as material becomes available and voluntary editorial resources and money permit.

Membership of BAHN is open to anyone with a significant interest in the history of the Brethren movement in all its manifestations. More details are available on the website (www.brethrenhistory.org).

Contents

Abbreviations xi
Contributors xiii
Introduction 1

Part 1: Introduction

Chapter 1 5
Bible Reading Through the History of the Church
JAMES M. HOUSTON

Part 2: The Bible and the Brethren

Chapter 2 17
Worn Symbols: Women's Hair and Head Coverings in Brethren History
NEIL DICKSON

Chapter 3 39
Samuel Prideaux Tregelles: A Nineteenth-Century Evangelical
Apology for New Testament Textual Criticism
DIRK JONGKIND

Chapter 4 51
In the World and of It Too:
Bible or Culture? The Role of Women in Brethren Assemblies 1880–1940
BETH DICKSON

Chapter 4 69
'You have to go by Scripture':
Taylorite Exclusive Brethren, the Bible, and the Holy Spirit
ROGER N. HOLDEN

Chapter 5 87
The Brethren and the Bible in Central Africa
KOVINA MUTENDA

Chapter 7 95
Brethren and Biblical Scholarship in Britain in the Twentieth Century
ALAN MILLARD

Chapter 8 107
Victor Danielsen (1894–1961): Teacher—Translator—Evangelist
TÓRÐUR JÓANSSON

Chapter 9 115
    Wilfred James Wiseman (1891–1970): The Bible Society and the Brethren
    IAN RANDALL

Chapter 10 133
    F. F. Bruce and the Bible
    TIM GRASS

Chapter 11 145
    Use of the Bible among the New Brethren in Flanders
    T. J. MARINELLO

Part 3: Theology and the Brethren

Chapter 12 157
    The Brethren and Systematic Theology:
    Outspoken Objectors; Unconscious Practitioners
    MARK R. STEVENSON

Chapter 13 171
    The Theology of George Müller
    NEIL SUMMERTON

Appendix 201
    Other examples of George Müller's gospel presentation

Chapter 14 203
    William Kelly and his Mystic Spirituality
    ANNE-LOUISE CRITCHLOW

Chapter 15 213
    A Darbyite Mystic: Frances Bevan (1827–1909)
    NEIL DICKSON

Chapter 16 249
    'I do not know that there is such a term in Scripture as eternal sonship':
    James Taylor and the Question of the Eternal Son
    ROGER N. HOLDEN

    Bibliography 275

TABLES

Table 1. Dahl and Danielsen: parallel translations into Faeroese 113

Table 2. Comparative comments on Faeroese translations 113

Abbreviations

BAHN	Brethren Archivists and Historians Network
BAHNR	*Brethren Archivists and Historians Review*
BDEB	*The Blackwell Dictionary of Evangelical Biography*, (ed.) Donald M. Lewis, 2 vols. (Oxford, 1995)
BHR	*Brethren Historical Review*
CBA	Christian Brethren Archive, the University of Manchester Library
CW	[J. N. Darby], *The Collected Writings of J. N. Darby*, 34 vols. [(ed.) W. Kelly] (?1867–1900)]
EQ	*Evangelical Quarterly*
H	*The Harvester*
IBHC	International Brethren History Conference
ODNB	*Oxford Dictionary of National Biography*, (eds.) H. C. G. Matthew and Brian Harrison, 60 vols. (Oxford, 2004)
SCH	Studies in Church History
SCHT	Studies in Christian History and Thought
SEHT	Studies in Evangelical Life and Thought
SBH	Studies in Brethren History
SKI	Scriptural Knowledge Institution
W	*The Witness*

Contributors

Anne-Louise Critchlow is an ordained Anglican chaplain for the Abbeyfield Society in the South West. She was awarded a Ph.D. by the University of Manchester for her research on the spirituality of William Kelly.

Beth Dickson is a Senior Lecturer in Education in the School of Education, University of Glasgow. As well as writing on teacher education, she is also interested in spirituality and has contributed 'Brethren Spirituality in the Mid-twentieth Century' to *Culture, Spirituality, and the Brethren*, a previous volume in this series.

Neil Dickson is the convenor of BAHN, editor of the *Brethren Historical Review*, and a contributing editor to Studies in Brethren History.

Roger N. Holden was born into an Exclusive Brethren family, and after spending many years among the Society of Friends (Quakers), he is now a member of a Reformed Baptist Church; although employed professionally in computing, is also academically qualified in history and spends much of his 'spare time' in a variety of historical pursuits.

James M. Houston is Emeritus Professor of Spiritual Theology and founding Principal of Regent College, Vancouver. He has written of edited over fifty books, most recently co-editing with Dr Jens Zimmerman, *Sources of the Christian Self: A Cultural History of Christian Identity* (2018).

Tórður Jóansson (now retired) was a teacher, lecturer, journalist, and writer in the Faeroes, and is the author of *Brethren in the Faroes* (2012).

Dirk Jongkind is Academic Vice Principal of Tyndale House, Cambridge, and Fellow of St Edmund's College. He is the editor of the *Greek New Testament Produced at Tyndale House* (2017), which started from the work of Tregelles.

T. J. Marinello is Professor of Systematic and Historical Theology at Tyndale Theological Seminary, the Netherlands, author of *New Brethren in Flanders* (2013), and co-editor of the Tyndale Theological Seminary Theses Series.

Alan Millard is Emeritus Rankin Professor of Hebrew and Ancient Semitic Languages, the University of Liverpool. He worked in the British Museum, was Librarian at Tyndale House, Cambridge, then taught at the University of Liverpool for thirty-three years. His publications include academic editions of Babylonian and Aramaic documents and many studies of the world of the Bible, including *Discoveries from Bible Times* (1997) and *Reading and Writing in the Time of Jesus* (2000).

Kovina Mutenda holds an M.Phil. from the University of Wales. He has written two books: *A History of the Christian Brethren in Zambia* (2002) and *The Christian Brethren in Zambia: their Origins, Beliefs and Practices* (2016).

Ian Randall is a Research Associate, the Cambridge Centre for Christianity Worldwide. He has written a range of books on the history of evangelical movements.

Mark R. Stevenson is Professor of Bible and Theology at Emmaus Bible College in Dubuque, Iowa. His University of Wales doctoral thesis was published as *The Doctrines of Grace in an Unexpected Place: Calvinistic Soteriology in Nineteenth-Century Brethren Thought* (2017).

Neil Summerton is an historian by training, was a civil servant, and led a research unit at Mansfield College, Oxford, on environmental ethics. He has written extensively in the areas between public policy, ethics, theology, and history.

Introduction

When Francis Newman first encountered J. N. Darby he discovered that he had 'had practically given up all reading except that of the Bible'.[1] The Brethren were 'people of the book', often of one book only. As Professor James Houston recalls in his contribution to this volume, his Glanton Brethren father was 'always reading the Bible' (chapter 1). It was not just individually that the Bible was read intensively, but 'Bible readings', conversational in nature, were for the Brethren, according to W. B. Neatby, writing at the turn of the nineteenth century, 'their principal recreation'.[2] Animated discussions of the Bible on Sunday evenings in the homes of the members were nothing unusual, even in the secular West.

The papers collected in this volume, with one exception, were presented at International Brethren History Conferences at Pilgrim Hall, East Sussex, on 15–17 July 2013, and Bishop Woodford House, Ely, on 6–8 July 2015. As the section on the Bible in this book demonstrates, Brethren individuals invested considerable energies in textual and biblical criticism (chapters 3, 7, and 10); translating the Scriptures (chapters 6 and 8); disseminating it through the Bible Society or in other ways (chapters 6, 8, and 9); and in using it pointedly as an evangelistic tool (chapter 11). Because the Bible was regarded, as Dirk Jongkind shows in his chapter on Samuel Prideaux Tregelles, 'to be verbally the word of God', it was most usually read in a literal manner (chapters 2 and 3). A particularly determined application of this principle was among the Taylor Exclusive connexion, as Roger Holden shows. There was no biblical text stating plainly the orthodox dogma that the Second Person of the Trinity was eternally the Son, and so the doctrine was rejected (chapter 16). Particularly problematic in the Open Brethren became those New Testament passages which related to women. First-century cultural customs or prescriptions for the primitive Church were mapped directly onto the twentieth. This was a difficulty as the role of women in Western society began to change during the nineteenth century and as fashions in hair and clothes altered with increasing rapidity. Most Brethren commentators resisted the culture shift in roles, while a small but influential minority of Open Brethren felt the Scriptures had been misapplied (chapters 2 and 4). Additionally, in the later twentieth century, some Open Brethren, like the wider evangelical world, became aware of hermeneutics which altered perceptions of biblical interpretation, although more conservative voices resisted this (chapter 2). Tim Grass, in a paper read at Tilsley College in Motherwell, demonstrates that probably the greatest of all Brethren biblical scholars, Frederick Fyvie Bruce, developed in the mid-twentieth century a more nuanced approach to matters of inspiration and interpretation (chapter 10), a path many Brethren were to follow into the present century. A more surprising turn was taken by the Taylor Brethren in applying Scripture to the new conditions of late modernity. They came to accept that

---

1. Francis William Newman, *Phases of Faith; Or Passages from the History of My Creed* (1850; rev. edn., 1853; Rationalist Press Assoc. edn., London, 1907), 26.
2. William Blair Neatby, *A History of the Plymouth Brethren* (2nd edn., London, [1902]), 278.

the Spirit speaks directly in the assembly though approved ministers, opening up as yet unrevealed fresh precepts (chapters 2 and 5).

The section on theology is slighter. This is largely because of the exigencies of organizing a conference and then progressing the papers to publication. It is also because, as Mark Stevenson demonstrates in his contribution, the Brethren 'vigorously opposed' systematic theology (chapter 12). It is one of the regrets of the editors that there is no chapter on dispensationalism. This system of biblical interpretation was undoubtedly the most distinctive contribution by the Brethren to transatlantic evangelical theology. The reader will have to look elsewhere for the historical relationship of the movement to this scheme of biblical interpretation, but thankfully there is no shortage of fine works which correct this deficiency.[3] Other aspects of theology are not absent, however, from the present volume. The Calvinist soteriology of the early movement is treated in chapters on George Müller and Frances Bevan, as is their very Brethren stress on sanctification entailing separation (chapters 13 and 15). Müller was also famed in Britain, and through his global tours, worldwide, as the preeminent contemporary practitioner of 'living by faith', the most distinctive Brethren contribution to international mission. It was a more immediate form of faith, as was the quasi-mystical theology that is to be found in both William Kelly and Frances Bevan, perhaps an aspect of Brethren theology that has been too little studied, but is represented by two chapters here (chapters 14 and 15). As has already been noticed, the Taylorite Exclusives, too, made their own distinctive mark on theology with their rejection of Eternal Sonship (chapter 16).

It is hoped that the collected papers, which are arranged chronologically, will stimulate further thought and research, as well as acting as an introduction to some of the ways in which Bible and theology have been understood and used within the Brethren movement.

Neil Dickson and T. J. Marinello

---

3. For the historical relations of dispensationalism and Brethren, see: Clarence Bass, *Backgrounds to Dispensationalism: Its Historical Genesis and Ecclesiastical Implications* (Grand Rapids, MI, 1960); Ernest R. Sandeen, *The Roots of Fundamentalism: British and American Millenarianism 1800–1930* (Chicago, 1970), 59–80; Mark S. Sweetnam, 'Tensions in Dispensational Eschatology', in Kenneth G. C. Newport and Crawford Gribben (eds.), *Expecting the End: Millennialism in Social and Historical Context* (Waco, TX, 2006), 173–92; Crawford Gribben and Mark S. Sweetnam, 'J. N. Darby and the Irish Origins of Dispensationalism', *Journal of the Evangelical Theological Society*, 52/3, (2009), 569–77; Thomas Ice, 'Left Behind and the Dispensational Tradition', in Crawford Gribben and Mark S. Sweetnam (eds.), *Left Behind and the Evangelical Imagination*, The Bible in the Modern World, 35 (Sheffield, 2011), 132–54; David J. Macleod, 'Walter Scott: A Link in Dispensationalism between Darby and Scofield', in Tim Grass (ed.), *Witness in Many Lands: Leadership and Outreach among the Brethren* (SBH: Troon, 2013), 111–31; Crawford Gribben, 'John N. Darby, Dispensational Eschatology, and the Formation of Trans-Atlantic Evangelicalism', *Schweizerische Zeitschrift für Religions—und Kulturgeschichte*, 110 (2016), 99–109; Donald Harman Akenson, *Discovering the End of Time: Irish Evangelicals in the Age of Daniel O'Connell* (Montreal, 2016), 445–56; id., *Exporting the Rapture: John Nelson Darby and the Victorian Conquest of North-American Evangelicalism* (New York, 2018), 5, 45–9, 280–1, 292.

PART 1

Introduction

CHAPTER 1

Bible Reading Through the History of the Church

James M. Houston

Bible reading is about God's speech; indeed speech originates from God.[1] This then, is a very ambitious survey to make, which I am only stimulated to do for two reasons. As the Apostle John reminds his readers, in the cycle of life, he calls on 'children' to start living in basic trust, which is implied in the experience that 'their sins are forgiven'. Now they can relate to God with no relational barrier of sin separating them and God. 'Young men' are those individuated by the Holy Spirit to be given a strong hope, with an identity 'in Christ', to 'overcome the evil one'. 'Fathers' are those at the end of the cycle of life, who have lived long enough to see many cultural changes, but through them all, to experience the eternal reality of the Father's love, knowing personally 'Him that is from the beginning' (1 John 1:12–14). This cosmic wide-angled lens helps us all to see the whole sweep of history within 'the Kingdom of his dear Son', under his sovereignty of love. Faith, Hope, and Love, these remain, says Paul in 1 Corinthians 13:13, 'but the greatest of these is love'. This is simply what 'reading the Bible' is all about.

    The second reason that stimulates me to prepare this survey is that I am actually co-editing with a colleague, Jens Zimmerman, a humanist philosopher, a major work on 'Sources of Christian Identity in the History of the Church', with some fifty contributors. We are covering many pivotal changes of western civilization in our survey. Detailed chronology is impossible, other than to identify significant markers. It is like visiting a public display in the British Museum of the biblical artefacts in the history of the Bible and making brief comments about each exhibit.[2]

Our personal Bible-reading narrative

I begin then with our own heritage in the movement of the Plymouth Brethren. As a child I still remember well, going to 'the Prayer Meeting' every Wednesday evening with my father, where we had Bible readings. In Sunday morning worship we had the same spontaneous readings, while at the annual conferences, where there was an 'open platform', often those who were the least equipped to expound were always fast on their feet to reach the pulpit—constrained by the Spirit of course—to exhaust the assembly's patience, time after time. Then at home, my father was 'always reading the Bible', despite my protests that there were lots of wonderful classics that fascinated me to read, in my reaction to my father's entire concentration on the Bible.

---

  1. Eugen Rosenstock-Huessy, *The Origin of Speech* (Norwich, VT, 1981), xv.
  2. Christopher de Hamel, *The Book: a History of the Bible* (New York, 2005), ix and *passim*.

Later, I learnt that John Muir, son of a lay preacher father who had joined the Disciples of Christ in Dunbar in East Lothian, felt so isolated by 'father always reading his Bible', that he reacted strongly to commune romantically with nature rather than with Nature's God.[3] Ironically, secular environmentalists today are unaware that their icon John Muir developed his passion for Nature through having a 'father-always-reading-his-Bible' upbringing. I, too, have to confess, I have never read the Bible innocently like many adult converts; it came only through long emotional struggles and in a series of prolonged, redemptive changes of attitudes. Thus I have sometimes counselled those with a neurotic devotional life to take a sabbatical from their practices of prayer and Bible reading, to begin freshly and in a redemptive re-reading! Our survey will show us that time and again Bible reading has been corrupted, requiring repentance and redemptive new approaches.

Orality as the cultural source of the Old Testament

While *homo sapiens* has been around for 30–60,000 years, the earliest script dates from only 6,000 years ago. The alphabet was a Semitic invention, the Canaanites being the first to use alphabet about 3,600 years ago.[4] Oral sounds transcribed into letters were originally a huge number; the ancient Babylonians of 1,600 BC had over 26,000, while ancient Chinese letters, possibly originating in the cracked bones of animal sacrifices with the exercise of necromancy, were also vast. Even as late as 1946, the Japanese tried to reduce the number of writing symbols to 1,850, of which 881 were to be taught in elementary schools![5] This may explain the hierarchical caste systems of ancient religions, where below the emperor were the scholars who alone were skilled to write and read. In contrast, the Hebrew language has had only twenty-two letters, simple for a child to learn, so that which God revealed in the Scriptures is a simple message even for 'the babes and sucklings', as well as for the uneducated and poor. As we shall see later, the great scholar Augustine of Hippo was amazed by both the simplicity as well as the depth of the biblical Scriptures.

In the oral cultures of the ancient world, literacy was only represented by a very small percentage of the population; possibly five per cent in ancient Mesopotamia and perhaps seven per cent in Egypt. Their scribes were the aristocrats by birth and sworn to secrecy in the practice of their arts.[6] Later the biblical prophets were to attack this system, as Jeremiah 8:8–9 does: 'How can you say , "We are sages, and we possess the Torah of Yahweh"? Assuredly, the deceitful pen of the scribes has turned it into a deception! The sages shall be put to shame, they shall be dismayed and caught. For they have rejected the word of Yahweh, so what kind of wisdom is theirs?'[7]

The distinctives of Old Testament reading

Very different were the Israelite Levites or scribes, teaching together and not esoterically. According to Nehemiah 8, Ezra was a *soper* or scholar scribe; he was assisted by a

---

3. Ferenc Morton Szasz, *Religion in the Modern American West* (Tucson, AZ, 2000), 65–7.
4. Joseph Naveh, *Origins of the Alphabet* (Jerusalem, 1994), 8.
5. Naveh, *Origins of the Alphabet*, 11.
6. Karel van der Toorn, *Scribal Culture and the Making of the Hebrew Bible* (Cambridge, MA, 2007), 65–9.
7. Unless noted otherwise, all Bible and Classical translations are by the author.

group of Levites together in his public reading of the Torah in the Temple: 'The Levites explained the Torah to the people, while the people remained in their places. And they read from the scroll, from the Torah of God, interpreting it and clarifying its meaning ; so they understood the meaning' (Neh. 8:7–8). No esoteric knowledge and no hierarchy of rank marked the corporate identity of the biblical writers. For all creation, as Genesis 1 describes it, is expressive of the speech of God, *creatio per verbum*.

Before Augustine ever wrote his *Confessions*, the confessions of Jeremiah were a unique document in the ancient world, since only the biblical God himself used 'speech' to communicate with his creature, man. So Jeremiah's calling is like that of Moses where God enters a dialogue with his servant (Jer. 1:4–10; 1:11–19). A biblical or real prophet then, is always pursuing an inner dialogue with God as the mark of bearing the *imago dei*. Biblical texts were for the ear to hear and to obey, not for the eyes to speculate about. Isaiah 29:18 predicts a time when the deaf also, 'shall hear the words of the scroll'. In Habakkuk 2:2, the prophet is commanded 'to write down the prophecy, and inscribe it clearly on tablets, so that a [town] crier may run with it'.

The books of the Old Testament may be more accurately conceived, then, as archival collections of sayings, composed late in Israel's history, possibly when they were already in captivity and exile. For the term '*biblia*' is a Greek word for 'the books', echoing from an age when the seventy-two Greek translators laboured to transcribe the Hebrew text into the books of the Old Testament just two to three centuries before Christ. The late prophet Daniel speaks of 'the books' (Dan. 9:2) of the Old Testament, while 1 Maccabees 12:9, speaks of 'the holy books'. The Hebrew word *qara* 'to read', literally means 'to cry, to speak out loud'. In Joshua 1:8, the urge to read assiduously is translated as 'not to allow the word to escape from his mouth'. The book we call Ecclesiastes clearly expresses this oral culture, for Qoheleth—meaning 'assembly speaker'—adverts to his writings as really being his speech.[8] 'Besides being wise, Qoheleth taught the people knowledge, and weighed, scrutinized, and arranged many proverbs. Qoheleth sought to find many pleasing sayings, and to write down true sayings with precision' (Eccles. 12:9–10).

In two very suggestive works, *Orality and Literacy* and *The Presence of the Word*, Walter Ong has contrasted the psychodynamics of speech and reading. He notes how sound interiorizes our consciousness, whereas light and reading diffuse us externally. Sound incorporates, requiring harmony, whereas sight isolates, generating curiosity.[9] The great biblical text then that converted the pagan rhetorician Augustine was 2 Corinthians 3:6, 'The letter kills, the spirit [literally, breath on which rides the spoken word] gives life'. In his friend's holiday villa at Cassiacum, he heard a child's voice, 'take up and read', and so conjoined hearing and reading, to unite them for the rest of his life.

Later Jewish Bible reading

By the exile, the Jews were being unwittingly prepared by the invention of the heavy book scrolls in the synagogues to abolish animal sacrifices. This occurred with the destruction of the temple in AD 67, distinguishing even further the Jews from the pagans, as now being solely 'the people of the Book'; the Torah was replacing the temple worship of animal

---

8. van der Toorn, *Scribal Culture and the Making of the Hebrew Bible*, 101.
9. Walter J. Ong, *Orality and Literacy* (London, 1982), 71–5.

sacrifice. Training their children to become 'Torah educated' then became far more ethical than any animal worshipper could ever have been. It was indeed the prelude to the advent of Christ, who came, as the epistle to the Hebrews so profoundly discourses, to displace all other sacrifices for sin.

Firstly, not all the books of the Old Testament were equally authoritative. The Torah, as the first five books of the Pentateuch, had special sanctity, the only books which the break-away sect of the Samaritans venerated. The Prophets were accorded a second level of sacred importance, and the remainder called 'the Hagiographa' had even less sanctity. Luke in his Gospel speaks of the life of Jesus having been predicted by the Law of Moses, the Prophets, and the Psalms (being the opening book of the Hagiographa). The distinction was maintained later in using the heavy and expensive scroll only for the Torah, in the synagogue worship, right into the late middle ages. If all the Old Testament was contained in a synagogue scroll, there were 'carpet pages' or full-page decorative tapestries, like lifting layers of differing carpets, to be read and studied differently.[10]

The second Jewish element in 'reading the Bible', was that in the development of the classic rabbinic culture from the second to the tenth centuries AD, a fluidity of questionable authority arose from it being 'a mixed' society, both oral and literate or written forms. Its orality remained archaic, but its textual interpretation kept changing with the cultural succession of rabbinical scholars, so that now their voices were authoritative as human interpreters.[11] This continues to the present time. A New York rabbi interpreting Psalm 22 today can solemnly announce the psalmist is describing his condition as suffering from diarrhoea and a fibrillating heart on his death bed, for 'all his bones were out of joint'.[12] This may be an extreme example, but it expresses the Jewish ambiguity of biblical authority and of its liberal reading. The use of scrolls for individual Bible books also meant there was no particular chronological order, in contrast to the later Christian use of the codex.[13]

The innovation of the codex

I suspect that the cultural change of wider use of papyri rather than of animal skins intensified with the abolition of animal sacrifices after AD 67. But the use of papyrus reed had earlier spread in antiquity from the Nile delta throughout the Mediterranean world of trade. This was utilized by classical culture later as the innovative source of the codex or book format.

Early Christianity, as transcribed by Paul's epistles or the Gospels, were read in bundles of hinged pages, still quite heavy to carry. But Paul is already speaking in prison of his need of 'the parchments'. This was a later innovation in the use of 'vellum', a light animal

---

10. de Hamel, *The Bible*, 44–5.

11. Yaakov Elman and Israel Gershoni, *Transmitting Jewish Traditions: Orality, Textuality and Cultural Diffusion* (New Haven, CT, 2000).

12. Martin Samuel Cohen, *Our Haven and our Strength: The Book of Psalms* (New York, 2004), 62.

13. John Barton, 'The Significance of a Fixed Canon of the Hebrew Bible', in Magne Sæbø (ed.), *Hebrew Bible/Old Testament: the History of Its Interpretation*, vol. 1, *From the Beginnings to the Middle Ages (until 1300)*, pt. 1, *Antiquity* (Gottingen, 1996), 81.

skin soaked, scraped, and dried under tension. For the early Christians, this became a new form of 'Bible reading', personal and easily portable, not like the synagogue scrolls. Such heavy and expensive book scrolls remained inevitably chained to the synagogue worship—memorized, but also repeatedly interpreted and copied by scribes, all within a deeply institutionalized religion.

We are still ignorant of a great deal of early Christian biblical scholarship, other than again to stress that the life of a scholar required great financial resources under rich patronage to collect priceless scrolls in a large library, with hired scribes to reproduce texts. It was not for monks in the desert until, as we shall see, Jerome made this possible later.

Bible reading, from the end of the first century until the middle of the second century, had a linkage to the personal memory of the apostles. But with the martyrdom of Polycarp, we have the last witness of one who as a boy remembered being in the presence of the Apostle John. This was a living text, both of 'who' an apostle was in his life and of 'what' he was in his text. For an apostle had witnessed and lived out what John's Gospel declares: 'the Word was made flesh and dwelt among us'. The next generation following Polycarp were now ready for their witness actually to become martyrs. Unlike any predecessor, Justin Martyr (c.100/110–165) becomes the transmitter of this new Christian tradition via his vast recitation of Old Testament quotations that all point to the reality of Jesus as the Messiah, the Son of God; of the changed role of the Law after Christ; and of the community of Christians now replacing the old Israel.[14] He now uses the biblical books as a codex in public as well as still using the scrolls in private.

Memory still provides him with two traits of an 'apostle': what he *remembers* about Jesus, what he said and did; and what an apostle taught about the Old Testament's predicting the coming of Jesus.[15]

The rise of biblical Christian scholarship

The scholar Origen (c.184–254) at the end of the second century wanted, as a teenager, to imitate his father as a Christian martyr, for to him a true Bible reader is martyred for his biblical faith. Possibly he actually did so at the end of his life. Instead, Origen, highly educated in classical *paedia*, is the first great Christian scholar—*sui generis*—more than a match for the finest pagan scholars (such as Celsus, Porphyry, and Plotinus). He was also a philologist, philosopher as well as exegete, producing a vast mass of biblical commentaries. He was the first comparative scholar to create the Hexapla, with its ten columns of variant versions of biblical script. He did this under rich patronage in Alexandria ('holy Ambrose'), where the Greek Septuagint had originally been translated from diverse Hebrew sources.

Origen defended Christianity as the best philosophy ever known and taught as well as to demonstrate it was the best way of living as a human being. For beyond remaining a *grammatikos* or teacher of Greek language and literature, Origen had a *metanoia* experience when he realized biblical or holy reading and its erudition is a 'spiritual' calling. He now pioneered reading Scripture in a strongly pastoral voice at three levels:

---

14. Oskar Skarsaune, 'The Development of Scriptural Interpretation in the Second and Third Centuries—except Clement and Origen', in Sæbø (ed.), *Hebrew Bible/Old Testament*, 389–409.

15. Oskar Skarsaune, 'Justin and his Bible', in Sara Parvis and Paul Foster (eds.), *Justin Martyr and His Worlds* (Minneapolis, 2007), 53–76.

literal, as grammatical and as historical; a mystical sense to be fulfilled in the future, as supremely so in Christ; and a moral sense, when by daily reading and transformation one is renewed day by day in the image of its Creator. Within the believing community of the Church, this moral reading and transformation takes place continuously.

Later medieval exegesis was to describe these readings as anagogy, tropology, and allegory, and to make a poem as the Dominican Dacia (d. 1253) does:

> The literal sense teaches what took place.
> The allegorical sense what you ought to believe.
> The moral sense what you ought to do.
> The anagogical sense what you must strive for.[16]

But Origen was dismissive of names and terms, so long as the transformative power of Bible reading was taking place in the reader.[17] Scholarship, asceticism, and martyrdom were all involved in developing Origen's person as a witness to God's word. So he was willing to die daily in rehearsal for the ultimate death of a martyr.

Eusebius of Caesarea (c.260–314) was Origen's successor, who went far beyond what Origen could have done in producing his *Onomasticon,* a commented list of biblical place names. Then he produced in AD c.300 his *Chronicle* or massive history, first in the *Chronography* , to synchronize the works of Greek, Roman, and Jewish chroniclers; and then in his *Canon*, to collate all the biblical rulers and sequences of other biblical characters into a historical frame. No doubt he got inspiration to do so from Origen's *Hexapla,* directed to it by his wealthy scholar-patron Pamphilus, whose library had vast resources.

Utterly selfless, Pamphilus shared his wealth to all eager to read and study the Scriptures, both men and women. He prepared many codices himself, and as Eusebius adds: 'so deep was his humility, however, that he wrote nothing of his own composition, except the letters that he now and then sent to his friends'.[18]

Building upon the scholarship of his two predecessors, Jerome (342–420) demonstrated a new life-style, being a desert monk, who could leave the patronage of the rich and their city libraries, and live in a humble hermitage near Bethlehem. He did so by creating a standardized Latin version of the Bible, much later called 'the Vulgate'. It was to profoundly influence all later western Christianity. He locked the door on variant readings which had generated doctrinal confusions throughout the fourth century. Yet paradoxically, he deepened the polyglot nature of the Old Testament by accepting esoteric elements of Jewish biblical exegesis in his 'hebraica'; for him these Jewish manuscripts had final authority over that of the Greek Septuagint. He was acting contrary to the spirit of the Old Testament Levites! Proudly, he claimed himself as *vir trilinguis,* 'the man of three languages'—Hebrew, Greek and Latin. This was a claim for more Hebrew expertise than he probably had, being reliant on Jewish scholars. Perhaps this ideal of trilingual scholarship

---

16. Susan K. Wood, *Spiritual Exegesis and the Church in the Theology of Henri de Lubac* (Eugene, OR, 2010), 27.

17. Henri de Lubac, *History and Spirit: the Understanding of Scripture according to Origen* (San Francisco, 2008), 166.

18. Anthony Grafton and Megan Williams, *Christianity and the Transformation of the Book* (Cambridge, MA, 2006), 181.

was somewhat fraudulent, becoming highly provocative, and yet also productive to later Renaissance and Reformation scholars.[19]

The inhibiting effect of the Western universal embrace of the Vulgate is still to be researched, but it meant that scarcely a dozen Christian Biblical scholars after Jerome knew Hebrew expertly, until the nineteenth century! The historical critical exegesis spawned by the Enlightenment meant that movements of Lutheran, French Huguenot, Puritan, Methodist, and central European pietism were all defenceless at the attacks of pseudo-Marcionite scholars concerning the morality of the Old Testament, which we continue to suffer from even in our own Evangelical Movement.

Oliver O'Donovan has stated succinctly: 'We will read the Bible seriously only when we use it to guide our thought towards a *comprehensive* moral viewpoint, and not merely to articulate disconnected moral claims. We must look within it not only for moral bricks, but for indications of the order in which the bricks belong together'.[20] In his strongly polemical book, Gordon Wenham takes Richard B. Hays in his *The Moral Vision of the New Testament* to task. Hays states discreetly: Christians 'will read the Old Testament in such a way that its portrayals of God's mercy and the eschatological restoration of the world will take precedence over the stories of justified violence'.[21] No, states Wenham: 'If the gap between divine ideals for human behaviour and the law's requirements witnesses to God's long-suffering and tolerance, the second clear point that the narratives demonstrate is his faithfulness to his promises despite the unfaithfulness of his people'.[22] As Psalm 103: 8, 10, 14 remind us: 'The Lord is merciful and gracious, slow to anger and abounding in steadfast love. He does not deal with us according to our sins, nor requite us according to our iniquities. For he knows our frame; He remembers that we are dust.'

Augustine's confrontation and ours

We can begin to see with Oliver O'Donovan, the need for an Augustinian base, from which to draw as much morality from the Old Testament as from the New Testament. So in reading the Bible, we turn now to how Augustine reads Scripture. He and Jerome are chilly contemporaries in this regard! While Augustine (354–430) was a decade younger than Jerome, his long polemical encounter with the Manichees—who wholly rejected the Old Testament yet considered themselves superior 'Christians'—placed Augustine as more deeply read in the Old Testament than Jerome. The latter had a friendly association with Jewish scholars. So did Augustine know and use Jerome's Latin version of the Septuagint, for they were in correspondence during the years 419–20?[23] As recent scholars

---

19. Grafton and Williams, *Christianity and the Transformation of the Book*, 237.
20. Oliver O'Donovan, *Resurrection and Moral Order: An Outline of Evangelical Ethics* (Leicester, 1986), 200.
21. Richard B. Hays, *The Moral Vision of the New Testament: Community, Cross, New Creation. A Contemporary Introduction to New Testament Ethics* (Edinburgh, 1997), 337.
22. Gordon J. Wenham, *Story as Torah: Reading Old Testament Narrative Ethically* (Grand Rapids, MI, 2000), 154.
23. It was only after the sixteenth century that it was popularly called the Vulgate.

have shown, Augustine was not impressed, and remained unshaken by his reliance upon the Septuagint.[24]

As Roland J. Teske has summarized it, the Manichees argued against the Old Testament on three counts: 1) It is its own undoing, since its prophecies have not been fulfilled, while its Law is immoral and grotesque; 2) Christ himself rejected the Old Testament; and 3) the very name 'New Testament' is a rejection of the 'Old'. Manichees sum up the Gospel, as the teaching of Jesus, excluding the Acts of the Apostles and Paul's epistles.[25] All this sounds familiar to modern liberalism! The Manichees have never died, for around Washington DC today, to appease Arab leaders politically, there are Christians who promote the love of Jesus, but who prohibit reference to the name of Jesus Christ.[26]

Like all sound scholarship today, Augustine was aware that the choice of method depends upon the type of text. While the Manichees refused to believe anything their mind-set could not accept, Augustine read in Old Latin the text of Isaiah 7:9, 'Unless you believe, you will not understand'.

Basic to Bible Reading is Humility
A humble intellectual submission to the Word of God is the first step to understanding the Scriptures. He read the Scriptures then, through the lens of Christ, as the two disciples heard from Jesus himself speaking of the Scriptures in this way. (Luke 24:25–27). 'This way' is the way of humility, so for Augustine the only way of reading the Scriptures is crucially pivoted on the hymn of the epistle to the Philippians, 2:6–11.

> Primordial to all his scholarship, all his pastoral life, all his prayers, all his identity was the humility of Christ, as the way of the incarnation, the way of the cross, the way of salvation and of future glory. It is all the *via humilitatis*! It anchors all Christian ethics, in faith, hope, and love, as we introduced our address. Christian morals are *in forma servis*, at the feet of those for whom Jesus was going to die, in obedient conformity to the will of his Father. All Christian life and behaviour is shaped by this divine humility.[27] This is how we have to interpret Augustine himself,[28] recognizing that he continued throughout his life to have not one, but many 'conversions'!

---

24. Annie-Marie La Bonnardiere, 'Did Augustine Use Jerome's Vulgate?', in Pamela Bright (ed.), *Augustine and the Bible* (Notre Dame, IN, 1986), 44.
25. Roland J. Teske, 'Augustine, the Manichees and the Bible', in Bright (ed.), *Augustine and the Bible*, 208–21.
26. American Bible Society, *Jesus* (1974; repr., n.d. [privately printed for the National Prayer Breakfast]).
27. Augustine, *In Iohannis evangelium tractatus*, 55.7 (Corpus Christianorum Latina [CCL]: Turnhout, Belgium, 1954), 36:466.
28. Albert Verwilghen, 'Jesus Christ: Sources of Christian Humility', in Bright (ed.), *Augustine and the Bible*, 301–12.

Figural Reading of the Bible is Personal

Augustine struggled to explain how in his divine nature Christ is called the Word, because he makes the Father known as a person uses words to make thoughts known.[29] He also struggled with Origen's use of 'the four senses of Scripture', which modern Catholic scholarship revived in Henri Lubac's massive scholarship and in the renewal of Cistercian contemporary devotion. Gradually, Augustine amalgamated allegory, typology, and anagogy, into a more general figural exegesis that deepened Christ as Exemplar and Mediator, in the unique paradigm of the incarnation. For no other book(s) can be 'read' like the Bible.

Many scholars today are trying to understand 'Augustine the reader', as Brian Stock has done,[30] but they fail to accept Augustine's own premises. I recommend to your perusal instead the rich reflections of Michael Cameron, *Christ Meets Me Everywhere*,[31] as he quotes Augustine's '*Against Faustus the Manichee*':

> But let us, who are now the body of Christ, acknowledge. . . .
> Christ meets and refreshes me everywhere in those Books,
> everywhere in those Scriptures,
> in their open spaces and in their hidden haunts.
> He sets me on fire with a desire that comes from
> having no little difficulty in finding him.
> But that only makes me eager to clutch whatever I find,
> to soak it deep into my bones,
> and hold it close for my salvation.[32]

The future of Bible reading?

To conclude this ambitious survey, we have not been able to describe the uses and abuses of Bible reading through the later centuries. With hoarding in the 'Dark Ages', richly illuminated Bibles in gold and richly ornate calligraphy were developed as the possessions of kings, abbots, and wealthy merchants. We have made only this mention of how the Gutenberg press revolutionized Bible dissemination in the Reformation. Nor have we referred to the establishment of the Bible societies, from the eighteenth century onwards, translating the Scriptures into thousands of languages. We simply ask what will be the fate of reading generally in this twenty-first century, which we now call the electronic age?[33] Susan Greenfield, among other voices, is now asking how digital technologies are leaving

---

29. Augustine, *Faith and Creed*, 4.6, quoted in Michael Cameron, 'The Christological Substructure of Augustine's Figurative Exegesis', in Bright (ed.), *Augustine and the Bible*, 81.

30. Brian Stock, *Augustine the Reader: Meditation, Self-knowledge, and the Ethics of Interpretation* (Cambridge, MA, 1996); id., *Augustine's Inner Dialogue* (Cambridge, 2010).

31. Michael Cameron, *Christ Meets Me Everywhere: Augustine's Early Figurative Exegesis* (Oxford, 2012).

32. Augustine, 'Contra Faustum', 12.27, in *Sancti Aureli Augustini* (Corpus Scriptorum Ecclesiasticorum Latinorum [CSEL]: Salzburg, Austria, 1891), 25/1: 356.

33. E.g., Sven Birkerts, *The Gutenberg Elegies: The Fate of Reading in an Electronic Age* (New York, 1994).

their mark on our brains? 'Climate change' seems a huge cultural and global event; could 'brain change' be even greater?[34] Is this why then, for Christians, a radical re-appraisal of our faith, requires us to become companions again of the early Fathers. For we have introduced them to help us face and challenge—not their classical civilization—but our own godless secularism today and tomorrow?

---

34. Susan Greenfield, *Mind Change: How Digital Technologies Are Leaving Their Mark on our Brains* (New York, 2015).

PART 2

The Bible and the Brethren

Chapter 2

Worn Symbols: Women's Hair and Head Coverings in Brethren History[1]

Neil Dickson

In a satirical piece of doggerel published in 1993 in *Assembly Testimony*, John Glenville, a preacher among the more conservative section of the Open Brethren in England, describes the problems for Brethren individuals holidaymaking in Europe and Britain. Although a holiday in Britain offered proximity to an assembly, the Brethren holidaymaker, according to Glenville's lines, might still find things to distress:

> The first Lord's Day brought tears, not smiles.
> Unhatted women, oh! how cute
> The one in the red trousered [*sic*] suit,
> That one who just escaped your gaze
> While your eyes were fixed on 'Power Praise'...[2]

By the time Glenville was describing his holiday difficulties, women with heads covered or uncovered had become one of the most visible signs in an assembly of whether it belonged to the conservative wing or what is often called the 'progressive' wing of the Open Brethren. Dress is one of the ways in which humans convey nonverbal information to each other, among other things, about gender.[3] It is not accidental that the satire juxtaposes 'unhatted women' and a woman in a 'red trousered suit'. Within the assemblies with which the holidaymaker would be familiar, wearing a hat in church instantly indicated femininity, just as trousers had been a signifier of masculinity in the wider society—the 1970s fashion of trouser suits for women could still be regarded among conservative dressers some twenty years later as a blurring of gender.[4] Gendered dress also carries with it a complex set of

---

1. An earlier version of this chapter appeared in *CHF Bulletin*, Spring 2016, 10–25.
2. J. Glenville, 'Holiday Dialogue', *Assembly Testimony*, Nov./Dec. 1993, 180; 'Power Praise' was a contemporary song sheet published for use in Charismatic praise-and-worship type singing. I am grateful to Dr Tim Grass for this information.
3. Joanne B. Eicher and Mary Ellen Roach-Higgins, 'Definition and Classification of Dress: Implications for Analysis of Gender Roles', in Joanne B. Eicher and Ruth Barnes (eds.), *Dress and Gender: Making Meaning in Cultural Contexts* (Oxford, 1992), 17–18.
4. Eicher and Roach-Higgins, 'Definition and Classification of Dress', 22–3, argue that the bid for equality implicit in the adoption of trouser suits by women is subverted by them being drawn into fashion, as has happened in the example discussed here through the colour of the trouser suit.

social expectations for behaviour which define the differences in status and power of the sexes.[5] Traditionally in the Brethren, women's dress had been expected to be modest and unassuming, but the red suit made this woman conspicuous. The visitor's concern over dress betrays wider anxieties. Women abandoning traditional feminine dress meant that the behavioural codes governing the assembly were in flux, especially those relating to the conduct of women. Subliminally or not, for a Brethren writer steeped in Scripture, the lady in red suggests the great whore of Babylon dressed in purple and scarlet, an image of corruption and worldliness in traditional Brethren exegesis,[6] problems which Glenville undoubtedly perceived in the assembly. Dress also indicates that one belongs to a certain group.[7] Women wearing hats in church was one significant indicator of belonging to the Brethren in late-twentieth-century British culture, even among conservative churches, as the anthropologist, Joseph Webster, still found in the next century in the Scottish fishing village of Gamrie.[8] The 'unhatted' nature of the women in the assembly Glenville had visited meant their dress no longer communicated a traditional Brethren identity, which is a significant reason for him feeling alienated. As will be seen later, there is probably a reason that hair styles did not draw Glenville's attention in the 1990s, but they, too, indicate identity. Anthony Synnott has argued that 'hair is malleable, in various ways, and therefore singularly apt to symbolize both differentiations between, and changes in, individual and group identities.'[9] For conservative assemblies, head coverings and long hair were symbols which ought to be worn—the issue was one of obedience to sacred Scripture; for progressive Open Brethren ones, they increasingly were symbols which were outmoded and therefore worn out—the issue was one of cultural appropriateness. Nevertheless, in a movement that has given such a central place to the Bible, its material dimensions had to be rooted in it. The divergent views on hair and head coverings of different streams within the Brethren movement demonstrate the evolution of differing identities which has implications for attitudes not only women and culture, but also Scripture.

Brethren interpretation

Despite perceiving themselves as a primitivist or a restorationist movement, returning the Church to truths found in Scripture that it had neglected,[10] the movement had many strands of continuity with the wider theology and traditions of evangelicalism, particularly on

---

5. Eicher and Roach-Higgins, 'Definition and Classification of Dress', 19–20.

6. For this theme in Brethren exegesis, see James Harding, *Babylon and Brethren: The Use and Influence of the Whore of Babylon Motif in the Christian Brethren Movement, 1829–1900* (Eugene, OR, 2015), 126–99.

7. Ruth Barnes and Joanne B. Eicher, 'Introduction', in Eicher and Barnes, *Dress and Gender*, 1.

8. Joseph Webster, *The Anthropology of Protestantism: Faith and Crises among Scottish Fisherman* (New York, 2013), fig. 1.4, 50–1.

9. Anthony Synnott, 'Shame and Glory: A Sociology of Hair', *The British Journal of Sociology*, 38/3 (1987), 381–413, spec. 381.

10. James Patrick Callahan, *Primitivist Piety: The Ecclesiology of the Early Plymouth Brethren* (Lanham, MD; 1996), 153–6. Callahan argues convincingly that the Exclusive Brethren were primitivists, as they did not look for the restoration of the Church, but the Open Brethren were restorationists.

issues of morality and culture. Attitudes to women were among them. Of course, the point for the Brethren was not this tradition, but the earliest Christian source of all for women covering their heads and having long hair: Paul's teaching in 1 Corinthians 11:2–16. Nevertheless, J. N. Darby is well within the classical Christian tradition in his *Synopsis of the Bible*, when he writes:

> The woman was to have her head covered, as a token that she was subject to the man (her covering being a token of the power to which she was subject). Man however could not do without woman, nor woman without man. Finally the apostle appeals to the order of creation, according to which a woman's hair, her glory and ornament, shewed, in contrast with the hair of man, that she was not made to present herself with the boldness of man before all. Given as a veil, her hair shewed that modesty, submission—a covered head that hid itself, as it were, in that submission and in that modesty—was her true position, her distinctive glory.[11]

Darby is closely following a commentator such as Calvin here—as he also did in his soteriology. The hair is a covering which in modesty itself must be covered.[12] No allowance was made for cultural relativity, a point explicitly made later by his disciple, William Kelly, in his commentary on 1 Corinthians. A covered head, Kelly wrote, 'is not argued on the grounds of habit, modesty or the like, but of the facts as revealed by God.'[13] As in the nascent stages of many other pietist movements, women can achieve a degree of equality through their perceived spirituality. Although insistent that women should be silent in church, Darby was not at all opposed to women participating in informal discussions, for in 'private meeting, it is merely a question of the modesty that becomes them',[14] and in such contexts he was happy that a woman was free to 'exercise her gifts'.[15] To avoid the obvious difficulty that the Corinthian passage refers to women praying and prophesying Darby argued: 'We are not as yet come to the order in the assembly. That commences with verse 17.'[16] But on those other occasions, to which he felt the passage referred, when using her gifts 'the woman's head was to be covered when under the power of the Spirit'.[17] Dress was expected to be simple. This that was not always observed, leading one

---

11. J. N. Darby, *Synopsis of the Bible*, <http://www.ccel.org/d/darby/synopsis/1Corinthians.html> [online text], accessed 6 Oct. 2011.

12. See also [J. N. Darby], 'Notes on a Reading of I and II Corinthians' in *CW*, 1:86; cf. John Calvin, *Commentary on the Epistles of Paul the Apostle to the Corinthians*, E.T. John Pringle, 2 vols. (Edinburgh, 1848), 1:356.

13. William Kelly, *Notes on the First Epistle of Paul the Apostle to the Corinthians with a New Translation*, (London, 1878), 173.

14. J. N. Darby, letter in 1861, in *Letters of J. N. D. Volume Three 1879–1882* (London, n.d.), 331.

15. J. N. Darby, letter in 1851, in *Letters of J. N. D. Volume One 1832–1868* (London, n.d.), 196.

16. Darby, *Synopsis*, 1 Corinthians 11, n.11. <http://www.ccel.org/d/darby/synopsis/1Corinthians_fn.html> [online text], accessed 6 Oct. 2011; see also J. D. Darby to a very dear sister, *Letters*, 1:197.

17. J. N. Darby, letter [n.d.], in *Letters of J. N. D. Volume Two 1868–1879* (London, n.d.), 206–7.

London pamphleteer to complain that if the true reasons for a woman's head to be covered were understood, 'there would be no unseemly bonnets or hats in our meetings'.[18] One woman, however, who first attended the Brethren in Bethesda Chapel, Bristol, in 1840 found the dress of the women to be 'grotesquely ugly', with on their heads 'a straight speckled straw bonnet with drab or brown veil, servants and mistresses all alike.'[19] Some twenty years later, Lizzie Douthwaite, a ladies maid, scandalized her fellow Open Brethren assembly members in Sheffield by wearing attractive bonnets and shawls. Her 'red bonnet with its jaunty plume', one individual had remarked to her (undoubtedly appalled by the associations of red), was 'an unchristian colour'.[20]

When the Brethren movement divided in 1848 into the Exclusive Brethren and the Open Brethren, most of the movement's early writers had followed Darby in the schism, but the Open Brethren continued to draw on their productions. In 1880 *The Northern Witness*, eventually the most widely-circulated journal among the Open Brethren in Britain, reprinted a letter to a female correspondent by Darby's follower, J. G. Bellett. In the reproduced extract Bellett maintained that 'Covering is the proper sign of woman', for 'the woman is mystically the Church'. Like the Church in relation to its Lord, her covering therefore expressed her subjection, but also the protection she receives, a lesser position than that of the man as 'mystically, the man is Christ'.[21] Earlier in 1878, *The Northern Witness* had carried a series of articles by an Open Brethren preacher on the ministry of women which also stressed a woman's covering as symbolizing her lesser position. These were by Anthony Oliver Molesworth, an English itinerant of aristocratic descent who was a retired lieutenant colonel.[22] In a passage discussing women's clothing in the New Testament he maintains that if women's 'appearance and conduct' was 'unrestrained', there would be 'fearful results in the Church'. God, knowing that it is 'Satan's aim, by the woman, ever to deceive and seduce man from spiritual obedience and fealty to Himself, caused to be written words which cut at the root of woman's fleshly pride and natural desire'. The thrust of the Corinthian passage, then, is that women should 'be hidden before men, and should, especially when worshipping God, not obtrude herself or her natural beauties before men, but remain veiled, positively covered with a veil, *or otherwise unnoticeable*,

---

18. William Dudgeon, *Questions as to the Public Ministry of Women* (London, [1905]), 7.

19. A[nne]. E[vans]., *The Brethren, as I knew them from 1840 to 1902* (Stroud, [?1902]), 9–10.

20. London, University of London, School of Oriental and African Studies, MS 381056, Douthwaite-Groves papers c.1975–2009, transcript of Arthur William Douthwaite's memoir; I am grateful to Dr John Owen for this reference.

21. J. G. Bellett, 'The Woman Covered'. I Cor. XI. 3–16', *The Northern Witness*, 10 (1880), 119; reprinted from J. G. B[ellett]., *"Showers upon the grass," being a few brief letters & papers addressed to C. E. M. Paul, of Exeter* (London, 1865).

22. 'Colonel A. O. Molesworth', *W*, 47 (Apr. 1917), 52; *Burke's Peerage, Baronetage & Knightage*, 3 vols. (107th edn., Wilmington, DE, 2003), 1: 1095: I am grateful to Dr Timothy C. F. Stunt for this last reference.

lest she prove a distraction and a snare'.[23] Molesworth was the father of nine children, and one does not need to be a Freudian to detect psychological projection at work here.[24]

The Open Brethren, then, continued the belief that long hair and a covered head were signs that women were in subjection to men.[25] In 1936, W. E. Vine had no apprehensions that women would fail to have their heads covered, which was something he felt had happened in first-century Corinth, but he was now worried that women might have their hair cut short, something he saw as springing 'from the motive of abandoning any mark of the subordination of the female sex'.[26] This concern reflected the trend in Britain from the 1920s of women having their hair 'bobbed', or adopting the even shorter 'shingled' hair. Bobbed hair, which first appeared in America during the First World War, was a blunt cut with the hair being shorn level with the ears.[27] It was an example of the permeation of contemporary fashion by Art Deco, the movement that expressed the streamlined post-war aesthetic of speed and mobility.[28] The new hairstyle received a boost from its adoption by such trendsetters as Coco Chanel and the silent-film actor Louise Brooks. Crucially, it allowed women more freedom, and it quickly came to be seen as a mark of rebellion.[29] The outrageous symbolism of the style can be seen in F. Scott Fitzgerald's short story of 1920, 'Bernice Bobs her Hair'. The eponymous heroine, in a bid to shed her dull, staid image among her peers, and egged on by her more worldly-wise cousin Marjorie, 'announced coolly' to one male friend: '"I want to be a society vampire, you see," . . . and went on to inform him that bobbed hair was the necessary prelude.'[30] She becomes a sensation among the boys.

In 1926, W. W. Fereday, a former Exclusive who had become a well-known itinerant Bible teacher among the Open Brethren, weighed in with a tract entitled *"Bobbed Hair" Is it Well-Pleasing to the Lord?*. Fereday, who had a reputation as having a dogmatic and irritable disposition, would be married three times over the course of his long life. In his pamphlet, he inveighed against the 'new fashion . . . that knows not God'.[31] He contended

---

23. A. O. M[olesworth]., 'The Ministry of Women', *The Northern Witness*, 8 (1878), 149; emphasis in original. For Molesworth on women's roles, see *intra*, 54, 67.

24. For a Freudian interpretation of hair, see Galia Ofek, *Representations of Hair in Victorian Literature* (Farnham, Surrey, 2009), 33–102.

25. Kenneth J. Newton, 'A History of the Brethren in Australia', Fuller Theological Seminary, Ph.D.. thesis, 1990, 216–22.

26. W. E. Vine, in C. F. Hogg, W. E. Vine and W. R. Lewis, *The Ministry of Women: A Study in the Scriptures* (London, [1936]), 24.

27. Richard Corson, *Fashions in Hair: The First Five Thousand Years* (London, 1980), 609–19.

28. Michael Windover, *Art Deco: A Mode of Mobility* (Quebec City, 2012), 13–18; W. Franklyn Paris, 'The International Exposition of Modern Industrial and Decorative Art in Paris, I. Interior Architecture', *Architectural Record*, 58/3 (1925), 263, quoted in ibid., 20.

29. Victoria Sherrow, *Encyclopedia of Hair: A Cultural History* (Westport, CT, 2006), 63–6.

30. F. Scott Fitzgerald, 'Bernice Bobs her Hair', in id., *Flappers and Philosophers* (New York, 1920), 175.

31. [W. W. Fereday], *"Bobbed Hair" Is it Well-Pleasing to the Lord?* (Waltham Abbey, [1926]), 3. The publication date is given in Corson, *Fashions in Hair*, 614, probably derived from the publication date of the contemporary critical discussion of Fereday's work in 'The Sin of Bobbing' by the Irish essayist, Robert Lynd in his *The Little Angel: A Book of Essays* (London,

that as '"bobbed" was another way of saying "shorn"', it meant that 'a "bobbed" woman is a disgraced woman'.[32] He concluded:

> The new mode is only one of the many symptoms of the universal revolt against every form of divine order. The restlessness of women in the outside world should have a warning effect upon those women who have been saved by grace. The refusal to utter the word "Obey" in the Marriage Service, the wearing of men's apparel when cycling, the smoking of cigarettes, and the "bobbing" of the hair are all indicative of one thing. God's order is everywhere flouted. Divine forbearance tolerates the growing evil for the present, but the hour of divine intervention in judgment approaches fast.[33]

Fereday was no alone in his condemnation of the latest fashion in hair. Henry Hitchman, an Open Brethren preacher from Exeter, declaimed against bobbing and shingling when on a preaching tour of New Zealand in 1928:

> The woman never shines so much when as when she answers to the purpose for which she was created. Satan's great object has been to frustrate that purpose, which is evidenced in the fall of man. The more woman tries to appear like a man, the more she falls short of God's will concerning her. The more feminine she is, the more pleasing she is to the Lord. A woman cannot be too feminine, because she is a woman; and it is the responsibility of every godly woman to avoid those fashions that would make her appear masculine.[34]

Noting that there was a time when 'practically every woman would have viewed it as a serious calamity to have been shorn of her locks, even if illness had necessitated it', Hitchman deplored that this had been changed by fashion, to which 'many believers have succumbed'.[35] That the new styles were being adopted by 'many' Christian women was also a reason for Fereday's ire.[36] Probably a greater degree of initial shock than that in the wider society was created in the very conservative movement by those Open Brethren women who had their hair bobbed. After looking approvingly at the more masculine look of their housemaid's newly-shorn hair, the young Margaret Anne Smith wanted her hair cut. Her father, Wilson Smith, was a senior consultant physician in Bath, and a member of the town's Manvers Hall, the assembly in which Vine was the leading elder. Smith

---

1926), chap. 16, 118–25. It is probable that the source of Corson's quotations is also Lynd's essay, which also does not name the author but has substantial quotations from the pamphlet. As Corson lists in his bibliography journals for which Lynd wrote, but does not list *The Little Angel* nor Fereday's pamphlet, it is probable that he read Lynd's essay in its original place of publication. The pamphlet was probably thought to be anonymous, as the front cover states it is 'From W. W. Fereday', and gives his home address in Waltham Abbey, Essex, as if he were the distributor rather than the author. For those not familiar with Fereday's publications, this might understandably create some confusion.

32. [Fereday], *"Bobbed Hair"*, 5.
33. [Fereday], *"Bobbed Hair"*, 7–8.
34. Henry Hitchman, *Some Scriptural Principles of the Christian Assembly: or Things which are most surely Believed among us* (1929; 2nd edn., Kilmarnock, [1930]), 176.
35. Hitchman, *Scriptural Principles*, 177.
36. [Fereday], *"Bobbed Hair"*, 3.

thought hair was a woman's crowning glory, and he was horrified. In one of her volumes of autobiography his daughter records: '"The girl's entirely ruined," my father retorted. "How incredibly foolish women are!"' But he allowed himself to be persuaded by the arguments of his non-Brethren brother-in-law who pointed out that Smith's mother, a Brethren seceder from Anglicanism, had short hair.[37] Others found the pressure to conform impossible to resist. Annie Morrison, a young woman who worked as a machinist in the textile industry, was a member of the Gospel Hall in the Plann, Ayrshire. When she had her previously long hair cut in the 1920s, she met with the shocked reaction of two of her contemporaries from a neighbouring assembly upon encountering them in a shop. She vowed never to have her hair cut again.[38] Henry Pickering, editor of *The Witness* (by then the shortened title of *The Northern Witness*), took a relatively nuanced approach to the issue. In 1929 one correspondent in the magazine's regular question-and-answer section asked whether a sister whose hair was bobbed should be refused fellowship. Pickering in reply made it clear that 'We have not an atom of sympathy with any *true* Christian woman who has her locks shorn under any of the popular terms used to designate modes of hairdressing.' He felt, nevertheless, that it was not Christ-like 'for anyone to think of *compelling* a sister how to adorn her person, under threat of expulsion'.[39] In a manner characteristic of the Open Brethren, then, there were a range of responses to the new fashion.

Vine, in his discussion of 1 Corinthians 11:5, which refers to a woman praying or prophesying being covered, had followed Darby by thinking that it 'cannot refer to the gatherings of an assembly. There are other occasions than that of an assembly gathering when a woman can exercise the oral ministry of prayer or testimony'.[40] The necessary corollary of denying the application of the passage to the church was that women had to be covered when praying outside the assembly. This gave rise to a debate in *The Witness* in 1930 on whether women should cover their heads when praying at home as well as in public.[41] Henry Pickering thought they should, as did the editor of the *Believer's Magazine*, William Hoste; but as the Open Brethren always allowed for some degree of variation in opinion, another leading itinerant, C. F. Hogg, thought it only applied to public occasions. It was perhaps possible to extend wearing hats to the domestic sphere because of traditional cultural norms,[42] but in attempting to stop Brethren women having their hair cut short the preachers and writers were fighting against contemporary trends. When the poet Patricia Beer was a child, the women of Littleham Gospel Hall in Exmouth in Devon, where her parents were members, had long hair. This insistence on having uncut hair was a source of intense embarrassment to Patricia and her sister when in the 1930s their classmates were beginning to have theirs bobbed. Their mother was completely deaf to their pleadings, adducing arguments, in addition to the Bible, from social propriety. But shorter hair came anyway for the sisters in the assembly, for by the end of the decade, they 'were as

---

37. Anne Arnott, *Journey into Understanding* (London, 1971), 185–7.
38. Oral information from Isobel Jack, Kilmarnock, 22 Nov. 2009.
39. *W*, 59 (Sept. 1929), 233.
40. W. E. Vine, *1 Corinthians* (London, 1951), 147.
41. *W*, 60 (Sept. 1930), 207.
42. Ofek, *Representations of Hair*, 6.

shorn as anyone else if they wanted to be, without a blow struck'.[43] In Scotland the trend was resisted in the mid-century by a school of working-class preachers who took every opportunity to stress that women's hair should be uncut.[44] One of them, Jimmy Paton, noted with satisfaction of his wife after her death: 'I never needed to alter my ministry to accommodate her lifestyle. Her hair was neither shorn nor braided, her dress was neither costly nor immodest.'[45] Its leader, John Douglas, in a retreat from the earlier position of Darby and Vine who had allowed a spoken ministry for women outside the assembly, strove to express the point in an epigram: "Two things God requires of women: hair and silence."[46] Even as late as the 1960s, many Brethren women were marked out by their hair. The writer Liz Lochhead, a native of Newarthill in Lanarkshire, where the stricter Open Brethren were well-represented, describes an open-air service of her childhood:

> Sunday, maybe later in the evening
> There'd be a Brethren Meeting.
> Plain women wearing hats to cover
> uncut hair. And
> singing, under lamp-posts, out in our street.[47]

Lochhead, however, is not reading the use of hats and long hair as a sign of women's subjection to men, but as a mark of the way Brethren appeared separate from the surrounding culture. The occasional, increasingly lonely voice might still be heard appealing for uncut hair, such as that of the English preacher Harold Butcher who felt that a '"half-length"' would not satisfy 'the godly sister'.[48] But in general among Open Brethren before the Second World War, the argument had already been lost. Post-war many Brethren women had their hair stylishly permanently waved or 'permed'. In the United Kingdom by the last two decades of the twentieth century, Open Brethren women with uncut hair were largely confined to the bastions of conservative Brethrenism in the north-east fishing communities of Scotland and Northern Ireland.[49]

Exclusive developments

According to one former Exclusive Brethren sister, who had been a member in the mid-twentieth century, 'nowhere is a woman's hat of greater significance than among

---

43. Patricia Beer, *Mrs Beer's House* (London, 1968), 131–4.
44. Neil T. R. Dickson, *Brethren in Scotland 1838–2000: A Social Study of an Evangelical Movement* (Carlisle, 2003), 234–7, 244–5.
45. Jimmy Paton, 'Men who Touched My Life for God', *Truth & Tidings* (Feb. 1999), 50/2, <http://truthandtidings.com/1999/02/men-who-touched-my-life-for-god/>, accessed 20 Sept. 2018.
46. Oral information, 3 Aug. 1993, from Margaret Cochrane, Newmilns, Ayrshire.
47. Liz Lochhead, 'The Offering', in *Dreaming Frankenstein and Collected Poems* (Edinburgh, 1984), 60–1.
48. Harold Butcher, *The Covering of a Woman's Head* (privately printed, n.d.), 3.
49. Dr Tim Grass to the writer, e-mail 9 Nov. 2009; Dr Grass was commenting on his observations during field study in Northern Ireland. When one woman visited Downshire Road Hall, Holywood, Co. Down, in 2004 she found that 'I was the only woman not wearing a hat!': 'Ship of Fools', <http://shipoffools.com/mystery/2004/827.html>, accessed 8 Apr. 2015.

Brethren.'[50] R. K. Campbell, the most prominent American writer in the Kelly-Lowe connexion, was also maintaining in the 1990s, in works that are still in print at the time of writing, that a woman should not cut any of her hair.[51] The Exclusive group which had become the most introversionist followed James Taylor, a New York linen merchant. Among them, there were developments which led to women's uncut hair and head covering becoming the most visible public signs of their identity. Taylor developed a theology which, though it did not supplant it, effectively placed his teachings on a par with that of the New Testament, and he introduced a new hermeneutic which allowed doctrine to be derived from the allegorical interpretation of the Old Testament.[52] It was under his son James Taylor Jr. that the centralisation implicit in the notion of teaching by the Holy Spirit being received through 'chosen vessels' became fully evident.[53] Roger Shuff, the historian of this period of Exclusive Brethrenism, states that the authority that Taylor Jr. had attained by the end of 1960 'was blatantly legalistic and coercive, and its status was boosted by the *quasi*-biblical status of the dogma he imposed.'[54] Among the Exclusives, the traditional hair style for women had been to pin their uncut hair in a roll or bun[55]—the style nicknamed 'the Brethren bun'— which was sign of adulthood. Perms and fringes were forbidden. Younger girls chose either pigtails, a pageboy style, or a more fashionable French roller. By the 1950s, at all times they wore a 'token' of their subjection to men on their heads, 'a small piece of ribbon tied into the hair or worn on a hair clip', and a scarf in public. They covered their heads at family prayer in their houses, often by using a handkerchief or serviette.[56] Taylor Jr., developing the interpretation of earlier Exclusive writers, such as J. G. Bellett, began emphasizing that there was a feminine aspect to the assembly, and within this context he also developed new symbolic significations for women's hair and head coverings. At a session of a conference held in Britain in 1963 which discussed the Corinthian passage on veiling, Taylor, alluding to the Church as the 'mystery' of Ephesians 5:32, maintained that men had 'the testimonial position, but the woman the mystery.' As

---

50. Joyce Harper, *Women and the Gospel: An Essay on the Scriptural Authority for the Ministry of Women in the Church, by a former Exclusive Sister* (CBRF Occasional Paper No. 5: Pinner, Middlesex, 1974), 23.

51. R. K. Campbell, *The Church of the Living God* ([1950]; 5th printing, Beamsville, ON, [1994]), 173. The book originated in a series of articles published in the magazine *Grace and Truth* during 1943–9. Campbell had revised the chapter on women's roles in the earlier editions of the book and had it separately published. He requested before he died in 1991 that future editions of the book should print this revised material, which posthumous ones did: Campbell, 'Preface', ibid., 5, and David A. Campbell, 'Preface to the Third Edition', ibid, 6. The publishing firm, The Believer's Bookshelf, keeps Campbell's works in print.

52. Roger N. Shuff, *Searching for the True Church: Brethren and Evangelicals in Mid-Twentieth Century England* (Carlisle, 2005), 121.

53. See Roger N. Holden, chap. 4, *intra*, 83–5.

54. Shuff, *Searching for the True Church*, 130; italics in original.

55. Shuff, *Searching for the True Church*, 252; see also Burns Singer, 'Fishermen of Scotland—2. Meeting the Brethren', *The Observer*, Sunday 11 Dec. 1960, on a visit to an Exclusive assembly in Peterhead, Aberdeenshire: 'The women were without make-up and their hair was uncut, coiled in buns at the back of the head or in rolls at the back of the neck.'

56. Ngaire Thomas, *Behind Closed Doors: A Startling Story of Exclusive Brethren Life* (2nd edn., Auckland, NZ, 2005), 95-6, 32.

such she had to be covered, for like the Ark of the Covenant, the coverings of which were also in the biblical passages under discussion, the assembly was 'not to be displayed, it is not for curiosity.'[57] His pronouncements often had a sexual undertone. The increasing introversionism of the sect was paralleled with a woman's covering, for neither assembly nor a woman's hair were for viewing by the public, but 'the woman has not to display her glory to anybody else but Christ.'[58] Because of this, Taylor maintained, 'what is seen in the woman leads to the thought of the feminine in the assembly.' Jacob's daughter Dinah, in being raped, 'exposed herself to the whole position, and so the female side, that relates to the assembly, was broken down.'[59] Such identification of the assembly with women did not raise their social status, however, and Taylor slid easily from an elevated symbolism to a belittling literalism. According to him 'the enemy is always at the feminine side. . . . he attacks that side through the weakness that exists, perhaps through the lack of subjection. That is the current need among us, that the sisters should be in their place.'[60]

New strictures on women's hair and head coverings were developed by Taylor in 1970. Hats among British Brethren Exclusives by the 1960s had been of a uniform type, being a pillar box without brims or trimmings, although the women were known for their taste in severe but expensive clothes. Throughout the 1960s, however, Taylor had entrenched the separation of the sect, and its members had to sever any links they had with other evangelicals, professional associations, and even family members who were not in the connexion. At a conference in March 1970 held in Cleveland, Ohio, at which the Corinthian passage on veiling was again discussed, Taylor rejected 'the Brethren bun' as a permissible hair style. Instead he advocated that a woman's hair, like Eve standing before Adam, should be 'hanging long' and unbraided:

> Why doesn't she show her glory? What are you sticking it up there for when your glory is to be seen? Oh, some painful faces are here now, very painful. You sisters, your hair is given to you—glory. Yes; and you mean to show it. Don't you hide it in some little nest up there, which you have to see whether there are any birds in there or what-have-you in there![61]

Taylor was also basing this new teaching on the woman who had washed the feet of Christ, and he observed that she could not be wearing a hat, and so 'What is important in scripture is covering, and then the token. That is the point here; that is the important point.'[62] Taylor was by this time given to long incoherent rambling and provoking laughter at his meetings. At the same conference session he mentioned, among other things, the members kissing their wives in bed, using Chanel No. 5, and playing chess, while simultaneously making personal comments about individuals present. According to a doctor who examined him,

---

57. J. T[aylor]. Jr., quoted in, 'The Trinity in Relation to the Local Assembly', in J[ames]. T[aylor]. Jr., *Revelation and Spiritual Growth and Other Ministry: Notes of Meetings in Hull, Blackburn, Glasgow and Sheffield, 1963*, 138 vols. (Hampton Wick, 1964), 22: 360.
58. T[aylor]. Jr., 'The Trinity', 362.
59. T[aylor]. Jr., 'The Trinity', 373.
60. T[aylor]. Jr., 'The Trinity', 378.
61. J. T[aylor]. Jr., *Features of Glory, Cleveland 1970* (Kingston-on-Thames, 1974), 134: 86.
62. T[aylor]. Jr., *Features of Glory*, 89.

he had been suffering from dementia.[63] His edict in the spring of 1970 that women should wear their unadorned, uncut hair down, and, shortly afterwards, that it should be covered at all times in public with a head scarf, was accepted worldwide throughout the sect within a matter of days of it being promulgated.[64] In the immediate aftermath of the 'Aberdeen Incident', as the allegations of scandal that irrupted around Taylor in the summer of 1970 came to be known, the most visible public sign that Exclusives in north-east Scotland had withdrawn from him was women reverting to the older hair styles.[65] On the other hand, maintaining his stipulations for women are at present the most visible public signs, among those now called the Plymouth Brethren Christian Church, of loyalty to the Taylorite succession. As with the Amish, the distinctive hair and head covering act as convenient ways of integrating the community through a shared sense of history and belonging while simultaneously marking the separation of its members from the wider society.[66]

Shuff has demonstrated how, despite their increasing isolationism, this branch of Exclusive Brethren were influenced by various aspects of the 1960s counter-culture.[67] The origin of the style in an era when the trend for long, straight hair had been popularized by celebrities such as Joan Baez, is one more such cross-fertilization. As it did in contemporary secular culture, the style cultivated a 'natural' look as opposed to the artificial constructs of fashion,[68] as was also true of the more informal style of wearing a head-scarf.[69] But it was a style which suited younger women and made much of their natural attributes, which in the male gaze indicated nubility.[70] The new teaching subverted the traditional practice among Brethren which was that a woman's glory should be hidden. Now it was to be openly displayed. Given how Taylor's imagination was clearly working,[71] his increasing loss of inhibition, and the biblical derivation of the new style in the freshly-created Eve before Adam, some verses in the Song of Solomon, and the prostitute who washed the feet of Christ, it is undoubtedly the case that it points to not only a pronounced gendering of body modification, but also the sexualisation of women.[72] Exclusive women had been put in their place.

---

63. Robert Gibb, *et al.*, notarized statement, Edinburgh, 11 Jan. 1988, reprinted as Appendix 2 in Shuff, *True Church*, 266–8; Roger Stott, 'The Aftermath of the 1970 Schism. Trauma Counselling', 1993, <http://wikipeebia.com/aftermath-1970-schism/>, accessed 11 Mar. 2017: the section relevant to Taylor's medical history is quoted in Shuff, *True Church*, 252.

64. Shuff, *Searching for the True Church*, 252.

65. Adam Borthwick, 'When Angels Fall Out', *Scottish Daily Express*, 14 Aug. 1970.

66. Donald B. Kraybill, *The Riddle of Amish Culture*, (2nd edn., Baltimore, 2001), 60–3, 79.

67. Shuff, *Searching for the True Church*, 239–55.

68. Arthur Marwick, *The Sixties: Cultural Revolution in Britain, France, Italy, and the United States, c.1958–c.1974* (Oxford, 1998), 410–11, 414.

69. Thomas, *Behind Closed Doors*, 139.

70. Thomas, *Behind Closed Doors*, 138, notes the stylistic inappropriateness of older women having to wear their hair down, ibid., 139.

71. For a catena of Taylor's sexually suggestive comments on women, see Shuff, *Searching for the True Church*, 250–2.

72. That the style was partly a fashion choice can be seen from there being no scriptural basis offered for the head scarf; when one English Exclusive enquired for its justification he was told, "Mr Taylor liked it." Roger Shuff to the writer, e-mail 11 Aug. 2010.

Open Brethren debates

Exclusive women dealt with the problem of split ends by singeing them, a tip that Open Brethren women also passed around.[73] By not cutting them, a maximalist interpretation of 'shorn', as meaning 'uncut', was preserved. The Northern Irish, Open Brethren missionary, David McAllister, with an obvious eye for hair care as a beauty aid, advocated in 2013 'the discreet removal of split ends; an action which will not noticeably affect the length of the hair, but which will promote healthy growth, and thereby, most likely, actually increase its length (and its thickness)'.[74] Among Open Brethren, however, the battle for uncut hair was largely a lost cause—as was noted earlier, Glenville in 1993 did not mention it in his holiday visit.[75] An increasing acceptance of the way things were can be seen in 2011 from the question-and-answer section of the conservative Open Brethren magazine, *Precious Seed*. A questioner asked whether it was wrong for a woman to cut her hair, and the reply, by a member of the trust which owns the magazine, compared the prescription for uncut hair to Eve's reply to the serpent, as both went beyond what God had said. No matter how godly and well-intentioned the source, the believer should not go beyond Scripture which merely specified the hair was to be long, which the writer admitted was a relative term, and not 'so short it looks like a man's hair'.[76]

What would become the new battleground over women's appearance was signalled in 1942 by J. B. Watson, the then newly-appointed editor of *The Witness*. Watson had been worried about the war breaking down gender distinctions, with women wearing 'uniforms of mannish design',[77] but he was equally unhappy that the Church of England was allowing women to attend public worship hatless.[78] Before the first half of the twentieth century, the Open Brethren debate over when a woman's head should be covered had been about praying in private houses, as the idea of respectable women being hatless in public, such as in the assembly hall, was culturally unthinkable. The lack of a hat was one way the Open Brethren itinerant G. H. Lang could readily indicate how 'unusual' the woman was that he met on Ostend quay in 1923, 'a militant English suffragette, hatless, with shock hair, stocky and aggressive.'[79] That this new fashion for being hatless in public, which became increasingly popular in post-war society, had implications for Brethren halls is shown by a question posted in 1948 in the *Believer's Magazine*: 'If an unsaved girl should come into the Gospel Meeting without a hat, should she be approached and told,

---

73. Exclusive practice from Thomas, *Behind Closed Doors*, 33; Jessica Westgate and Lucy Koorey, *The Cutting Edge*, ABC POOL, Sydney, 2012; oral information on the Open Brethren from Iris Gooding, Sept. 2009.

74. David McAllister, 'Godly Women in Paul's Epistles', in [Roy Reynolds (ed.)], *The Glory of Godly Women* (Belfast, 2013), 202. McAllister was aware, doubtless from his Zambian missionary context, 'that not every woman has been given long hair by God.', but that 'long' meant a woman's 'natural length' ('Godly Women', 201, 202).

75. However, the Glasgow Open Brethren firm, Gospel Tract Publications, reprinted Hitchman's *Scriptural Principles* with its strictures on women cutting hair, in 1982.

76. Richard Collings, 'Question Time', *Precious Seed*, 66/3 (Aug. 2011), end pp.

77. J. B. W[atson]., 'Witness Watchtower', *W*, 72 (Jan. 1942), 9; id., 'Witness Watchtower', *W*, 72 (Nov. 1942), 100.

78. W[atson], 'Witness Watchtower', 100.

79. G. H. Lang, *An Ordered Life: An Autobiography* (London, 1959), 195.

or turned away at the door?'[80] Eventually by the 1960s it was not just the 'unsaved' that were discarding their hats, and some tried to find a half-way position for women between hats and being uncovered. Writing in 1969, Paul Marsh, a former missionary to Pakistan, in his commentary on 1 Corinthians for *A New Testament Commentary*, a work that was perceived as the product of an emerging progressive Brethrenism in Britain, was critical of hats, 'decorative, attractive and often obstructive',[81] but he wanted some cultural equivalent to the first-century head covering:

> That western culture has no means of expressing woman's subordination—having abandoned the concept is perhaps the strongest argument for the retention of the 'token' veil, signifying a divinely appointed status. To be quietly, though not dowdily dressed, in all aspects of one's person is perhaps the most effective way in our western culture of fulfilling the injunctions and principles of scripture.[82]

Many women, however, abandoned their hats with relief. What might happen when Brethren women were away from the restrictions of their assemblies was seen at the Billy Graham crusade of 1959 in Australia, at which, according to one critic, they 'took their places in the Graham Crusade choirs bare-headed'.[83] Now, what was also liable to happen if head coverings were insisted upon, was evident in an incident in the 1960s in an assembly adjacent to an American university campus. One of the older men, who had collected surplus hats from the older women, posted himself by the door and issued them to bare-headed students. Very quickly, they stopped attending.[84] Increasingly, however, there were others prepared to go further than Marsh had done and defend the removal of head coverings altogether. The Christian Brethren Research Fellowship (CBRF), founded in 1963, was an increasingly emboldened ginger group for the more progressive thinking. In 1971, in an occasional paper published by it, the American missionary Leroy Birney had advocated a limited public role for women wearing head coverings.[85] The subsequent paper in the series, published in 1974, was by Joyce Harper, a former Exclusive and by then an Anglican, who argued for the equality of status and roles between the sexes. 'To many of us a hat has no special religious significance' she wrote. If they were to be worn, they should be regarded as 'light-hearted bits of decoration'.[86] When Birney repeated his position in the CBRF journal in 1982, the editors printed after it a critique of his views

---

80. 'The Believer's Question Box', *The Believer's Magazine*, 58 (Oct. 1948), 237.
81. Sally Hogg, *Invisible Women: A History of Women and the Church* (Raleigh, NC, 2012), 6, growing up in south-west England in the mid-twentieth century found Brethren women 'wore smart hats.'
82. Paul W. Marsh, 'The First letter to the Corinthians', in G. C. D. Howley et al. (eds.), *A New Testament Commentary* (London, 1969), 397, ii.
83. D. O. Murray and H. E. Messer, *Word and Work* (1963), 46, quoted in Newton, 'Brethren in Australia', 227.
84. Prof. Ward Gasque to the writer, e-mail 7 June 2007.
85. Leroy Birney, *The Role of Women in the New Testament Church* (CBRF Occasional Papers, No.4; Pinner, 1971), 8–14.
86. Harper, *Women and the Gospel*, 28, 24; the editor, D. F. Murray, however, noted in his preface that he had not been convinced by all Harper's conclusions, ibid., 4.

by the Baptist theologian Mary J. Evans, who questioned the need for head coverings and Birney's views of women's subjection.[87]

Joyce Harper had argued that Paul had been mistranslated in 1 Corinthians 11 and was thus able to retain the continuity of first-century meaning with one that appropriated liberation from hats and rejected the subjection of women. The leading Brethren revisionist on women's head coverings, however, allowed for cultural relativity in interpretation. F. F. Bruce, the Rylands Professor of New Testament Criticism at the University of Manchester, who responded to questions for a number of years in *The Harvester*, confessed that he could not treat enquiries about 'women's headgear and other articles of apparel' with the same degree of seriousness as did the questioners.[88] For Bruce, Scripture was not a form of canon law, but itself displayed the 'phenomenon of cultural relativity, with the adaptations it imposes'.[89] He distinguished between what he termed 'principles' and 'patterns'. The New Testament, he argued, did not contain the latter, but the former. Women having their heads covered in the first century was a matter of public seemliness and how that might be expressed varied in different cultures.[90] In his commentary on 1 Corinthians, Bruce maintained that 'standards of propriety or social convention change from time to time and from place to place', and what Paul was recommending was 'a scrupulous maintenance of social decorum' to give the lie to, if not then, certainly later, 'the most scandalous rumours of what went on at Christian meetings'.[91] Within his own family, however, the practice was more conservative as his wife continued to wear a hat in church to avoid offending others.[92] Nevertheless, he had lent his considerable authority to the trend for Brethren women to be in church with uncovered heads. An additional critique of traditional Brethren teaching on 1 Corinthians 11:2–16 was offered by biblical hermeneutics for Rex Koivisto, an Open Brethren biblical theologian who was a professor at the non-denominational Christian Multnomah University in Portland, Oregon. In his book *One Lord, One Faith*, first published in 1993, Koivisto's concern was for catholicity in the context of the pluriformity of American Protestant denominations. To isolate core orthodoxy that would unite Christians, he proposed recognizing the role of 'interpretive tradition', which was evidently derived from the concept of 'interpretive communities' popularized by the literary theorist, Stanley Fish.[93] Interpretive tradition, maintained Koivisto, explained the differences between Christian denominations, which preserve and transmit their own distinctive doctrines and practices, but it also has a mediatorial function,

---

87. Leroy Birney, 'The Role of Women in the New Testament Church', *Christian Brethren Review Journal*, 33 (1982), 15–32; Mary J. Evans, 'A response to L. Birney', ibid., 33–40.

88. F. F. Bruce, 'Lessons I have Learned', *H*, 54 (June 1975), 154.

89. F. F. Bruce, 'Women in the Church: A Biblical Survey', *Christian Brethren Review Journal*, 33 (1982), 7.

90. F. F. Bruce, 'Practice or Principle', *H*, 68 (Jan. 1989), 13.

91. F. F. Bruce, '1 Corinthians', in id. (ed.), *1 and 2 Corinthians* (London, 1971), 107. Bruce also noted elsewhere about the veil in Corinth: 'With that symbol of authority she had liberty to pray or prophesy in meetings of the church.' (Id., *Answers to Questions*, (Exeter, 1972), 247).

92. Tim Grass, *F. F. Bruce: A Life* (Milton Keynes, 2011), 59.

93. Stanley Fish, *Is There A Text in This Class? The Authority of Interpretive Communities* (Cambridge, MA, 1980), 303–55. Koivisto, however, does not cite Fish as a source.

like a lens through which to view Scripture.[94] Among other examples, he illustrated its functioning in his own Brethren churchmanship in the demand for head coverings even when a woman was not praying or prophesying. This example of 'interpretive selectivity', in a passage that was difficult to interpret, demonstrated for Koivisto that an interpretive tradition was at work.[95] Women not covering their heads became widely accepted public practice in the last three decades of the twentieth century, as also largely happened throughout evangelicalism, among what were undoubtedly the most substantial numbers of Open Brethren in the English-speaking world.[96] One reason for the change was to achieve freedom from what were perceived as the more sectarian features of Brethrenism, and this necessarily involved emancipation from an outmoded fashion. To a greater or lesser degree, such congregations often ceased to identify themselves with the movement.

More conservative Open Brethren, however, have a fundamentalist biblicism. They reject the idea that the teaching of Scripture might be refracted through a cultural prism and feel that the plain sense of the text, which is universal and applicable to every society, should be adhered to. A key text for this hermeneutic with regard to head coverings is 1 Corinthians 1:2, which states the letter is addressed to 'all that in every place call upon the name of Jesus Christ our Lord'. Being in the introduction to the epistle, the verse is taken to set the context for reading the whole letter, which, as the verse is taken self-evidently to mean, includes present-day Christians. In his one-volume Bible commentary, first published in 1989, William MacDonald, the principal of Emmaus Bible College, the most influential Open Brethren tertiary education institute in America, propounds the commonsense view, which fundamentalists tend to favour. He notes that some interpret the Corinthian passage as being culturally relative, or that its teaching was a result of Paul's bachelorhood, but then affirms: 'Still others simply *accept* the teaching of this portion, seeking only to *obey* its precepts even if they do not understand them all.'[97] A later lecturer at Emmaus, John Fish, rejected Koivisto's use of interpretive tradition, as in his opinion it makes everything 'simply a matter of "perspective" or "preference."' He too favoured the commonsense view that there was a clear biblical mandate to insist women cover their heads.[98] The editor of the Canadian magazine, *Truth & Tidings*, Alexander J. Higgins, a New Jersey physician, rejects the very notion of contextualizing

---

94. Rex A. Koivisto, *One Lord, One Faith: A Theology for Cross-denominational Renewal* (1993; 2nd edn., Eugene OR, 2009), 114–15, 167–8, 201–4.

95. Koivisto, *One Lord, One Faith,* 321–3.

96. See, for example, Newton, 'Brethren in Australia', 240.

97. William MacDonald, *Believer's Bible Commentary: New Testament* (Nashville, TN, 1989; rev. edn, 1990), 601.

98. John H. Fish III, 'Brethren Tradition or New Testament Church Truth', *Emmaus Journal*, 2/2 (Winter 1993): 127, 145, Koivisto responded to Fish's critique in the second edition of his book, citing G. H. Lang as one Brethren individual who had no difficulty in seeing that 1 Corinthians 11:5–6 supported women praying publicly. He also notes that his own interpretation (if he gave it) would undoubtedly differ from Fish's: Koivisto, *One Lord, One Faith*, 321 n.26. He also argues that his citation of multiple interpretations of 1 Corinthians 11 and Brethren inconsistency of interpretation between it and 1 Corinthians 14 demonstrate that the former 'should not be used as a basis for a doctrine', a principle the Reformers had recognized: ibid., 323 n.32. I am indebted to Prof. T. J. Marinello for these sources.

Scripture. In an editorial in 1997 entitled 'History, Culture and Revelation', he argued that insisting that the historical and cultural background of a passage be understood before its meaning can be determined creates difficulties in his view specifically for the traditional stances on 'the ministry of women, the head covering and long hair of the sister, baptism and church order'. He maintains it is inadmissible for three reasons: the bias of the historian who studies the cultural context; the 'revisionism' that arises through the re-interpretation of each generation; and, most significantly, because it means the interpreter has to go outside the word of God to understand it. He concludes: 'we can be confident that with the Word of God before us and the Spirit of God indwelling us, we have all the tools which are needed to understand the clear teaching of Scripture.'[99]

One other fundamentalist rhetorical strategy which is employed is to quote selectively from church history and scholarship to show that contemporary teaching is in complete accord with them. In 2002 the American full-time Bible teacher, Warren Henderson, in *Glories Seen & Unseen*, perhaps the most thorough treatment of head coverings from a conservative perspective, gives a catena of quotations from historical texts stretching over eighteen pages and ranging from *The Shepherd of Hermas* to the current practice of the Russian Orthodox Church, sources he would otherwise disagree with profoundly on a number of points. In a series of articles on 1 Corinthians in *Precious Seed,* Malcolm Horlock, then one of the committee which oversees the magazine, cites a paper by the Southern Baptist scholar Thomas R. Schreiner to support his argument that a woman's head covering alludes to the authority of men.[100] Schreiner's paper, while it supports Horlock's interpretation of male authority, has exactly the opposite conclusions from the latter on several crucial aspects of the Corinthian passage, although the reader would not know this from Horlock's article. Schreiner thinks that Corinthians demonstrates women have a public speaking role and should wear, not a head covering, but a culturally equivalent expression of femininity.[101] As James Barr has noted, the purpose of much fundamentalist rhetoric is to reassure the reader that there is scholarship on its side, giving him comfort and assuring him of the certainty of his position.[102] One other marked fundamentalist trait in much of this writing is the manner in which it associates women removing a head covering with other perceived evils. For R. K. Campbell, it comes from 'present movements such as "Women's Lib" and "Unisex".'[103] One American Open Brethren preacher notes that confusion of the sexes has always been a mark of depravity. He asks rhetorically where the fashion for long hair in men comes from. Not from the Beatles, he answers, but from the hordes of hell which have, according to Revelation 9: 7–8, '*the faces of men and the*

---

99. A. J. Higgins, 'Editorial: History, Culture and Revelation', *Truth & Tidings*, 48/11 (Nov. 1997), <http://truthandtidings.com/1997/11/editorial-history-culture-and-revelation/ >, accessed 20 Sept. 2018.

100. Malcolm Horlock, '1 Corinthians 11 (1)', *Precious Seed*, 62/2 (2007), <http://www.preciousseed.org/view.php?id=2203>, accessed 13 June 2011.

101. Thomas R. Schreiner, 'Head Coverings, Prophecies and the Trinity: 1 Corinthians 11:2–16', in John Piper and Wayne Grudem (eds.), *Recovering Biblical Manhood and Womanhood: A Response to Evangelical Feminism* (Wheaton, IL, 1991), 124–39.

102. James Barr, *Fundamentalism* (London, 1977), 16.

103. R. K. Campbell, *Headship and Head Covering According to Scripture* (Sunbury, PA, [1984]), 10.

hair of women.¹⁰⁴ These writers reveal an anxiety that the removal of what is for them key ways in marking gender would inevitably lead to alternative ways in constructing sexual identity. Hostility such as this towards societal trends which are felt to be out of control is among the roots of fundamentalism.¹⁰⁵

One further marker of the anxiety felt over societal trends is that the numerous magazines which serve the conservative Brethren constituency regularly carry articles arguing for the necessity of women covering their heads, and in the last decade especially, a number of monographs on the topic—some books but mostly pamphlets—have been published. One feature of these publications is the minutiae in which they engage, a hermeneutical strategy which attempts to supply a hedge around the Corinthian passage. The most basic one is what constitutes a head covering, and while all are agreed that it should be ample, the answers suggest veils, mantillas, hats, or a simple piece of cloth placed on the head.¹⁰⁶ The debate has recurred over whether the Corinthian passage applied to the assembly or all places. One Canadian reasoned that it could only apply within the assembly: 'The Bible was written for people in the frozen regions of the north', he maintained, and so uncovering one's head elsewhere would 'put men in danger of severe frostbite.'¹⁰⁷ Warren Henderson engages in a gynaecological discussion of pubescent girls to establish when it is proper for them to begin wearing a covering.¹⁰⁸ In general, these writers are keen to establish they are dealing with a issue of significance, and, alongside the appeal to the commonsense understanding of the passage, the principal means by which this is done is through establishing an entirely novel theology of ecclesial ordinances that has been developed at least since the mid-1960s, but which could be found earlier within American fundamentalism.¹⁰⁹ Henderson regards hair and head coverings as 'symbolic

---

104. J. B. Nicholson, *The Head Covering: A Biblical Perspective* (Port Colborne, ON, 2006), 24. Emphasis in original.

105. George M. Marsden, *Fundamentalism and American Culture: The Shaping of Twentieth-Century Evangelicalism 1870–1925* (Oxford, 1980), 199–201.

106. At the time of writing, the Brethren publisher John Ritchie Ltd., in its bookshop in Kilmarnock sells 40 different women's berets in a variety of colours and degrees of stylishness which can also be purchased online: <https://www.ritchiechristianmedia.co.uk/christian-gifts/berets>, accessed 3 Oct. 2108.

107. John Dennison, 'Questions from an Assembly Observer: Head Coverings', *Truth & Tidings*, 59/2 (Feb. 2008), <http://www.truthandtidings.com/issues/2008/t20080206.php>, accessed 13 June 2011.

108. Henderson, *Glories Seen & Unseen*, 97–9; cf. Romel Ghossain, *Indispensible Ordinance: Baptism, the Lord's Supper, Head Covering* (Bristol, 2013), 128, which maintains the decision depends on a sister's 'spiritual maturity and conscience'.

109. H. Wingfield Graham, 'Symbolic Declarations', *Assembly Testimony*, 80 (Nov./Dec. 1965), 89, quoted in Grass, *Gathering to His Name*, 419–20. The earliest example that I have found of representing long hair as an enduring ecclesial symbol is in a work by the American arch-fundamentalist and independent Baptist evangelist, John R. Rice (1895–1980), *Bobbed Hair, Bossy Wives and Women Preachers: Significant Questions for Honest Christian Women Settled by the Word of* God (Murfreesboro, TN, 1941), 70–1. Rice's symbols also include ordination and anointing the sick.

truth', which he defines as 'an act or object that epitomizes a spiritual fact'.[110] Head coverings, therefore, have been elevated alongside the dominical institution of baptism and the Lord's supper to being an enduring symbol, neatly caught in the title of a book by the Scottish physician, Norman J. Gourlay: *Church Symbols for Today: The Water, the Head, the Bread and Wine*.[111] Mark Sweetnam, an assistant professor of English at Trinity College, Dublin, prefers the term 'ordinance', the word the Brethren use, in common with other low-church traditions, rather than 'sacrament' in which the notion of receiving grace is additionally implicit. The three ordinances of baptism, the Lord's supper, and the head covering Sweetnam maintains, to avoid an obvious difficulty, have been given to the Church, not by Christ, but by the Holy Spirit.[112] The case is reinforced for these writers by the second half of 1 Corinthians 11 being concerned with directions for the Lord's supper, allowing them to ask on what principle can one set of symbols be retained and the other rejected.[113] David Gooding, emeritus professor of Greek at Queen's University, Belfast, argues that from the teaching of the Corinthian passage 'we gather at once what an important thing headship is in the realm of redemption: under God everyone, whether man, woman or Christ himself has a head.'[114] As a result to accept the teaching of the passage on head coverings is to 'gladly and voluntarily to submit to his gracious government and to accept the leadership and headship which he appoints for us'.[115] A head covering mediates divine transcendence, but also a reified social order.

One of the rare female voices in the works arguing for retaining head coverings comes from Hazel Dixon, the wife of an English full-time worker in the Glanton Exclusive connexion. Dixon, writing in 2003, imaginatively develops a sacramental theology with reference to C. S. Lewis's epithet in his Narnia stories, 'daughters of Eve'. Quoting a male Exclusive writer of her connexion to the effect that the powers of darkness have always tried to dominate the woman, she notes that a fallen angel was a witness to Eve acting in independence from her head and husband, but now women, whom Paul states must have their heads covered 'because of the angels', 'have the honour of proclaiming to those same witnesses of her fall (for angels are deathless) our loyalty to His wise designs by this simple sign which they can read—the covering on our head.'[116] For this woman at least, like the North-American women in the Anabaptist tradition responsible for numerous postings on

---

110. Henderson, *Glories Seen & Unseen*, 6. Cf. John Calvin, *Institutes of the Christian Religion* (1559), 4: 14; The Thirty Nine Articles (1562), XXV.

111. N. J. Gourlay, *Church Symbols for Today: The Water, the Head, the Bread and Wine*, (Kansas City, KA, 1999).

112. Mark Sweetnam, *There am I: The Purpose and Pattern of the New Testament Church* (Cookstown, 2015), 47. Sweetnam's definition of ordinances is that they 'give physical expression to spiritual realities.' Ibid.

113. Edwin Taylor, *The Head-Covering. Does it Really Matter?* (Aberdeen, 2004), 26–8; Campbell, *Headship and Head Covering*, 8.

114. David Gooding, *Symbols of Headship and of Glory* (Belfast, n.d.), [2].

115. Gooding, *Headship and of Glory*, [3].

116. Hazel Dixon, 'Head Covering—Cultural or Cosmic?', in [Jane Worsley and Hazel Dixon], *Head Covering*, (Morpeth, 2003), 9.

head coverings on Internet sites, or the *hijab* for many Muslim women,[117] her covering is an important symbol of her identity, but one that enchants the cosmos.[118]

Conclusions

The changes in women's hair and head coverings in the Brethren could be paralleled in a variety of twentieth-century Christian denominations in the West. Perhaps what distinguished the Brethren was the central place the issues were given in their debates, how protracted the process was among them, and the conservative retrenchment. The retired Canadian missionary, T. Ernest Wilson, listed women's silence and covered heads as among the distinctive doctrines which the Brethren maintained that had been lost or altered—presumably by other Christians.[119] However, in the Open section, maintaining a woman's head covering as being, in the title of one work, an 'indispensible ordinance',[120] created tensions. Some of the frustrations can be seen by the *reductio ad absurdum* of the debate in an article in the youth magazine of one Scottish assembly. It imagined an elders meeting in 2050 discussing what to do with teenagers visiting from Mars, especially the female of the species. One elder states: 'I thought we had decided that if any alien had multiple heads they would be expected to cover at least one of them.'[121] In the late 1970s, one progressive Open Brethren assembly in north-west England decided to reverse its practice and insist on head coverings at the breaking of bread, even going so far as to purchase a set of veils to issue to women who did not bring a covering. This was due to the influence of a number of former Exclusive Brethren who had become elders, and the pastor, although he disagreed with the policy, had to announce it. There was considerable resistance among the members. After one week, the veils mysteriously disappeared, some women had to be reprimanded for non-compliance, and one couple left the fellowship.[122] The tensions could lead to more open schism. In Malaysia, the influence of the Northern Irish missionary, Tom Bentley, led to a division in 1963 among the English-speaking Chinese assemblies, and one of the key issues was an objection to head coverings no longer being insisted upon at all assembly gatherings.[123] Throughout the English-speaking world there were many more unrecorded cases of individuals transferring allegiance to

---

117. John R. Bowen, *Why the French Don't Like Headscarves: Islam, the State and Public Space* (Princeton, NJ, 2007), 71.

118. Webster, *Anthropology*, 160–1.

119. T. Ernest Wilson, 'Appendix I: Who are the Brethren?' in Fredk. A. Tatford, *That the World May Know*, 6: *Light over the Dark Continent* (Bath, 1984), 485–9, spec. 488.

120. Ghossain, *Indispensible Ordinance*.

121. 'Elders Meeting 2050. Part 2', *Youth News*, c.2000, Greenview Evangelical Church, Glasgow; the elder quoted would have been readily identifiable by the readers.

122. E-mails to the writer from Prof. John Coffey, 19 May 2015 and 21 May 2015.

123. Grace Bentley, *A Biography on [sic] Thomas Bentley* (Newtonards, 2012), 87; Samuel T. W. Wee, *Simply Gathered in the Malayan Peninsula: A Historical Reflection on Assembly Testimony in Malaysia and Singapore 1860–2010. A Sesquicentennial Essay* (Singapore [2010]), 66–8; see also, Peter H. L. Wee, *The Woman's Head Covering and the Glory of God* (Singapore, 1983).

neighbouring assemblies or churches in protest at either the insistence on head coverings or allowing their removal, which usually, as was the case in Malaysia, involved other issues.[124]

The material dimensions of women's hair and head coverings illustrate the varying Brethren responses to Western culture in the last 100 years perhaps better than any other aspect of the movement. Not surprisingly, given the public status women traditionally had, the discourse was conducted almost exclusively by men. It is significant than when CBRF had published works in the 1970s by women arguing for the non-necessity of head coverings, they were written from ones outside the movement—an Anglican and a Baptist. The men who wrote and spoke about women strove to control women's behaviour and bodies in ways that were patriarchal, and which could be, at their most extreme, at best, sexist, and at worst, misogynistic and prurient. Women's appearance in a time of social flux created a deep sense of anxiety, and the virtues which were consistently praised were meekness and submissiveness. In the concentration on a woman's hair, a symbol of sexuality was being focused on; differences in hair and head coverings also stressed gender difference. Traditional notions of society were being preserved. The attitudes can therefore be readily calibrated with attitudes to female emancipation. Those who quietly accepted dress trends in society belonged to the denominationalizing trend within twentieth-century Open Brethren which increasingly permitted a more tolerant attitude to integration with the wider Church and society.[125] Many Open Brethren women, particularly those in the more cosmopolitan middle classes, had undergone social and cultural transformation.[126] Consequently, men who also had shared in these cultural processes were increasingly willing to permit wider roles within their assemblies to women, though this was a process which was slow and partial.[127] Those who maintained the conservative view on head coverings, however, also rejected any changes in a woman's role. They wanted to pull up the drawbridge to keep the wider society outside, and to be a bastion of a traditional social order. Theirs was a sectarian response. This was seen most markedly in the Taylorite innovations, bequeathed to the Plymouth Brethren Christian Church, in which women's hair and head coverings established a strong group identity that set them apart from outsiders. They are also signifiers of an assembly's identity—as one contemporary belonging to the non-Taylorite Exclusives noted, '"You can tell if a place is right or not by if the women wear head coverings."'[128] Henderson concludes his book in hortatory mode. The Lord 'did not entrust the visual beauty of the local assembly unto the brothers, but to the sisters. Sisters, you're on display for the entire universe to see. The angels are watching you.'[129] There are more earthly audiences. In cultural and fashion writing, conservative early-twentieth Brethrenism has come to represent the rebarbative, not to say the ridiculous, nature of religion, through Fereday's pamphlet becoming a

---

124. Wee, *Simply Gathered*, 53–69, also cites greater cooperation with other Christian bodies, an informal approach to worship, blurring of male/female roles, and reception of non-Brethren Christians to the Lord's table.

125. Bryan R. Wilson, 'An analysis of sect development', in id. (ed.), *Patterns of Sectarianism*, 23–5; Dickson, *Brethren in Scotland*, 367–71.

126. Sheila Westbury, 'Women in the Church', *H*, 71 (Mar. 1992), 17–18.

127. Grass, *Gathering to His Name*, 455–7.

128. Webster, *Anthropology*, 145.

129. Henderson, *Glories Seen & Unseen*, 120.

stock reference in the literature.[130] Brethren women, too, are instructed in their behaviour and identity through the discourses on head coverings and hair. It is the lot of Brethren women that their appearance should be the language which speaks in several different registers to themselves, to fellow assembly members, and, perhaps more faintly to those in a secularized society who deign to listen, about relationships between Church and society.

For most Brethren women there were no great arguments. Patricia Beer maintained of change in the Brethren of her childhood: 'I realised it was not a question of principle at all, but of the passage of time. The Brethren moved with the times in the worst possible sense: they did not rethink their rules in a mood of enlightenment working on social change; they just gradually stopped forbidding.'[131] This is fair as a comment on how the change was achieved for many ordinary believers, but not, as this chapter has made clear, as a criticism of the movement as a whole. For most, religion is not reasoned logically. When symbols become worn out, they fall into desuetude. Elizabeth Street Chapel in Wellington, New Zealand, gradually accepted the long-term social trends in the 1980s of women no longer wearing hats to avoid what they felt was the rigour of fundamentalism, but the elders were acutely aware it was 'more in keeping with the fashion of the day than with any clear policy and practice based solely on the Bible.'[132] But in a movement that gives the Bible such a central place in its practice, the divisions that opened up in the Brethren made questions of hermeneutics as impossible to avoid as fashion trends had been. Those who had interacted with significant modern cultural trends, such as changes in the status and roles of women, had revaluated ecclesiastical traditions and long-held biblical interpretations and found the teaching of the Bible to be other than what it traditionally seemed to be, or found new ways of interpreting it. They were part of the growing awareness among evangelicals of hermeneutics, which, as Brian Stanley has noted, was no longer confined to the university, but intruded into church life. What the biblical text meant in the different context of contemporary Western society had to be established.[133] To conservative Brethren this was surrendering to secular society. Sweetnam argues that 'the hermeneutical contortions and exegetical gymnastics performed by expositors who will not allow God's Word to mean what it says' would be 'risible', if it

---

130. This is due to generous quotation from it in a standard work of reference, Corson, *Fashions in Hair*, 614–5. Corson does not identify either the author or his ecclesiastical loyalty. For quotation from Corson, see: Jill Rudd and Val Gough, *Charlotte Perkins Gilman: Optimist Reformer* (Iowa City, IA, 1999), 228; Karen Stevenson, 'Hairy Business: Organising the Gendered Self', in Ruth Holliday and John Hassard (eds.), *Contested Bodies* (London, 2001), 137–52, spec.141–2; Patricia Wynn Brown, *Hair-A-Baloo: The Revealing Comedy and Tragedy on Top of Your Head*, (Lincoln, NE, 2005), 71; Caroline Cox and Lee Widdows, *Hair and Fashion* (London, 2005), 52; Steven Zdatny, *Fashion, Work, and Politics in Modern France*, (London, 2006), 63; Patricia Malcolmson, *Me and My Hair: A Social History* (Gosport, Hampshire, 2012), 72.

131. Beer, *Mrs Beer's House*, 133–4.

132. Harvey G. Rees-Thomas, *100 Years on the Street: A Story of God's Grace* (Wellington, NZ, 2017), 163.

133. Brian Stanley, *A History of Evangelicalism: People, Movements and Ideas in the English-Speaking World*, vol. 5: *The Global Diffusion of Evangelicalism: The Age of Billy Graham and John Stott.* (Downers Grove, IL, 2013), 211–13.

were not for 'the fundamental seriousness of seeing Scripture denigrated and disregarded'. In not following the 'the plain—though unpopular—teaching' of 1 Corinthians 11, 'it is the strident cry of society that is heard and heeded, and the clear commands of God's Word set aside'.[134] In this view, hermeneutics has become one more site for the contest in pluralistic societies between accommodation and entrenchment in religious belief and practice.[135] But conservative commentators, too, were perhaps not as isolated from cultural influences as they thought. The appeal to the role of angels as a witness to women's head coverings, which occurs in much of the more recent conservative Open Brethren literature, seems an obvious response to the disenchanted universe of secularization.[136] Both they and the Exclusives took a symbolic turn in seeking to justify long hair and head coverings from the mid-twentieth century onwards. Traditionally fundamentalist exegesis had been heavily propositional, arising, as it did, out of the strain of rationalism within it, but in a society alive to the semiotics of dress, and influenced by the postmodern embrace of the visual, it is significant that in a more diluted and tentative manner the arguments employed appealed to the symbolic. Cultural trends of late modernity had made an impact on all shades of Brethren, influencing their biblical exegesis.

---

134. Sweetnam, *There am I*, 48.
135. Peter L. Berger, *The Sacred Canopy: Elements of a Sociological Theory of Religion* (New York, 1967), 153.
136. Henderson, *Glories Seen & Unseen*, 77–82; Ghossein, *Indispensible Ordinance*, 124–5; anon., *Focus on the Head-Covering* (Kilmarnock, 2008), 14–15; Dixon, 'Head Covering', 7–10; Sweetnam, *There am I*, 50–1.

CHAPTER 3

Samuel Prideaux Tregelles: A Nineteenth-Century Evangelical Apology for New Testament Textual Criticism

Dirk Jongkind

The nineteenth century was an exciting time when it comes to the study of antiquity and especially in the field of manuscript studies. The scholarly world became increasingly aware of new materials that were useful to publish new critical editions of ancient texts. Libraries were combed for hidden treasures, and expeditions to the Orient were undertaken in search of manuscripts.[1] However, the field of the New Testament did not behave like, for example, the field of Classics, where there was no perceived problem in replacing older with newer editions. Within Christian scholarship and the Christian church there was a resistance to change, even though since the sixteenth century (and also before) scholars were fully aware of the existence of differences in the wording of the text between Greek manuscripts. However, since the publication of the first Greek New Testament in 1516, the *Novum Instrumentum* edited by Erasmus, to the early nineteenth century, the text in use had not been updated to reflect the increased knowledge of the textual transmission. The text of Erasmus had set the norm and reflected fairly well—though not at all exactly—the text of the Byzantine medieval church.

By the seventeenth century, the text of Erasmus had become the 'text accepted by all' (*textus receptus*),[2] and none ventured to introduce changes to the received text, even though it was admitted that in particular the Greek text of Revelation was not of high quality. However, with the growing publication of collations of manuscripts and further theoretical reflections throughout the eighteenth century by people such as Gerhardt van Maestricht and the great pietistic scholar Johann Albrecht Bengel, it was only a matter of time before a new generation of Greek New Testaments was published. The first was published in 1831 by a German classicist, Karl Lachmann, who set himself as a goal to reconstruct the Greek text as it existed in the fourth century AD.[3]

---

1. For a recent biography of the efforts of one of the most prolific scholars in the area of the Greek New Testament, Constantin Tischendorf, who among others brought the fourth century manuscript *Codex Sinaiticus* to the attention of the European scholarly world, see Stanley E. Porter, *Constantine Tischendorf: The Life and Work of a 19th Century Bible Hunter* (London, 2015). Given the cultural context of the 19th century perhaps more surprising is the contribution of two sisters to manuscript discoveries. See Janet Soskice, *Sisters of Sinai: How Two Lady Adventurers Found the Hidden Gospels* (London, 2009).
2. An expression used in the Greek New Testament of Elzevir in 1633.
3. *Novum Testamentum Graece: Ex Recensione Caroli Lachmanni* (Berolini, 1831). Lachmann sets out his goals and methods in a separate article published a year earlier:

It is in this context that Samuel Prideaux Tregelles did his work, and he is the first British scholar to publish any part of the Greek New Testament as a new critical enterprise that is not dependent on the *textus receptus*. In 1844 he published a Greek text of Revelation,[4] but set himself the task to work on the whole of the New Testament. Throughout his work, Tregelles was always conscious about issues of method and questions of theology. This makes him a valuable starting point to reflect on some of the issues at stake.

The theory and theology of textual criticism

Tregelles was by no means the first to write on theoretical questions of textual criticism, but his contributions, and those of many before him, suffer from being overshadowed by the influential work of B. F. Westcott and F. J. A. Hort, who published their edition and theoretical framework within a decade after Tregelles's death.[5] There is some justification for the notion that the major theoretical developments of modern textual criticism did not start with Westcott and Hort, but actually ended with these two scholars.[6]

The theory of Westcott and Hort is based on the notion of text-types, groupings of manuscripts based on affinities in their text, that is, shared readings in places where there is variation between manuscripts. In itself this was nothing new and the notion goes back to the early eighteenth century when Bengel suggested that manuscripts could be divided into various groups which he called 'nations'.[7] Westcott and Hort, though, gave a lucid account of how the relationship between the various text-types could be conceived. The later Byzantine text is the synthesis of the Alexandrian and Western text. The Alexandrian text is a development of the pure 'Neutral' text, while the Western text is admittedly old but shows paraphrastic and expansionary tendencies. Westcott and Hort's text is based on the notion that the best manuscript of the best text-type will provide the most important voice. However, considerations of style and internal probability lead to frequent deviations from this important voice (*Codex Vaticanus*) in favour of readings provided by other manuscripts or even other text-types.

'Rechenschaft über seine Ausgabe des Neuen Testaments', *Theologische Studien und Kritiken*, 3 (1830), 817–45.

4. Interestingly, also Kelly published a Greek text of Revelation (William Kelly, *The Revelation of John: Edited in Greek with A New English Version and A Statement of the Chief Authorities* [London, 1860]).

5. B. F. Westcott and F. J. A. Hort, *The New Testament in the Original Greek*, 2 vols. (London, 1881).

6. I have considerable sympathy for Eldon Epp's assessment of the situation: 'The Twentieth-Century Interlude in New Testament Textual Criticism', in Eldon J. Epp and Gordon D. Fee (eds.), *Studies in the Theory and Method of New Testament Textual Criticism* (Grand Rapids, MI., 1993), 83–108; originally published under the same title in *Journal of Biblical Literature*, 93 (1974), 386–414. Also id., 'A Continuing Interlude in New Testament Textual Criticism?', in Eldon J. Epp and Gordon D. Fee (eds.), *Studies in the Theory and Method of New Testament Textual Criticism* (Grand Rapids, MI, 1993), 109–23.

7. This part of the history of textual criticism is well recorded in Tregelles's *An Account of the Printed Text of the Greek New Testament: With Remarks on Its Revision Upon Critical Principles* (London, 1854).

Tregelles is fully aware of the existence of text-types and in a sense he foresees some of the dangers of applying the strict macro-genealogical approach of Westcott and Hort. He refuses to reduce the voice of any text-type to a single voice; the boundaries between the text-types are too vague to posit that any text-type goes back to a single recension at any one particular point in time.

Besides considerations such as these, which are relevant to every practitioner within the discipline, there is also the question of the right theological framework for textual criticism. John Owen had argued in his 1657 essay, 'Of the Integrity and Purity of the Hebrew and Greek Text of Scripture', that bringing together in an uncritical way a great number of variant readings was of no other use 'than merely *to create a temptation* to the reader that nothing is left sound and entire in the word of God'.[8] Tregelles was all too aware of the sensitivity of surrounding textual criticism and the wide-spread trust people had in the *textus receptus*, which was also by Owen held as the standard.[9] Rather than charging those who held a different view with ignorance, Tregelles took serious the task of providing an explanation of, or perhaps better, an apology for the discipline of textual criticism. This paper will trace the positive argument for textual criticism Tregelles made in his introduction to his edition of the Greek text of Revelation, published in 1844.

Samuel Prideaux Tregelles was born into a family in the Quaker tradition in the early nineteenth century, but was for most of his life closely associated with B. W. Newton, who stood in the middle of some of the earliest controversies in the Plymouth Brethren.[10] Tregelles is described as never to have identified himself fully with the Brethren movement, but at the same time never to have attached himself to any of the denominational churches.[11] Tregelles has, as far as his dislike of liberal theology goes, an impeccable track record, yet he does not always show the conciliatory attitude one might expect or hope for. For example, in his translation of Gesenius' Hebrew Dictionary, he warns the reader from the outset against the unnecessary, liberal ideas promoted in particular lemmas and adds that he has put in a serious effort to provide his own view in the translation.[12] His dates (1813–75)

---

8. John Owen, 'Of the Integrity and Purity of the Hebrew and Greek Text of Scripture with Considerations on the Prolegomena and Appendix of the Late "Biblia Polyglotta"', in William H. Goold (ed.), *The Works of John Owen, DD* (New York, 1853 [1659]), 345–421 (cited 364). Emphasis in the original.

9. Owen, 'Of the Integrity and Purity of the Hebrew and Greek Text of Scripture', 366.

10. For a rather fragmentary overview of the life of Tregelles, see George H. Fromow, *B. W. Newton and Dr. S. P. Tregelles: Teachers of the Faith and the Future* (2nd edn., London, 1969).

11. So e.g. F. F. Bruce, 'Samuel Prideaux Tregelles', *H*, 54/7 (Aug. 1975), 211–12.

12. Wilhelm Gesenius, *Gesenius' Hebrew and Chaldee Lexicon to the Old Testament Scriptures*, ET Samuel Prideaux Tregelles (London, 1857), preface v: 'It has been a special object with the translator, to note the interpretations of Gesenius which manifested neologian tendencies, in order that by a remark, or by querying a statement, the reader may be put on his guard. And if any passages should remain unmarked, in which doubt is cast upon Scripture inspiration, or in which the New and Old Testaments are spoken of as discrepant, or in which mistakes and ignorance are charged upon the "holy men of God who wrote as they were moved by the Holy Ghost,"—if any perchance remain in which these or other neologian tendencies be left unnoticed—the translator wishes it distinctly to be understood that it is the effect of inadvertence alone, and not of design.'

are very similar to Constantin Tischendorf (1815–74), the better known German text-critic with whom Tregelles was in frequent correspondence and even spent time with in Leipzig.

Introduction to the Greek text of Revelation, 1844

At the age of 31, Tregelles published his edition of the Greek text of Revelation.[13] He does not mention in the introduction to the text that he had collated any manuscript himself—there is no evidence at all in this work that he had actually seen any Greek manuscript in person. At this stage of his grand project, Tregelles relies solely on the collations and transcripts of manuscript published by others.

He relates how it had struck him that the Greek text of the book of Revelation had particularly been subject to not a few corrections in recent editions of the Greek New Testament (e.g., those of Johann Scholz; Johann Griesbach).[14] As Revelation in particular presents itself as a book with the specific solemn injunction to hear the words and keep the things written in it,[15] Tregelles set out to present the text 'as correctly as possible'.

In his introductory essay Tregelles uses this phrase 'as correctly as possible', or words to a similar effect, a number of times. For him, restoring the text and making critical judgements is a process of approximating the true text instead of presenting the assured results that lie beyond any shade of doubt. This entails the acknowledgement that, firstly, there is no quick solution to textual criticism (against the defenders of the *textus receptus*), and, secondly, textual criticism is a complex process of fallible decisions. Because of this acknowledgement of the complexity of the process, Tregelles can be described as a methodological eclectic: no single manuscript gives us the exact text of the original. Tregelles could only hope to contribute to a more precise approximation of the original wording of the Greek New Testament.

Inspiration and textual criticism

How does Tregelles as a conservative Christian see the relation between Scripture as inspired by God and the necessity of critically addressing the form and shape of the actual Greek text? His argument starts by stating his commitment to the verbal inspiration of Scripture. He writes, 'I avow my full belief in the absolute, plenary inspiration of Scripture, 2 Tim 3.16. I believe the sixty-six books of the Old and New Testaments to be verbally the word of God, as absolutely as were the ten commandments written by the finger of God on the two tables of stone.'[16] This statement does not mean necessarily that Tregelles held that all Scripture was dictated in a similar way, but it does mean that the end result of enscripturation had taken the form as intended by God.

---

13. S. P. Tregelles, *The Book of Revelation in Greek: Edited from Ancient Authorities; with a New English Version and Various Readings* (London, 1844).

14. Though the Byzantine text is fairly uniform in the rest of the New Testament, it is much less so in Revelation, leaving plenty of room for editorial decisions even by those who wanted to present the traditional text.

15. Tregelles, *The Book of Revelation in Greek*, i: 'No book of the New Testament is pressed upon our attention with more solemn sanctions; "Blessed is he that readeth, and they that hear the words of this prophecy, and keep the things which are written in it"' (Rev. 1:3).

16. Tregelles, *The Book of Revelation*, iii.

From this point a number of possibilities lay open. Some have used the notion of verbal inspiration to argue that inspiration therefore entails the necessity of providential preservation. That is, since God inspired Scripture verbally, he must have preserved it for us somehow, an argument used both positively within the King James-only movement who will argue that God did so indeed by giving us the *textus receptus* and by those who are critical of any notion of inspiration who will argue that since God did not preserve Scripture without error there cannot have been inspiration in the first place.[17]

Tregelles starts from a different point: 'now I wish most distinctly to state that because I reverence Scripture as being the word of God, I believe it to be of importance to bring every aid in our power to bear upon its text, in order that we may as accurately as possible read it in the very words in which it was given by the Holy Ghost.'[18] So, because God inspired Scripture verbally, it is actually important to establish the exact words of Scripture. We might tease this out a little further by saying that if one confesses that only the message of Scripture was inspired, and that this inspiration does not extend to the very words, then indeed there is little intrinsic need for textual criticism that often occupies itself with the tiny details of the text. Tregelles underlines that his aim is positive: 'because *I thus fully believe in its verbal inspiration, I judge that it is not labour ill bestowed to endeavour to search into the evidence which is obtainable as to what those words are, and to exhibit the results of such investigation*'.[19]

In a later work from 1852, Tregelles simply dismisses a relation between verbal inspiration and perfect preservation. Elaborating on the notion that the Bible was subject to similar processes as non-inspired literature, he says,

> Some have thought that such an idea would cast a kind of reflection upon God—as if He would permit the perfection of Scripture to be impaired. All we need say is, that the fact is such; Scripture has been subject to just the same casualties as other books; copyists have made mistakes (just as compositors in printing may do) in transcribing Scripture, exactly the same as if they had been engaged on secular writings. As things are so, we know that God has permitted this to take place.[20]

Tregelles uses a truly empiricist argument in constructing his theology. Given the existence of differences in wording between manuscripts, and given God's sovereign rule over all, it follows that God must have allowed this situation to arise. Tregelles does not go into

---

17. See e.g. the following quotation from the popular book by the text-critic Bart Ehrman. 'For the only reason (I came to think) for God to inspire the Bible would be so that his people would have his actual words; but if he really wanted people to have his actual words, surely he would have miraculously preserved those words, just as he had miraculously inspired them in the first place. Given the circumstance that he didn't preserve the words, the conclusion seemed inescapable to me that he hadn't gone to the trouble of inspiring them.' Bart Ehrman, *Whose Word is It?: The Story Behind Who Changed the New Testament and Why* (London, 2006), 211. Similar sentiments can be found also in Islamic apologetic literature against Christianity.

18. Tregelles, *The Book of Revelation*, iii.

19. Tregelles, *The Book of Revelation*, iii. Emphasis added.

20. S. P. Tregelles, *A Lecture on the Historic Evidence of the Authorship and Transmission of the Books of the New Testament* (London, 1852), 98.

any speculation as to the reasons why God would have allowed this, but at this point the simple acknowledgement of the existing situation is sufficient theologically.

Tregelles readily admits that textual criticism may affect texts that have been traditionally used to establish the divinity of Christ or the doctrine of the Trinity, two of the core doctrines of the Christian church.[21] He has two things to say on this. The first argument is that though some passages in Scripture can no longer be used to uphold certain doctrines, this does not weaken the doctrine itself. On the contrary, support that should never have been used in the first place is removed with the result that the doctrine is more fully grounded in the true text of Scripture. Healthy critical work in the word of God provides a safeguard against ignorance and heterodoxy. Secondly, he again presents an argument based on observation:

> It is indeed a cause for thankfulness that God has preserved the Scripture unto us in such substantial integrity: it has been subjected to many casualties, it has passed through the hands of many copyists, but in doctrine and precept it is unchanged. I believe that it may most truly be said that the most faulty copy presents to us the doctrines and the duties of Christianity devoid of any material alteration.[22]

That is to say, within all the textual corruption that has affected the text, the doctrine or ethical commands have not been altered. Though Tregelles does not claim that God was going to ensure that the Bible would be transmitted with its teaching intact, or that God had put himself under an obligation to do so, he does note that it is a cause for thankfulness that God had done exactly this. Yet, Tregelles hastens to add, 'Of course the more exactly we know the very words of Scripture as originally inspired by the Holy Ghost, the more exactly have we the declaration of His mind set before us.'[23]

In 1854, in his *Account of the Printed Text of the Greek New Testament*, published ten years after the edition of the Greek text of Revelation, Tregelles discusses the previous editions of the Greek New Testament and the theoretical contributions of the editors.[24] Besides the now sharper articulated view on the limited validity of the theory of early text-types, there is comparatively little change in the fundamentals underlying Tregelles's approach to textual criticism though there is a further refinement of the theological reflection on the absence of providential preservation. 'If God had so pleased, he could have preserved its text from all the casualties of transcriptural error: but the text has not been so preserved; it is therefore no reflection on the divine wisdom, no want of

---

21. Most likely Tregelles refers to the variant in 1 Tim. 3: 15 where he would opt for the reading 'who was revealed in flesh' rather than 'God was revealed in flesh', and to his leaving out the Trinitarian formula in 1 John 5: 7–8 'For there are three that bear record in heaven, the Father, the Word, and the Holy Ghost: and these three are one'. One must bear in mind that Tregelles was writing at a time where every printed English Bible contained these words.

22. Tregelles, *The Book of Revelation*, v.

23. Tregelles, *The Book of Revelation*, v.

24. S. P. Tregelles, *An Account of the Printed Text of the Greek New Testament: with Remarks on its Revision upon Critical Principles. Together with a Collation of the Critical Texts of Griesbach, Scholz, Lachmann, and Tischendorf, with that in Common Use* (London, 1854).

reverence for God's inspired word, to admit the fact.'[25] Tregelles is careful to state God's omnipotence, 'he could have preserved the text', and his sovereignty, 'the text has not been so preserved'.[26] God made a sovereign choice to commit the transmission of Scripture to the normal patterns of history. 'God did not see fit to multiply the copies of his Scripture for the use of mankind by miracle; and just as He left it to the hands of men to copy His Word in the same manner as other books, so was it left exposed to the same changes, from want of skill in copyists, from carelessness or misapprehension, as affect all other ancient writings.'[27]

However, surveying the quantity and quality of the evidence that is available to do proper textual criticism, Tregelles does not hesitate to ascribe the survival of so many manuscripts to God. 'To this, however, it should be added (even though it be by anticipation), that the providence of God has transmitted to us far more ample materials for the restoration of the text of the New Testament, than we have in the case of any other work of similar antiquity.'[28]

In his 1844 introduction to the text of Revelation, Tregelles is aware of an accusation that so much of Biblical criticism is carried out by liberals and rationalists. This he addresses by making two points. First, he acknowledges freely that many of these liberals (but certainly not all) have made good critical choices, and besides also orthodox scholars such as Bengel, a little over a century before Tregelles, have been active in the field. But then, in a nice twist of the argument, Tregelles adds, 'instead of leading those who hold orthodox sentiments to avoid the subject, ought to induce them to take it up themselves, in order that they might not be under the necessity of receiving critical texts from doubtful hands'.[29]

The practice of textual transmission and textual criticism

Having set out the theological parameters within which Tregelles intends to work, he describes the actual work that needs to be done. As said above, Tregelles does not make a difference between the transmission of secular books and Scripture—both are copied by fallible scribes. 'The fact of [the Scriptures] having been "given by inspiration of God", has not and could not ensure perfection in the transcripts made, unless the copyists were also inspired.'[30] However, Tregelles does not drive the point of similarity between the transmission of the Bible and of secular literature to its logical conclusion. When it comes to conjectural emendation he hastens to state that there is no space within the textual criticism of the New Testament to suggest a wording of the text that is not found in any actual manuscript. '[But] to use critical conjecture with regard to the word of God is to act in a manner wholly unjustifiable. When this is done, then charges of innovation and want of reverence for God's holy word may indeed be brought'.[31] In this context, though, he justifies his rejection of conjectural emendation for Scripture by pointing out

---

25. Tregelles, *An Account of the Printed Text of the Greek New Testament*, 37.
26. Tregelles, *An Account of the Printed Text of the Greek New Testament*, 37.
27. Tregelles, *An Account of the Printed Text of the Greek New Testament*, 37.
28. Tregelles, *An Account of the Printed Text of the Greek New Testament*, 38–39.
29. Tregelles, *The Book of Revelation*, iv.
30. Tregelles, *The Book of Revelation*, vi–vii.
31. Tregelles, *The Book of Revelation*, xix.

the difference in the amount of available evidence between the New Testament and other literary works from antiquity. Yet it is clear that Tregelles's conviction is informed by his theology and does not solely rest on critical assumptions. Incidentally, for Tregelles the charge of innovation was apparently a real one, as further down in his introduction he brings 'innovation' up again and distances himself again from it. '. . . I may here remark, that no charge of innovation can be fairly brought against the text here adopted. The innovation really has been the adoption and use of modern readings instead of ancient'.[32]

This brings us to Tregelles's evaluation of the text as printed by Erasmus, and especially, as we are dealing here with Tregelles's 1844 introduction to his text of Revelation, how Erasmus handled the text of the last book of the New Testament. The one manuscript Erasmus used for Revelation was defective, which problem was remedied by Erasmus by translating the existing Latin text back into Greek. Tregelles is clear in his condemnation of such practice, and expects other Christians to agree immediately.

> It must be obvious to the Christian reader that the word of God ought never to have been edited with such precipitancy,[33] or with such liberties taken with the text: indeed it may be regarded as a cause for thankfulness that more incorrect readings were not thus introduced into the printed copies than was actually the case.[34]

The word of God cannot be treated as lightly as Erasmus had done; it should never have been edited so hastily. The result could have been much worse, but the editorial process was irresponsible. In light of this, and now armed with better material than available to either Erasmus or the editors of the *Complutensian Polyglot*, which was published shortly after Erasmus's first edition, Tregelles feels completely free to re-edit the text without ascribing independent authority to the earlier printed texts, even though he sees himself standing in their line and tradition, working as an editor just as they were.

> In forming the Text, no prescriptive right was allowed to the Received Text; the principles on which readings were approved, were the same that I should have adopted, had the critical materials been before me without such a thing as a printed edition in existence;—in fact, I put myself in the place in which the Complutensian editors or Erasmus would have been, had they the various collations before them; and it was now my place to act as they, according to my judgment, ought in such circumstances to have acted.[35]

The principles according to which Tregelles edited the text are by and large those of current textual criticism, with one particular characteristic, which would prove to be defining in Tregelles's later text-critical work, and that is the emphasis on the importance of evidence. Though all modern text-critics would be quick to agree, Tregelles works this out in how he appreciates the manuscript tradition. There are early manuscripts and there are late manuscripts. When late manuscripts have readings not found in early manuscripts or in

---

32. Tregelles, *The Book of Revelation*, xxxvii.
33. OED, 'precipitancy: 1. Excessive haste in action or thought; rashness, hastiness; (also) a rash or hasty act.'
34. Tregelles, *The Book of Revelation*, xiv.
35. Tregelles, *The Book of Revelation*, xxiv–xxx.

other early evidence, then there is in principle no reason to prefer the later above the earlier reading. The criterion of age receives a high prominence. Tregelles makes exceptions to this rule, and he takes care to list those readings from the earliest manuscripts which he does not adopt.[36] From this it becomes apparent that one of the reasons to reject the oldest attested reading is the tendency of copyists to harmonize to the immediate context by, for example, adjusting case endings to that of preceding words.

A further corollary of Tregelles's emphasis on evidence is his already mentioned aversion to text-types and text-groupings, which have a certain artificiality over them.[37] Though the situation for the Greek manuscript of Revelation is quite different than that in the rest of the New Testament, still Tregelles concentrates on the witness of the individual, oldest manuscripts.

The text-critic

Writing as a Christian to Christians, Tregelles feels free to discuss two points normally not seen in an introduction to textual criticism. The first is that of the influence of already held convictions. Unlike the current, post-modern tendency of self-disclosure and subsequent relativizing and individualizing of scholarly output, Tregelles claims a critical distance to his work. He does not believe that his theology or his exegetical opinions have influenced the text-critical choices he made.[38]

> No thoughts of my own on the subject of interpretation have, I believe, in a single instance influenced my judgment as to the adoption of readings; on the contrary in many places preconceived thoughts on particular passages had to give way before what I saw, on sufficient grounds of evidence, to be 'the words of the Holy Ghost'.[39]

There is an interesting parallel with what Tregelles said earlier about those texts that are used in support of certain doctrines but which may be affected by critical work. In that context Tregelles demonstrated a deep faith in the truth of these doctrines and their rootedness in Scripture, and he was not afraid to go where the evidence would lead him. If some passages turn out not to support these doctrines, nothing is lost and something is gained. The doctrines end up having a more secure support from Scripture than before when partially supported by suspect texts. In the case of Tregelles's textual criticism and the relation to exegesis, he makes a similar move; again he is not afraid to go where the evidence leads him. The word of God, when established more precise than before, should keep its potential to change opinions and convictions. If that means that if he needs to

---

36. In his work on other parts of the New Testament this would lead to a rejection of the Byzantine text as a valuable voice. Tregelles could not see any evidence that the text found only in late manuscripts was early.

37. This notion is fully worked out in Tregelles's later work, particularly in his *Account of the Printed Text of the Greek New Testament*, for example, in his discussion of Griesbach's classification of text-types (pp. 90–1).

38. Compare this to the declared interest Tregelles took in the translation of Gesenius' Hebrew dictionary where there was a clear absence of critical distance to the task of translation.

39. Tregelles, *The Book of Revelation*, xxxvii–xxxviii.

change his opinion on the exegesis of certain texts after he has established the true text, so be it. Nothing lost, but truth gained.

The second point Tregelles addresses in his introduction is the role of the devotional life of the text-critic. He comments on the role of prayer in doing textual criticism.

> I may here again remark that I believe it to be the privilege and duty of a Christian editor to pray that he may be enabled to collect the evidence which is needful, and to form a right judgment on evidence so collected. It is true that this will not make him infallible; but just as in every matter of daily life it is our place to pray for Divine guidance that we may act as disciples of Christ, and just as every Christian must acknowledge that this has been often vouchsafed to him, so surely we may seek in this matter to be guided aright in judgment on evidence, both as to the principles and their application in particular instances. Whatever *approximation* to truth may be made in the statement of results or probabilities may be thus thankfully ascribed to Him who can bestow the needful diligence, application, and vigilance.[40]

Tregelles points out that the Christian editor has the privilege and duty to pray. In practice this prayer should be for the careful collection of the evidence, which, as Tregelles described elsewhere, is a long and arduous task. In addition, prayer for right judgements should be made. For Tregelles this is certainly not a guarantee for good results or for infallibility, but much more a way to ensure that whatever progress may be made, this will be ascribed to God rather than to one's own effort. One cannot boast on having achieved a result when one has asked God first to give this result.

Evaluation

From the above, it should be clear that Tregelles took the task of justifying his involvement in the fast emerging discipline of New Testament textual criticism very seriously. There is a clear theological justification for what textual criticism is and why it is a good thing to be involved in it. Though he worked 150 years ago, a number of his specific ideas still deserve attention because of the positive contribution they make both to the discipline and any evangelical reflection on the discipline.

First, belief in verbal inspiration should lead to a greater concern for these words. Though this argument has often been used in the case for precise, word-by-word translations of Scripture, this applies equally to ascertaining the precise wording of the original text for Tregelles.

Secondly, Tregelles is modest in what textual criticism can actually achieve. There can be only an approximation—not a final resolution. The result will be imperfect but may improve on what has been done before. To state the notion of approximation more positively, the more exactly we have the wording, the more exactly we have the expression of God's mind. A modern equivalent of Tregelles's approximation would be that of digital images. Low-resolution images allow only for a limited level of zoom. Beyond this level, the image becomes pixelated, and the finest details remain hidden even though the overall image is clear and beyond dispute. A high-resolution image allows for the study

---

40. Tregelles, *The Book of Revelation*, xxxi.

of details otherwise hidden, and it is here that further approximation of what is out there becomes possible.

Thirdly, rather than accepting a theology that necessitates a doctrine in which God would be under some sort of obligation to preserve his Word, Tregelles sees the existing integrity of Scripture as a reason for thanksgiving. On the one hand, the situation could be far worse than it actually is; on the other hand, for most practical purposes the theologian and exegete has a sufficiently precise text to do their work.

Fourthly, Tregelles held a strong conviction that theology and exegesis should come after the text, not the other way around. There is an inherent authority in Scripture that overrules the scholar's interpretations and conclusions. Stylistic arguments and considerations based on the flow of thoughts have only limited value.

Fifthly, Tregelles does not forget that the discipline is carried out by human beings, and in his case, by someone who is a devoted Christian and who is under an obligation to take care to integrate his discipline with his spiritual life.

What questions, then, could be asked of Tregelles's theological framework for doing textual criticism? A genuine question that remains is to what extent the emphasis on the evidence of 'facts' is indirectly an admission of some sort of providential preservation, albeit a sufficient rather than a perfect preservation. Tregelles states so much when he says that God 'in his providence' provided us with a wealth of material and that Christians should be thankful for this act of mercy. Still there is an important difference between acknowledging that God has preserved the integrity of the text and given us an abundance of manuscripts and versions to work with, and the notion that God providentially has kept the text clear from any corruption.

A second possible question is related to the previous point. Is it really possible to dismiss a text in use by the church for over a 1000 years (such as the Vulgate) or 300 years (*textus receptus*) with a single stroke? But again, this may be a case of stating the issue in the wrong terminology. The 'text' is not rejected and replaced with something else, but rather, one edition of the text is replaced with another, more careful edition of the same text. It is exactly this process that is described by Tregelles's emphasis on approximation.

Lastly, Tregelles did not use any model of the early history of the transmission of the text. Though he made a distinction between early manuscripts and late (and therefore held a suspicion against readings exclusively attested in the Byzantine text) and also acknowledged the peculiar character of many of the readings in manuscripts such as *Codex Bezae* (what many would call Western readings), he did not formulate a historical theory that would explain the development of the text. Though the advantage of this approach is that every variant reading is taken seriously and that no summary judgement is made on groups of readings, it has the disadvantage that it forces the text-critic to use an atomistic approach whereby one moves from variant unit to variant unit. The danger is that such an approach blinds one to detailed knowledge of manuscripts and their particular tendencies—a manuscript is more than a collection of unconnected variant readings. Furthermore, as with almost any theory of textual criticism, Tregelles was unable to solve the tension between the possibility that a true reading could be preserved in any manuscript and the observation that some manuscripts contain better readings than others.

At the same time, Tregelles's reluctance to accept any reconstruction of the early transmission history may prove a helpful correction to the ideas of some practitioners in the field and, for example, stands in stark contrast to Westcott and Hort after him. Yet it seems that one cannot do without some rudimentary notion of what happened in the early centuries. At the very least, a tacit assumption of Tregelles seems to be that the early transmission of the text must have been highly convoluted and is now impossible to disentangle on the basis of current evidence. However, this question is not crucial to any theology of textual criticism and moves already into actual praxis. Certainly it does not take away from the valuable contribution Tregelles makes to the development of an evangelical view of what text-critics of the New Testament are doing.

CHAPTER 4

In the World and of It Too: Bible or Culture? The Role of Women in Brethren Assemblies 1880–1940

Beth Dickson

> Thus we hold that the mind of the woman is equally perfect with the mind of the man, but perfectly different. No amount of education will obliterate this essential difference; and no theories of our modern scientists to the contrary will do other than introduce mischief into the hive of the commonwealth. When we read the noble poem of the German Schiller on the praises of woman,[1] we see that we are not alone in believing that woman is the great civilizer. Woman's love of what is decorous and beautiful supplements well man's love of truth, and his admiration of practical wisdom. Yes, woman in her right place is the great civilizing power; but alas for civilization if she should adopt the theories objected to.
>
> John Eliot Howard, 'The Early Dawn of Civilization Considered in the Light of Scripture', *Journal of the Transactions of the Victoria Institute*, 9 (1876), 242.

John Eliot Howard was a former Quaker who joined the Brethren in 1838 and founded Brook Street Chapel in Tottenham. He was a noted scientist and manufacturer of quinine.[2] In objecting to the theories of the physicist John Tyndall, whom Howard saw as promoting an Epicurean atheism, he was representative of his time in believing in essential differences between men and women. As he wrote elsewhere: 'Man is the expression of the *majesty*, woman of the *beauty* of Creation.'[3] These differences were expressed in the public lives of men and the domestic lives of women, and many other dualities were laid across this binary, notably reason and emotion. John Ruskin, art critic and social commentator, in a

---

1. This is an allusion to Friedrich Schiller's 'Würde der Frauen' ['Dignity of Women'] (1795), in which women were praised as more having greater sensibility and being more civilized and civilizing than men, with superiority in knowledge and poetry, and remote from war; see Matthew Head, *Sovereign Feminine: Music and Gender in Eighteenth-Century Germany* (Oakland, CA, 2013), 233–7.

2. Gerald T. West, *From Friends to Brethren: The Howards of Tottenham—Quakers, Brethren, and Evangelicals*, (ed.) Tim Grass (SBH: *Subsidia*; Troon, 2016).

3. John Eliot Howard, 'Creation and Providence with Special Reference to the Evolutionist Theory', *Journal of the Transactions of the Victoria Institute*, 12 (1879), 207.

series of lectures dating from 1864 (fifteen years earlier than Howard) makes a similar set of points:

> We cannot determine what the queenly power of women should be, until we are agreed what their ordinary power should be . . . And there never was a time when wilder words were spoken, or more vain imagination permitted, respecting this question—quite vital to all social happiness. The relations of the womanly to the manly nature, their different capacities of intellect or of virtue, seem never to have been yet estimated with entire consent. We hear of the mission and of the rights of Woman, as if these could ever be separate from the mission and the rights of Man . . . .[4]

The lecture, addressing the question of the sort of education which would benefit women, dates from 1864 and is evidence of the extent to which the role of women was a matter of general cultural discussion on which three contemporary views can be identified. The first, contained in the 'ideology of domesticity', was a view of the relationship between the sexes which aligns easily with the teaching about the role of women which Brethren interpreted as being the teaching of the New Testament, particularly in the Pastoral Epistles. Brethren believed that a woman's place was in the home and that public duties and employment outside the home were the preserve of men. The language of 'separate spheres' was commonly used to establish this gendered binary between private and public.[5] However, both Eliot and Ruskin believed in educational opportunities for women and in women's role as teachers, especially of the young. This demonstrates a second view towards the topic which is prepared to concede that in the modern world there might be more expanded roles for women—Florence Nightingale was a pioneer for this position.[6] The Brethren, perhaps more than might be supposed, given the rigour of their rhetoric, provided, through their lay movement, expanded roles for women. However, this expansion was set firmly within the binary with Eliot's warnings about the end of civilisation and the 'wild words' to which Ruskin refers, being spoken by those who argued for a third position: a maximalist position, that there should be equality between women and men. Howard and Ruskin's anxiety about equality was shared by most Brethren writers. This cultural ferment surrounding the role of women was taking place as the Brethren were moving from their revivalist phase in mid-Victorian Britain to an institutional phase.[7] As they sought to order and codify their meetings, this chapter will argue that they accepted the first and second cultural positions but rejected the third position, except in a handful of notable cases. The chapter will also argue that the Brethren did not think of themselves as existing within culture, accepting or rejecting cultural positions, but outside culture, judging it by the teaching of Scripture

---

4. John Ruskin, 'Of Queens' Gardens', in *Sesame and Lilies:* (1865; rev. edn., New York, *c.*1891), 103, online text at <http://www.archive.org/stream/sesameliliesthre01rusk#page/n7/mode/2up>, accessed 19 Mar. 2012.

5. Mary Lyndon Shanley, *Feminism, Marriage, and the Law in Victorian England, 1850–1895* (Princeton, NJ, 1989), 5.

6. Lawrence James, *The Middle Class: A History* (London, 2006), 343–60.

7. Neil Dickson, 'Modern Prophetesses: Women Preachers in the Nineteenth-Century Scottish Brethren', *Records of the Scottish Church History Society*, 25 (1993), 111.

which they regarded as outside, above, and impervious to, culture. I will also look briefly at the ways they read Scripture to produce such interpretations.

Six pamphlets will be considered. Three of the pamphlets have no date, and the dates assigned to them here, determined on historical grounds, are approximate ones. The six are: A. O. Molesworth's *The Ministry of Women* ([1878]), which was first published as a series of magazine articles and in its pamphlet form it had an appendix by the magazine editor, J. R. Caldwell (1839–1917), who would also later write on the same topic in the magazine;[8] William Hoste's *The Service of Sisters, Its Service and Scope* ([1909]); *A Plea for the Sisters of our Lord Jesus Christ* (1912) (anonymous but written by 'four of His [Christ's] servants'); J. J. Sim's *"My Handmaidens Shall Prophesy"* (1913); J. A. Anderson's *Woman's Warfare and Ministry* (1921); and finally *The Ministry of Women* (1936) by C. F. Hogg, W. E. Vine, and W. R. Lewis.[9] These six pamphlets will enable us to examine a variety of opinions on women's roles within the Brethren movement, from the majority anti-expansionist position to the decidedly minority voices of those who argued for expanded roles and even for a maximal public one for women.

Anti-expansionsists

Brethren decisively rejected progressive elements of the cultural discussion about the role of women, although they were aware of its topicality. 'One of the world's ungodly themes in these last days is "Women's Rights"', concludes Caldwell. 'Take heed, lest the leaven which is working in the world around be permitted to do its deadly work within the assemblies of the saints'.[10] For William Hoste (1861–1938), a former Anglican and a later editor of *The Believer's Magazine*, it is a 'burning issue', but the claims for gender equality cut no ice with him being merely 'the boasted advances of our day in education and civilisation'.[11] Some women obtained the vote in 1918, and in 1928 the franchise was extended to all women over 21. In 1936, writing about the passages in the Pastoral Epistles dealing with women's roles, William Edwy Vine (1873–1949), a lay theologian and an editor of the missionary magazine *Echoes of Service*, warned that 'professing Christian teachers' should teach the 'the plain instructions given in these passages [1 Cor. 11: 14 and 1 Tim. 2: 5] and beware of relegating them to a past period, as if they were inapplicable to modern conditions.[12] He is aware of the argument that these passages of Scripture as culturally conditioned, but rejects it. Charles Frederick Hogg (1861–1943), a former

---

8. J. R. Caldwell later published a pamphlet entitled *The Ministry of Women* (Glasgow, [1895]) which reprinted a series of his articles in *The Witness* in 1895.

9. A. O. Molesworth, with appendix by J. R. Caldwell, *The Ministry of Women . . .* (Glasgow, [1879]); William Hoste, *The Service of Sisters: Its Sanction and Scope, with special reference to "The ministry of women" by A. J. Gordon* (Glasgow, [1909]); J. J. Sims, *"My handmaidens shall prophesy": An Exegesis and Review, in which certain teachings concerning the public ministry of women are brought under the searchlight of truth and examined* (London, 1913); Four of His Servants, *A Plea for the Sisters of Our Lord Jesus Christ* (Oxford, 1912); John A. Anderson, *Woman's Warfare and Ministry* (2nd edn., Stonehaven, 1921); and C. F. Hogg, W. E. Vine and W. R. Lewis, *The Ministry of Women: A Study in the Scriptures* (London, [1936]).

10. J. R. Caldwell 'Appendix', in Molesworth, *Ministry of Women*, 32.

11. Hoste, *Service of Sisters*, 17.

12. Vine, *Ministry of Women*, 24.

missionary to China and a prominent full-time minister of the word among the Brethren in the early twentieth century, too warns of being influenced by 'the modern defiance of God in the refusal of the Divine, and natural order. In the world, the usurpation by women of the functions of men is everywhere in evidence. The windows of the churches are open to the world, its atmosphere enters insidiously, and all unawares we become conformed to "this present age"'.[13] By contrast, 'God's order is universal, and vindicates itself everywhere'.[14] During this period, the Brethren view was remarkably consistent. It regarded progressive views about women's role as antithetical to its view of the teaching of Scripture. Brethren believed they were aware of the cultural influences on them and were able to recognize and judge them as wrong in the light of Scripture. The content of their views aligns them with those who held culturally conservative views. However, this alignment was either of no importance—or invisible—to them.

These anti-expansionist pamphlets made no distinction between the teaching of Scripture and the 'ideology of domesticity'. Anthony Oliver Molesworth (1839–1917), a retired lieutenant colonel who had become an itinerant preacher, argues that the veil makes a woman '*unnoticeable*' in public worship, 'lest she prove a distraction' to male worshippers.[15] Caldwell struggles with the depiction of Deborah as a judge and strategist, writing that 'it does not appear that she left the shade of the palm tree where she dwelt' (for 'under the palm tree', read 'private sphere'). He continues: 'The utmost discretion seems to have been used by Deborah to avoid, in the most responsible position that perhaps God ever called a woman to occupy among His people, even the appearance of going beyond what was strictly a woman's place.'[16]

Keen though Caldwell is to cast this passage as an exception, he nevertheless respects Deborah's actions as divinely sanctioned, although he gives her behaviour a Victorian cast in terms of anxiety about woman's place. The anti-expansionists all use the language of 'separate spheres'.[17] The most unguarded of the writers, William Rhodes Lewis (1877–1964), a lawyer and another editor of *Echoes of Service*, states that the private, domestic sphere where a woman has 'personal equality' because she can influence other women and children, is 'perfectly consistent with administrative subordination' which he goes on to characterize much more by restriction than by equality. He writes that a woman has to be accepting of 'the limitation of her sphere of action and of her subordination'.[18] The writers also produce common contemporary stereotypes of women. Hoste's pamphlet was a polemic directed against *The Ministry of Women* (1894) by the American Baptist, Adoniram Judson Gordon (1836–95), who argued for a public role for women in the church. In arguing against the importance which Gordon gave to Priscilla, Hoste uses a transferred epithet to characterize the weakness of Gordon's argument by saying it rests on

---

13. Hogg, *Ministry of Women*, 9.
14. Hogg, *Ministry of Women*, 17–8.
15. Molesworth, *Ministry of Women*, 6.
16. Caldwell 'Appendix', in Molesworth, *Ministry of Women*, 23.
17. Molesworth, *Ministry of Women*, 18; Caldwell, 'Appendix', in Molesworth, *Ministry of Women*, 31; Hoste, *Service of Sisters*, 25; Vine, *Ministry of Women*, 20.
18. Lewis, *Ministry of Women*, 38.

Priscilla's 'frail shoulders'.[19] Hogg believes that men are rational and women emotional.[20] Lewis writes 'the woman's shorter stature, her slighter frame, her higher pitch of voice, and more graceful form and movement are indications that she is intended for private ministries, and especially for those of home-life rather than for general public service in the world'.[21] Thus Brethren writers reproduced the ideology of domesticity in their writing. They never acknowledge that this is a way of behaving that is largely shared by their fellow-citizens. Although they do sometimes use 'Nature' to reinforce the rightness of their position, it is likely that they were thinking of the created order rather than a culturally-constructed social order. Because of their belief in the necessity of conversion, if they had thought about why those they characterized as 'sinners' behaved to all intents and purposes like children of God with regard to the role of women, they would perhaps have concluded that good works, no matter how admirable, provided no grounds for salvation. Thus only when this behaviour was the outcome of a converted life, would Brethren take notice of it. Their view of themselves as a separated community inside an unconverted culture, able to recognize and reject cultural influences, blinded them to the extent to which the cultural conservative norms of their society permeated the church and were, indeed, reproduced by it, often in the familiar shape of the women sitting next to them in the assembly, their wives. They became in spite of their best efforts 'all unawares conformed to "this present age"'.[22]

However, cultural influences are not so clearly demarcated, and the arguments which caused Brethren writers most difficulty were those which originated from within evangelicalism and which advocated an expanded role for women. It was the abiding Brethren passion for evangelism which was the source of the difficulty as arguments derived principally from home missions, especially those in the revivalist tradition from which the Brethren sprang and with which they had considerable sympathy, and foreign missions in which Grass has calculated that between 1874 and 1913 at least fifty per cent of Brethren missionaries were women.[23] These areas were not the exclusive preserve of Brethren, and they had to interact with other evangelicals who held opposing arguments but who held them from presuppositions about how to read the Bible which were very much like their own. These interlocutors were not so easy to reject or ignore.

The historical record, as found in Dickson and Grass, demonstrates that women, as well as men, though not in the same numbers, founded Brethren assemblies. 'Mary Hamilton and Mary Paterson were widely used in Brethren church planting,' writes Dickson, 'including the formation of congregations at Larkhall and Motherwell, later two of the most influential Scottish assemblies.'[24] The Irish female preacher Isabella Armstrong preached widely in Scotland supported and encouraged by the revivalist Gordon Forlong

---

19. Hoste, *Service of Sisters*, 7. A version of the male-female binary underlies this as men are associated with strength and women with frailty; it is difficult not to hear echoes of Shakespeare's 'Frailty thy name is woman'.

20. Hogg, *Ministry of Women*, 17.

21. Lewis, *Ministry of Women*, 35.

22. Hogg, *Ministry of Women*, 9; 'this present age' is a quotation from Galatians 1:4 (RV)

23. Tim Grass, *Gathering to His Name: The Story of Open Brethren in Britain and Ireland* (Milton Keynes, 2006), 184.

24. Dickson, 'Modern Prophetesses', 98.

who became associated with the Brethren.[25] John Wardrop, the leading member of the assembly in Wishaw, Lanarkshire, in the later nineteenth century and James Stone, a founder member of the assembly in East Kilbride, also in Lanarkshire, encouraged the ministry of women.[26] In England, Anne Evans, Grass states, 'one of the first seven to break bread at Bethesda, Bristol in 1832, moved to Brimscombe and began a fruitful outreach work, opening mission rooms in the Stroud area.'[27] J. R. Caldwell knew that some Scottish assemblies had been founded by women evangelists, and he himself acknowledged that he had, as a young preacher, been much encouraged by an older Christian woman who invited him to preach in her kitchen meetings.[28] He sees nothing wrong with '[sisters] visiting in cottages in a dark country district'; indeed he believes that 'visitation in the homes of the poor is a sphere where women's ministry is specially calculated to be fruitful … But the moment she steps from beneath the roof of a home to the platform of a public place of assembly, she leaves the private sphere and enters upon the public' thus usurping a man's authority'.[29] This view, he maintains, is 'gathered from Scripture as a whole', but Caldwell seems unaware that he is reading a nineteenth-century distinction between public and private into the New Testament. Elsewhere Brethren writers are quick to point out that the body of Christ is not be confused with the ecclesiastical buildings in which it assembles, but here the building in which the church meets does determine the extent to which women can minister. There is another interesting vignette which shows Caldwell's struggle. He describes an incident in which a 'sister who was accustomed publicly to preach the gospel, was excluded from the fellowship for so doing, whilst seven of those converted through her ministry were received.' While his rhetoric is more than capable of judging this a right action, Caldwell continues, 'We should like to know upon what authority such an one was excluded.'[30] Although Caldwell immediately categorizes this evangelism as an exception, and therefore divinely, if inconveniently, permitted, his likely actions are far more just than his rhetoric would predict. The effectiveness of women in evangelism *did* carry enormous weight with individuals such as Caldwell. Here experience acts against cultural conservatism and his interpretation of Scripture in a way which he finds uncomfortable. However, he speaks only in terms of stories he has been told, and in his pamphlet he does not remember explicitly the women evangelists who began the movement. Therefore their stories are already beginning to be lost to his readership. Of potential cultural narratives about women, the anti-expansionists, aided by their reading of Scripture, reflected only the dominant one.

---

25. For Forlong, see Hy Pickering (ed.), *Chief Men Among the Brethren* (2nd edn., London, [1931]), 67–9.
26. Dickson, 'Modern Prophetesses', 104–8.
27. Grass, *Gathering to His Name*, 182.
28. Dickson, 'Modern Prophetesses', 114.
29. Caldwell, 'Appendix', in Molesworth, *Ministry of Women*, 30.
30. Caldwell, 'Appendix', in Molesworth, *Ministry of Women*, 29.

An expansionist

John J. Sims (*fl*.1891–1930) was a Canadian evangelist who preached to gatherings of 4,000 in Glasgow's largest civic venue in 1893.[31] *"My Handmaidens Shall Prophesy"* is a vigorous recommendation of an enlarged sphere for women. Driven by the compulsion to preach the gospel in conditions where many people were positively affected by it, Sims could see that women considerably expanded the evangelistic labour force. In some ways, Sims is close to the traditional Brethren view. He does not believe that women are able to teach, and that as a sign of their subjection, they should have their heads covered. 'Her status in creation, her action at the Fall prohibit her taking the place of authority. She is not a Leader but a Helper.'[32] Although he sees this teaching as self-evident, he cannot express it without stressing that 'In that place of quietness and subjection, she is responsible to exercise the gift that is in her'.[33]

Given this restriction, his understanding of Scripture is more open. He argues that the woman with the issue of blood is the authority for women publicly testifying to Christ's power; that the woman of Sychar's well authorizes women to preach the gospel; and that the instruction to Mary Magdalene to tell the disciples about the resurrection authorizes women to deliver 'messages' to the assembled saints.[34] If a woman is gifted, Sims argues that she *must* use her gift. If women preach and sinners are converted, it demonstrates God's approval of the preacher. Sims has no difficulty in reading the New Testament as a manual for revivalist meetings. His list of what a woman can do is notably energetic:

> She may take a Hall, and preach the Gospel, or speak in the open air, or give a Bible Reading, so long as she does it in the spirit of subjection, of which the covering on her head is a sign. We have seen that knowledge and prophesying are not necessarily teaching in the Apostolic sense of the word. So in a Bible Reading, she may help the saints by a word of knowledge, or comfort, or exhortation. In the Church and connected with it, she is subject to its scriptural rule. In the exercise of the gift the Lord has bestowed on her she is responsible to the Lord alone, and any brother or sister who seeks to hinder her, is disobeying the direct command of the Apostle, "Judge nothing before the time, until the Lord come"—*(I. Cor. iv)* Christian men and women must not allow themselves to be brought under bondage to others.[35]

The extent to which women could inhabit such an enlarged sphere depended on the nature of the assembly they worshipped in. The more evangelistically inclined the assembly, in terms of home or foreign mission, the more likely it was that women could be teachers of other women, children, the poor or the inhabitants of developing countries. The more the assembly was predicated on producing ecclesiastical purity, the less likely these outlets were to be open to women. There were no female Sunday school teachers in the strict assembly in the mining village of Shotts in Lanarkshire until after the Second World War, a long time, therefore, after women school teachers had become culturally acceptable in

---

31. Grass, *Gathering to His Name*, 137.
32. Sims, *"My handmaidens shall prophesy"*, 40.
33. Sims, *"My handmaidens shall prophesy"*, 40–1.
34. Sims, *"My handmaidens shall prophesy"*, 11–13.
35. Sims, *"My handmaidens shall prophesy"*, 46–7.

Scotland.³⁶ Only after women had died did the language men used to describe them publicly change. Obituaries in *The Witness* and *The Believer's Magazine* were written in kinder language than the language surrounding the limitation and restriction of role. Margaret Haldane 'gave devoted service to the Lord'; J. S. Anderson's wife was 'A devoted wife and energetic worker'. All the inhabitants of the village of Busby in Renfrewshire drew their blinds as Mrs Duff's cortege passed, 'as a token of respect to one who had lived and manifested Christ in her life among them'.³⁷ This language shows a benign patriarchy able to honour the work of women with tenderness. However, it does leave unanswered the question, why did the Brethren insist on the necessity for orderly behaviour from women given that so many Brethren women would never have dreamt of challenging the norms of behaviour prevalent in church and society?

The second area from which Brethren were assailed by arguments for an expanded role for women was foreign missions. In *The Service of Sisters: Its Sanction and Scope*, Hoste identifies the Welsh awakening and A. J. Gordon's pamphlet *The Ministry of Women* (1894) as two sources which make the Brethren wonder about expanded roles for women.³⁸ Gordon was a regular evangelist at Dwight L. Moody's Springfield convention and founder of Gordon College and Seminary. The pastor of one of Boston's largest Baptist churches, he was also chairman of the American Baptist Missionary Union. He wrote a brief pamphlet in year before he died in which he treats the main New Testament passages about the role of women and concludes that there is nothing to stop them preaching or teaching.³⁹ The quality of the arguments adduced from Scripture and the authority of the man who made them drew a response from Hoste who writes that 'clearness, and clearness alone demands a frequent reference by name to the late Dr. Gordon, whose memory is so widely honoured as an earnest servant of Christ, especially in the sphere of Missions'.⁴⁰ Names were not usually cited in pamphlets, but here in order to refute Gordon, Hoste has to follow him so closely that he cannot but name him.

Gordon's argument depends on re-arranging the scriptural passages where the more positive passages are to be considered more important than the less positive ones: so the key texts are Acts 2: 17 and Galatians 3: 18. Priscilla's teaching of Apollos is more important than the injunction against teaching in 1 Timothy 2 which Gordon regards as an injunction to orderly behaviour in prayer and insists that it should be interpreted in the light of the New Testament as a whole. Hoste counters simply by stating that texts such as 1 Corinthians 14 and 1 Timothy 2 are the texts which govern the rest. Gordon concludes that experience has a place in interpreting Scripture:

---

36. Oral information from John Jack, July 2007.
37. *W*, 66 (Nov. 1936), 264; *W*, 49 (Jun. 1919), 99; *Believer's Magazine*, 47 (Jan. 1935), 28.
38. Hoste, *Service of Sisters*, 5, and 'Preface'.
39. A. J. Gordon, 'The Ministry of Women', *Missionary Review of the* World, 7 (Dec. 1894), 910–21. The article was published as a pamphlet with the same title; online text at <http://xythos.gordon.edu/Archives/Gordon_Herritage/Ministry%20of%20Women.pdf>, accessed 15 Mar. 2012. Gordon was published in Britain by Pickering & Inglis, and G. H. Lang cited with approval the remark by A. T. Pierson that along with Bethesda Chapel in Bristol, Gordon's church in Boston, MA, was 'one of the two truly apostolic churches he knew': G. H. Lang, *The Local Assembly* (Walsham-le-Willows, 1942), 50.
40. Hoste, 'Preface', *Service of Sisters*.

> The final exegesis is not always to be found in the lexicon and grammar. The Spirit is in the Word; and the Spirit is also in the Church . . . To follow the voice of the Church apart from that of the written Word has never proved safe; but, on the other hand, it may be that we need to be admonished not to ignore the teaching of the deepest spiritual life of the Church in forming our conclusions concerning the meaning of Scripture.[41]

Hoste dismisses experience as a guide to the interpretation by characterizing it as a method of interpretation 'dangerously like that of Rome'.[42] He notes that women missionaries may find themselves in 'anomalous positions by force of circumstances, by the absence, or even by the supineness, of brethren, as in the case of Deborah of old; but this would not be the same as voluntarily taking up an unscriptural position or retaining it longer than was necessary'.[43] Gordon's pamphlet had been occasioned by being present at a summer conference where a young woman missionary was withdrawn from the programme because of the scruples of those who believed she should not be addressing a mixed audience. Later in the pamphlet he gives two examples from experience, and although Hoste is not explicit about this, they may provide the 'anomalous positions' to which he had earlier referred. Gordon cites the American Baptist missionary in Burma, Marilla Baker Ingalls (1828–1902), who 'though not assuming ecclesiastical functions, yet by force of character on the one hand, and by the exigencies of the field on the other, . . . had come to be a virtual bishop over nearly a score of churches, training the native ministry in theology and homiletics, guiding the churches in the selection of pastors, and superintending the discipline of the congregations'. He continues with a description of the work of another American Baptist, Adele Fielde (1839–1916), whom he characterizes as 'that brilliant missionary to China'. She had been recalled by her board because other missionaries complained that she was

> transcending her sphere as a woman . . . She replied by describing the vastness and destitution of her field—village after village, hamlet after hamlet, yet unreached by the Gospel—and then how, with a native woman, she had gone into the surrounding country, gathered groups of men, women and children—whoever would come—and told out the story of the Cross to them. "If this is preaching I plead guilty to the charge," she said. "And have you ever been ordained to preach?" asked her examiner. "No," she replied with great dignity and emphasis—"*no; but I believe I have been foreordained.*"[44]

William Hoste edited the work of these remarkable women out of his argument, referring to it, if at all, as 'anomalous'. A conservative view of culture and a conservative view of Biblical interpretation combine to enable Hoste to ignore historical evidence from a reliable source which contradicts and challenges the *status quo*. Brethren orthodoxy rejected the pragmatic arguments of the expansionists.

---

41. Gordon, 'The Ministry of Women', 918–19.
42. Hoste, Preface, *Service of Sisters*.
43. Hoste, *Service of Sisters*, 4.
44. Gordon, 'The Ministry of Women', 920; emphasis in original.

Maximalists

John Arthur Anderson (1862–1959) was born and brought up in Rhynie, Aberdeenshire. Rhynie was unique among Scottish assemblies because it allowed the public participation of women in church services from its revivalist foundation until it closed around the end of the nineteenth century. Anderson's mother participated in church services, and to her and to his wife, Ina Ross Anderson, he dedicated his pamphlet, *Women's Warfare and Ministry: what saith the scriptures?*. The refusal of this remote village, which is not on any main thoroughfare, to give up its unique position on women's ministry led to it being ostracized by other Scottish assemblies.[45] Anderson, after qualifying as a doctor, became a missionary with the China Inland Mission but returned to a 'very active retirement in Aberdeen'.[46] He was an energetic writer with great reserves of confidence and no little intellectual ability.

Having lived in another culture made Anderson, as it made other missionaries, much more aware of culture as culture, rather than as the norm or the invisible 'way things are', which characterizes the way British writers react. His discussion of the veil shows an understanding that in some cultures it is a symbol which allows women to move freely in public.[47] He adds this to his understanding that the veil is a sign of a woman's authority rather than her subjection. He is much more aware that 'subjection' can mean the degradation, humiliation, and abuse of women.[48] This shows the extent to which culture reigned in the anti-expansionists. Although they used the terms 'subjection' and 'subordination', these were governed by the prevailing cultural norms of the 'ideology of domesticity'. Compared with cultures in which women were regarded as slaves or property, Brethren behaviour assumed a level of respect for women which its explicit rhetoric did not necessarily imply. Anderson is aware, also, of the progressive beliefs of his own society and is happy to endorse them when he thinks they can be justified from scripture. Unlike the anti-expansionists, he is aware of an interplay between culture and Scripture. So when he describes Christ as 'the Emancipator', he is deliberately (and provocatively) choosing to characterize Christ in the political language of nineteenth-century anti-slavery campaigning.[49] He does argue for an expansion of women's role, but his vision is more profound and begins to address some of the debate's underlying issues. From the outset, Anderson understands women as being totally and completely human. Even when he is describing them in the house, he shows how much agency he regards them as having: '[Homes cannot be happy] unless a woman is accorded a worthy place . . . with freedom of action, with a consciousness of responsibility, and with the right, unfettered by circumstance or prejudice to develop all that is best and noblest in her to the utmost perfection.'[50]

---

45. John A. Anderson, *Autobiography of John A. Anderson* (2nd edn., Aberdeen, 1950), 21–2.
46. F. F. Bruce, *In Retrospect: In Remembrance of Things Past* (London, 1980), 54.
47. Anderson, *Women's Warfare*, 24.
48. Anderson, *Women's Warfare*, 5–6.
49. Anderson, *Women's Warfare*, 14.
50. Anderson, *Women's Warfare*, 12. Anderson quotes from James Donaldson, *Woman: Her Position and Influence in Ancient Greece and Rome* (London, 1907). Donaldson argues that although women are prominent in the Gospels, their status in the Roman world suffered degradation in the post-apostolic period. Anderson follows Donaldson closely. He quotes

That he knows about the prejudices which affect women is shown by the pamphlet's first quotation from the classical and biblical scholar Sir James Donaldson, who argues that 'The first condition of the successful study of women's history is to come unbiased to the task . . . [trying to hold opinions in abeyance] for all opinions on women are apt to be intense'.[51] To explain the scope and longevity of misogyny, Anderson argues that insufficient attention has been paid to Genesis 3:15—'I will put enmity between thee and the woman'.[52] Anderson regards women as being specially singled out by Satan for attack because Eve revealed his role in the temptation, and it was through her seed that his eventual destruction was prophesied. He is pre-feminist here in his desire to find some all-encompassing argument for the historical repression of women. Like feminists, he bases his viewpoint on a continuing power struggle, not between man and woman, but between the Enemy of Souls and the victory of God.

He proceeds to work through the list of Old Testament women maximizing their stories as effectively as others had minimized them. According to Anderson, 'In his first recorded word to woman, God empowered her to rule and to judge', and he has no difficulty in believing that Deborah exercised gifts of leadership and strategy. She had 'faith, hope and ability' when no-one else had, 'She appointed Barak . . . she it was who gave directions for the final battle . . . she ruled Israel and judged the princes and people for years, during which time God smiled upon them . . . On Meroz and its associates, the curse of God was called down because they refused to follow the lead of Deborah.' His vigorous support for women even has him seeing Pharaoh's daughter as 'worthy to be numbered among women of strong character.[53]

His theological argument continues by asserting that, in what he calls 'apostate Israel', views of women were misogynistic. In the oral law he says that both Deborah and Hulda are given the demeaning names BEE and CAT.[54] Christ came with a revolutionary attitude to women which was reinforced by the work of the Spirit at Pentecost. However, this antagonized Satan, and through Judaisers who supported the oral law, contempt for women was present in the early Church and therefore in the Scriptures. He is clear that 1 Corinthians 14:34–5 is a direct quotation from the oral law. He argues that since the silence of women is contradicted by the experience of Pentecost and after, it is 'preposterous' to suppose that Paul could ever have written these words as they contradict the principles of freedom announced in 1 Corinthians 11:2–16.[55]

His attitude to 1 Timothy 2 is equally bold. He regards the Pastoral Epistles as having been written by Paul but expressing more cautious Christian behaviour because of the Neronian persecution which he judged was ongoing at the time they were written. These were 'special conditions which called for special treatment'. He envisages the context of

---

Donaldson quoting Plato on the belief of the equality of the sexes (p.12) but the two quotations following are Donaldson's interpretation (pp.191, 35), not translations from Plato.

51. Anderson, *Women's Warfare*, title page; the quotation is from James Donaldson, *Woman*, 2–3.

52. Anderson, *Woman's Warfare*, 7.

53. Anderson, *Women's Warfare*, 6; 10–1; 10.

54. Anderson, *Women's Warfare*, 12; the block capitals are in the original.

55. Anderson, *Women's Warfare*, 12–3; 19; 16–7; 19–23.

1 Timothy 2:11–12 as the home in which a Christian wife was attempting to convert a non-Christian husband, and the advice is that, particularly in these dangerous times, she should do this quietly. 'The manner in which the wife must not instruct her husband is the subject dealt with. It is not the question of instructing or teaching him, but the manner of doing it'.[56]

Like Gordon, Anderson also gives examples from contemporary evangelicalism such as Mrs William Booth and two of her daughters, who won thousands of souls for Christ. 'These then are "the seal of their apostleship in the Lord"', proclaims Anderson, unconstrained in using the title of apostle to dignify the evangelism of women.[57] That title was never even used among Brethren to characterize the evangelistic endeavours of men, being retained uniquely for the Eleven and Paul.

Anderson, however, goes further in marrying his interpretation of the Bible to his interpretation of culture. Women should minister, not only because it is taught by Scripture, and because they are effective evangelists and loving worshippers, but also because they are intellectually capable:

> For intellectual ability the Universities place women students practically on the same level as their brothers. The same is true in the practice of the different professions. Women now graduate in theology . . . while women's sphere centres in the home, where her influence is great beyond calculation, it is reaching far afield. She is alongside of her brothers in the work of the farm, the office, the mart, the shop, and the professions. If she has grace and gift for public service for Christ, no man has a right to hinder her.[58]

This vision of the potential of women was not attained by many Brethren churches until the late twentieth century, and in its fullness of understanding of women's ability to lead has been realized by few. It was and is anathema to conservative Brethren of all complexions.

The anonymous pamphlet *A Plea for the Sisters of our Lord Jesus Christ*, which almost certainly has a Brethren provenance, is interesting because of its approach to the problem.[59]

---

56. Anderson, *Women's Warfare*, 25–6.
57. Anderson, *Women's Warfare*, 30.
58. Anderson, *Women's Warfare*, 30; cf. Ruskin who believed that theology was a 'dangerous science' for women because they were simply unable to comprehend its mysteries: Ruskin, *Sesame and Lilies*, 121–2.
59. I am grateful to Dr Samuel McBride for drawing this pamphlet to my attention. The British Library catalogue attributes its authorship to William Adams, Ellen Martha Adams, William Trelawney Adams, and Frances Adams, who have links with Australia and South Africa. Another work which is more ascertainably by members of the Adams family, *Round the World: Notes by W[illiam. and E[llen]. M. A[dams].* (Hobart, Tas: Davies Brothers, 1914), on textual grounds does not evidently have a Brethren provenance. Dr Elisabeth Wilson made extensive searches in Australian newspapers for the Adams family members and did not find any connection to the Brethren, although they were clearly committed Christians (e-mail to Neil Dickson, 6 June 2014). Almost certainly, the British Library's attribution is mistaken. Dr McBride's copy of *Plea for the Sisters*, which is the reprint in 1922 of Horace Hart's first edition of 1912, has a hand-written note, which (as he understood from the reputable second-hand dealer he acquired it from) he takes to be genuine. It is immediately below the reprint date and states: 'by Pickering & Inglis Glasgow N[orth].B[ritain].' This is also puzzling as Pickering

Rather than considering those texts which form the substance of the debate, instead, its four anonymous authors look at those texts which relate to all Christians and argue that they apply as fully to women as men. A repeated text is Ephesians 4:16: 'From whom the whole body fitly joined together and compacted by that which every joint supplieth, according to the effectual working in the measure of every part, maketh increase of the body unto the edifying of itself in love.' The pamphlet argues that it is wrong for one group of Christians to have authority over another; instead the focus is on mutual submission. It makes links with the arguments for the abolition of slavery and is quite outspoken in description of the pervasiveness of male authority as 'the idol of masculine supremacy'.[60] It argues that there was equality of access to roles in the New Testament Church but that this has been overtaken by customs which do not express the fullness of the revelation of Christ. As men have benefited from the insight that the role of clergy was inconsistent with the freedom of all male believers, they should ensure that this freedom is extended to women in worship. The writers think that without this equality, meetings lose out as love is inadequately expressed and that, further, women are frustrated or stunted in their Christian growth. This pamphlet attempts to think from scratch about the roles of men and women in the light of the New Testament and does this by generating new arguments and resting on contradictions—foremost here is that women can write hymns and tunes and can sing them, but cannot engage in the distinctively Brethren practice of individuals stating which hymn is to be sung during open worship.[61]

Reading strategies

Central to this relationship between the Bible and culture are the reading practices which produced the interpretations. All the writers discussed in this essay regard Scripture as pre-eminent. All seek to work out what the scriptural texts say and what they mean.[62] All seek to grapple with the New Testament languages whether they had been trained in them or not. Caldwell hoped to come to the New Testament 'unbiased'.[63] The principle that what is clear should be used to govern what is less clear is also accepted by all, but the clear starting point is disputed. The anti-expansionists wanted to use 1 Corinthians

---

& Inglis publications sided with Brethren orthodoxy on the role of women, but it may be their Glasgow press merely reprinted it for the anonymous authors. The pamphlet does use Brethren ecclesiastical jargon, and there is a copy in the CBA which also suggests a Brethren connection. Prof. Peter Lineham argues for a Brethren provenance. He writes: 'A Plea for the Sisters is very obviously a Brethren work given page 16 "she must on no account give it out to be sung" which refers to a distinctively Brethren practice. Also the list of hymn writers on pages 26–28—these are very well known hymns in Brethren circles alone, I would say. But to be published privately by Horace Hart, University Printer at Oxford in 1912 and then reprinted by Pickering and Inglis in 1922 suggests that it was someone British probably English with excellent connections. Could there be a connection with G. H. Lang? I see no hints of an Australasian link.' (e-mail to Neil Dickson, 10 June 2014).

60. *Plea for the Sisters*, 6.
61. *Plea for the Sisters*, 15–16.
62. Molesworth, *Ministry of Women*, 2; Caldwell, 'Appendix', in ibid., 32; Hoste, *Service of Sisters*, preface; Hogg, 'Preface', *Ministry of Women*.
63. Caldwell, 'Appendix', in Molesworth, *Ministry of Women*, 28.

14:34-5 to control other texts where the expansionists preferred Acts 2:17 or Galatians 3:21. Generally they treated the passages concerning publicly active women as exceptions (as does Caldwell on Deborah) or they minimized the importance of what the women were doing (as does Hoste on Priscilla).[64]

Vine believed that the meaning was 'clear' and that Scripture could not contradict itself.[65] However, textual knots of obscurity and contradiction were encountered. When it comes to the relevant scriptural passages, the text is sometimes quite obscure. Even Hogg says, 'The reference of the clause "because of the angels" in 11:10 is not obvious'.[66] Hoste notes that the movement in Paul's writing between seeming to grant freedom of women to worship in public and then outlawing it has been prefigured by a similar wavering over the issue of eating food presented to idols in 1 Corinthians 8: 'Where no moral evil is directly involved, he does sometimes treat questions in this piecemeal fashion, for the sake of important lessons to be learnt in the process.'[67]

This is a good example of someone reading Scripture with great care and noticing the structural similarities in the formation of teaching on two key issues for the Church. However, it is also a good example of the way in which Hoste's principles of interpretation constrain him. Because he believes Scripture cannot contradict itself, Hoste cannot, and therefore does not, use the word 'contradiction' in this context. He resolves the two positions by using the argument about the gradual method of teaching which Paul used. Although Hoste does not point this out, this is a concession (caused by an apparently contradictory text) to the principle that the meaning of Scripture is plain. Although this apparent contradiction could have been resolved in various ways, anti-expansionists agreed on the fact that the apparent contradiction must be resolved against the public participation of women. When this happened, other reading strategies taken from the level of belief, rather than semantics or morphology, were being invoked. This, of course, is Gordon's point and the one which Hoste attacks with some force. Although Hoste can see how Gordon is interpreting by using experience (since Gordon has helpfully made this explicit), Hoste does not seem to be aware of the process that in order to make the Bible prohibit the public participation of women, he himself also uses strategies from levels other than the textual—since Paul was an apostle then why was he not simply laying down the law? Why was there an awkward lacuna in this teaching? Why was the Bible not crystal clear on a topic on which Brethren writers were clear? These sorts of hermeneutical questions presuppose a level of critical perspective which seemed irrelevant to most Brethren people.

The ways in which the Biblical passages are written suggest that pamphleteers fall back on their own presuppositions which have been coloured by the conservative views of their culture. Because the Bible is assumed not to contradict itself, when it appears to do so,

---

64. Caldwell, 'Appendix', in Molesworth, *Ministry of Women*, 23; Hoste, *Service of Sisters*, 7.

65. Vine, *Ministry of Women*, 23; for Vine's biblical interpretation, see Neil T. R. Dickson, 'William Edwy Vine (1873–1949) and Brethren Biblical Interpretation: A Case Study', in Tim Grass (ed.), *Witness in Many Lands: Leadership and Outreach among the Brethren* (SBH; Troon, 2013), 147–60.

66. Hogg, *Ministry of Women*, 14.

67. Hoste, *Service of Sisters*, 13.

the move to resolve the contradiction distracts attention from the cultural assumptions on which the resolution is made and forecloses on further exploration of whether there may or may not be any other undergirding principles on which a resolution might be achieved—both Gordon and Anderson argue that what leads to freedom should be given more weight than what leads to restriction, a position notably taken up subsequently by F. F. Bruce.[68] It is not that one side is impervious to culture while the other is influenced by it; both sides are profoundly influenced by culture. Conventional Brethren writers condemn its progressive influence, but are unaware of the extent to which they expressed its conservative influences uncritically. Progressive writers are aware of themselves accepting and rejecting from both conservative and progressive cultural influences simultaneously. Reading practices are the means by which the relationship is expressed. The ways of reading were as sacrosanct as the text which was to be interpreted and it was when other interpretations were seen to be based on other methods of reading that the anti-expansionists had their most powerful reasons for rejecting them.

The expansionists use a wider range of reference. We have seen how Gordon, Sims, and Anderson appeal pragmatically to experience. Additionally, Gordon and Anderson invoke names from Christian history, but the Brethren can be elitist in their sectarianism, making Lewis uncertain if Clement can be regarded as a reliable historical source.[69] Anderson's reference to progressive secular culture would have seemed irrelevant to Brethren as they did not think they had anything to learn about morality from those they regarded as 'sinners'. Anderson also raises the point that translation itself was vulnerable to misogynistic influence, and that what Brethren thought of as 'Christian' culture was actually 'pagan'.[70]

Although it is not commonly referred to in terms of reading non-fiction, imagination also plays a part in these reading strategies. All of the writers with the exception of Gordon move fairly uncritically between the contemporary world and the world of the New Testament. They do not systematically distinguish between Christian and secular culture in the New Testament and Christian and secular culture in Britain at their various times of writing, and this also reveals something of their reading practices. Ironically Hogg appears to be aware of this need to distinguish at the very point at which he fuses the present and the past:

> We too readily read the conditions of our own day into the Apostolic age, when church buildings and halls did not exist. It is not possible to imagine the Apostle sharing a pulpit or platform with these women, or standing with them in the Synagogues or on Mars' Hill, though we can see them visiting homes and teaching women and children.[71]

Hogg's inability to imagine women in a sphere other than the one allotted to them by his culture is obvious here, and it is possible that this failure of imagination reinforced his conservative reading practices, not allowing him to sense either from the text or from

---

68. F. F. Bruce, 'Women in the Church: A Biblical Survey', *Christian Brethren Review Journal*, 33 (1982), 7–14, 11.
69. Lewis, *Ministry of Women*, 37.
70. Anderson, *Woman's Warfare*, 8–9.
71. Hogg, *Ministry of Women*, 19.

experience possibilities seen by others. Hoste is similarly incapacitated when writing on Priscilla that 'No one would feel more surprised, we are sure, than this good sister herself at being styled a "theological teacher".'[72]

Sims spends the last part of his pamphlet in a sustained imaginative reconstruction of life in the church at Corinth and seems to be using his imagination as a way of synthesizing his reasoning. The church is described both before and after Paul's letter and hinges on the sentence, 'The elders were at their wits end'.[73] Unlike their twentieth-century British contemporaries, these imagined elders were in the fortunate position of being able to request and then act on divinely inspired advice. As soon as Paul's letter appears, church disorder ceases. This too may be an imaginative failure. The more likely position is that Paul's letter defused some tensions but not all as some would simply disagree with him.[74] Like Hoste's problem with Paul's wavering, Sims assumes that God's will can be and, for the most part, is, revealed with all the precision of a railway timetable. But the record of faith shows that it is not always easy to discern God's will, and that this discernment happens slowly through much effort in prayer and reflection on Scripture. Even when his will is discerned, it is entirely possible that other believers will not receive it, especially if it advocates change from tradition as happened in the case of Jesus of Nazareth. Until a more complex hermeneutic was adduced, some arguments based on Scripture could only exist at the level of assertion.

Anderson's imagination and ready empathy is evident in the following description of Priscilla:

> Paul wrote this Epistle from the house of Aquila and Priscilla in Ephesus, where they were again his fellow-labourers, and no doubt he had Priscilla in his mind when he wrote of the woman with long hair having authority to minister without the veil. Doubtless Paul read this to Aquila and Priscilla. Priscilla listens, and a tear trickles down her cheek, for she knew she was hated by the Judaisers, an influential part of the Church, but that God had inspired Paul to write this.[75]

This is the only explicit attempt in all of the pamphlets to access the feelings of a believing woman who had the ability to teach in the context of a church which was hostile to the practice of that gift. Gordon's pamphlet is a close second because it was written from the sense of injustice he felt at the treatment of women missionaries. That he sensed injustice implies his empathy. Both these men could imagine what it would be like to be a gifted and talented human being whose deepest motives and worthiest actions were consistently belittled and attacked by fellow-Christians. It is not reason alone which produced interpretations of Scripture which dignified women but the empathetic powers of imagination—love, by another name.

---

72. Hoste, *Service of Sisters*, 7.
73. Sims, *"My handmaidens shall prophesy"*, 56.
74. See David G. Horrell, *The Social Ethos of the Corinthian Correspondence: Interests and Ideology from 1 Corinthians to 1 Clement* (Edinburgh, 1996).
75. Anderson, *Autobiography*, 221.

Conclusions

During their institutionalizing phase, many Brethren individuals were preoccupied with what they called 'church truth'. This phrase contained their understanding of how their assemblies should be organized. Given the highly charismatic way in which many of the churches came into existence in the wake of the revivalism of the later nineteenth century, and the importance Brethren placed on the leading of the Spirit in structuring church meetings, and the gifts of the Spirit being freely available to unordained individuals—a very counter-cultural strategy—it is perhaps not surprising that they sought to impose order on such a potent and unpredictable mix. Although they could be counter-cultural in their understanding of every-member-ministry, their radicalism was not through-going. From Scripture they understood public ministry as a male preserve—a principle which took precedence over any giftedness to which women might lay claim. Thus the institutionalizing tendency circumscribed the charismatic impulse of the movement. Women were seen as a threat to order which had to be consistently and comprehensively anticipated and resisted. Thus the strictures on what women could not do, could not ask, and could not wear meant that the assembly became for some women an ecclesiastical corset which defined spiritual role and restricted spiritual movement.

The very few radically progressive voices which the movement produced were isolated. Of the anti-expansionist pamphlets, one was by a future editor of *The Believer's Magazine*, two authors of another were editors of *Echoes of Service*, and a third, Molesworth's, first appeared as articles in *The Northern Witness* and additionally carried an endorsement by the editor. These represented the principal magazines of the period, the key media for disseminating Brethren orthodoxy. On the other hand, Sims and Anderson were peripheral figures, as also were the anonymous 'Four of His Servants'. Because Anderson's voice was marginal, major cultural developments in equality in political discourse stemming from, among other sources, American ideas of emancipation for slaves and then for women,[76] tended to go unmodified by Christian thought and belief; this was not a conservatism possessed only by Brethren. Generally speaking the Church had longer, more painful journeys to make before the extent to which it was understood that there were other ways of understanding how Scripture related to such an emancipatory trajectory.

However, the Brethren passion for evangelism loosened the ecclesiastical corset laces somewhat as women were enabled to evangelize and teach other women, children, and indigenous believers in countries out of sight of the sending churches. This expansion of their role was common in evangelicalism generally. Lynn Abrams notes that, in Glasgow in 1895 'two-thirds of the 10,766 Sunday School teachers were female' and argues that this fostered general cultural forces for expansion of women's roles.[77] In this way, where the Brethren were not aware of any scriptural prohibition—there were no Sunday Schools in the New Testament—the movement can be seen in a more progressive light.

---

76. Lynn Abrams, *The Making of Modern Woman: Europe 1789–1918* (New York, 2002), 243–64.

77. Abrams, *Modern Woman*, 221.

CHAPTER 4

'You have to go by Scripture':
Taylorite Exclusive Brethren, the Bible, and the Holy Spirit

Roger N. Holden

The Taylorite Exclusive Brethren, here called the Brethren for short, have always maintained that they go by Scripture. The international website of the Plymouth Brethren Christian Church, as they now publicly call themselves, states that they are 'a Christian fellowship based on the Holy Bible as the Word of God'.[1] The name 'Taylorite' comes from James Taylor, senior, acknowledged leader from around 1903 until his death in 1953.[2] He made the assertion 'You have to go by Scripture' during a meeting at Barnet in 1929 and in doing so he may be seen as simply uttering a Protestant commonplace.[3] But this was during the meeting when he denied the Eternal Sonship of Christ and my other chapter in the present book suggests that there might be rather more to the statement than a reiteration of a Protestant truism since Taylor subsequently claimed the Spirit's leading for what he said.[4]

The relationship between the word of Scripture and the current working of the Holy Spirit has been seen variously by different groups and people throughout church history and the first section of this paper provides a brief overview of the subject to provide a context for the subsequent exploration of the Brethren's views on the subject. This proceeds by examining the key figures in Brethren history, those who came to be regarded as the 'Ministers of the Lord in the Recovery' and granted a status akin to apostolic, J. N. Darby, F. E. Raven, and James Taylor, senior. We also look briefly at two ministers, J. B. Stoney and C. A. Coates, who were not granted this status but were nevertheless highly regarded

---

1. Plymouth Brethren Christian Church, 'What We Believe', <www.plymouthbrethren-christianchurch.org/beliefs/what-we-believe>, accessed 31 Mar. 2018.

2. Note that here the name 'James Taylor' without qualification will always refer to James Taylor, senior, and not James Taylor Junior.

3. J. Taylor, 'The Divine Standard of Service (2)' [Barnet, 1929], in [James Taylor], *Ministry by J. Taylor*, (new series) 100 vols. (Kingston-on-Thames, n.d), 29:368. The published ministry of J. B. Stoney, F. E. Raven, C. A. Coates, and J. Taylor consists largely of notes from meetings and where the date and place are known these will be quoted in square brackets after the title. In this chapter references to the ministry and letters of J. B. Stoney, F. E. Raven, C. A. Coates, and J. Taylor have been taken from the Ministry Search Engine CD-ROM (2005) produced by Ian Purdy and available from the Kingston Bible Trust; this gives pagination as in the original published volumes. Available online at <http://www.mcclean.me.uk/mse/>, accessed 31 Mar. 2018.

4. See Roger N. Holden, chap.16, *intra*, 249–74.

and influential. Finally we consider what happened after the death of Taylor, senior, as the views the Brethren had come to accept from these leaders led them into what many would see as disaster under the leadership of James Taylor, junior.

The Bible and the Holy Spirit

By way of orientation in what is a large topic, we shall present here three basic views, that we shall call the Catholic, the Reformed and the spiritualist views. In many ways these represents points on a spectrum, or perhaps more accurately a field, of views around which people have moved.

The Catholic view arises in the pre-Reformation tradition of the Western Church, formalized by the Council of Trent (1545–63). The Catholic view acknowledges the present working of the Holy Spirit but this is institutionalized within the procedures of the Church hierarchy. The Church is the body of which Christ is the head and the Temple of the Holy Spirit, the Holy Spirit working through the church hierarchy, that is the Supreme Pontiff, who is the visible head of the church on earth, and the bishops.[5] As interpreter of the word of God, the Church is the ultimate authority, the word of God consisting of both Scripture and tradition. *The Catechism of the Council of Trent* states that 'all the doctrines of Christianity, in which the faithful are to be instructed, are derived from the word of God, which includes Scripture and tradition', and thus the faithful should yield 'unhesitating assent to whatever the authority of our Holy Mother the Church teaches'.[6] The Church hierarchy, then, is the ultimate authority.

This view came under scrutiny at the time of the Reformation, resulting in the Reformed view. The Reformers saw Christ as head of the Church and that he has ordained ministers in the church, but denied the claims of the Pope to be the visible head of the Church on earth.[7] Scripture is authoritative as being the word of God and is the sole authority, there are no authoritative interpreters. Article VI of the Thirty-Nine Articles of the Church of England of 1562 makes a simple statement that 'Holy Scripture containeth all things necessary to salvation: so that whatsoever is not read therein, nor may be proved thereby, is not to be required of any man, that it should be believed as an article of the Faith, or be thought requisite or necessary to salvation'.[8] The Westminster Confession of 1647 asserts the sufficiency of Scripture in that all things necessary for salvation, faith and life are 'either expressly set down in Scripture, or by good and necessary consequence may be deduced from Scripture' and nothing may be added to this 'by revelations of the Spirit or traditions of men'.[9] We are not confined to the mere words of Scripture but may freely express what is contained in it or may by 'necessary consequence' deduced from it.[10]

---

5. *The Catechism of the Council of Trent*, ET, J. Donovan (Dublin, 1829), 70–9. *Catechism of the Catholic Church*, ET (rev. edn., London, 1999), paras 752, 792, 797, 807, 837, 857, 880–3.

6. *Catechism of the Council of Trent*, 18. This remains the doctrine of the Catholic Church, see *Catechism of the Catholic Church*, paras.76, 84 & 85.

7. The Westminster Confession of Faith (1647), 25.1, 3, & 6.

8. Article VI. The Thirty-Nine Articles are printed at the end of *The Book of Common Prayer* (1662).

9. Westminster Confession, 1.6.

10. The derivative Second London Baptist Confession (1689) replaces the wording 'by good and necessary consequence may be deduced from Scripture' by the slightly more restrictive

Understanding of what is contained in Scripture may develop over time, both personally and collectively in the Church. While recognizing that 'all things in Scripture are not alike plain in themselves, nor alike clear to all', yet all necessary truth is presented in such a way that it may be understood by all, whether learned or unlearned.[11] Therefore no infallible teaching authority is needed. This is what has come to be known as the doctrine of the perspicuity, or clarity, of Scripture.[12]

That the Spirit still speaks directly is rejected—in the words of the Westminster Confession 'those former ways of God's revealing His will unto his people being now ceased'.[13] But the continued working of the Spirit is affirmed in other ways. The Holy Spirit is still active in and through Scripture, the mere words of Scripture being of no value without this. As Calvin says in his Commentary on Ezekiel 2: 1–2 'Certainly God works effectively through his Word but we must affirm that its efficacy is not contained in the sound itself but comes from the hidden power of the Spirit. . . . the work of the Spirit is joined with the Word of God.'[14] Scripture and the Holy Spirit are connected in three ways: the Holy Spirit is the ultimate author of Scripture; the Spirit confirms to the believer that Scripture is the Word of God and the Spirit leads the believer and the Church to a right understanding of Scripture.[15] These may be categorized as inspiration, inward witness, and interpretation.

The spiritualist view challenges the Reformed view by asserting that the current working of the Spirit is prior to Scripture. In England the spiritualist view was held by the Society of Friends, or the Quakers. One day George Fox interrupted the sermon in the church at Nottingham, crying out 'Oh no it is not the Scripture' and told the congregation that it was 'the Holy Spirit, by which holy men of God gave forth the Scriptures, whereby opinions, religions and judgements were to be tried; for it led into all Truth, and so gave knowledge of all Truth.'[16] Robert Barclay, the Quaker apologist, formalized Fox's views, insisting that revelations of God by the Spirit, outward voices and appearances, dreams, or inward manifestations in the heart—what the Westminster Confession referred to as 'former ways'—were still the primary means. These inward divine revelations would not contradict the outward testimony of the Scriptures, but neither should they be subject to test by the Scriptures.[17] This is the doctrine of 'the light' or 'the inward light'.[18] The

---

'necessarily contained within the Holy Scripture.'

11. The Westminster Confession, 1.7. Robert Letham, *The Westminster Assembly: Reading its Theology in Historical Context* (Phillipsburg, NJ, 2009), 120–58.

12. For a recent defence see: Mark D. Thompson, *A Clear and Present Word: The Clarity of Scripture* (Nottingham, 2006).

13. The Westminster Confession, 1.1. The Scripture quoted in support of this view is Heb. 1: 1–2.

14. John Calvin, *Old Testament Commentaries: Ezekiel I (Chapters 1–12)* ([1565]; Carlisle, 1994), 59.

15. Wayne R. Spear, 'Word and Spirit in the Westminster Confession', in J. Ligon Duncan, III (ed.), *The Westminster Confession into the 21st Century*, 3 vols. (Fearn, 2003), 1: 39–56.

16. John L. Nickalls (ed.), *The Journal of George Fox* (London, 1975), 40.

17. Robert Barclay, *An Apology for the True Christian Divinity* (1678), Prop. 2, online text, Quaker Heritage Press, <http://www.qhpress.org/texts/barclay/apology/>, accessed 9 Mar. 2018.

18. Note: not at this point 'the Inner Light', which is a later expression.

Quakers, notably George Fox himself, claimed inward voices teaching and instructing them what to do. The spiritualist dilemma is: how can one be sure what is the authentic voice of the Spirit? In response to this the Quakers developed a collective view of testing what were right leadings of the Spirit within a hierarchy of meetings, the Yearly Meeting having power to decide what was binding on members of the Society. Ultimately this did not lead to claims of new doctrine but rather to quietism and a scrupulousness of behaviour.

J. N. Darby

The United Kingdom version of the Plymouth Brethren Christian Church website states that they 'continue to follow the principles elucidated by Mr Darby in full'.[19] So it is with John Nelson Darby we must start. Darby did not write systematically, most of his voluminous *Collected Writings* being occasional pieces written in response to particular situations or notes of Bible readings or lectures given by him. The most substantial sections on Scripture are found in volume 23, which is entitled *Doctrinal No.7*. But there are references elsewhere and his views can of course be inferred from his use of Scripture. 'What Do I Learn from Scripture?', which can be dated to 1871, was written in response to someone who asked him for a statement of his faith.[20] In this he states:

> I learn from the example and authority of the Lord and His apostles that the scriptures of the Old and New Testament are inspired of God, and are to be received as the word of God, having His authority attached to it, and which works effectually in those that believe; and that the testimony of the Lord is sure, making wise the simple, discerning the thoughts and intents of the heart, being understood, not by the wisdom of man, but by the teaching of God, being spiritually discerned, they are revealed, communicated, and discerned by the Spirit.[21]

This is not the only place where Darby asserts his belief that the Scriptures are inspired and possess absolute authority as the word of God.[22] Darby defended these views against contemporary critics who sought to deny this inspiration and authority. Thus, while accepting that science is not the object of Scripture, Darby disagrees with the views of Alexander Raleigh, expressed in his address as Chairman of the Congregational Union of England and Wales in 1868, that there are mistakes and errors in the Bible that do not affect the substance of its inspiration nor the complete communication of divine meaning.[23]

---

19. Plymouth Brethren Christian Church, 'What We Believe'. The statement on the UK website in fact comes from documents resulting from an investigation by the Charity Commission for England and Wales: Gov.UK, 'Preston Down Trust', <www.gov.uk/government/publications/preston-down-trust>, accessed 31 Mar. 2018.
20. J. N. Darby, 'What Do I Learn from Scripture?', in *CW* (repr. Kingston-on-Thames, 1956), 23: 127–33. *Dates of J. N. Darby's Collected Writings* (Chessington, 2013), 56.
21. Darby, 'What Do I Learn from Scripture?', 132.
22. Darby, 'Letter on the Divine Inspiration of Scripture or Remarks on the Letter of Resignation of M. Le Professeur Edmond Scherer', in *CW*, 23: 13.
23. Darby, 'Remarks on "Christianity and Modern Progress" by the Rev. A. Raleigh, D.D.', in *CW*, 23: 72–81. This has been dated to 1868 (*Dates of J. N. Darby's Collected Writings*, 56). Raleigh was chair of the Congregational Union of England and Wales in 1868 (*The Congregational Year Book* (1928), xviii).

To Colenso's argument that the Scriptures never affirm their own infallibility, Darby responds that they affirm that they are inspired by God and therefore have His authority.[24]

But the quotation given above from 'What Do I Learn from Scripture?' also shows that Darby saw the work of the Holy Spirit as necessary in order to understand and apply Scripture. Merely examining Scripture and the external evidences does not produce faith; the Holy Spirit has to use the Scriptures and give faith to those who receive them.[25] On the other hand the authority of Scripture remains irrespective of the effect it produces.[26] The teaching of Scripture is not to be understood by the wisdom of man but by the Spirit.[27] The Holy Spirit speaks through Scripture, and so Darby disagrees with Edmond Scherer's view that rejecting the inspiration of Scripture will allow the Holy Spirit to operate.[28] He is in accord with what we have called the Reformed view, but the above passage with its emphasis on teaching being revealed, communicated, and discerned by the Spirit suggests that he also inclines towards the spiritualist view. This can be seen elsewhere, for example:

> If I were to take the Word of God by itself and say I can judge of it and understand it, then I am a rationalist; it is man's mind judging the revelation of God. But where we get God's mind communicated by the Holy Ghost, and the Holy Ghost [gives] the power to receive it, then I get God's mind. There is just as much wisdom and power from God for us to meet the state of ruin in which we now are, as there was at the first when He set up the church; and that is what we have to lean upon.[29]

The presence of the Holy Spirit is fundamental to what the Brethren called the truth as to the assembly. The Church, Darby maintained, has 'grievously forgotten the presence and authority of the Holy Ghost dwelling in her.'[30] Darby's tract *The Notion of a Clergyman Dispensationally the Sin against the Holy Ghost*, written in 1836 but not published until 1873, came to be regarded as a fundamental text of the Brethren.[31] Here Darby states that the presence of the Holy Ghost is a cardinal principle, the assembly depending wholly upon His power and presence.[32] He repeats this elsewhere, for example 'I believe that the

---

24. Darby, 'Dr. Colenso and the Pentateuch', in *CW*, 23:87. This was written in response to Dr Colenso's book *The Pentateuch Critically Examined* (1862).
25. Darby, 'Divine Inspiration of Scripture', 21.
26. Darby, 'Divine Inspiration of Scripture', 45.
27. Darby, 'What Do I Learn from Scripture?', 132.
28. Darby, 'Divine Inspiration of Scripture', 42.
29. Darby, 'The Faith once delivered to the Saints', in *CW*, 32:391; insertion in square brackets mine.
30. Darby, 'Divine Inspiration of Scripture', 42.
31. It is explicitly referenced in the 'Statement of Core Doctrine', on 'Preston Down Trust'.
32. Darby, 'The Notion of a Clergyman Dispensationally the Sin Against the Holy Ghost', in *CW*, 1:36. The original title was: 'The Connexion of the Term Clergy with the Penal Guilt of the Present Dispensation & the Sin against the Holy Ghost', and when published in 1873 a preface was added. Peter J. Embley, 'The Origins and Early Development of the Plymouth Brethren', University of Cambridge, Ph.D. thesis, 1966, 47, n.98.

Holy Ghost dwells *in the Church*.³³ This indwelling of the Holy Spirit in the assembly is to be distinguished from the indwelling in the individual.³⁴

Thus any human appointing of ministers with sole authority to preach and administer the sacraments, 'clericalism' in Brethren shorthand, was a denial of the Headship of Christ and the presence of the Holy Spirit in the Church. The Spirit gives the testimony of the Lord Jesus Christ to whomever he chooses and the notion of clergyman, a humanly appointed minister, contradicts this principle.³⁵ Thus all meetings should be held under the guidance of the Spirit. Ministry should not be prepared in advance as the Holy Spirit would lead and guide people to speak, although Darby did not like using the word 'impulse' to describe this.³⁶ This applied not only to preaching and Bible study, but also to who should pray and what hymns were to be sung. In their regular Sunday and mid-week Bible readings it was practice for local meetings to work through a book of the Bible, which retained some connection to the Reformed expository tradition, but what was said and discussed in such readings was as the Spirit led and not pre-meditated. It should be noted, however, that one of the sub-series of Darby's *Collected Writings* was entitled *Expository* so he did not totally reject the exposition of Scripture but affirms that exposition of a passage of Scripture requires taking account of what precedes and follows it.³⁷

Darby became the most prominent leader of the Exclusive section of the Brethren after the split between Open and Exclusives in 1848. Towards the end of his life, in 1875, he warned against the view that the Brethren had something that other Christians had not.³⁸ Clearly by that time some Brethren had developed very high views of themselves. Although Darby did not claim it himself, he was given a status that verged on the apostolic as the Brethren came to believe that the Lord had spoken uniquely through him. This view may not have been articulated during his life time, but certainly it was accepted by 1910 when a contributor to a meeting in Indianapolis said the 'The Lord made known to J.N.D. the truth of union with Christ'.³⁹ Although the Brethren viewed the Reformers as instruments of God in recovering the truth as to the doctrine of justification by faith, they were considered to have failed to allow for the Lord's own place in the assembly by the Holy Spirit.⁴⁰ Instead

---

33. Darby, 'A Few Remarks Connected with the Presence and Operation of the Spirit of God in the Body, the Church', *CW*, 3:320. Emphasis in the original. This has been dated to 1845 (*Dates of J. N. Darby's Collected Writings*, 12).

34. Darby, 'A Letter to the Saints in London as to the Presence of the Holy Ghost in the Church', in *CW*, 3:349. Here Darby quotes 1 Cor. 6:9 as referring to the presence of the Holy Spirit in the believer and 1 Cor. 3:16–17 as the presence in the assembly.

35. Darby, 'The Notion of a Clergyman', in *CW*, 1:39.

36. Darby, 'The Presence and Operation of the Spirit of God in the Body', in *CW*, 3:334. The twenty-first century mind will notice an unspoken restriction to this—it applied only to men, not to women.

37. Darby, 'The Gospel According to Matthew', in *CW*, 24:1.

38. Darby to J. Leslie, 8 April 1875 in [J. N. Darby], *Letters of J. N. D.*, 3 vols. (Kingston-on-Thames, n.d.), 2:339. This also appears in Darby, 'Correspondence on Recent Matters', in *CW*, 31:371.

39. Taylor, 'Reading' [Indianapolis, 1910] in *Ministry*, 3:249.

40. G. H. S. Price, *A Brief Synopsis of the Public History of the Church* (Kingston-on-Thames, 1950), 44.

they set up man-made organisations, 'system' in Brethren short-hand, and it was left to Darby and the early Brethren to recover the truth. As A. J. Gardiner later said 'the Lord showed [Darby] that He was Head of the assembly, which was his body, united to him by the Holy Spirit, and that each believer was a member of that body.'[41]

J. B. Stoney and F. R. Raven

One might have thought that Joseph Butler Stoney, who lived until 1897, would come to be regarded as Darby's successor as spiritual leader of the Brethren after his death in 1882. Stoney was one of the early Brethren who had met in Dublin but was fourteen years younger than Darby. His ministry was always highly regarded, being reprinted in the 1960s, but it was Frederick Edward Raven who came to be acknowledged as Darby's successor. Raven was a close friend of Stoney and held him in high regard, saying 'there is no one on earth whose ministry and self have produced so lasting a moral effect on me as Mr. Stoney'.[42] Stoney is seen to be mystical and because of his evident influence on Raven needs to be considered before moving on to the latter.

Stoney clearly regarded Scripture as authoritative and stated that we should not use wording that is not found in Scripture.[43] But on the other hand his views on the necessity for the Spirit in understanding Scripture, such that a spiritual person will discern in Scripture things that are not seen in the literal word, move in a spiritualist direction:

> It is only the spiritual mind which can adapt and perceive what is the mind of the Spirit in any case, and thus be able to wield the word of God effectually therein. Hence a spiritual man can apply Scripture, and discover the mind of the Lord in figures and allegories, in a way which is quite foreign and incomprehensible to the man who has learned the Scriptures only as a science.[44]

Raven came into fellowship in 1865 at the Priory Meeting in north London, which at that time was Darby's local meeting. This meeting subsequently moved to Islington Park Street and Raven moved to Greenwich where he was civilian secretary to the Royal Naval College. But it does not seem that Darby in any way marked out Raven and indeed he does not seem to have been recognized as spiritual leader until 1890 when his ministry on the person of Christ and eternal life caused division amongst the Brethren. The published ministry of Raven consists of notes of Bible readings, addresses, and his letters. Apart from an isolated letter dated 1867,[45] the earliest published letters are dated 1888 and are

---

41. A. J. Gardiner, *The Recovery and Maintenance of the Truth* (2nd edn., Kingston-on-Thames, 1963), 3.

42. F. E. Raven, extract from letter, 19 Dec. 1895, in [F. E. Raven], *Ministry of F. E. Raven*, (new series) 20 vols. (Kingston-on-Thames, n.d.), 3:303.

43. J. B. Stoney, *Letters of J. B. Stoney*, 3 vols. (Kingston-on-Thames, n.d.), 1:123.

44. J. B. Stoney, 'Spirituality and its Hindrances', in *Ministry by J. B. Stoney* (new series), 13 vols. (Kingston-on-Thames, n.d.), 10:358.

45. Raven, letter, 2 Nov. 1867, in *Ministry*, 20:287–90.

in connection with the controversy raised by his teachings.[46] The earliest dated items of ministry are from 1895.[47]

In the Reformed view, the Holy Spirit is prior to Scripture, but the Spirit spoke the words of Scripture and now speaks through it. By contrast Raven was declared by Neatby to be 'pre-eminently the apostle of the inner light' because he emphasized the direct speaking of the Holy Spirit in a manner characteristic of the spiritualist view:[48]

> As regards the Scriptures I have always maintained most carefully that as being the inspired record of God's communications it is the word of God. But the word of God has in my mind a different force. It means to me the revelation of God and of His mind directly or immediately to man.... I think that it is extremely important to see that God's communications to man are directly by the Spirit of the living God.[49]

But on the other hand he did 'not care to put out anything which cannot be substantiated from scripture'.[50] Similarly 'we have to learn everything from Scripture; it is no good bringing preconceived thoughts to Scripture, because that is not subjection to the Spirit of truth nor to the word of God'.[51] By way of reconciling these statements he said 'I get the benefit of the word in some way or other, and then I go to Scripture to substantiate it.'[52]

Raven has a reputation for being obscure and mystical, rather than readily intelligible.[53] Nevertheless, what he says in his ministry concerning the relation between Scripture and the Spirit may be summarized in a number of points, although overlapping and even contradictory in places:

1. The Spirit is the truth and is prior to Scripture.[54]
2. Christianity was established before the New Testament was written and thus Christianity does not depend on Scripture.[55]
3. The Spirit is a living voice, to be distinguished from the letter, by which God communicates and teaches directly, therefore the presence of the

---

46. Raven to Mr. Bradstock, 1 May 1888, [F. E. Raven], in *Letters of F. E. Raven* (Kingston-on-Thames, n.d.), 1–2.
47. Raven, 'The Spirit's Day—Jesus Glorified and the Spirit Given' [1895], in *Ministry*, 1:1–133. Not all of Raven's published ministry is dated so it is possible that some pre-dates 1895.
48. William Blair Neatby, *A History of the Plymouth Brethren* (London, 1901), 320.
49. Raven, letter, 28 Mar. 1900, in *Ministry*, 3:315.
50. Raven, 'The Spirit's Day', in *Ministry*, 1:2.
51. Raven, 'The Gift of the Spirit and Eternal Life', in *Ministry*, 7:282–3.
52. Raven, 'Faith' [Peckham, 1899/1900], in *Ministry*, 13:216.
53. Neatby, *Plymouth Brethren*, 317–8. Tim Grass, *Gathering to His Name: The Story of Open Brethren in Britain and Ireland* (Milton Keynes, 2006), 205.
54. Raven, 'Readings on Philippians' [Greenwich], in *Ministry*, 9:372; 'The Presence of the Spirit Here' [Battersea, 1899], *Ministry*, 13:87.
55. Raven, 'Philippians' [Greenwich], in *Ministry*, 9:372; 'Fruit-Bearing and Witness' [Quemerford, 1900], in *Ministry*, 20:195–6.

'You have to go by Scripture'

Spirit is primary, contra the Catholics who look to the Church or the Protestants who look to Scripture.[56]

4. The term 'Word of God' refers primarily to Jesus Christ, not Scripture; he is the final revelation, being before Scripture.[57]
5. As an inspired record of God's communications, whose author is the Holy Ghost, the Bible is the inspired word of God and thus carries authority.[58]
6. The Spirit has no new revelation and what the Spirit communicates directly will be substantiated from Scripture.[59]
7. We have to learn everything from Scripture, we should study Scripture and should not accept anything that is not found in Scripture.[60]
8. Scriptural expressions are to be preferred to human expressions, such as the Trinity.[61]
9. The Spirit is needed to lead beyond the letter of Scripture to what it is making known and without the Spirit the study and exposition of Scripture is of no value.[62]
10. The Spirit will bring out things that cannot be directly discerned in the letter of Scripture.[63]
11. A true minister will not just minister from his knowledge of Scripture, but from what he truly knows by the Spirit.[64]
12. The Spirit has imparted particular light to certain individuals to draw attention to things that are in Scripture which are important for that

---

56. Raven 'The First Epistle of Peter, Chapter 2', in *Ministry*, 4:26; 'Readings on the Gospel of John, Chapter 14', in *Ministry*, 5:296; 'Christ at the Right Hand of God' [London, 1898], in *Ministry*, 11:69; 'The Calling of God' [USA & Canada, 1898], in *Ministry*, 12:137; 'The Presence of the Spirit Here' [Battersea, 1899], in *Ministry*, 13:87; 'Christ's Word of Counsel' [USA & Canada, 1902], in *Ministry*, 17:134.

57. Raven, 'Faith' [Peckham, 1899/1900], in *Ministry*, 13:216–7; 'The Sanctuary (1)' [Park Street, London, 1900], in *Ministry*, 14:5.

58. Raven, 'The Gravity of the Moment' in *Ministry*, 2:295; 'Deliverance from Law' [1895], in *Ministry*, 2:335; 'Faith' [Peckham, 1899/1900], in *Ministry*, 13:216–7; 'Fruit-Bearing and Witness' [Quemerford, 1900], in *Ministry*, 20:195–6.

59. Raven, 'Faith' [Peckham, 1899/1900], in *Ministry*, 13:216–7; 'Christ's Word of Counsel' [USA & Canada, 1902], in *Ministry*, 17:134.

60. Raven, 'The Spirit's Day', in *Ministry*, 1:2; letter, 23 Nov. 1898, in *Ministry*, 3:313; 'The First Epistle of Peter, Chapter 2', in *Ministry*, 4:26; 'The Gift of the Spirit and Eternal Life', in *Ministry*, 7:283.

61. Raven, 'Various Names of Christ and their Import (1) The Mediator' [1898], in *Ministry*, 11:364.

62. Raven, 'The Head Over All Things', in *Ministry*, 2:224–5; 'The First Epistle of Peter, Chapter 2', in *Ministry*, 4:43; 'The Inheritance' in *Ministry*, 4:244; 'Readings on the First Epistle to the Corinthians—Chapter 3' [Weston-super-Mare, 1897], in *Ministry*, 10:49; 'Christ at the Right Hand of God' [London, 1898], in *Ministry*, 11:69; 'In Christ' in *Ministry*, 13:123–4; 'God's Word, The Principle of Life in the Soul' [1899], in *Ministry*, 13:175.

63. Raven, 'God's Word, The Principle of Life in the Soul' [1899], in *Ministry*, 13:175.

64. Raven, 'The Presence of the Spirit Here' [Battersea, 1899], in *Ministry*, 13:91.

particular time; Luther and Darby in particular. Both received light from the Spirit and were then led to find this in Scripture.[65]
13. The Spirit speaks particularly in the church, the assembly.[66]

As laid out here, these points in a sense take us round a circle, starting with the Holy Spirit and taking us back to the Holy Spirit. If not contradictory, certainly they are in tension at a number of points—particularly the emphasis that we should take everything from Scripture but that on the other hand the Spirit can bring out things in Scripture that are not immediately evident. This may be seen as contrary to the doctrine of the perspicuity of Scripture and was to become of increasing significance amongst the Brethren when combined with the view that the Spirit works through particular individuals in bringing out truth. Yet the emphasis on the Spirit is coupled with an insistence on the exact words of Scripture, a viewpoint also found amongst the early Quakers.

In retrospect Raven's two visits to North America in 1898 and 1902 were of particular importance. The volumes of published notes of meetings during these visits were prefaced by an introduction written by J. S. Allen of Birkenhead describing the order of these meetings and some of the most important subjects that came under consideration.[67] Some of this concerned Raven's controversial views on eternal life and the person of Christ, but his views on Scripture and the Spirit were also expressed. James Taylor was present at many of these meetings and his contributions evidently impressed Raven, which may thus have suggested Taylor as being his successor.[68] In turn Taylor was clearly impressed by Raven and learned much from him; as my other chapter contributed to this book shows, Taylor later claimed that he had learned his controversial views on the Eternal Son from Raven during these visits, although the remarks were not published at the time.[69] On one occasion, in the context of a discussion on 'gifted persons', James Taylor asked the question 'Is it by studying Scripture [that a gifted person brings light]?' and received the reply 'No. The anointing which you have of him teaches you.'[70] In the same meeting Raven made the assertion that 'if I had to live over again I would study Scripture less and pray more.'[71] At the end of their lives most Christians no doubt feel they should have prayed more, but probably also that they should have studied Scripture more, not less.

On his second visit in 1902 Raven again made significant remarks concerning the Spirit speaking in the church and the necessity of those who are spiritual to discern this:

> the thing is to get out to where the Spirit is, and there you will find understanding of the oracles of God. I mean that individually you come to where the spiritual man discerns

---

65. Raven, 'Faith' [Peckham, 1899/1900], in *Ministry*, 13: 216–7.
66. Raven, 'Readings on 1 Corinthians (1)' [USA & Canada, 1902], in *Ministry*, 17: 121.
67. Raven, 'Introduction', by J.S.A., in *Ministry*, 12: 1–7; 'Introduction', by J.S.A., in *Ministry*, 17: 1–6. For the identification of 'J.S.A.', see Raven, *Letters*, 190.
68. 'Historical Reference', in [James Taylor], *Letters of James Taylor*, 2 vols. (Kingston-on-Thames, 1956), 2: 413.
69. See Holden, chap. 16, *intra*, 253.
70. Raven, 'The Calling of God' [USA & Canada, 1898], in *Ministry*, 12: 136. Here Raven is simply quoting 1 Jn. 2: 27 (King James Version).
71. Raven, 'The Calling of God' [USA & Canada, 1898], in *Ministry*, 12: 137.

all things . . . When we left system we did not understand much about the temple. We connected the Spirit very much with the individual. There was no idea of the Spirit in the company. I think when we were delivered from those things we began to get some apprehension of the temple of God and of the presence of the Spirit of God, not merely in the individual, but in the temple.[72]

Implicitly this makes a very high claim for the Brethren—here was where the Spirit was speaking and spiritual persons were present to discern this. But to be fair, it should also be pointed out that he said: 'Now brethren are not a remnant because there are a great many really in the church who are not among brethren. We are so liable to get into a kind of brethrenism. You must recognise the entire circle.'[73] He agreed with a comment made in response to this that 'the only company we could recognize in Indianapolis is all the Christians in Indianapolis.'

James Taylor

Raven died in 1903, and by 1905 it would appear that James Taylor was becoming to be regarded as his successor. Taylor had clearly assimilated Raven's teaching. In one of his earliest published items of ministry, an address given in New York in 1903, Taylor said 'I always read a Scripture myself when I try to speak, and it is necessary to support everything you state by Scripture, but the basis of your preaching is not exactly Scripture.'[74] The notes of meetings held in Chicago over New Year 1904–5 provoked some controversy, particularly in Britain. In the light of this, Taylor in fact revised the notes but he maintained that what he said was in accordance with Scripture and was 'substantially the truth which the Lord has been calling our attention to for some years', which was the importance of the assembly as a sphere of practical salvation from the world.[75] As in his later denial of the Eternal Sonship of Christ, this leading seems to be some general inward sense, not direct direction by voices, as in the early Quakers, nor direct visions and prophecies as claimed by more recent charismatic leaders.

Taylor may have been referring to the 'Chicago Notes' controversy when, in 1910, he said 'The line of attack in connection with the receiving of the Spirit . . . was against the subjective side'.[76] Certainly Alfred J. Gardiner, writing many years later, in *The Recovery and Maintenance of the Truth* (1963) stated that 'the opposition that arose at that time was an effort of the enemy to use objective truth to deny or obscure the importance and value of the presence in the assembly of the Holy Spirit and His resulting work in the saints . . . many who refused a subjective line of ministry . . . were carried away at the time of the

---

72. Raven, 'Readings on 1 Corinthians (1)' [USA & Canada, 1902], in *Ministry*, 17:121.
73. Raven, 'Readings on the First Epistle of John (5)' [USA & Canada, 1902], in *Ministry*, 17:329.
74. Taylor, 'Christ in Authority' [New York, 1903], in *Ministry*, 1:37.
75. Taylor, 'Preface to Readings and Addresses at Meetings held in Chicago [31 December 1904 to 2 January 1905]', *Ministry*, 1:111. Taylor to Mr. John Henderson, 15 Jan. 1906, in *Letters*, 1:31–3.
76. Taylor, 'Reading' [Indianapolis, 1910], in *Ministry*, 3:250.

Glanton issue.'[77] The subjective line of ministry implies the direct speaking of the Spirit. Ultimately it is Christ, the Lord, who is speaking but he speaks through the Spirit, 'the Spirit speaks...in a subjective way . . . as dwelling in the Church'.[78] Others remarked upon 'the importance of being on the line of the Spirit' and that 'If you speak it should be by the Spirit'.[79] Speaking should be by the Spirit while hearers must be able to discern the speaking of the Spirit. Taylor emphasized the presence of the Spirit in the assembly, to the detriment of the Spirit in the individual believer.

This raises the question of exactly how the Spirit speaks in the assembly. Increasingly the answer to this can be seen in an emphasis on what is 'authoritative'. Sometimes the use of these terms is innocuous enough, referring to Scripture, the prophets of the Old Testament or the apostles of the New. But other references are referring, not to the authority of Scripture, but to an authority that is present here and now, that comes from the Spirit in the form of authoritative ministry or authoritative teaching. Associated with this is the use of the term 'anointed'. Some of these statements are ambiguous, particularly as Taylor on occasions makes bold statements but later says something to soften the edge.[80] Sometimes he may be implying that all ministry can be authoritative, whoever it is given by, rather than claiming that only his ministry in particular is authoritative, a claim he never explicitly makes.

The word 'authoritative' first occurs in Taylor's published ministry in 1919 in connection with the Spirit speaking in the assembly.[81] It is first explicitly connected with 'ministry' on two occasions in 1925, where he speaks of 'the general principle of ministry is authoritative' and then more emphatically that 'All ministry should be authoritative'.[82] But he suggests that not that all that is said in conversational Bible readings has this character, and the Bible is the ultimate test.[83] At meetings in Surbiton in south-west London in March 1929, that were—significantly—shortly before the Barnet meetings in north London, he says 'the servant carries authority in his ministry if it is rightly presented in an anointed mouth; but there is authority in it.'[84] In the immediate context he is referring to Moses and Aaron, but can fairly be read as having a wider implication, as explained in an address 'Divine Anointing' that he gave when he returned to Barnet in the following year, 1930.[85] Here he says 'the idea of the anointing has a very wide bearing, and brings God in authoritatively and in suited dignity in the instruments used'. Initially, here he is talking about Ezekiel, but towards the end of the address he refers unambiguously to the existence of anointed

---

77. Gardiner, *Recovery and Maintenance of the Truth*, 153. For the Glanton issue see: Grass, *Gathering to His Name*, 205–6.
78. Taylor, 'The Order Marking the Church at the Outset' [Toronto, 1908], in *Ministry*, 2:83.
79. Taylor, 'The Order', in *Ministry*, 2:83–4. Remarks made by 'F.L.' and 'G.A.T.'
80. Roger Shuff, *Searching for the True Church: Brethren and Evangelicals in Mid-Twentieth-Century England* (Carlisle, 2005), 118–9.
81. Taylor, 'Spiritual Education (2)' [Belfast, 1919], in *Ministry*, 10:370.
82. Taylor, 'The Assembly' [Melbourne and Adelaide, 1925], in *Ministry*, 23:71–72; id., 'How Living Conditions are Promoted' [Manchester, September 1925], in *Ministry*, 23:205–6.
83. Taylor, 'The Assembly' [Melbourne and Adelaide, 1925], in *Ministry*, 23:71–72.
84. Taylor, 'The Service of God (2)' [Surbiton, 1929], in *Ministry*, 30:81.
85. Taylor, 'Divine Anointing' [Barnet, 1930], in *Ministry*, 32:200–212. This is repeated in 36:245–57.

servants today: 'The point is what God has to say as to the saints *now*' concluding 'that the idea [of anointing] may pervade us all as it pervaded the tabernacle, and that it may be seen especially in those who are ministering the word, that the Scriptures may be brought to bear on us today in power.'[86] An address 'Inscrutability', given in Edinburgh in 1932, can be seen as a defence of his statements on the Eternal Sonship. While not actually using the word 'authority', he states 'The Lord sees the need of correcting His people, but if the correction or adjustments He makes are disregarded, we can no longer plead ignorance. There is the refusal of what the Spirit says.'[87] Still responding to the reaction following his denial of the Eternal Sonship, two reading meetings held in England at Birmingham in 1933 were published under the title 'Authority in Doctrine and Fellowship'.[88] The word 'authority' occurs sixty-six times in these meetings. In opening the first of these readings Taylor remarked that 'It seems as if the Lord, whilst ministering to His people freely, would stress from time to time, that the teaching He furnishes has authority in it, and that the fellowship bound up with it also involves authority. . . . These facts remind us of the need of experience with the Lord in relation to His people so that ministry or teaching should be authoritative.'[89] In the context, this might be seen as asserting the authority of his own ministry and some may have seen this as making a claim to apostolic authority, leading him to qualify this in his opening remarks to the second reading. 'It is not intended to suggest that we have any such authority [as held by the apostles] vested in any man now', then adding, 'but [it is intended] to show that there *is* authority. The presence of the Holy Spirit, a divine Person, continuing on with the assembly, and in it, and speaking, necessarily carries the thought of authority.'[90] This leaves unclear the distinction between apostolic authority and present-day authority.

We can summarize Taylor's teaching in the following points:

1. The speaking of the Holy Spirit is authoritative, it is the speaking of Christ, the Lord, himself.
2. Scripture is authoritative as it is given by the Holy Spirit.
3. The Spirit speaking in the assembly is authoritative.
4. The Spirit speaks through authoritative ministry.
5. Authoritative ministry is based on Scripture.

As with Raven, these do not necessarily follow logically, may overlap, and are potentially contradictory.

---

86. Taylor, 'Divine Anointing' [Barnet 1930], in *Ministry*, 32:212 (emphasis in original).
87. Taylor, 'Inscrutability' [Edinburgh, 1932], in *Ministry*, 13:207.
88. Taylor, 'Authority in Doctrine and Fellowship' [Birmingham, 1933], in *Ministry*, 34:257–91.
89. Taylor, 'Authority in Doctrine and Fellowship (1)' [Birmingham, 1933], in *Ministry*, 34:257–8.
90. Taylor, 'Authority in Doctrine and Fellowship (2)' [Birmingham, 1933], in *Ministry*, 34:274.

Like Raven before him, Taylor diminished the expository, asserting that Scripture can only be understood by those in the light of the assembly.[91] There is nothing new about typological, or allegorical, interpretation of Scripture, as it was one of the four senses of Scripture used in medieval interpretation.[92] But Taylor increasingly used typological interpretation of the Old Testament in a way that enabled phrases to be used with little regard for context. He began moving in this direction very early in his ministry in a tentative or, as he put it, undogmatic, manner. An address given in Wallington, in the London Borough of Sutton, in 1912 entitled 'The Life Line' is on the rather gruesome tale in 2 Samuel 8:2 where David lays out the Moabites in three lines, two to die and one to live. Taylor presents these three lines as representing the Law and the Prophets; Christ down here in the flesh; and Christ in resurrection. Clearly aware that such interpretation may be controversial he adds:

> You will understand that in using a scripture in this way from the Old Testament it is not to present it in a dogmatic sense. I think we are allowed by the Lord great latitude in ministry, in the use of the Scriptures. They are said to be "profitable for doctrine, for reproof, for correction, for instruction in righteousness", (2 Timothy 3:16); and I think a minister is given, as it were, certain latitude, by the Spirit, in his use of them. They are said to be profitable; that is to say, they help in the ministry of the truth, they help in the way of showing how it is set, its bearing; and I would say in that connection that the Old Testament is as much for us as the New. We read: "Whatsoever things were written aforetime were written for our learning", (Romans 15:4). So that you will understand, that in using these Scriptures, I do it to endeavour to make the truth clear to you.[93]

Despite the arbitrary nature of such typological use of the Old Testament, Taylor came to rely on it more and more, basing authoritative requirements on it. Roger Shuff discusses his later use of Numbers 21:17 to support singing to the Holy Spirit, something that previously, following Darby, the Brethren had not done.[94] Those who queried this use of the Old Testament, seeking New Testament confirmation, were accused of effectively saying that the Old Testament was not inspired Scripture.[95] Support for authoritative ministry was found in Ecclesiastes 12:11 'The words of the wise are as goads and the collections of them as nails fastened in: they are given from the one shepherd'. Taylor himself quoted this with this implication in 1925 and when quoted by Percy Lyon in 1948 he could well be implying that the 'one shepherd' is the one authoritative minister, that is Taylor himself.[96]

---

91. Taylor, 'Intelligence to Mark the Assembly' [1925], in *Ministry*, 15:441, 447; id., 'Intelligence in the Assembly' [Birkenhead, 26 Jul. 1925], in *Ministry*, 95:2, 9. These are evidently two versions of the same reading.

92. Alister E. McGrath, *Christian Theology: An Introduction* (2nd edn., Oxford, 1994), 207–8.

93. Taylor, 'The Life Line' [Wallington, 1912], in *Ministry*, 5:116.

94. Shuff, *Searching for the True Church*, 118–9.

95. Taylor, letter of Sept. 1942, *Letters*, 2:285.

96. Taylor, 'How Living Conditions are Promoted' [Manchester, September 1925], in *Ministry*, 23:205–6; id., Taylor, 'Divine Persons and Our Relationships with them' [Toronto, October 1948], in *Ministry*, 72:213. Toronto, 1948. The 'P.L.' who made this statement is almost certainly Percy Lyon.

Having moved in the spiritualist direction, in answering the spiritualist dilemma of how one knows the current speaking of the Spirit the Brethren moved towards the Catholic view of authoritative interpreters. However, for the Brethren there is still a dilemma as to how such persons are to be recognized as they do not have the institutional framework that answers that question in the Catholic Church.

C. A. Coates

Charles Andrew Coates was not seen as one of the line of 'Ministers of the Lord in the Recovery', but was one whose ministry was nevertheless highly regarded and put into print. Born in 1862, he came amongst the Brethren in 1878, dying in 1945 and so spanning the eras of Darby, Raven, and Taylor. He wrote a lengthy defence of Taylor's views on the Eternal Son.[97] In ministry given during the 1940s, Coates particularly emphasizes that the Spirit speaks through 'spiritual persons' and does so calling attention to specific matters at particular times. In Luther's time the Spirit said much about justification, but recently he has been speaking about Christ as head of the assembly and no spiritual person would care to be out of the line of what the Spirit is saying.[98] In the context of ministry on Zechariah chapter 4 he says:

> It is not enough that we should recognise that the Spirit is here—that this is the Spirit's day—but we should be greatly concerned to be spiritual. It is only in spiritual persons that there can be the flow of what is spiritual, and without this the assembly cannot be in any real way the vessel of spiritual light. The Spirit Himself acts in the assembly, but in a general way the service there is through spiritual persons; of course, in the power of the Spirit.[99]

To a direct question, 'You would not hesitate to say that J. N. D. was an apostle [?]', Coates does not clearly respond either 'yes' or 'no' but says 'I believe he was distinctly sent to restore the truth of the headship of Christ and what stands vitally connected with it; and that his mission was universal in its scope, an apostle in that sense, if you like.'[100]

After James Taylor

Although as we have seen it had roots in the ministry of F. E. Raven, some Brethren had evidently begun to feel unease at the direction Taylor's later ministry was taking, as it seemingly gave ministry the same authority as Scripture. One of these was Robert Grubb of Norwich who after Taylor's death wrote and circulated a pamphlet entitled *Brief Remarks on the Unique Authority Attaching to the Holy Scriptures*. This was essentially a defence of what we have called the Reformed view, warning the Brethren against the view that ministry has an equal authority. Grubb argues that the Scriptures alone are authoritative; all ministry is to be tested by Scripture and it is the right of every Christian to do this. This led to correspondence with E. J. Boyt of Manchester, with subsequently the resulting correspondence and the original pamphlet being privately published in a booklet of the

---

97. See Holden, chap. 16, *intra*, 265.
98. C. A. Coates, *An Outline of the Epistle to the Ephesians* (Kingston-on-Thames, n.d), 58; id., *An Outline of some of the Minor Prophets* (Kingston-on-Thames, n.d), 103.
99. Coates, *Minor Prophets*, 102.
100. Coates, *Ephesians*, 58–9. Question mark not in original, but is implied.

same title as the original.[101] Boyt's response shows how the teaching of Raven and Taylor had been absorbed by the Brethren. Boyt makes the common Brethren criticism that what Grubb is saying would lead to 'independency'.[102] An individual's understanding of Scripture may be wrong and Grubb has 'exalted my own independent judgement as to what the scripture means above light which God may give through vessels of his own choosing.'[103] The Spirit speaking in the assembly carries authority, the right response of every member being to receive this instantly and obediently. This should not be seen as onerous but a pleasure and delight. This of course raises the question of how the Spirit speaks and the answer is through authoritative ministers:

> we are not all level in the assembly, for God has set certain in the assembly as it has pleased Him, and we must recognise that he has done that, and bow to it. I like to feel that I, with the Bible in my hand, am a match for anyone . . . but the fact remains that I must accept that I am not: God has put His authority in persons as He has thought fit.[104]

In other words, what is a right understanding of Scripture is that taught by authoritative ministers and it is through them that the Spirit speaks in the assembly. This authority is something additional to the Scriptures, but coming from the same source, the Spirit, it will not contradict them.[105] Through such ministers the Brethren have come to understand that some Scriptures do not mean what they had always thought they had meant. As an example of this, Boyt uses one that comes from Taylor's denial of the Eternal Sonship:

> Have we not constantly had to be taught, in ministry, that a scripture meant something quite different from what I myself had thought before? Did we not all read "The Father has sent the Son" as meaning that the Father sent the Son into manhood, until we had to be taught that the Son had previously come, voluntarily into manhood before He was sent by the Father?[106]

The Spirit's speaking in the assembly is thus not something general that can come through anyone, but something that comes through specific persons. Boyt does not discuss the question of how such persons are to be recognized and this is indeed the fatal flaw in what he says. The correspondence between Grubb and Boyt took place the year after Taylor had died when there was something of a power struggle developing as to who would be the next anointed leader. From this struggle, James Taylor Jr. emerged triumphant. In the light of what happened under his leadership, many will find that Boyt's words have an ominous note to them. When Boyt urges Grubb to withdraw his statements 'for the sake of . . . the sheep', some may feel that the sheep should have heeded Grubb's warning.[107] Taylor Jr.

---

101. R. Grubb, *Brief Remarks on the Unique Authority Attaching to the Holy Scriptures* (London, 1955).
102. Grubb, *Brief Remarks*, 10. 'Independency' refers to the position taken in 1848 by the Open Brethren concerning the independence of local assemblies.
103. Grubb, *Brief Remarks*, 11.
104. Grubb, *Brief Remarks*, 22. Emphasis in original.
105. Grubb, *Brief Remarks*, 22.
106. Grubb, *Brief Remarks*, 11. Emphasis in original.
107. Grubb, *Brief Remarks*, 22.

exploited to the full his father's concept of authoritative ministry, coupled with typological use of Scripture while claiming the leading of the Spirit, to exert an increasingly rigorous and arbitrary rule over the Brethren. New teaching on separation in 1959 resulted in many leaving.[108] The Brethren had never engaged in missionary work, but the increasing emphasis on separation meant that the notice boards on Brethren meeting rooms, inviting people to hear the gospel, were removed.[109] The Brethren might possess the 'truth' but it was something to be kept to themselves and not proclaimed. The Brethren came to expect a continuous stream of new teaching, which had to be acted upon immediately and unquestioningly even though it became increasingly bizarre as the 1960s progressed—for example, that clocks were to be removed from meeting rooms and Brethren were not to wear watches to meetings.[110] The tradition of meetings working through a book of the Bible in their Sunday and mid-week Bible Readings was abandoned; instead the passage of Scripture to be considered was to be based on 'impressions', thus severing any links with the expository tradition. Taylor Jr. was referred to as 'The Man of God' and proclaimed as 'the present day Paul', abandoning earlier cautions about claiming apostolic status.[111] But appearances suggested to some persons that he was being driven not by the Holy Spirit but by an addiction to alcohol.[112] As a result many left in 1970, concluding that neither his teaching nor his behaviour were scriptural. Others however remained, either dismissing the reports of alcoholism as lies or claiming that, whatever outward appearances might be, Taylor Jr. was a spiritual person who was not to be judged by the unspiritual;[113] these now use the title Plymouth Brethren Christian Church.

What shall we say to these things?

We could respond with the Preacher of *Ecclesiastes*, 'there is nothing new under the sun.'[114] As with the debate over the Eternal Sonship, the Brethren in some respects had traversed familiar territory in relating the present work of the Holy Spirit and the Bible. Darby's views on Scripture are in line with what we have called the Reformed view: that the work of the Spirit is necessary but always works through Scripture which is the sole authority. But his emphasis on the presence of the Holy Spirit in the assembly leaned in the spiritualist direction and this tendency was amplified in the teaching of Stoney and Raven. Under Taylor's ministry this increasingly came to be seen as the Holy Spirit speaking

---

108. Gardiner, *Recovery and Maintenance*, 316. Shuff, *Searching for the True Church*, 176–84.

109. Roger N. Holden, '"Sending out missionaries is not scriptural at all": An Exclusive View of Missions', in Neil T. R. Dickson and T. J. Marinello, *Brethren and Mission: Essays in Honour of Timothy C. F. Stunt* (SBH; Glasgow, 2015), 107–115, spec. 114. Roger Shuff has discussed the paradox that, despite this, 1960s culture in many ways infiltrated the Brethren, particularly through Taylor Jr. himself. Shuff, *Searching for the True Church*, 245–53.

110. Personal recollection of the author. This was justified by appeal to Psalm 31:15, our 'times are in thy hand.'

111. Personal recollection of the author.

112. Shuff, *Searching for the True Church*, 245–53.

113. A document subsequently circulated, seeking to explain Taylor's behaviour in 1970, effectively incorporates both these views: Shuff, *Searching for the True Church*, 266–8.

114. Eccles. 1:9.

through one anointed leader whose authority had to be accepted. Biblical exegesis, the understanding of Scripture in context, was increasingly set aside allowing texts to be used typologically and without attention to context. This took away the right of Brethren to understand Scripture for themselves, removing congregational checks and balances. This can be seen as a move in the direction of the Catholic view, authoritative teaching having to be calmly accepted. Darby, Raven, and Taylor came to be accorded apostolic authority. In the hands of James Taylor Jr. this was to lead the Brethren into what many would see as disaster in the 1960s as it became impossible to question the authoritative leader. Despite continuing claims to be based on Scripture, the teaching of this line of ministers became all important. These issues are relevant to the Church today, with, for example, some sections of the charismatic movement emphasizing visions and prophecies to provide direction.[115]

---

115. For example: Terry Virgo, *No Well-Worn Paths* (Eastbourne, 2001), 143–4.

Chapter 5

The Brethren and the Bible in Central Africa

Kovina Mutenda

The title of this chapter refers to an area in Africa referred to by Brethren historians as 'the Beloved Strip', comprising the three countries of Angola, Congo, and Zambia. Congo, which was originally called Belgian Congo, is now the Democratic Republic of Congo, but in this chapter will be referred to simply as 'Congo'. The Beloved Strip is the area with the greatest concentration of Brethren churches in Africa. In this paper I shall briefly show how the message of the Bible has affected the people of Africa not only to change their way of thinking but their way of life. There is a significant difference between other Christian groups and the Brethren, and the difference lies in what they believe about the Bible. There were many missionaries who brought the Bible to Africa but their message or application of the message did not change the lives of the people to whom they ministered. To those missionaries and their converts, the Bible did not seem to have had any real lasting spiritual effect. It is like what Paul describes in 2 Timothy as 'a people having a form of godliness but denying its power'.[1] But the message that the Brethren missionaries preached changed the lives of the people to whom they ministered, and changed them from spirit worshippers to born again believers in Christ. To those who came into contact with the Brethren, the Bible was to them a spring of living water, a life changing and living book, and as the apostle Matthew rightly expresses the situation as 'a source of light for people living in darkness.'[2]

The Brethren, like other evangelicals, believe that the Bible comprising of the sixty-six books of the Old and New Testament Scriptures, is given by verbal inspiration of God or 'God-breathed', that is to say that the Holy Spirit directed its writing. And that the Bible is a divine book, it is the real word of God. The Bible is not man's reasoning, nor man's conclusions, but God's absolute authority over men in all that we believe and practise. Man's word may be questioned, but God's word must be obeyed, or man must suffer the consequences. The Bible reveals the way of life for those who will obey and believe, and the way of death for those who disobey and reject it. This paper shall look at the impact the Bible had on the Africans from a historical rather than from a contemporary point of view. And almost all that shall be said in this paper will make reference to Christian Brethren who came to this part of Africa—the Beloved Strip.

---

1. 2 Tim. 3:5. All biblical quotations are from the NIV.
2. Matt. 4:16.

The Brethren mission to Africa

As a result of their conviction about the Bible, when Brethren missionaries came to Africa, they were determined not only to preach the gospel of the Bible but also to teach the Bible so that the national believers would live a life of obedience to God and his word. But how could the missionaries teach the Bible if the people could not read the Bible for themselves as their languages were not written? The early missionaries then preached the gospel with one hand and with the other they worked on the language and grammar, and they opened schools to make the people literate. This is confirmed by one Brethren missionary, Kitty Fisher, in her autobiography, when she describes her husband's initial approach to the people:

> Soon after we arrived, Singleton called village elders to a camp-fire discussion. He explained that we had come to teach them about *Nzambi* whom they knew as creator, and about Jesus. We would give them medicine, and we would help to deliver them from their fears of witchcraft. We would teach them to read and give them God's book, the Bible, in their own language. But we have not come to clothe them and feed them and do the things which they could quite easily do for themselves.

On the next page of her book, Kitty Fisher writes: 'As people began to learn to read, we started a class on Friday afternoons, which we called, *Kulumbulula,* which means 'to unravel the tangle, to explain'. Singleton believed in letting the Bible itself teach and convict, and as each book was translated and printed, we studied that book, starting with Genesis.'[3]

And when the people learnt how to read and write, the next step was to have the Bible in their mother language. One of the most important and outstanding contributions to missionary work in Africa was the translation of the Bible and other literature in local languages. One of the early translations in Luvale was *Pilgrim's Progress*. The book was eventually chosen as a school reader for African schools in Zambia. The work of translation also included the production of hymnbooks into the vernacular. Hymns are of great importance in witness and in worship, and also for teaching doctrine to non-readers. However, their doctrinal content had to be carefully considered, something that is not always done with hymns in English, when often-sung sentiments are not always scriptural. Emmaus courses were translated into local languages and through these courses many people, both believers and unbelievers, studied God's word. Brethren missionaries also taught the Bible through the literature that was published by Everyday Publications Inc. in Canada. Several titles were translated into local languages.

In more recent years the Brethren have continued to teach the truths of the Bible through the distribution of the same literature, but for English speakers more Emmaus courses and Everyday Publications books have been made available. John Ritchie publications from Scotland have been promoted alongside William McDonald's two-volume Bible commentary. Magazines such *Uplook*, *Counsel*, *Precious Seed*, and *Truth & Tidings* have been freely distributed for readers in Zambia. Everyday Publications books have been

---

3. M. K. Fisher, *Lampposts to Searchlights: 'The Brighter Side of Missionary Life'. Memories of M. K. Fisher* (Iklenge, Zambia, 1994), 65, 66.

translated into French and Swahili and distributed in Congo and also into Portuguese and distributed in Angola. Every effort has been made using literature to encourage people to read and study the Bible. The Brethren effectively used carefully selected and translated literature to teach Bible truths so that the Africans might grow and be grounded in their faith.

Bible translation

During the Reformation, William Tyndale became convinced that England would never be evangelized using Latin Bibles because 'it was impossible to stablish the lay people in any truth, except the scripture were plainly laid before their eyes in their mother tongue.'[4] Convinced of exactly the same truth, Brethren missionaries translated the Bible into five languages spoken in the Beloved Strip. Translation is not a work to be lightly undertaken by anyone. In the case of the word of God it involves a great responsibility. Translation demands the most meticulous care to obtain accuracy of rendering. Translation is not a case of word-for-word transference from one language into another. In many cases phrases must be re-arranged and sentences entirely recast. For example, quoting from Albert Horton's biography, this is how John 3:16 reads in the Luvale Bible and when literally re-translated back into English it reads like this,

> In-this-way indeed in-he-them-loved God those-of-earth, to-give-for-them Son-his one only of the finger, so-that (he-intended) whoever will-him-accept should-be-without perishing, but (he-intended) he-should-be-sitting with-living of-whereon-go years all.
>
> Romans 6:2: Forbidden! We who-became-separated from-sin by-dying, we-shall-be-sitting-therein how?
>
> 1 John 1:5: this this-is news this we-heard already from Him, this-which we-tell to you saying, God He is sunlight, and in Him in-is-not darkness even a-little.[5]

The above sentences will be perfectly understood by a Luvale speaker like myself. In the beginning, portions of Scripture were translated, for example, the Gospel of Mark.

Horton, an American missionary, engaged in Bible translation at Kavungu in Angola in the heart of Luvaleland. In 1944 he produced the New Testament, a revision of the work previously done by Gavin H. Mowat and George Suckling of Chitokoloki in Zambia, and the following year 10,000 copies were made available to the public. The Old Testament was completed in 1956 as a separate volume. The New Testament was again revised and finally in 1961 the complete Luvale Bible was done. Horton was helped by two Luvale believers only identified as Mako and Ngongo.

The Lunda Bible was translated at Kasaji in Congo by William Singleton Fisher, the son of Dr Walter Fisher of Kalene Mission. Singleton, as he was known to his missionary colleagues, was born at Kavungu in Angola and brought up at Kalene. Hugh Cunningham of Kalunda in Angola started the translation work on the Lunda Bible. Cunningham sent the draft New Testament manuscript to Singleton Fisher to check through. And this opened

---

4. William Tyndale, 'Preface to The Pentateuch' (1530), quoted in *Opal News* (Spring 2015), 1.

5. Albert E. Horton and Petronella D. Horton, *'Africa, oh Africa!' Reminiscences of Fifty-Two Years in Africa* (1977; 3rd edn., Spring Lake, NJ, 1979), 87.

the door for him to do a complete translation of the Bible into Lunda. Singleton was helped by a blind-man, Chamuwana; by Manase Kapanga, who became his chief collaborator; Kutela; and then Edomi who was an excellent reader. The completed manuscripts were sent to Tom Rea, an expert in Lunda, for checking, and the suggestions made by Rea led to an even better translation. Towards the end, Singleton's wife Kitty and Nessie Riddel of Kalene joined the team. The Lunda Bible was completed in 1962 and in its first edition 15,000 copies were printed.

David Long, from Northern Ireland, a missionary based at Luma-Kasai in Angola translated the Bible into Chokwe with the assistance of Crawford Allison and Donald McLeod. He completed his work in 1970. The fact that all these three languages, Luvale, Lunda, and Chokwe, spoken by more than a million people in each of the languages in Angola, Congo, and Zambia, reveals the unpardonable sin committed by the Berlin Conference in 1886 when those who shared these languages were arbitrarily divided by colonial-era borders.

Lesley G. Barham, a missionary commended from Zimbabwe—formerly Southern Rhodesia—based at Kalundu in Zambia translated the Bible into Cibemba. He was assisted by people from the Church of Scotland, Mr MacMinn and Paul Mushindo of Lubwa Mission, who did the initial translation work. The joint work was done in order to harmonize the Cibemba spoken in the Northern area and that spoken in the Luapula. The Cibemba Bible was completed and printed in 1956. The Cibemba Bible is used in Zambia and Congo.

Dan Crawford first translated the Bible into Luba-Sanga in 1928. It was later decided that another translation be produced to improve on what Crawford had done. A committee consisting of three church groups was put in place to supervise that work, but the text was to be produced by the Brethren missionary, John Alexander Clarke.[6] Grace Tooley, a British missionary based at Bunkeya in Congo, spent many years revising the work previously done by Crawford and Clarke. With the help a national Job Kiyana, a new translation of the Kisanga Bible was completed in 1984. Eunice Rhoades from Australia helped to type the manuscripts and Ethel Hamilton also from Australia helped in preparing the translation for publication.

The missionaries encountered some problems in Bible translation and one such example was the word 'snow'. There is no snow in Africa with the exception of a few areas in South Africa, the Mediterranean coast, and on Mount Kilimanjaro. The majority of Africans who have never travelled to snowy countries have never seen snow and hence the absence of the word for 'snow' in most African languages. Albert Horton translated 'snow' into Luvale as 'the rain of the winter' but this did not help the people—they know the summer rain but have no idea about the winter rain. And in the Cibemba Bible 'snow' is translated as 'white rain', although the Bemba people do not have a slightest idea of what the white rain looks like. In the original Lunda Bible manuscript 'snow' was translated as 'the rain of the winter' but as that made no sense to the Lunda people, they ended up translating the word 'snow' as 'whitewash', to convey the idea of whiteness. In the Luchazi Bible

---

6. David Maxwell, 'The Creation of Lubaland: Missionary Science and Christian Literacy in the Making of the Luba Katanga in Belgian Congo', *Journal of Eastern African Studies*, 10/3 (2016), 367–92, spec. 373–5.

'snow' is translated as 'solidified water' (ice)—here again the problem is that the majority of the people in the rural areas who have no fridges have never seen solidified water. There were other words and concepts that posed a big challenge to Bible translators, but space does not allow going into such details.

One problem encountered in translating the Bible into Lunda was how to translate the word 'gods' as in heathen gods. The missionaries wanted to use the name for 'God' but in plural, 'anzambi'. The Lunda people strongly reacted: "'We thought there was only one Nzambi (God) until the missionaries told us there were many.'"[7] They ended up using another word akin to ancestral spirit-gods. However, this problem did not occur in other languages such as Luvale, Luchazi, and Chokwe where they pluralized the name for God with a small letter.

Over the years these five translations have been used of the Lord in his sovereign will for preaching the gospel, which has resulted in the salvation of thousands of people. And the national believers have also learnt to accept the Bible as the real word of God as the Psalmist testifies 'Your word is a lamp to my feet and a light for my path.'[8] In one rural district of Zambia, people had gathered for a Sunday morning church service, but on that particular day there was no one to read from the Bible because all those present were illiterate. The church then decided to go and look for someone in the village to come and read God's word. They finally found one man who was drunk, gave him the Bible and he read the Bible to them.[9] This true story shows how the national believers have come to appreciate the value of the Bible and at the same time demonstrates the desperate need for literacy. The translation of the Bible into the Africans' mother tongues resulted in many being saved and increased understanding in biblical truth ultimately leading to spiritual growth and service to God.

African Traditional Religion

When Brethren missionaries came to Africa they intended to teach the nationals God's message from the Bible by which they could be saved and direct their daily lives. But they found that the people had their own religion—animism or better defined as African Traditional Religion (ATR). ATR had three main components: belief in God, belief in the spirit world, and belief in mystical powers. The African believed in a God who is the Supreme Being and creator of all things. For many Africans the worship of God is mixed with petitions and sacrifices offered to the ancestral spirits and not directly to God. Sacrifices and offerings are a common form of worship in Africa. These offerings are directed at the ancestral spirits for the purpose of appeasing the offended ancestors. The African people worshipped the spirits of their ancestors by bringing offerings at the shrines daily or on special days. They would pour oil, beer, crops or animal blood. Each village had its own shrine in form of a tree.

Traditionally Africans thought that God is basically unknowable for he is mysterious and distant from people. The people believe that God creates, sees and knows, but they have no concept of personal relationship with God. They did not know him as one who

---

7. Fisher, *Lampposts and Searchlights*, 159.
8. Ps. 119:105.
9. Story told by Wathabu Simfukwe of Samfya Bible School.

would personally sustain and guide them day-by-day. The Africans had general revelation but no special revelation. The words of the apostle Paul in Romans 10:14 and 15 found and still find application to both the missionaries and the Africans:

> for, "Everyone who calls on the name of the Lord will be saved." How, then, can they call on the one they have not believed in? And how can they believe in the one of whom they have not heard? And how can they hear without someone preaching to them? And how can they preach unless they are sent? As it is written, "How beautiful are the feet of those who bring good news!"[10]

The Brethren taught the people from the Bible to abandon their animistic practices. In 1 Thessalonians 1:9 it is said of the Thessalonian Christians that, 'for they themselves report what kind of reception you gave us. They tell how you turned to God from idols to serve the living and true God.'[11] In the same way the Bible as taught by the Brethren missionaries turned many thousands of Africans from their idols and spirits to trust in the true living God.

What is written about some of the early converts who became preachers testify to this fact:

> These men from time to time were sent by missionaries into needy areas that they might live among the people and witness not only with their message, but especially with their lives. Each time the trials of serious illness or loss of children came to test them they faced great pressures from their unsaved relatives to return to the witch doctors and worship the spirits. These happened to most national workers but their perseverance in the faith gave them victory and gave credibility to the message they preached.[12]

Much of ancestral worship has disappeared from Central Africa but the influence of the witchdoctor and diviner still rules supreme. The temptation for Christians, even in a well-taught, Bible-based Brethren church, to turn back to ATR in times of sickness and suffering is very real. Such situations can be solved by much teaching and counselling based on the Bible. The Brethren effectively taught and used the Bible to change the Africans from animism to faith in Christ.

Bible Schools and religious education

Brethren missionaries did not restrict the teaching of the Bible to Sunday and Bible-study meetings only. They set up Bible schools of various types. There were some very short-term, others long-term, some temporary, and others permanent Bible schools, most of which were established at mission stations. For very short-term schools people would gather for one week or two, bring their own food, and sleep in grass shelters. For long-term and more permanent schools, facilities such as classrooms and dormitories were

---

10. Rom. 10:14–15.
11. 1 Thess. 1:9.
12. Kovina Mutenda, 'An Evaluation of Gospel Work in Zambia', in Neil T. R. Dickson and T. J. Marinello (eds.), *Brethren and Mission: Essays in Honour of Timothy C. F. Stunt* (SBH; Glasgow, 2016), 207–18, spec. 213.

built for that purpose. Different topics were taught ranging from Christian marriage to Bible doctrines. The teaching was tailored according to the levels of literacy and spiritual maturity.

In the early days, Brethren missionaries taught in these Bible schools, but over the past thirty years, the old-generation missionaries have either retired to their homelands or gone to be with the Lord. Although the number of missionaries has drastically reduced, the work of many Bible schools has been taken over by capable and responsible nationals. There are still a good number of Bible schools in Angola and Congo. Currently there are four Bible schools in Zambia which offer residential training of nine months and longer: Kashikishi Bible School in Nchelenge; Samfya Bible School in Samfya; Kalobwa Bible Training Institute in Chienge in the Luapula Province; and Discipleship Training Centre under the wider ministry of Gospel Literature Outreach (GLO) in Ndola in the Copperbelt Province. Over the years, many have been trained from these schools and have laboured for the Lord among the churches and their ministry has been greatly appreciated. It is not easy to evaluate the effectiveness of Bible schools in a publication like this one. However, the most important fact is that the Brethren have effectively used Bible schools to teach the Bible so that the African students are grounded in sound doctrine and are in a position to teach the same to others.

The teaching of religious education (RE) as an examination subject in government schools in Zambia has been part of the curriculum for many years and is still the case. Many Brethren missionaries took up the opportunity by offering to teach Scripture in secondary schools on a voluntary basis and the Zambian government gladly accepted their services. Whereas school authorities were happy that the pass rate in the RE classes taught by missionaries was high, the missionaries were grateful to God that the Scriptures were being taught. The attitude of the missionaries was not only to teach RE but to impress upon their pupils the fact that the Bible is God's infallible word. The missionary teachers also took the liberty to explain the gospel and in that way the seed of salvation was being planted.

Many of the missionary teachers of RE also became involved with the work of Scripture Union (SU) in the secondary schools where they taught. SU was founded with the aim of encouraging Bible study through Bible reading. The contribution of Brethren missionaries to the growth and development of SU in Zambia was outstanding. The writer of this paper personally benefitted from the teaching of RE and the spiritual growth received from an American Brethren missionary through SU at the secondary school he attended in the early 1970s. The missionaries effectively used RE and SU to teach the Bible thereby laying a solid spiritual foundation for a countless number of pupils. And it is this very foundation which led the writer of this paper to answer God's call to full-time Christian ministry and later to pursue theological training. Many in Zambia of the writer's generation who were taught by missionaries are now Bible teachers themselves and church elders, and others are leading key Christian ministries.

Conclusion

What the Brethren missionaries did then is still being done today by national full-time Christian workers and other believers who are working alongside and in some cases have taken over the work previously done by expatriate missionaries. I want to conclude this paper by quoting evangelist Mavumilusa Makanzu of Congo, who may not be Brethren, but captures the heart and soul of the Brethren and the Bible.

Where the West is retreating spiritually, Africa is advancing. The African has decided to love the Bible with all his heart. Keep your novels and horoscopes and sell us your Bibles. We prefer to die rather than end up as candidates for atheism. Not the horrors of modern war, or the sufferings of famine, nor pounds sterling, or anything else will turn us into atheists. We love the Bible more than our earthly lives. It is not only a book of God, but a letter written by God to the African soul.[13]

---

13. Mavumilusa Makanzu, quoted in Kovina L. K. Mutenda, *A History of the Christian Brethren in Zambia (Christian Mission in Many Lands—CMML): One Hundred Years of God's Faithfulness in the Gospel (1898–1998)* (Chingola, Zambia, 2002), 196.

CHAPTER 7

Brethren and Biblical Scholarship in Britain in the Twentieth Century[1]

Alan Millard

Biblical scholarship was at home among the early Brethren—witness the work of S. P. Tregelles, B. W. Newton, Henry Craik, all concerned to ensure that readers of the Bible had the necessary tools for its sound understanding, with John Kitto especially aware of discoveries in ancient Assyria.[2] For a century or more, biblical scholarship has been widely equated with biblical criticism. The largely negative results of such studies concerning biblical history and faith in the later decades of the nineteenth century is probably a reason why biblical scholarship was long treated with suspicion, if not disdain, in Brethren circles. At the start of the twentieth century, the emphasis on evangelism in Brethren circles and, after the Schofield Bible had been published, on eschatology, was another reason, diverting attention from contextual studies of biblical passages. Bible studies and teaching in churches and in home groups tended to be expositional and devotional, rather than exegetical. In common with most evangelical Christians, the Brethren showed little concern for biblical scholarship in the early years of the twentieth century. Evangelism at home and abroad coupled with aversion to the self-proclaimed 'assured results' of liberal biblical criticism meant there was little to encourage able young Christians to take up such studies, except for those who needed to learn Greek or Hebrew for Bible translation work. Another reason for the lack of biblical scholarship among Brethren churches in the earlier part of the twentieth century was the doctrine of 'the priesthood of all believers'. What need was there for academic study when the Scriptures were available for everyone and everyone could interpret them? Of course, the consequences of that concept were frequently disastrous: poor or wrong teaching resulting from 'zeal without knowledge' and the departure of able minds to other church fellowships (such as the New Testament scholar G. R. Beasley-Murray).

For many, a strictly academic study of the Bible should affirm natural cause and effect and be conducted irrespective of religious commitment, following where the evidence,

---

1. Contrary to usual editorial practice, in bibliographical information in footnotes for this chapter, the publisher is stated. This is to show the range of publishers with which the scholars discussed were publishing. Additionally, due to the number of publications cited, if the title of a work is given in the text, it is not repeated in a footnote, but merely the place and date of publication along with the publisher.
2. See Dirk Jongkind, 'Samuel Prideaux Tregelles: A Nineteenth-Century Evangelical Apology for New Testament Textual Criticism', *intra*, chap. 3.

carefully considered, may lead, in order to understand the ancient books better. As knowledge of the ancient languages and civilizations has accumulated, so new insights can be gained and need to be assessed, then publicized. While most biblical scholars hold a religious commitment of some sort, they should take care to avoid it prescribing their results; atheists should be alert to the same problem.

I am not aware of any Brethren who were professionally involved in biblical scholarship during the first three decades of the century. To read Theology for a degree was considered the first step to liberalism or loss of faith, but to read Medicine, History, English, or Sciences was acceptable, leading to significant numbers becoming doctors, teachers, or entering other professions. Some studied Classics and some learnt biblical languages, often teaching themselves. From such men came a few who read the mainstream works widely and interacted with current ideas. We may term them *forerunners*.

Forerunners

Most notable is William Edwy Vine (1873–1949), who wrote books attacking liberal views, beside many expository commentaries. He completed his major work, An *Expository Dictionary of New Testament Words* in 1939 (since reprinted many times). His *Expository Dictionary of Old Testament Words* was published posthumously in 1979, edited by F. F. Bruce. At the start of the century, one who was sometimes associated with the Brethren, was Sir Robert Anderson (1841–1918), Assistant Commissioner of the London Metropolitan Police, from 1888 to 1901, who attempted in several books to counter the works of S. R. Driver and his colleagues: examples are *The Bible and Modern Criticism* (1902), *Pseudo-criticism, or the Higher Criticism and Its Counterfeit* (1904), *Daniel in the Critics' Den* (1909).

The Professor of Surgery at Bristol University from 1933 to 1946, Arthur Rendle Short (1880–1953), deserves attention for the scope of his interests, which came to fruition in his books *The Bible and Modern Research* (1933), *Modern Discovery and the Bible* (1942), and *Archaeology gives Evidence* (1951). He was aware of the need for evangelical work to counter the modernist and liberal movements exemplified by the Student Christian Movement after the First World War, and each of his books shows knowledge of current opinions and recent discoveries in the Near East that can be related to the reliability of the Bible. They were widely read and reprinted. (The writer was privileged to revise the last one in 1971.) Rendle Short was the senior advisor to Inter-Varsity Fellowship from its inception in 1928, and through it, supported three significant figures to whom we shall shortly turn.[3]

Contemporary with Rendle Short was Percy John Wiseman (1888–1948), an accountant who set up the infant Royal Air Force's book-keeping system. From service in Iraq, 1923–25 and 1931–33, arose a fascination with ancient Babylonia and ways in which Babylonian texts might illuminate the Bible. His *New Discoveries in Babylonia about Genesis* (1936) was a pioneering publication. He argued that Genesis was constructed from tablets ending with colophons ('these are the generations of') in Babylonian scribal manner. At the time, John Wenham thought it 'made one feel that the world of Wellhausen's

---

3. See W. M. Capper and D. Johnson, *The Faith of a Surgeon. Belief and Experience in the life of Arthur Rendle Short* (Exeter: Paternoster, 1976).

J E and P was quite anachronistic'.[4] In *Creation Revealed in Six Days: The Evidence of Scripture Confirmed by Archaeology* (1948) he maintained that the 'days' of Genesis 1 record a revelation made over six days.[5] While neither hypothesis can be upheld today, the attempt to use ancient customs and linguistic knowledge to delineate the history of a biblical book opened a new path of positive research.

Three prime movers

Three scholars appeared on the scene in the 1930s whom we may call the *prime movers* of biblical scholarship among the Brethren.

The first was William James Martin (1904–80), son of a farmer in County Antrim, who received his BA from Trinity College, Dublin, in 1927, and then, as a good Presbyterian, went to Princeton Theological Seminary, aiming for the church's ministry, graduating B.Th. in 1929. That was the time of the division which led Gresham Machen and his friends to leave Princeton to found Westminster Theological College. The impact on Martin was determinative. He departed to study ancient languages in Germany, I think at R. D. Wilson's suggestion, seeing proficiency in the languages as the entry to better understanding of the Bible and its world, and study at the highest level as the only way for evangelical Christians to be heard in the academic world. He studied in Berlin and Leipzig, from 1929–35, completing a doctoral dissertation in Assyriology (published as *Tribut und Tributleistungen bei den Assyrern*, Helsinki, 1936), having taken courses in ancient Egyptian, Hebrew, and Arabic. Cuneiform texts and biblical Hebrew remained his main interests, so he spent some months at the British Museum in 1931–2, cataloguing and drawing one hundred clay tablets, letters written early in the second millennium B.C., the days of the Patriarchs, which Sir Leonard Woolley had excavated at Ur of the Chaldees.[6] In 1937 he was appointed Rankin Lecturer in Hebrew and Ancient Semitic Languages at the University of Liverpool, teaching there until 1970, when he moved to become Vice-Principal of Regent College, Vancouver, with Jim Houston as Principal. How early he began to associate with the Brethren I do not know, but he was a member for many years of Hoylake Chapel when he lived on the Wirral in Cheshire.

The majority of students who came to Martin were ordinands from the Anglican St Aidan's College in Birkenhead, but a few came to learn ancient Egyptian and, occasionally, Assyrian. I have no record of any from Brethren churches, except John Ruffle, who worked for his Master's degree on the alleged relationship between the Book of Proverbs and the

---

4. John Wenham, *Facing Hell: The Story of a Nobody. An Autobiography 1913–1996* (Exeter: Paternoster, 1998), 88.

5. Both books were combined as *Clues to Creation in Genesis*, (ed.) Donald J. Wiseman (London: Marshall, Morgan and Scott, 1977), published in the U.S.A. by Thomas Nelson Publishers as *Ancient Records and the Structure of Genesis: A Case for Literary Unity* (Nashville, TN, 1985). See David F. Payne, *Genesis One Reconsidered* (London: Tyndale Press, 1964)..

6. His work was eventually published in H. H. Figulla and W. J. Martin, *Letters and Documents of the Old Babylonian Period*, vol. 5, Ur Excavations: Texts (London: British Museum, 1953).

Egyptian work, 'The Wisdom of Amenemope'.[7] Ruffle became an Assistant Keeper at Birmingham City Museum, then Keeper of the Oriental Museum in Durham.[8] He attended assemblies in Liverpool and Birmingham, but later ceased.

At Liverpool, Martin wrote papers on Hebrew language and gave lectures to other bodies. His Tyndale Lecture, *Stylistic Criteria and the Analysis of the Pentateuch* is probably his most memorable publication,[9] although all his studies deserve attention. Their number is rather small for a career of thirty-three years; one former student unkindly said they could be listed on the back of a postage stamp! However, in his later years he played no small part in the creation of the *New International Version* of the Bible.

Where Martin's significance lies is, rather, in personal contacts through which he enthused others with his vision of evangelical Christians working at the highest scholarly levels to uphold the objective study of Scripture and its trustworthiness. In 1941 he proposed to the infant Biblical Research Committee of the Inter-Varsity Fellowship (IVF; now Universities and Colleges Christian Fellowship), the establishment of a library for biblical research, a concept he had been promoting since 1937. He was a friend of (Sir) John Laing on whom he impressed the need for a centre where biblical Christian faith could be fostered and defended. Roy Coad quotes Laing, writing of Martin: 'you inspired me with the thought of Tyndale House and the real value it might be for Evangelical Bible Scholarship'.[10] Tyndale House was founded as a residential library for biblical research in 1944, under the auspices of the IVF. When he was in his eightieth year, Sir John wrote with relish to Martin about a tour on the Continent with him. Martin's most vivid memory was of a visit to a motorway bridge under construction across a deep valley. 'The work was perhaps not more than two-thirds completed and there were still here and there on the roadway great squares unlaid with a drop of several hundred feet to the floor of the valley. Sir John seemed to be in his element and kept moving from place to place, while I followed like a petrified dunlin'.[11]

The second of the Prime Movers is so well known that much less need be said: Frederick Fyvie Bruce (1910–90).[12] Born into a Scottish Brethren family, he remained faithful to that tradition throughout his life. His brilliant academic career culminated with the Rylands Chair of Biblical Criticism and Exegesis at Manchester, which he held from 1959 until he retired in 1978. His own memoir, Tim Grass's biography, and Peter Oakes' essay cover his career well.[13]

---

7. J. Ruffle, 'The Teaching of Amenemope and its Connection with the Book of Proverbs', *Tyndale Bulletin*, 28 (1977), 29–68.

8. *Durham University Gazette*, 25/1 (31 Jan. 1980), 6–7.

9. London: Tyndale Press, 1955.

10. Roy Coad, *Laing. The Biography of Sir John Laing (1879–1978)* (London: Hodder, 1979), 190–1.

11. Coad, *Laing*, 198–9. Martin had asked Coad to present his memory anonymously, but he told the writer the story himself.

12. See, Tim Grass, 'F. F. Bruce and the Bible', *intra* Chap. 10.

13. F. F. Bruce, *In Retrospect: Remembrance of Things Past* (Glasgow: Pickering and Inglis, 1980); Tim Grass, *F. F. Bruce. A Life. The Definitive Biography of a New Testament Scholar* (Milton Keynes: Paternoster Press, 2011); Peter Oakes, 'F. F. Bruce and the Development of Evangelical Biblical Scholarship', *Bulletin of the John Rylands Library*, 86/3 (2004), 99–124; see

The British Society for Old Testament Study recognized his scholarship by electing him president for 1965, as did the international Society for New Testament Study for 1975; his election as a Fellow of the British Academy in 1973 and the award of its Burkitt Medal for Biblical Studies in 1979 were further accolades, as were his honorary degrees. (With typical modesty, he does not mention the medal in his *In Retrospect*, but he was obviously very pleased when he showed it to me!) The existing assessments of his work make a lengthy account unnecessary. His classical training in languages and history enabled him to become a model to his students and many others as a positive biblical critic, respectful of ancient texts. That objectivity led him to consider the ideas, opinions, hypotheses, and theories other scholars proposed with care and balance. Often he was able to expose the weaknesses of others' views, sometimes widely fashionable ones, in a short paragraph stating his reasons clearly and concisely. Yet he always treated courteously even those whose work was least agreeable to him. In 1947 he set out his understanding of evangelical biblical scholarship at the establishment of the Tyndale Fellowship for Biblical Research.[14] Faith in Scripture as the word of God does not preclude the application of critical methods in its study; the scholar should be prepared to follow wherever the evidence leads, acknowledging presuppositions and being ready to modify them, honestly evaluating the evidence, with every alternative assessed. Conclusions should not be tailored to any audience! As a consequence, some Brethren would have nothing to do with him, while numerous others heard him gladly!

The third Prime Mover is slightly younger—P. J. Wiseman's son, Donald John Wiseman (1918–2010). In 1936 he enrolled at King's College, London, to read History and Latin. However, his father sent him to meet a friend who lived in Hoylake on the Wirral in Cheshire, W. J. Martin, who persuaded him to turn his attention to the world of the Bible. King's let him change courses to read Hebrew and Assyrian. He won an Exhibition in Oriental Studies at Oxford, but the Second World War intervened. (He tells of his significant wartime service in his privately published memoirs, *Life Above and Below*, 2003.) At Oxford he shared digs with Jim Houston and introduced him to the assembly at James Street! After graduating in 1948, Wiseman was appointed an Assistant Keeper at the British Museum, charged with editing cuneiform tablets unearthed by Sir Leonard Woolley in Turkey. His publication, *The Alalakh Tablets*, which he had to prepare within a restricted time, has become a source for scholarly study ever since.[15] Museum duties involved study and publication of some of its treasures, notably the tablet recording Nebuchadnezzar's capture of Jerusalem on 16 March 597 B.C., and allowed him to join excavations in Iraq, especially those at the Assyrian city of Nimrud, directed by Max Mallowan, whose wife Agatha Christie was the photographer. Significant documents found there were entrusted to him for publication. In 1961 the University of London appointed Wiseman to its Chair of Assyriology, which he held until 1982. He was elected a Fellow

---

also David F. Payne, 'F. F. Bruce as a Teacher', *Christian Brethren Research Fellowship Journal*, 22 (Nov. 1971), 15–16.

14. 'The Tyndale Fellowship for Biblical Research', *EQ*, 19/1 (1947), 52–61, reprinted as Appendix F in Thomas A. Noble, *Research for the Academy and the Church, Tyndale House and Tyndale Fellowship: the First Fifty Years* (Leicester: Inter-Varsity Press, 2006).

15. London: British Institute of Archaeology at Ankara, 1953.

of the British Academy in 1969. Although cuneiform texts formed the major part of his academic study, from the first he was alert to their possible relevance for biblical studies, publishing papers in the *Journal of the Transactions of the Victoria Institute* in 1951 and later. Incidentally, the scholar who taught Wiseman elementary Assyrian at King's was Samuel H. Hooke, Professor of Old Testament Studies, whose early years were spent among the Exclusive Brethren, but who joined the Church of England when a student. In a curious link, Wiseman's teacher was a greatly admired friend of F. F. Bruce, who edited a Festschrift for him.[16]

At the Museum, Wiseman dealt with many inquirers. If he found they were Christians, he encouraged them in their faith, emphasizing the value of exhibits that show the historical accuracy of biblical passages. That culminated in his *Illustrations from Biblical Archaeology*[17] and numerous entries in Bible dictionaries and commentaries. He had served on the IVF's Biblical Research Committee and so was invited to set up an Old Testament Study Group for the new Tyndale Fellowship, which met in 1951, concomitantly with the New Testament Study Group led by F. F. Bruce. The Fellowship was intended for scholars who knew Hebrew and Greek and were involved in 'Biblical Studies and research in a spirit of loyalty to the Christian Faith'.[18] All concerned were urged to recruit suitable young people to devote themselves to this end. Wiseman was particularly effective at that, building up the Old Testament Group and leading it for thirty years. Like Bruce, Wiseman spoke in churches, Brethren and others, at conferences and student groups, both as a gospel preacher and as a Bible teacher, specifically drawing on his archaeological knowledge. With Martin, he had a large role in the translation of the New International Version of the Bible. As a child, Donald attended various assemblies with his family, at one in Sydenham, meeting my father who was twelve years older, but who had a clockwork railway train that he allowed Donald to play with. Years later, that contact was resumed, and Donald turned the writer's interest from British archaeology to the biblical world![19]

One man whose Bible teaching brought 'a fresh and invigorating wind' of thought to Brethren circles was Harry L. Ellison (1903–83).[20] He was involved with the Tyndale Fellowship from 1952 onwards, with his 1953 Tyndale Lecture being entitled *On the Centrality of the Messianic Idea for the Old Testament*.[21] His career as a teacher at London Bible College was ended in 1955 by regrettable misunderstanding of something he had written, ultimately to the benefit of Moorlands [Bible] College. His studies and experience resulted in valuable presentations of scholarly calibre on Old Testament books *Men Spake from God* (1958), *Ezekiel: The Man and His Message* (1956) *From Tragedy to Triumph* (1970), many 'study guide' volumes and his instructive *The Household Church: Apostolic Practice in a Modern Setting* (1963). His major commentary on Jeremiah, which is often

---

16. See Bruce's *In Retrospect*, 150, 164–9, 182–4, etc.
17. London: Tyndale Press, 1958.
18. Noble, *Research for the Academy and the Church*, 56.
19. In addition to Wiseman's autobiography, *Life Above and Below*, see the writer's memoir, 'Donald John Wiseman 1918–2010', *Proceedings of the British Academy*, 172 (2011), 379–93.
20. Bruce, *In Retrospect*, 115.
21. London: Tyndale Press, 1953.

undeservedly overlooked, appeared only in instalments in *The Evangelical Quarterly* from 1959 to 1968.[22]

Increasing engagement

The greater availability of university education after the Second World War[23] made it easier for the Three Prime Movers and others to encourage embryo scholars to take up subjects related to biblical studies, while the growing recognition gained for evangelical scholarship by these three men helped to reduce the barriers to employment that dominated colleges and universities. The parade of Brethren engaged in biblical scholarship in Britain began to grow! To name everyone is outside the writer's range—additions will be gladly accepted!

An area little known to most members of Brethren churches was the focus of David W. Gooding's academic research: the Septuagint. He wrote his doctoral dissertation on 'The Greek Deuteronomy' at Cambridge (1954),[24] going on to publish three monographs and a string of essays on the Septuagint, notably on its renderings of passages in the books of Kings. Queen's University, Belfast, where he had taught Classics for several years, recognized his contributions by creating a personal chair for him in Old Testament Greek in 1977. In the same year he was elected to the Royal Irish Academy. His inaugural lecture, *Current Problems and Methods in the Textual Criticism of the Old Testament*, summarizes his work.[25] He is also well-known as a Bible teacher in Britain and abroad and author of many expository volumes, most recently *The Riches of Divine Wisdom. The New Testament's Use of the Old Testament*.[26]

Joining Gooding to teach at Queen's was David F. Payne, the first student F. F. Bruce taught at Sheffield (1949–52). He became Senior Lecturer and Head of the Department of Semitic Studies, then moved to become Academic Dean of London Bible College (now the London School of Theology). He delivered the Tyndale Old Testament Lecture for 1962,[27] produced various academic papers and wrote the volume *Kingdoms of the Lord: A History of the Hebrew Kingdoms from Saul to the Fall of Jerusalem* (1981) for a projected series on the history of Israel. He authored several study guides and the textual notes for the major two-volume *International Critical Commentary on Isaiah 40–55*, with John Goldingay providing the exegesis (2006).[28]

A New Testament Commentary

The list of contributors in *A New Testament Commentary* (1979), edited by Cecil Howley, with F. F. Bruce and H. L. Ellison, demonstrates the growth of Brethren biblical scholarship,

---

22. Other publications include (all Exeter: The Paternoster Press): *Prophets of Israel: From Ahijah to Hosea* (1969); *From Babylon to Bethlehem: The Jewish people from the exile to the Messiah* (1976); *Mystery of Israel* (1976); *Fathers of the Covenant: Some Great Chapters in Genesis and Exodus* (1978); *The Servant of Jehovah* (1983).

23. F. R. Coad, *A History of the Brethren Movement* (Exeter: Paternoster Press, 1968), 219.

24. *The Account of the Tabernacle: Translation and Textual Problems of the Greek Exodus* (Cambridge: Cambridge University Press, 1959) is a by-product of his dissertation.

25. Belfast: Queen's University, 1979.

26. Belfast: Myrtlefield House, 2013.

27. Published as *Genesis One Reconsidered* (London: Tyndale Press, 1964).

28. London: T&T Clark, 2006.

for all were drawn from Brethren churches in Britain and abroad. Only four of the twenty-five contributors were not British. Seven taught in British universities or Bible Colleges and two in Higher Education colleges. Ten years later *A Bible Commentary for Today*, with forty-three contributors, had wider ecclesiastical scope, and added three more British Brethren university teachers.[29]

We may list the university teachers and others who qualify as biblical scholars by virtue of their publications, with brief comments.

Leslie Allen taught at London Bible College, but moved to Fuller Seminary in California in 1983 after criticism of his commentary suggesting that the Book of Jonah is fiction.[30] He has written other commentaries, for example *Jeremiah: A Commentary* and *Ezekiel 1–19* and *Ezekiel 20–48*.[31]

F. F. Bruce, University of Manchester, has already received attention!

David Clines began to teach at the University of Sheffield in 1964 and subsequently became Professor of Biblical Studies. His reputation will last as originator and editor-in-chief of *The Dictionary of Classical Hebrew*. Completed in 2011 in eight volumes, with subsidiary volumes expected, it is more comprehensive and up-to-date than standard dictionaries of biblical Hebrew. It may be noted it received a subvention from the Laing Trust. Clines' prodigious output contains major commentaries on Ezra-Nehemiah and Job[32] and numerous essays, from straightforward textual studies to post-modernist readings, often deliberately provocative. In 1976, he and two colleagues founded the *Journal for the Study of the Old Testament*, published by Sheffield Academic Press, which has also published scores of volumes in biblical studies, then, after Bloomsbury Press (as Continuum) took it over, he set up the equally prolific Sheffield Phoenix Press. As well as serving as President of the Society for Old Testament Study in 1996, he was elected President of the American Society of Biblical Literature in 2009, the first British scholar to hold the position, and in 2015 he received the British Academy's Burkitt Medal. Attached to a Brethren church in his native Australia, he kept those links for some time, but has said, 'I make it a policy not to put my present religious opinions and affiliations on any public record.'

H. L. Ellison, David Payne, and Donald Wiseman have been mentioned.

Robert Gordon, a protégé of David Gooding in Belfast, studied Hebrew and Aramaic at Cambridge, taught at the University of Glasgow from 1968 until 1979 when he was appointed to a lectureship in Cambridge. There, in 1995, he was promoted as Regius Professor of Hebrew, retiring in 2012. He was elected as a Fellow of the British Academy in 2011. His publications range from the ancient versions of the Old Testament to commentaries on the Books of Samuel and the Epistle to the Hebrews, to comparison of

---

29. F. F. Bruce (ed.), *The International Bible Commentary with NIV* (London: Marshall Pickering); US edn., *The New Layman's Bible* Commentary (Grand Rapids, MI: Zondervan, 1986).

30. *The Books of Joel, Obadiah, Jonah and Micah*. New International Commentary on the Old Testament (Grand Rapids, MI: Eerdmans, 1976).

31. Old Testament Library (Louisville, KY: Westminster John Knox, 2008); Word Biblical Commentary, vols. 28 & 29 (Waco, TX: Word Books, 1994 and 1990).

32. *Ezra, Nehemiah and Esther*, New Century Bible (London: Marshall, Morgan and Scott, 1984); *Job*, Word Biblical Commentary, 3 vols. (Waco, TX: Word Books, 1998–2011).

Babylonian and Hebrew prophecies.[33] Throughout his residence in Cambridge, Robert has worshipped at, and been an elder at, Panton Hall.

Alan Millard taught at the University of Liverpool from 1970 to 2003, being awarded a Personal Chair in 1992. He was involved with the NIV and TNIV (see below).

More scholars

Not a contributor to the *Commentary,* but a notable scholar with strong Brethren association, is Hugh Williamson. He read Theology at Cambridge, with emphasis on the Old Testament and Biblical Hebrew, obtaining his Ph.D. in 1975. He taught at Cambridge from 1974 until elected to the Regius Chair of Hebrew at Oxford in 1992, retiring in 2014. He was elected a Fellow of the British Academy in 1993. Among several books and essays, notably on Isaiah, should be noted the first two volumes of his International Critical commentary on Isaiah 1–27.[34]

Professor of New Testament Studies, King's College London since 2014 is Edward Adams who grew up in Irvine in Ayrshire, attending Central Gospel Hall there. He gained his Ph.D. at Glasgow in 1995 and has taught at King's since 1996. He has published his research on Pauline language, the Gospels, and his extensive argument that early Christians met in other places beside houses.[35]

Mention may also be made of Donald F. Murray who took degrees in Sydney and Cambridge (where he attended Roseford Hall) and taught at the University of Exeter, now living in his native Australia. He published studies on the historical books of the Old Testament and a volume *Divine Prerogative & Royal Pretension in a Narrative Sequence about David (2 Samuel 5.17–7.29)*, finding an opposition between David and the Lord.[36] In Scotland, Kenneth T. Aitken was Lecturer in Hebrew Bible at the University of Aberdeen in Scotland. He contributed 'Proverbs' to the *New Daily Study Bible* in 1986. A lecturer at the University of St Andrews was Peter W. Coxon who studied Aramaic and published significant essays on its use in the book of Daniel.

A one-time member of Brethren churches in Liverpool and Birmingham was the already mentioned John Ruffle whose Liverpool Master's thesis made a valuable contribution

---

33. [32] *Studies in the Targum to the Twelve Prophets: From Nahum to Malachi* (Leiden: Brill, 1994); *1 and 2 Samuel. A Commentary* (Exeter: Paternoster, 1986; repr. Grand Rapids: Zondervan, 2004); *Hebrews. A Commentary* (Sheffield: Phoenix Press, 2000; 2nd edn. 2008); *Hebrew Bible and Ancient Versions, Selected Essays* (London: Routledge, 2006); *'Thus Speaks Ishtar of Arbela': Prophecy in Israel, Assyria, and Egypt in the Neo-Assyrian period* (co-ed. with H. M. Barstad) (Winona Lake, IN: Eisenbrauns, 2013).

34. *A Critical and Exegetical Commentary on Isaiah 1–27*, vol. 1: *Commentary on Isaiah 1–5;* vol.2: *Isaiah 6–12*, The International Critical Commentary (London and New York: T&T Clark International; Continuum, 2006, 2018).

35. *Constructing the World: A Study in Paul's Cosmological Language*, Studies of the New Testament and its World (T. &T. Clark, Edinburgh, 2000); *The Stars Will Fall from Heaven: 'Cosmic Catastrophe' in the New Testament and its World*, Library of New Testament Studies, 347 (London: T&T Clark International, 2007); *Parallel Lives of Jesus: Four Gospels, One Story* (London: SPCK, 2011); *The Earliest Christian Meeting Places: Almost Exclusively Houses?* Library of New Testament Studies, 450 (London: Bloomsbury, 2013).

36. London: Bloomsbury Press, 1998.

to the study of the Book of Proverbs and who became Keeper of the Oriental Museum in the University of Durham. James Houston, formerly lecturer in Geography at Oxford University, founder and Principal of Regent College, Vancouver 1970–78, now Professor of Spiritual Theology, gains a place here for his essays on 'The Environmental Background' of the Old and New Testaments in the *Commentary*.

One of the earliest and most faithful members of the Tyndale Fellowship's Old Testament Study Group was John P. U. Lilley who, after studying Hebrew at Oxford, became an accountant and tax inspector, yet found time to make the books of Joshua and Judges his speciality, writing papers for learned journals and the 'Joshua' entry in the *Bible Commentary for Today*. He and his wife were members of the assembly in Horley where they led a Crusader class, eventually moving to Norwich.

Professor Robert Gordon kindly contributed this paragraph about the present writer:

The work of Alan Millard has focussed on the Bible and on the ancient Near East more generally, with the two interests often combining in his publications. He has also been highly successful in mediating the findings of modern archaeological research to a wider general readership, and some of his writings have been published in up to a dozen languages. Alan studied Ancient Semitic Languages at the universities of Oxford and London, and worked in the Department of Western Asiatic Antiquities at the British Museum. After serving as Librarian at Tyndale Library for Biblical Research in Cambridge for seven years, he began lecturing at the University of Liverpool in 1970, and was appointed to a personal chair as Rankin Professor of Hebrew and Ancient Semitic Languages in 1992. He has been a member of the Tyndale Fellowship since his student days, and served as secretary and chairman of two of its study groups. He has also served as Chairman of the Tyndale House Council, representing the House on the UCCF Trust. Alan's interests centre on the ancient languages and history of the Near East, and on the Bible as a product of that ancient world. Motivating much of his work has been the desire to 'help others to appreciate Scripture more positively as God's Word'. One of his special interests has been the uses of writing in ancient Israel and neighbouring countries. This has involved questions of literacy and book production, and examining biblical narratives in the light of developing knowledge about the society, culture and thought of those times. He has written extensively about these topics in Bible dictionaries and handbooks, and in several of his own books—notably *Treasures from Bible Times* (1985) and *Discoveries from the Time of Jesus* (1990) (issued in a single volume in 1997 as *Discoveries from Bible Times*), and *Reading and Writing in the Time of Jesus* (2000). In academic circles he is also well known for his work on such topics as Babylonian flood traditions (with W. G. Lambert), Near-Eastern onomastics, and Assyrian state officials (eponyms). For much of his career Alan and his wife Margaret were members of Hoylake Chapel, but, following his retirement, they have more recently settled in Leamington Spa [R. P. Gordon].

It is amazing that almost simultaneously near the end of the twentieth century, the Regius Professors of Hebrew at Oxford and Cambridge, the Professor of Old Testament Greek at Belfast, the Professor of Old Testament at Sheffield, and the Professor of Hebrew and Ancient Semitic Languages at Liverpool were men who currently or previously were members of Brethren churches—Williamson, Gordon, Gooding, Clines, and Millard!

Conclusion

Biblical scholarship began to flourish among the Brethren when the emphasis on biblical knowledge was married to an openness to wider knowledge of Scripture and its world and as suspicion of academic study in the churches diminished. The scholars mentioned above have, in turn, promoted this attitude. Regrettably, that has sharpened the division between the type of church they attend, or have attended, and more traditional ones that insist, for example, on reading from the Authorized Version and countenancing only a dispensationalist outlook.[37] (The strong reaction to the *New Testament Commentary* gives evidence of this.) Whether remaining with the Brethren, or not, their scholarly attitude is ecumenical, sharing with scholars of various persuasions and being accepted as writers in standard publications. Besides Bruce and Wiseman, Clines, Gordon, and Williamson have been presidents of the British Society for Old Testament Study (1996, 2003, 2004 respectively); Bruce seems to have been the only one in the international Society for New Testament Study. Clines was the first scholar from Europe to become President of the American Society of Biblical Literature (2009). Publications by these scholars gain respect at the highest levels so those they produce intended for the wider Christian public can be accepted as reliable guides. There is no school of Brethren Biblical Research—and we trust there will never be one! As we have seen, there is a line of scholarship at university level running from the 1930s until today, with primary study of ancient languages consistently represented. All enjoy the liberty Bruce championed—which permits disagreement within an overall loyalty to Scripture as God's inspired word, so that one author may argue for dating the Book of Daniel in the sixth century B.C., another in the second. New discoveries require assessment, old ones reassessment; new hypotheses and new fantasies continually appear, demanding critical, informed responses. Finding younger scholars to be enthused and encouraged is always a necessity, for the benefit of all and for the glory of God.

---

37. See Neil T. R. Dickson, 'The Authorised Version and the Brethren', *BHR*, 7 (2011), 1–16.

CHAPTER 8

Victor Danielsen (1894–1961): Teacher—Translator—Evangelist

Tórður Jóansson

Before introducing the great second generation Brethren leader, Victor Danielsen, who was a teacher, preacher, poet, translator of more than a thousand hymns, nineteen books, and author of two rapture novels, and who also made the first translation of the whole Bible into Faeroese, it seems necessary to put his enormous achievements into historical context. One of the consequences of the Reformation in the Faeroe Islands in 1538/9 was that Danish became the sole language in church and all official matters, later also the only language of instruction in the schools.[1] There was no written Faeroese language until the nineteenth century, and very few Faeroe Islanders were aware that their own language was special until the end of that century. Not until after the Second World War was Faeroese a fully accepted language and a subject in schools, and not until the 1960s were there textbooks in most subjects in the language.[2]

The archipelago was first part of the Danish-Norwegian Kingdom, then a county in the Danish Kingdom until 1948, when it got a kind of home-rule; the county council became a local parliament and Faeroese the first language in the islands with Danish as a required second language. However, the changes from a medieval, agricultural and backward society, spread over eighteen islands with around fifty villages, started around the middle of the nineteenth century when new attitudes in Denmark and the Faeroes paved the way for the modern welfare society that we know today. In 1816 Danish authorities appointed a commission to improve the administration, industries and trade in the Faeroe Islands; and subsequently a number of commissions worked on these matters. This resulted in the formation of a local council in 1852,[3] and free trade in 1856.[4] Gradually the whole society went through enormous changes: the first of many seafaring fishing smacks, mainly bought in Britain, were introduced; farmhands and maids left the agricultural villages and moved to the newly founded fishing ports; new towns emerged and farming villages declined; universal primary education and improved health provision were introduced; and

---

1. John F. West, *Faroe: The Emergence of a Nation* (London, 1972), 9.
2. Tórður Jóansson, *English Loanwords in Faroese* (Tórshavn, 1997), 29.
3. '*Løgting*', Faeroese for 'law' and 'thing', i.e. 'assembly'.
4. Tórður Jóansson, *Brethren in the Faroes: An Evangelical Movement, its Remarkable Growth and Lasting Impact on an Island Community* (Tórshavn, 2012), 61.

eventually a flourishing fishing industry paved the way for the socio-economic conditions which made the Faeroes unrecognisable half a century later.[5]

The Brethren movement was introduced in the islands in the middle of this turbulence, in 1865, and in the following decades it gained considerable ground, especially among fishermen and workers. So much so, that from the middle of the twentieth century it was the most numerous Brethren movement in the world per head of the population—at the beginning of the twenty-first century, around fourteen per cent of the 50,000 inhabitants.[6]

Biography

Victor Danielsen (1894–1961) was the son of Sheriff Daniel Jacob Danielsen, a good friend of William Gibson Sloan (1838–1914), the first Brethren missionary who came from Scotland. He was the youngest of seven siblings, born in 1894, but he lost his mother only one week after his birth. Consequently his father's sister took over the responsibility of nurturing the young boy. Victor was physically weak, suffering from a leg-disorder, and also had a serious bout of life-threatening pneumonia when a small child.[7]

In spite of this, the boy later became arguably the most industrious and innovative Brethren leader in the Faeroes and one of the most influential figures in the emerging Faeroese nation-building of the twentieth century. His name will hardly ever be forgotten in the histories of the nation, church, or assemblies in the Faeroe Islands. What he lacked physically was made up by other abilities, especially his intelligence and his extraordinary memory and learning capabilities, combined with exceptional will-power and diligence. Today he is best-known as the composer and translator of more than 1,000 hymns and songs and the man who first translated the whole Bible into Faeroese.[8]

In 1911 Victor entered the Teachers' Training College in the islands' capital, Tórshavn, from which he graduated with the best marks in 1914, aged 20. Jákup Dahl, later Dean of the Faeroes and one of pioneers in the struggle for Faeroese self-government and the vernacular, was Victor's teacher in that language; and Dahl had noticed his student's extraordinary linguistic and literary abilities.

During his stay in Tórshavn, Victor went through a deep spiritual and religious crisis, especially in the autumn of 1913—his last year at college. Later in life, he explained this period in some of his many messages at Brethren meetings. First he went to an abstinence meeting where the distinguished English Brethren missionary, Arthur Brend (1880–1959), spoke. Victor felt that there was a personal message to him—this was the first time he experienced that God called him. Then he got in touch with the other evangelical movement, the Danish Home Mission, introduced in the islands decades later than the Brethren. One of their missionaries especially, Ryvang-Jensen (1878–1948), later a Lutheran clergyman, helped Victor, as he put it, in seeing the importance of the

---

5. West, *Faroe*, 74–5, 97.
6. Jóansson, *Brethren in the Faroes*, 18.
7. Zacharias Zachariassen, *Bíblian á føroyskum í hálva øld* [*The Bible in Faeroese for Half a Century*] (Gøta, 2000), 21–2.
8. Jóansson, *Brethren in the Faroes*, 215–18.

light in Jesus Christ and faith in his name. At this stage Victor Danielsen experienced an evangelical conversion.[9]

After graduation, Victor was a teacher in his home village for some months, but he felt that his field of work was to be within evangelicalism and he did not agree with the teachings of the established school, heavily dominated by the Danish Lutheran State Church.[10] His work as an evangelist started with Christian meetings in the school where he was working; and in the beginning he read homilies, but soon started preaching himself. This led to many conversions before the authorities stopped these meetings, but Victor continued his work in the local dance hall where the awakenings continued. Soon both Victor and his followers concluded through reading the Bible that it was necessary to be baptized. So in 1916 most of them were baptized in the sea by the village, and from then on Victor became an energetic Brethren worker travelling around the islands with the new Christian message.[11]

Life work: new approaches

Victor Danielsen used to call the established Danish brand of Lutheranism '*vanakristindomur*', which means 'habit Christendom' or 'Christianity of habit'. The kind of Christianity introduced in the remote islands from around AD 1000, and especially after the Reformation around 1538/39, could be seen as an alien religion, imposed by rulers abroad, first from Norway, then Denmark. So not until the Brethren movement was introduced by the Scottish missionary William Gibson Sloan in 1865 can we talk about a home-grown Christian movement, based on the three 'S-es': self-supporting, self-propagating, and self-governing assemblies.[12] The established Lutheran Church was not devolved to Faeroese authorities until 2007, so it was always an integral part of the colonial system. Out of 'habit' and tradition this church was—and still is—seen by the majority of the population as the only valid form of Christianity.[13]

Victor Danielsen was opposed to this state of affairs, both for religious reasons and for cultural ones. According to his way of thinking the Established Church did not follow what the Bible says. And true to the principles of the Reformation, he was opposed to using a foreign language in worship. For centuries Danish, not Faeroese, had been the language of the Church and in all official matters, also in the schools until the Home Rule Act of 1948. Victor thought that this was unreasonable, unjustifiable, and had to change. He became one of the main figures in the struggle against foreign authoritarianism—as well as one of the most important and industrious fighters for the Faeroese language.

Like the early Brethren in Britain, Victor was very much influenced by Calvinist thought such as predestination, and the concept of the elect. This is clear from a letter that Victor wrote to the newly converted Jóan Petur Vang (1879–1933) of Kaldbak in 1919 after he

---

9. Petur Háberg, 'Victor Danielsen', *Lív og læra*, 15 (14 Sept. 1961).
10. Zachariassen, *Bíblian á føroyskum*, 25–6.
11. Jóansson, *Brethren in the Faroes*, 166–7.
12. Tórður Jóansson, 'William Gibson Sloan (1838–1914): Mission Strategy in the Faeroes', in Neil T. R. Dickson and T. J. Marinello (eds.), *Brethren and Mission: Essays in Honour of Timothy C. F. Stunt* (SBH; Glasgow, 2016), 131–7, spec. 135.
13. Jóansson, *Brethren in the Faroes*, 64.

and a couple of fellow villagers had been baptized by Victor in his village on another island.[14] He later translated works by D. L. Moody, however, whose soteriology tended towards Arminianism.

In 1920 Victor married Henrikka Malena Olsen (1896–1997), daughter of one of the newly converted Brethren members. They had nine children, the eldest ones born at Søldarfjørður on Eysturoy, the second largest of the islands, but in 1928 they moved further north on Eysturoy to Fuglafjørður where Victor became the driving force of the Brethren assembly, Siloa, until his death in 1961. But he also visited other assemblies in the islands; and his son Richard told me shortly before his own death that they felt like the other children in the village—most men were fishermen and therefore at sea most of the year, and Victor was also away for long periods preaching and organizing in numerous villages. It should be added that in the 1920s and 30s the Brethren movement grew enormously and the halls of most assemblies were built during these two decades in spite of economic crises and widespread poverty.[15]

Victor Danielsen was primarily an evangelist and saw it as his calling to make people turn to Jesus. He concentrated on missionary work for the remaining forty years of his life. In spite of weak legs, he visited all the towns and villages in the islands. Travel was difficult in those days because there were few roads, so he had to sail in open boats or walk over mountains to reach the many places he visited. At Victor's funeral, a fellow Brethren worker stated that once they had had sixty-nine meetings in forty-nine villages in only fourteen days.[16] He was a brilliant and inspiring preacher and succeeded in persuading many individuals towards the new Christianity of evangelicalism. Of course many regarded him as an unreasonably harsh and fiery preacher, giving little room for compromises. For him faith was a question of life and death, of Heaven or Hell, and many church-people saw him as a *helvitispredikant*—a preacher of brimstone and fire. He was accused of scaring and threatening people into belief. However, it was not only Victor who was accused of this in those days. Home Mission preachers, as well as some clergymen, used the same methods. And reading some of his talks, written down from recordings later, he does not seem to have been particularly fierce. Often people misunderstood him, harassed him and sometimes persecuted him.

In private Victor was a humble man, a sincere, loving, and genuinely honest and emotional person who would never hurt anybody. He was known as an energetic, fiery and popular preacher in his lifetime, and later he has been regarded as one of the most industrious writers, translators and poets of his generation. In 1917 he translated his first hymn into Faeroese, and it was 'After the earthly shadows have lifted'. Then, Brethren assemblies and individuals asked him to make the first Faeroese hymnary, and this was published in 1920, comprising eighty-five hymns in the vernacular. In the following years, Victor edited ten further hymnaries, the second one in 1922 with 121 hymns, and the last one edited by him in 1952, comprising an astonishing 1,125 hymns. A new Brethren hymnary is being published at present, and contains more than 1,500 hymns and songs.[17]

---

14. Victor Danielsen to Jóan Petur Vang, 20 Jan. 1919, quoted in Jóansson, *Brethren in the Faroes*, 194.
15. Jóansson, *Brethren in the Faroes*, 127–8.
16. Jóansson, *Brethren in the Faroes*, 167.
17. Zachariassen, *Bíblian á føroyskum*, 28–9, and Jóansson, *Brethren in the Faroes*, 145.

The Bible translation

Victor translated eighteen books from other languages, mainly from English, into Faeroese, the best known probably John Bunyan's *Pilgrim's Progress,* in Faeroese *Pílagrímsferðin,* published in 1946. Also Victor wrote two rapture novels, *Aðru ferð* [*Second Time*] in 1927, and *Nei, lyftið sveik ikki* [*No, the Promise Wasn't Broken*] in 1947. The first one is about the second coming, imagined as taking place in an ordinary Faeroese village; the second one is on the same theme but seen from the angle of those who were taken away. Both novels had considerable influence on many people.

Today Victor Danielsen is best known as the translator of the Bible into Faeroese. In 1930, the assembly in Tórshavn, Ebenezer, had asked Danielsen to translate it into the Faeroese, and they were so pleased with the results that he was asked to translate the entire New Testament. It appeared in 1937, and subsequently the whole Bible was published in 1948/9. Although another translation of the New Testament was completed by the above mentioned Dean Jákup Dahl, and published by the Danish Bible Society a few weeks after Victor's, the Established Lutheran Church did not have its complete Bible translation until 1961, the Old Testament translated by K. O. Viderø.[18] Danielsen did not know Greek and Hebrew, so he translated both his New Testament and, later, the whole Bible from Scandinavian languages, especially the Danish one of 1907, the Norwegian of 1904, and the Swedish one of 1917; but he also used the Icelandic one of 1866. He also used the Elberfelder Bibel German translation of 1871, associated with J. N. Darby, and the English King James Version of 1611. In addition he also made use of Thomas Newberry's *The Englishman's Bible* (1884), with its aids for Greek tenses, and Robert Young's *Literal Translation of the Bible* (1862/1898).[19] The two clergymen Dahl and Viderø, however, translated from Greek and Hebrew.

Victor Danielsen's language was good, ordinary Faeroese, close to the spoken language, and this made it easier to read for the majority who read Danish only. His view was that writers had to compromise because even radical Faeroese papers were still printed in Danish, and a high, purist style would prevent ordinary people from reading their own language. Here Victor thought that islanders were in the middle of a linguistic evolution and that it would take decades to get people used to reading and writing proper Faeroese. In this matter he disagreed with Jákup Dahl and others who thought that writers should aim at a purist or final written language right away. But further developments proved that Victor was probably right.

Faeroese people, however, still discuss the merits of two translations, and many find them not all that different. The Lutheran Church minister and linguist Elsa Funding wrote a dissertation *Føroyskar bibliutýðingar* [*Faeroese Bible Translations*], published in 2007, which includes linguistic analysis of the two translations.[20] Funding's book is the only Faeroese scholarly work on Bible translations, and she gives a good brief historical and theoretical overview, going back to the sixth century BC Targum and the later Septuagint, as well as explaining the difference between literal and idiomatic, metaphrase and paraphrase.

---

18. Zachariassen, *Bíblian á føroyskum,* 103–49.
19. Zachariassen, *Bíblian á føroyskum,* 46; Jóansson, *Brethren in the Faroes,* 217.
20. Elsa Funding, *Føroyskar bibliutýðingar* [*Faeroese Bible Translations*], Setursrit 4 (Tórshavn, 2007).

Funding then analyses and discusses the eight translations into Faeroese, starting with J. H. Schrøter's Gospel of Matthew of 1828; but the main emphasis is on twentieth-century translations of the whole Bible—Dahl/Viderø (1937/1961) and Danielsen (1937/1949). A revised version of Danielsen was published in 1974, bringing the language closer to modern written Faeroese, a generation after the vernacular had been accepted as the principal language in the archipelago and Faeroese had been established as the language of education in the Home Rule Act of 1948. Her conclusions point out that many of the grammatical constructions in the two versions are quite similar, such as the use of the genitive case, and that it is dubious whether Danielsen's translation is so much closer to the spoken language as some have claimed in the past.

Table 1 sets out Dahl's and Danielsen's parallel versions of the Gospel of John 1:1–5, and Table 2 makes some comparative comments by the present writer on the two translations. From the samples in these tables, it can be seen that Elsa Funding is correct in concluding that Danielsen's translation is not that much closer to the spoken language than that of the Established Church. It seems quite clear that in some cases Danielsen uses a register quite similar to that of Dahl/Viderø, nevertheless in others he uses a more commonplace language. He used to read passages from his manuscript to ordinary people (fishermen, workers, housewives, children, and the like) and asked them for suggestions. In the Faeroes, when teenagers went for preparation for confirmation at age 14 in the Danish State Church's, some clergymen would recommend Danielsen's translation because it was easier to read, and it still sells in greater numbers than the Dahl/Viderø version. This has given Danielsen's translation an important place not only in the Brethren, but in the wider community.

Table 1. Dahl and Danielsen: parallel translations into Faeroese.

Verse	New King James Version	Dahl's translation	Danielsen's translation
1	In the beginning was the Word, and the Word was with God, and the Word was God.	Í fyrstuni var orðið, og orðið var hjá Guði, og orðið var Guð.	Í upphavi var Orðið, og Orðið var hjá Gudi, og Orðið var Gud.
2	He was in the beginning with God.	Hetta var í fyrstuni hjá Guði.	Hann var í upphavi hjá Gudi.
3	All things were made through Him, and without Him nothing was made that was made.	Allir lutir eru vorðnir til við tí, og uttan tað varð einki til av tí, sum til er vorðið.	Alt er vorðið til við Honum, og uttan Hann er einki vorðið til av tí, sum til er.
4	In Him was life, and the life was the light of men.	Í tí var lív, og lívið var ljós menniskjunnar.	Í Honum var lív, og lívið var ljós menniskjanna.
5	And the light shines in the darkness, and the darkness did not comprehend it.	Og ljósið skínur í myrkrinum, og myrkrið tók ikki við tí.	Ljósið skínur í myrkrinum, og myrkrið skilti tað ikki.

Table 2. Comparative comments on Faeroese translations.

Verse	Comments
1	Only one word differs: Dahl uses 'í fyrstuni', meaning 'at first', 'in the beginning' or 'to begin with', while Danielsen uses the more poetical and archaic 'í upphavi', meaning 'originally', 'in the beginning' or 'genesis'; so here we might argue that Danielsen's word is more puristic than Dahl's. The other difference is that Danielsen consistently uses capital letters when referring to God, Jesus, the Spirit, or the Word; here 'Orðið', the definite form of 'Word'.
2	Here there is some discrepancy, because while Danielsen uses the pronoun 'hann' ('he'), Dahl uses the neuter pronoun 'hetta' ('this'), and again they use different words for 'in the beginning'. And as in the first verse, Dahl spells 'God' with 'ð', 'Guð', while Daniensen spells it with 'd', 'Gud', which is also how it is pronounced / gu:d/, while 'ð' is mute in most cases in Faeroese.
3	These are two quite different translations. While Dahl writes 'allir lutir', meaning 'all things', Danielsen just writes 'alt', meaning 'everything'; and while Dahl writes 'eru vorðnir til við tí' ('are become into existence with it'), Danielsen writes 'er vorðið til við Honum' ('is created with/by Him'). So here the latter is closer to the NKJV. And while Dahl writes 'uttan tað varð einki av tí, sum til er vorið' ('without it became nothing of that which is in existence'), Danielsen uses the more straightforward style 'uttan Hann er einki vorðið til av tí, sum til er' ('without Him is nothing in existence of that, which is').
4	Again Dahl writes 'í tí var lív' ('in it was life'), compared with Danielsen's 'í Honum var lív' ('in Him was life'); but the second half is the same apart from the two slightly different genitive forms of 'menniskja' ('man/human being') because the noun has two genders, so Dahl's is feminine, genitive, plural; Danielsen's neuter, genitive; and both are the plural of 'menniskja'.
5	The only difference in the first part is that Dahl starts with the conjunction 'og' ('and') here; but 'comprehend' is translated in different ways. Dahl uses the slightly archaic phrase 'tók ikki við tí' (literally 'did not take with it') while Danielsen uses the more everyday phrase 'skilti tað ikki' ('understood it not').

Conclusion

Victor Danielsen was among the most important figures in the Faeroese nation-building process, especially in the linguistic and literary fields. That is why a beautiful statue by the Faeroese sculptor Hans Pauli Olsen, was erected in the centre of Fuglafjørður in his memory in 2008 (see the front cover). It consists of a life-size statue of Danielsen, leaning on a walking stick and standing on a large slab on which is superimposed over its entire area a greatly enlarged version of the first page of his manuscript of Genesis, dated 21 March 1937, and on which a giant hand is writing. Danielsen was the most important pioneer of the second generation of Faeroese Brethren, and certainly contributed to the growth of the movement in the islands, so that the percentage of assembly members increased from around five per cent of the population to more than twice as many by the time of Victor Danielsen's death.

CHAPTER 9

Wilfred James Wiseman (1891–1970): The Bible Society and the Brethren

Ian Randall

In 1938 Wilfred J. Wiseman (1891–1970) wrote an article in *The Witness*, entitled 'The Bible Society and the Brethren', which concluded with words written by Anthony Norris Groves in 1832 to the British and Foreign Bible Society (BFBS): 'May every blessing attend all your persons and all your deliberations, and may the work of the Lord abundantly prosper in your hand.'[1] When he wrote this article, Wiseman was responsible for Bible Society work in parts of Europe and also Equatorial Africa. Tim Grass notes that while Brethren disapproved of missionary societies, seeing them 'as lacking New Testament precedent and interfering with the worker's direct responsibility to the Lord', they did support the Bible Society. Many worked with the Society as translators, and many more circulated the Bibles produced by the Society.[2] Wiseman, however, is one of the few examples up to the mid-twentieth century of someone from the Brethren who took on a wide-ranging role in the Society's work. Another is James W. Wiles, a Cambridge graduate who lectured in English literature at Belgrade University from 1913 and was the Society's Agent in South-Eastern Europe from 1920 to 1940.[3] The particular significance of Wiseman, who began to work for the Bible Society in 1923, is the breadth of his involvements: in various parts of Europe, in Asia, and in Africa. He relished challenges, especially when associated with travel. James Roe, a historian of the Bible Society, notes with reference to the African period how Wiseman, in typical fashion, 'threw himself enthusiastically into the work'.[4]

Wilfred Wiseman wrote an unpublished autobiography, 'In Journeyings Oft', and in this he began by relating the circumstances of his birth. He wrote, 'Life began for me with what can surely be called a divine interposition of God.' He was apparently still-born and there was nothing the doctor considered could save his life. Then a family friend Elisabeth Cornelia Waldegrave, who was known for her evangelical work among naval personnel and was the sister of Lord Radstock, intervened, telling the doctor—in what Wiseman described as the 'aristocratic manner of the [eighteen] nineties'—that he must 'send immediately

---

1. W. J. Wiseman, 'The Bible Society and the Brethren', *W*, 68 (1939), 133.
2. Tim Grass, *Gathering to His Name: The Story of Open Brethren in Britain and Ireland* (Milton Keynes, 2006), 271.
3. James M. Roe, *History of the British and Foreign Bible Society, 1905–1954* (London, 1965), 259, 423.
4. Roe, *History*, 397.

for a pump'. It was the next Lord Radstock who told Wiseman of his aunt's successful intervention.[5] Wiseman's family lived in Portsmouth, and at one stage his father was naval tutor to the future King George V.[6] The family moved to Wales, living there from 1892 to 1897, before returning to Portsmouth. The young Wilfred developed a love for the Welsh language. Later, he noted, he would use 'a dozen foreign languages'.[7] Wiseman wrote that his father built up the Open Brethren Assembly at Rudmore Hall, Southsea, to well over 300 people. He died suddenly in 1905 as he was preparing to visit Wales to experience the Welsh Revival.[8] Wilfred studied at Portsmouth Technical College and then worked in yacht design.[9] He married in 1918, when holding what he called 'an executive position in war service', and he and his wife Jennifer moved to Bristol, where Wilfred took up a business partnership. He spoke of the 'holocaust' of the War being followed by 'impressive movements of the Spirit of God', and he promoted ventures such as Sunday evening after-church services which filled large cinemas in the city. Because of a 'particular blessing' in business, as he put it, 'I was able to provide the Bristol Assemblies with a tent holding 2,000 people'.[10] Donald J. Wiseman, the biblical scholar and Professor of Assyriology at London University, who was Wilfred's nephew, spoke of his uncle leaving 'a prosperous business career' to join the Bible Society.[11] In this study I want to look at Bible Society-Brethren dynamics through a focus on the entrepreneurial Wiseman.[12]

The Bible Society and the Brethren

The BFBS, formed in 1804, became 'one of the most dynamic and successful institutions spawned by the great evangelical awakening of the late eighteenth and early nineteenth century'.[13] Its aim was 'to encourage a wider circulation of the Holy Scriptures at home and abroad' and in its first fifty years the Society issued nearly 28 million copies of the Scriptures (in whole or part) in 152 languages and dialects. The majority of these versions were in the languages of Europe and Asia.[14] The Bibles sold were to be 'without note or comment', so that there could be no allegations of denominational bias.[15] In Europe, where Wiseman was to do much of his work, the Bible Society was one very important

---

5. Cambridge University Library, Bible Society archive [hereafter BSA], BSA/F3/Wiseman/22, W. J. Wiseman, 'In Journeyings Oft' (unpublished, undated), first draft, 1. Two drafts exist of the autobiography. I am grateful to Dr Onesimus Ngundu, the Society's Librarian, for his help.

6. BSA/G1/3/67, *The Bible in the World* [hereafter *B in W*], 32 (Mar. 1936), 35. The family treasured an autographed photograph of the King which he gave to Wiseman's father.

7. Wiseman, 'In Journeyings Oft', first draft, 1.

8. Wiseman, 'In Journeyings Oft', first draft, 2.

9. Grass, *Gathering*, 312.

10. Wiseman, 'In Journeyings Oft', second draft, 2.

11. Donald J. Wiseman, *Life Above and Below: Memoirs* (Tadworth, 2003), 11.

12. I am grateful to Anthony Harrop, who has held senior Bible Society posts, for his insights.

13. Stephen Batalden, Kathleen Cann, and John Dean (eds.), *Sowing the Word: The Cultural Impact of the British and Foreign Bible Society, 1804–2004* (Sheffield, 2004), 1.

14. Roger Steer, *Good News for the World: The Story of Bible Society* (Oxford, 2004), 222.

15. Batalden, Cann, and Dean (eds.), *Sowing the Word*, 4–5.

channel through which currents of evangelical Christianity flowed. In the second half of the nineteenth century, a pattern of influential territorial 'Agencies' developed, along with the establishment of permanent Bible Depots and the employment of travelling salesman—'colporteurs'. Their responsibility, under the supervision of a regional Agent, was to sell and distribute Bibles.[16] Wiseman undertook several BFBS regional Agency roles from his appointment in 1923 until his retirement in 1950. He was therefore well placed to reflect on central aspects of the Society's activities.

Wiseman's 1938 article in the *Witness* began: 'The name of Anthony Norris Groves has a deservedly honourable place in the early records of the missionary service of those connected with Assemblies of the Brethren.' Wiseman then quoted from a Bible Society Report of 1831: 'Mr Groves, residing at Baghdad, has furnished an interesting account of his proceedings and pointed out the great advantage of that place for promoting the dissemination of the Scriptures.'[17] The Society had put Bibles, New Testaments, Psalters, and Gospels in Arabic, Armenian, and other languages at the disposal of Groves. In response, Groves said he would do all he could for the Society. Wiseman also spoke of how J. N. Darby had produced a translation of the Bible in German, the Elberfeldt Version, with tens of thousands of copies of this translation having been circulated by the Bible Society. The names of eighteen members of the Brethren who had translated the Bible into African languages were then listed by Wiseman, with Dan Crawford, well-known for his work in Africa, at the head of the list. Wiseman emphasized that Brethren workers listed with Christian Missions in Many Lands devoted their energy to 'evangelistic service' rather than 'large educational and social service institutions'; given that focus, the Bible Society was 'heavily drawn upon'. It was, Wiseman said, beyond the means of the Brethren to engage in the translation and dissemination of the Bible on the massive scale on which the Bible Society operated.[18] Wiseman was arguing for the coherence of Brethren and Bible Society commitments.

This overview by Wiseman was reproduced twelve years later by W. T. Stunt, in *Echoes Quarterly Review*. Stunt's article was entitled 'The Bible Society and Missionaries from Assemblies'.[19] It is intriguing that although for much of his article Stunt drew his material from what Wiseman had written—with minor changes of wording—Stunt did not acknowledge his indebtedness to Wiseman or make reference to the *Witness*. Towards the end of his article, Stunt added three paragraphs of his own. He quoted J. Alexander Clarke, of Katanga, Central Africa, who wrote appreciatively in 1935 about the BFBS. As Stunt noted, this was almost a hundred years after Groves wrote in support of the Bible Society. For Clarke, the Society was 'the handmaiden of all the missionary churches and all the missionary churches must stand behind the Bible Society.' Clarke argued that it was 'incumbent on us all' to help the Society since 'there would be no Bible in the different dialects of Africa if there were no Bible Society'. His plea was for Brethren recognition

---

16. See I. M. Randall, 'Nineteenth-Century Bible Society Colporteurs in Eastern Europe', *Journal of European Baptist Studies*, 12/3 (2012), 5–25.
17. Wiseman, 'The Bible Society and the Brethren', 133.
18. Wiseman, 'The Bible Society and the Brethren', 133.
19. W. T. Stunt, 'The Bible Society and Missionaries from the Assemblies', *Echoes Quarterly Review* (Apr.–June 1950), 41–2, 57.

of the 'bounty' received from the Society and for their response to be co-operation with it.[20] Stunt reproduced Wiseman's list of Brethren involved with the Bible Society as translators, and added, in conclusion, reference to a number of Brethren involved in the BFBS as home Committee members, such as George Goodman, General Sir William Dobbie, and John Laing. Stunt noted two current BFBS overseas staff members from Assemblies: Ernest Tipson, in Malaya, and Wiseman, whom Stunt identified as responsible for Southern Europe.[21]

Wiseman was recruited to the Bible Society by John H. Ritson, who had been the visionary Secretary of the BFBS since 1899. Ritson, a Wesleyan Methodist minister (President of Conference in 1925–6), was the Society's Free Church joint Secretary. He was inspired by the way the Society offered 'a wider base of service for the Kingdom of God'.[22] Ritson's experience coupled with (as Rose put it) his 'quasi-imperial statesmanship' meant that by the 1920s he was 'in a position of effortless and virtually unassailable authority in all aspects of the Society's work'.[23] Ritson wrote to Wiseman in May 1923 asking if he would be willing to meet to talk about possible Bible Society work.[24] It is likely that Ritson had heard of 'Back-to-the-Truth' evangelistic campaigns that Wiseman had been helping to organize.[25] Ritson was impressed by those who combined what he called 'sterling Christian qualities' with business experience and financial acumen.[26] When Wiseman received Ritson's letter, he was about to leave home (in Bristol) for Norwich on a business trip. Without knowing what exactly Ritson was wanting to say, Wiseman and his wife had 'a brief prayer' and decided that on the way to Norwich Wiseman would call at the Bible Society offices in London. There Ritson convinced him that there was a call from God to leave his business—despite the fact that he had a diary full of engagements for the next two years—and to serve the strategic work of the Bible Society.[27] Within a month, in June 1923, Wiseman was on his way to Constantinople, to the South-Eastern Europe BFBS Agency.[28] His assignment was to replace A. L. Haig, who had moved to Berlin to take charge of the Central European Agency.[29]

Although Wiseman's priority would now be the work of the Bible Society, he continued to draw support from Brethren connections and to follow developments in the Brethren. He spoke of the debt he owed to the wisdom of Edward Short, 'father and grandfather of seven [medical] doctors', and the encouragement of William Bergin, the Director of the Müller Homes. Bergin wrote to Wiseman every week after the latter left Bristol.[30] One of Wiseman's continuing interests was the magazine *The Harvester*, which charted

---

20. Stunt, 'The Bible Society and Missionaries from the Assemblies', 42, 57.
21. Stunt, 'The Bible Society and Missionaries from the Assemblies', 57.
22. John H. Ritson, *The World is our Parish* (London, 1939), 48–9. There were Anglican and Free Church joint secretaries.
23. Roe, *History*, 226.
24. Wiseman, 'In Journeyings Oft', second draft, 4–5.
25. Wiseman, 'In Journeyings Oft', second draft, 2.
26. Ritson, *The World is our Parish*, 55.
27. Wiseman, 'In Journeyings Oft', second draft, 4–5.
28. Wiseman, 'In Journeyings Oft', second draft, 5–6.
29. Roe, *History*, 275.
30. Wiseman, 'In Journeyings Oft', second draft, 4.

evangelistic endeavours. The *Counties Quarterly* became *The Harvester* in 1922, and Wiseman was asked by a Home Workers' Conference to become its editor.[31] Wiseman was well known in these circles: he reported in his autobiography convening a Home Workers' Conference which attracted 1,100 people, filling the largest Brethren Hall in Bristol.[32] Circulation of *The Harvester* reached 7,000 copies, with Wiseman providing significant funding. He noted: 'It meant quite a considerable drain on my income.' Later Fred Tatford, who had been a young man in Wiseman's Assembly, took over editing *The Harvester*.[33] When Tatford wrote about Wiseman, he referred to him as 'an assembly worker' with the Bible Society.[34] In line with his ongoing commitment to the Brethren's evangelistic work, Wiseman described in 1940 how Brethren had circulated very large numbers of Scriptures in parts of Europe. He traced their activities from Lapland to the Romanian border. His survey took in Assemblies in Estonia, Latvia, Silesia and German Poland. In Czechoslovakia there were nearly 100 Assemblies and Wiseman reported that despite war conditions one Czech leader, Jan Siracky, was visiting Assemblies in Yugoslavia. Wiseman concluded: 'The lights of the Gospel testimony are burning low in Eastern Europe today and some lamps are going out. The darkness is increasing. It is always darkest before dawn.'[35] Brethren witness retained its importance for Wiseman.

The place of the Bible

Both the Bible Society and the Brethren saw the Bible as central to their work. When Wiseman joined the Society the challenge to which he responded was Ritson's message that in all service for God, 'the Bible must have the primary place for it is the Word of God'.[36] After joining the Society, Wiseman soon had opportunity to put into practice that belief. He arrived in Turkey just as the Treaty of Lausanne of 1923 came into effect, under which many privileges and immunities for foreigners in Turkey were cancelled.[37] A Turkish government official arrived to close down the Bible Society work in Constantinople. Wiseman had to act quickly. There was no time to consult J. W. Wiles, who was Wiseman's senior colleague in the region. Wiseman, who could speak Turkish, engaged the government representative in conversation and found a beautifully bound Turkish Bible which he presented to the official, conveying to him that the gift was very precious. Wiseman commented in his autobiography that whereas in England the custom was to 'depreciate what you give', in Turkey it was the reverse.[38] Several bowings took place, with Wiseman becoming quite fascinated by the official's 'massive watch-chain', hanging over his 'enormous abdomen' as if over 'a precipice'. In the course of answering questions, Wiseman told the official there could be nothing anti-Islamic in what was done by the Bible Society since the Society was distributing the Bible, and 'Moslems only began their understanding of religion

---

31. Grass, *Gathering*, 312–13.
32. Wiseman, 'In Journeyings Oft', second draft, 3.
33. Wiseman, 'In Journeyings Oft', second draft, 4.
34. F. A. Tatford, *Red Glow over Eastern Europe* (Bath, 1986), 84–6.
35. F2/3/3/10, BSA, W. J. Wiseman, 'In Eastern Europe Today', ([1940]?), no pagination.
36. Wiseman, 'In Journeyings Oft', second draft, 5–6.
37. Roe, *History*, 275.
38. Wiseman, 'In Journeyings Oft', second draft, 8.

seven centuries after Christ had died'.[39] Whether as a result of the gift, the argument, or something else, the Bible Society was allowed to continue to function.

A further encounter which also involved the presentation of a Bible to an official took place the following year in Greece. When Greece was declared a Republic in 1924, Wiseman immediately went to meet with the Greek Prime Minister, Alexandros Papanastasiou. There had been a two-year hold-up in a Greek customs warehouse of a consignment of modern Greek New Testaments.[40] With this in mind, Wiseman presented a beautifully leather-bound copy of the Bible in contemporary Greek to the Prime Minister, who apparently received it with 'real pleasure'. Wiseman then raised the issue of the customs authorities, who he said had demanded £4,000 in duties for Bibles to be imported. The Prime Minister considered this was beyond any reasonable figure, and he ensured that Bibles were allowed in free.[41] Although Wiseman served in the South-Eastern Europe Agency of the Society for only two years, this period gave him important insights into how to negotiate on behalf of the Society's work. He was able to visit Palestine, and in 1925 described how being there 'makes the Bible stories appeal to one far more than when it is just left to a Westerner's imagination'.[42] Some years later Wiseman wrote, with reference to his period in Constantinople: 'To the credit of the Turks we must say that their new-found place and power in European matters brought officials often into my office for talks on various subjects. They trusted me and we became very friendly. The result has been that our colporteurs have been able to continue right on till the present, and for long this was the only Christian work allowed.'[43]

Early in 1925 Wiseman was re-allocated by the BFBS to take charge of the North-Eastern Europe Agency, responsible for Russia, Finland, and the Baltic states. He was followed in Constantinople by J. S. St Clair, an Evangelical Anglican whose wife was Armenian. Wiseman encouraged St Clair about possibilities in the region. St Clair was interested in the Holy Land, and Wiseman spoke from his experience of the Holy Land about the way in which he found it to be a place that drew Christian believers 'closer to Him who has for ever hallowed these scenes by His wonderful death and life'.[44] In north-eastern Europe, Wiseman immediately sought to understand the history of Bible Society work in the region. The Russian Bible Society had operated from the early nineteenth century.[45] In 1855 Tsar Alexander II gave his blessing to a new translation of the Bible into Russian—the Synodal Bible.[46] By the early twentieth century BFBS agents directed a massive Russian colportage operation, and the BFBS was the main purchaser of the

---

39. Wiseman, 'In Journeyings Oft', second draft, 8–9.
40. Roe, *History*, 276.
41. BSA/G1/1/78, 'In Journeyings Oft', second draft, 12; *Bible Society Annual Report* [*BSAR*], 78 (1924), 107–8.
42. BSA/F2/3/1/6/2, W. J. Wiseman to J. S. St Clair, 14 May 1925.
43. Wiseman, 'In Journeyings Oft', first draft, 4.
44. BSA/F2/3/1/6/2, Wiseman to J. S. St Clair, 14 May 1925,
45. See J. C. Zacek, 'The Russian Bible Society and the Russian Orthodox Church', *Church History*, 35 (1966), 411–37.
46. S. K. Batalden, 'The BFBS Petersburg Agency and Russian Biblical Translation, 1856–1875', in *Sowing the Word*, 179.

Synodal New Testament.⁴⁷ William Kean, who led Bible Society work in Russia from 1895 to 1918, supervised the circulation throughout Russia of over eleven million copies of the Scriptures.⁴⁸ Wiseman's immediate BFBS predecessor was Walter Davidson, a much-respected figure who had been with the Society since 1885, spending most of his time until 1920 in the Russian Empire, principally in Siberia. Wiseman, however, faced a situation in which no Bible Society work was allowed in Russia. There was hope that the Bolshevik government's policy might change, but the Society's optimism, which was shared by Wiseman, was, as James Roe put it, as 'as boundless as it was baseless'.⁴⁹

Initially, Wiseman and his wife settled in Riga, the capital of Latvia.⁵⁰ He was soon reporting to Ritson about Bible distribution in the Baltic countries and beyond, where he had identified thirty-seven languages being spoken, with Russian, German, Finnish, Estonian, Latvian, and Lithuanian being the most common. In a letter in May 1925, Wiseman said he had met Adam Podin, a Baptist leader born in Latvia who lived in Estonia.⁵¹ It was while living in London that Podin had experienced evangelical conversion, and he had wide connections in international Baptist and Evangelical Alliance circles.⁵² Podin was based in Keila (Kegel), Estonia, and when Wiseman met him, Podin spoke about an offer he had received from J. H. Rushbrooke, a British Baptist minister who was the Baptist World Alliance's full-time Commissioner for Europe. Rushbrooke had offered Podin Bibles and New Testaments at half price for Estonia. Wiseman, in response, pointed out to Podin what an adverse effect this would have on wider Bible work in Estonia, since such reduced prices would be expected but could not be sustained. Podin accepted the point and said he would not pursue the offer.⁵³ Two months later Wiseman wrote to Kitson to report: 'I have had the pleasure of meeting Dr Rushbrooke.' The conversation had been helpful. Rushbrooke had explained that he was simply passing on to Podin an American Baptist offer. Wiseman and Rushbrooke also discussed Russia, which stimulated Wiseman's desire to go there.⁵⁴ Rushbrooke had crucial Russian contacts. At the Baptist World Alliance Congress in Stockholm in 1923, Rushbrooke found it particularly

---

47. S. K. Batalden, 'Colportage and the Distribution of Holy Scripture', in Robert P. Hughes and Irina Paperno (eds.), *Late Imperial Russia* (Christianity and the Eastern Slavs, vol. 2), California Slavic Studies, vol. 17 (Berkeley, CA: University of California Press, 1994), 83–5.

48. Roe, *History*, 64; Batalden, 'Colportage and the Distribution of Holy Scripture', 83–5.

49. Roe, *History*, 259.

50. For Bible Society work here, see Valdis Tēraudkalns 'Bībeles biedrības Latvijas teritorijā 19. gadsimtā un 20. gadsimta sākumā' ['Bible Societies in the territory of Latvia in the 19th century and the beginning of the 20th century'], in V. Tēraudkalns, (ed.), *Bībele: Raksti, teksts, kultūrvide* [*Bible: Articles, Text, Cultural Environment*] (Rīga, 2005), 214–39.

51. BSA/F2/3/1/1/5, W. J. Wiseman to J. H. Ritson, 19 May 1925.

52. See Toivo Pilli, 'Adam Podin: An Estonian Baptist with International Links and Pan-Evangelical Vision', in P. J. Lalleman, P. J. Morden, and A. R. Cross (eds.), *Grounded in Grace: Essays to Honour Ian. M. Randall* (London, 2013), 103–17.

53. BSA/F2/3/1/1/5, W. J. Wiseman to J. H. Ritson, 19 May 1925.

54. BSA/F2/3/1/1/5, Wiseman to Ritson, 16 July 1925.

significant that a large delegation from Russia was able to attend. The leader was Ivan Prokhanoff, President of the All-Russian Evangelical Christian Union.[55]

At the time the name Ivan Prokhanoff did not mean a great deal to Wiseman. However, with his knowledge of the Russian language, Wiseman soon began to gather information about everyone in Russia who might be able to further Bible distribution. With Prokhanoff, some surprises were in store. Wiseman found in a copy of a Russian Bolshevik newspaper a statement signed by Prokhanoff and others, which said: 'The All-Russian Union of Evangelical Christians, which embraces about two million members and followers, sees in the Soviet Government the most brilliant expression of the nation's will, and the system of Government in its idea is close to the heart of the Russian people.'[56] It was now easier to understand why Prokhanoff had been allowed to take a large Russian delegation to Sweden. Wiseman wondered whether Prokhanoff had the influence necessary to find channels for Bibles to be printed in Russia. In 1927, in response to one idea—the printing of 50,000 Gospels and Psalms—Prokhanoff expressed his view forthrightly to Wiseman: 'We are obliged to mention that you do not quite understand our real life.' One issue was that the Russians could not pay for the printing of scriptures in advance. The only money available would be after they were sold. He also told Wiseman that Russian evangelicals preferred the whole Bible, or at least the New Testament, not just the Gospels.[57] Two years later, by which time Prokhanoff was in Berlin, his admiration for the Bolshevik regime having evaporated, Wiseman wrote to him to ask if there was 'anything I can do for Russia'. He wondered if there could be a Bible Depot. Prokhanoff replied that a Depot was 'very impracticable' as it would be seen as 'an agency of a foreign Society'.[58] Wiseman consistently explored possibilities for the place of the Bible.

Evangelistic vision

Although the Bible Society did not officially allow its Agents and colporteurs to engage in evangelistic work—their focus was to be the Bible alone—in practice it was impossible to draw such clear boundary marks. Wiseman, not surprisingly, drew inspiration from Brethren figures who had engaged in evangelistic ministry in the area in which he was now living. He spoke of there being 27,000 Brethren in Soviet Russia in 1914, and as he surveyed Russian evangelical history, he described Friedrich Wilhelm Baedeker, who had died in 1906, and E. H. Broadbent (1861–1945), as the 'best known among the brethren'. He noted that Baedeker had been converted through Lord Radstock's preaching in Weston-Super-Mare.[59] Radstock had spoken to great effect in St Petersburg in the 1870s, and Baedeker had lived and worked in Russia from 1877, undertaking a remarkable ministry

---

55. Bernard Green, *Tomorrow's Man: A Biography of James Henry Rushbrooke* (Didcot, 1997), 98–100.
56. BSA/F2/3/2/1/4, copy held in Wiseman papers, dated 12 Aug. 1923.
57. BSA F2/3/1/5, Ivan Prokhanoff to W. J. Wiseman, 14 Dec. 1927.
58. BSA/F2/3/1/5, W. J. Wiseman to Ivan Prokhanoff, 19 Jan.1929; 4 Feb.1929; Prokhanoff to Wiseman, 27 Jan. 1929. Prokhanoff died in Germany. In 1935 A. L. Haig wrote to Wiseman, 'You will be sorry to hear that our old friend Ivan Prokhanoff died in a German hospital on Sunday morning 6th inst.' BSA/F2/3/3/6, A. L. Haig to W. J. Wiseman, 19 Oct.1935.
59. 'In Journeyings Oft', second draft, 13.

in Russian prisons.[60] Baedeker also encouraged Ivan Prokhanoff.[61] Wiseman was inspired by Baedeker's travels, often with Ivan Kargel, a German-Russian evangelical leader, and Wiseman noted that Baedeker 'received the Scriptures from the Bible Society in very large quantities, for every prisoner who would accept a copy, and these were supplied almost without any cost'.[62] In the 1920s Broadbent was still acting as a kind of 'roaming bishop of Eastern Europe'.[63] Wiseman wrote that his 'valuable experience and most gracious statesmanlike advice had been of the utmost assistance to the simple leaders of small churches, far and wide across Russia'.[64] This, for Wiseman, was Brethren ministry at its best.

Wiseman's admiration was in no way limited, however, to Brethren preachers. It is clear that Wiseman felt an immediate rapport with Podin, a Baptist leader. Wiseman was deeply moved when he was invited to Podin's house, which Podin explained had been 'destroyed by the Bolsheviks and Germans but now repaired'.[65] An early experience Wiseman had in Estonia was accompanying Podin to an Estonian young offenders' prison to distribute New Testaments. One copy was given to each of the 200 prisoners, most of whom were aged 12 to 18. Wiseman reported in the 1926 *Annual Report* of the Bible Society not only about the Bibles, but also about how '[t]he story of the love of Christ had a most telling effect.' He added for the benefit of especially his British readers that an English woman supported the spread of the Bibles in Estonia.[66] In 1927, by which time the Wisemans had moved to Helsinki (Helsingfors), Wiseman returned to speak in Estonia, no doubt at the invitation of Podin. On Whit Monday, Wiseman addressed a large crowd, about 2,000 people, at a united conference of Christians in Estonia. The chairman requested those present at the gathering to show their appreciation of the Estonian Pocket Bible. Wiseman was exhilarated at the sight of so many 'upraised hands' and 'upraised Bibles'.[67] Wiseman's Brethren and Bible Society aspirations were fully satisfied.

While Wiseman's instincts were to co-operate with all those who were involved in evangelistic work and Bible distribution, he was aware that the Bible Society was sensitive about its rules of engagement. On 5 April 1928 he wrote to A. L. Haig, then the Society's Secretary for Central Europe, who was based in Berlin, to ask for advice: 'We have an enquiry through an Estonian friend acting for the Scripture Gift Mission of London, for 10,000 copies of the Gospel of John in Estonian. If the S. G. M. supply you with pictures for the covers, what price would these Gospels be? Have you had any dealings with the S. G. M. in Central Europe and on what terms?'[68] It was widely known that the SGM

---

60. R. S. Latimer, *Dr. Baedeker and his Apostolic Work in Russia* (London, 1907).
61. I. S. Prokhanoff, *In the Cauldron of Russia* (New York, 1933), 97–100.
62. 'In Journeyings Oft', second draft, 13. For Ivan Kargel, and his travels with Baedeker, see G. L. Nichols, *The Development of Russian Evangelical Spirituality* (Eugene, OR, 2011).
63. Tim Grass, 'Edward Hamer Broadbent (1861–1945): Pilgrim Churchman', in Tim Grass (ed.), *Witnesses in Many Lands* (SBH: Troon, 2013), 137, citing Stuart Hine.
64. 'In Journeyings Oft', second draft, 13.
65. F2/3/1/6/2, Podin to Wiseman, 21 Apr. 1925.
66. *BSAR*, 80 (1926), 84. BSA/G1/1/80. For Podin's prison ministry see Pilli, 'Podin', 108–10.
67. BSA/G1/1/82, *BSAR*, 82 (1928), 87.
68. BSA/F2/3/1/2, W. J. Wiseman to A. L. Haig, 5 Apr. 1928.

had distributed many millions of Gospels and New Testaments during the First World War, and Wiseman appreciated them as a thoroughly evangelistic agency. Haig replied, however, with words of warning: 'We have never had any dealings with the Scripture Gift Mission in the Agency hitherto. . . . As you no doubt know the S. G.M. are rather free and easy gentry and sometimes are inclined to appropriate our editions without in any way seeking for permission.' Also, Haig emphasized, we are 'not allowed by London to put pictures on the covers'. The only exception, he acknowledged, was in certain Roman Catholic editions of the Bible.[69]

There were occasions when Wiseman himself was cautious. In June 1926 a translator and evangelist, F. W. Kingston, who claimed to be linked with a Baptist publishing house in Poland (Kompas Press), called at the BFBS headquarters in London, bringing a recently published copy of Luke in the 'Belarusian' (often referred to in English-speaking circles as 'White Russian') language. Kingston spoke of plans to publish the entire New Testament. The Society, however, was doubtful about the status of 'Belarusian'. The BFBS editorial superintendent, Robert Kilgour, who had been a missionary with the Church of Scotland in India, said he had been told 'White Russians' could understand the Scriptures in Russian. Wiseman was also doubtful because there were suggestions that Kingston was Brethren, but he had apparently never had any previous contact with the Bible Society. In a letter to Kilgour, Wiseman commented with some incredulity: 'Surely he cannot be a so-called "P.B." if he has never come into contact with the work of the B.F.B.S.!'[70] But after two years of investigation, Wiseman came to a different conclusion about Kingston's work. In a long letter to Ritson, Wiseman pleaded the cause of the twelve million Belarusians who he now believed to be 'without the New Testament in their own tongue'. He asked the Society to produce the New Testament and Psalms in Belarusian and held out a vision of the evangelistic impact on the readers.[71] Wiseman was persuasive. Ritson replied to say it had been agreed that the BFBS would initially supply to the Synod of the Orthodox Church 1,000 copies of the scriptures in Belarusian.[72]

Wiseman's commitment to evangelistic ministry did not mean that he failed to focus on his work as a Bible Society agent. In Estonia he met the Estonian Minister of Education to talk about Bibles in schools. The Ministry later recommended that every pupil should have a New Testament.[73] When Wiseman was invited to speak at larger gatherings, his message was often related specifically to the Bible Society. He was pleased to report to Ritson and to Rushbrooke about several significant gatherings. Wiseman told Rushbrooke in September 1925 that he 'had the privilege of speaking at the opening meeting of the Baptist Seminary in Estonia', and had also addressed anniversary meetings in Matthew [Mateja] Baptist Church and the Seminary Church in Riga. Wiseman gave an account of his talk: his theme had been the beginnings of the Bible Society, especially the famous

---

69. BSA/F2/3/1/2, Haig to Wiseman, 11 Apr. 1928.
70. BSA/F2/3/1/1/11, W. J. Wiseman to Robert Kilgour, 23 June 1926.
71. BSA/F2/3/1/1/8, W. J. Wiseman to J. H. Ritson, 24 Oct. 1928.
72. BSA/F2/3/1/1/8, Ritson to Wiseman, 30 Oct. 1928.
73. BSA/G1/1/81, *BSAR*, 81 (1927), 83.

story from Wales of Mary Jones and her Bible.[74] He also told Rushbrooke that John Frey (Janis Freijs), the leading Latvian Baptist pastor, had spoken of the impact of Wiseman's message. One example Frey had given was of an old Latvian lady who rarely read the Bible but following Wiseman's challenge was now reading it every day.[75] Rushbrooke replied immediately to emphasise his 'great delight' at 'meeting with Mrs Wiseman and yourself'. Rushbrooke continued: 'I am glad that you appear to be having pleasant fellowship with our Baptist people in Estonia and Latvia. I look forward to a renewed fellowship at an early date.'[76] To Ritson, Wiseman described speaking in Latvia to a capacity congregation of 1,500—with all the aisles in the building filled—on the subject of Mary Jones and the Baptist pastor asking the whole assembly to stand in recognition of BFBS work. Wiseman added—perhaps so that Ritson would not feel he was in danger of becoming too close to radical Baptists—that he had also preached at St Saviour's Anglican Church in Riga.[77] For Wiseman, an evangelistic vision was entirely consistent with his Bible Society role.

Itinerancy: 'In Journeyings Oft'

The work to which Wiseman gave himself in the Bible Society involved an enormous amount of travel. He reckoned he had visited a remarkable 141 countries, and he revelled in writing travel narratives, a number of which were published in the Bible Society's publication, *The Bible in the World*.[78] His nephew Donald at one time contemplated missionary service, partly 'fired by tales told by my uncle' about his exciting travels.[79] In 1925 Wiseman described travelling from the Macedonian frontier to the Adriatic coast. Travel, he informed Bible Society readers, was in a vehicle in which 'you will sit or crouch upon a short plank, a box, a bundle, a barrel, or a roll of leather, or anything else that can serve the purpose of a seat, and wedging yourself into a corner, you hang on tight – thinking not too much of the precipices down which a few months before (or it may be only days) a whole lorry went hundreds of feet to destruction.' He added: 'The drivers are splendid: always very young men with no nerves.'[80] Another journey, in Albania, was '[i]n inky darkness, illuminated only by brilliant flashes of lightening, we went careering along precipices at a fearful pace . . . It was flirting with death, and very thrilling.'[81] Travel on behalf of the Society was something encouraged by the Society leadership. Ritson,

---

74. Bible Society, 'Our history', <https://www.biblesociety.org.uk/about-us/our-history/>, accessed 15 Aug. 2018.
75. BSA/F2/3/1/6/2, W. J. Wiseman to J. H. Rushbrooke, 21 Sept. 1925.
76. BSA/F2/3/1/6/2, Rushbrooke to Wiseman, 25 Sept. 1925.
77. BSA/F2/3/1/1/5, W. J. Wiseman to C. H. K. Boughton, 21 Sept. 1925.
78. In Europe Wiseman visited Northern Ireland, Eire, France, Belgium, Holland, Denmark, Norway, Sweden, Finland, Poland, Estonia, Latvia, Lithuania, Germany, Austria, Hungary, Yugoslavia, Romania, Czechoslovakia, Bulgaria, Turkey, Greece, Albania, Italy, Spain, Switzerland, Liechtenstein, Portugal, Russia, Ukraine and Georgia.
79. Wiseman, *Life Above and Below*, 11. Although Donald Wiseman did not follow in Wilfred's footsteps in the realm of overseas Christian service, he was active in the Bible Society Translations Committee. See ibid., 109–13.
80. BSA/G1/1/79, *BSAR*, 79 (1925), 109.
81. Wiseman, 'In Journeyings Oft', second draft, 42–3.

before he retired through ill health in 1931, was himself an 'intrepid traveller'.[82] He visited the Southern Seas, parts of Africa, Europe, Russia, China, Japan, and the Middle East.[83] Brethren figures such as Groves, Baedeker, and Broadbent were also models for Wiseman. 'One realises', he commented on one travelogue, 'that some parts of the work of a Bible Society Agent are not "mere book distribution".'[84]

During his time in charge of the North-Eastern Europe Agency, Wiseman took a particular interest in people living beyond the Arctic Circle. This appealed to his sense of adventure. He described in his autobiography and in a shorter published report a journey north by train, bus, and steamboat which took him 800 miles within the Arctic Circle to see the Lapps. His companion was a Russian-Ukrainian, Pastor A. Dobrinin, who worked part-time for the BFBS. On the bus leg of the journey, the roads gave the vehicle, said Wiseman, 'perpetual motion' and 'frequent contact with the roof'. Wiseman commented ruefully that he had never realised he 'had so many bones in my body'. Another memorable aspect of the journey was a 'terrific storm' which blew up in the Arctic Ocean. Wiseman and Dobrinin were in 'a mere cockleshell of a steam boat'.[85] When they arrived, a meeting was held in one of the houses. The air was so bad that the hurricane lamp went out. Those present said this was all right and in any case it was too cold to open a window. Wiseman kept to himself his thought: 'It might have been alright for them, but it was pretty tough for me.' Wiseman carried on speaking for half an hour 'explaining the meaning of the cross', and five present were converted to Christ. Later there were large orders for copies of the scriptures. He found that there were several languages spoken in the area, and he was able to follow up this discovery by seeking scriptures in these languages.[86]

In 1929 Wiseman was asked by the Bible Society to move from Europe to India, initially to support Bible Society work in the Punjab. The Wisemans, who by now had a young son, Ian, went in 1930 from the bitter cold of Finland to India's extreme heat. They settled for a time in Calcutta with Wiseman taking on the role of BFBS Acting Secretary. He noted in 1931 that it was 120 years since the Calcutta Auxiliary Bible Society was founded, and he recalled the efforts at that time of Henry Martyn and David Brown. The early Bible translation and distribution work in that region was for Wiseman a 'magnificent venture of faith'.[87] In Calcutta Wiseman made many cross-denominational contacts: Anglican, Baptist, Presbyterian, and Methodist.[88] From Calcutta he was asked to go to Rangoon, Burma. At the end of these assignments, Wiseman took a period of leave, while his family returned home, and he visited—at his own expense—Malaya, China, Japan, Australia, New Zealand, and the Pacific Islands. He then obtained a tourist visa to travel through a large part of Russia, fulfilling a long-held ambition. He noted that in Russian cities it was most unusual to observe attitudes of religious reverence. 'Holy Russia', he wrote,

---

82. Roe, *History*, 33.
83. Ritson, in *The World is our Parish*, gives details.
84. *BSAR*, 79 (1925), 110. BSA/G1/1/79.
85. Wiseman, 'In Journeyings Oft', second draft, 35–6; W. J. Wiseman, 'A Journey to the Land of the Aurora Borealis', *B in W*, 32 (March 1927), 40.
86. Wiseman, 'In Journeyings Oft', second draft, 39.
87. BSA/G1/1/85, *BSAR*, 85 (1931), 149.
88. BSA/G1/1/86, *BSAR*, 86 (1932), 156.

was now a 'misnomer'.[89] In the countryside, however, Wiseman heard that atheist orators had little success. They believed they were successful in attacking Christianity, but 'then a wandering Baptist, or other evangelical preacher arrives, and the very people whom the atheist regarded as safe were soundly converted and became members of the local church, in spite of much opposition'.[90] Wiseman reported to the Bible Society Committee members in London on Russia, and the response was that they had 'seldom, if ever, been more absorbed by an address in the Committee Room'.[91]

Wiseman's hope was that when he returned in 1933 from Asia he might be able to cover a part of Europe again. In 1932 he wrote to Arthur H. Wilkinson, the BFBS Anglican joint Secretary, rehearsing the way he had enabled Society work in Europe to prosper. Wiseman argued that the challenges of Bible Society ministry in Europe demanded 'experience and organising capacity of no mean order'. He believed that was what he could offer.[92] Wilkinson replied to say that some BFBS re-organization was going on in Europe.[93] In the event, Wiseman's wish was granted, and in 1934 he resumed his work with the North-Eastern Europe Agency.[94] The Wisemans did not return to Helsinki, but settled in Bristol and Ian, their son, later went to Monkton Combe School in Bath. However, Wiseman was determined to seek to continue to meet the special challenges he saw across Europe. He firmly believed that what he saw as his particular expertise had made and could make a significant difference. Ever the businessman, Wiseman counted BFBS circulation figures, noting that 33,170 copies of the scriptures had circulated in 1924, when he took over North-Eastern Europe, and 147,000 copies had circulated in 1929, when he left. In his three-year absence the figure had dropped to 75,162. However, numbers were 144,106 by 1936 after two years of his leadership.[95] This leadership involved extensive travels in Finland and the Baltic states. In 1936 he spoke of the continued work of the colporteurs and of those who supported them, such as Jonas Inkenas, a Lithuanian Baptist pastor whose help had been 'consistently extended' to the Bible Society. His apartment in Šiauliai functioned like a BFBS storage depot.[96]

Two final Bible Society assignments given to Wiseman: Equatorial Africa, which he combined with a Russian watching brief, followed by South-Eastern Europe. From 1937 Wiseman, as Equatorial Africa Secretary, travelled widely across Africa, usually for several months at a time. On one trip he discussed issues relating to translations into fifty-six languages. In the Gold Coast (Ghana) he was delighted to meet the King of Ashanti, Nana Prempeh II, a Bible Society supporter whose 'wide versatility and intimate acquaintance with modern problems', Wiseman commented, 'shows how African rulers

---

89. Wiseman, 'In Journeyings Oft', second draft, 29.
90. Wiseman, 'In Journeyings Oft', second draft, 30–1.
91. *B in W*, 30 (Dec. 1934), 190. BSA/G1/3/65.
92. BSA/F2/3/3/3, W. J. Wiseman to Arthur H. Wilkinson, 3 Oct. 1932.
93. BSA/F2/3/3/3, Wilkinson to Wiseman, 8 Nov. 1932.
94. BSA/G1/1/89, *BSAR*, 89 (1935), 71..
95. Wiseman, 'In Journeyings Oft', second draft, 53.
96. BSA/G1/1/90, *BSAR*, 90 (1936), 79. For Inkenas see Lina Andronoviena, 'Jonas Inkenas and Forgiveness Lived Out: An Experiment in Biography as Narrative Theology', *American Baptist Quarterly,* 22/2 (2003), 247–61. I am indebted to Lina, the grand-daughter of Jonas, for her help.

today are in touch with world affairs'.[97] The 1938 *Annual Report* of the Bible Society noted: 'For the first time the vast territory from Lake Chad to the Congo was visited by a representative of the Society, and the language survey made then will be of great benefit to us in the future.'[98] During a trip through East Africa, Wiseman reckoned he addressed a total of 30,000 people. This included a large congregation in Namirembe Cathedral, Kampala, Uganda.[99] In May 1939 he was asked to supervise Society work in Italy, Spain, Portugal, Yugoslavia, Albania, and Romania. True to form, he set off almost immediately, but found himself by mistake on a train to Vienna and jumped off as it was moving. He commented that he might have ended up in a Nazi prisoner of war camp.[100] In 1946, Wiseman's wife Jennifer died.[101] From later in that year to his retirement in 1951, his focus was on South-Eastern Europe. He married again, and he and his wife Dorothy lived in Minster House, Leominster, opposite the Brethren assembly's Brook Hall. The house was filled with artefacts and furniture from the many countries Wiseman had visited in the course of his remarkable global ministry.[102]

An enabling ministry

From his early evangelistic initiatives in Bristol onwards, Wiseman's vision was of enabling God's work to go forward. His personal investment was wholehearted and at the same time he wished to enable others. An example of this enabling was his appointment and training of BFBS depot managers and colporteurs. In Riga he appointed Fricis Anderson, who had been a foreman in the 'Non-Poisonous Department' of a match factory. Anderson wondered if his not being an ordained minister was an issue, and Wiseman, with his Brethren outlook, assured him that being a lay person was not a hindrance. He wrote: 'You need not feel at a disadvantage in the fact that you are not an ordained minister. In some places we have ministers, in others laymen. The main thing is living the right life and efficiently doing the task to which God has called us.'[103] Wiseman gave guidance to Anderson about undertaking ministry in hospitals, suggesting that in hospital a small light book like St John's Gospel was much better than a heavy Bible which a person would find hard to hold.[104] In Memel (now Klaipeda), Lithuania, Wiseman made a very different appointment. He reported to Ritson that he had been able to recruit Dr Wilhelm Gaigalaitis, a Lutheran priest and academic who had a local religious bookshop. The previous Bible Society representative

---

97. W. J. Wiseman, 'A Tour in West Africa', *B in W*, 34 (September 1938), 138. BSA/G1/3/69.
98. *BSAR*, 92 (1938), 128. BSA/G1/1/91.
99. *BSAR*, 93 (1939), 108. BSA/G1/1/93.
100. Wiseman, 'In Journeyings Oft', second draft, 59.
101. I am grateful to Dr Alison Stacey, archivist at Tyndale House, Cambridge, for her note about Jennifer Wiseman's funeral on 11 Jan. 1946.
102. I am grateful to the younger members of the Wiseman family for their memories of the latter part of Wilfred Wiseman's life. Peter and Angela LeRoy speak of visiting 'Uncle Bill' and Dorothy and recall 'their impressive limousines, including a "Lanchester" kept in a stable building behind Brook Hall'. E-mail, 28 June 2016.
103. BSA/F2/3/1/3/1, W. J. Wiseman to F. Anderson, 10 Apr. 1928.
104. BSA/F2/3/1/3/2, Wiseman to Anderson, 18 Sept. 1928.

had apparently not been doing anything: Wiseman found him living out in the forest.[105] Wiseman also facilitated support of colleagues. In Tallin, Estonia, he was happy to tell the BFBS representative, H. Kokamägi, that a gift of £20 for his support had been received via E. H. Broadbent from Mrs Greenaway in Australia.[106]

The reference to a representative who had been doing nothing highlights the business-like aspect of Wiseman's vision. His Brethren context was one in which businessmen were often in Christian leadership. Part of the challenge Wiseman had received from Ritson was whether 'as a business man', he would meet the high standards required for 'The Father's Business' in the BFBS.[107] With evident admiration, Wiseman spoke of Ritson's 'soundness of judgment, experienced Christian statesmanship, and exceptional business capacity and integrity'.[108] In similar vein, Wiseman described Broadbent as 'a very consecrated business man' and one who 'because the word "missionary" was not written in his passport, could travel widely'.[109] Wiseman believed sound administrative procedures enabled the BFBS to be effective. Writing to J. S. St Clair in 1925, Wiseman informed him, with no trace of false humility, that '[m]any people in Constantinople remarked to me what a great change for the better I had been able to effect'. Wiseman spoke of difficulties in 'managing the older men and their muddles', and dealing with very antiquated systems.[110] St Clair, however, was not enthusiastic about what he inherited from Wiseman. He considered Wiseman should have reported the poor state of affairs.[111] It is likely that Wiseman was not confident enough when in Constantinople to send such a report to London, but from then on he made sure he placed on record all the business affairs of the Society. In Riga and Helsinki, for example, he carefully documented sales, costs, and quality. He told Ritson he did not wish to criticize Walter Davidson's work in Riga, but 'as far as booking-keeping goes the present system here is far from satisfactory.'[112] Wiseman's message to Anderson, as the latter took over the Riga Depot, was clear: 'I can soon tell the difference between a care<u>ful</u> man and a care<u>less</u> man.'[113]

Local Brethren assemblies had shaped Wiseman, and he saw the work of the Bible Society as enabling local churches to fulfil their ministry. When he first moved to Riga in 1925, Wiseman felt the lack of 'spiritual fellowship', but he affirmed 'the presence of the Lord Jesus Christ' as what mattered. He continued: 'He can hallow the humdrum, transfigure the troublesome, consecrate the commonplace and gild with the glory of God the ordinary paths of life.'[114] However, Wiseman wanted more than 'humdrum' church life. In September 1925, referring to the Estonian Baptist Preachers' Seminary, of which Adam Podin was director, he told Podin that he had 'very happy memories' of time spent at this school for the 'sons of the prophets'. Wiseman was delighted that the students would be

---

105. BSA/F2/3/1/1/5, W. J. Wiseman to J. H. Ritson, 30 June 1925.
106. BSA/F2/3/1/4/4, W. J. Wiseman to H. Kokamägi, 14 May 1926.
107. Wiseman, 'In Journeyings Oft', second draft, 5–6.
108. Wiseman, 'In Journeyings Oft', second draft, 4.
109. Wiseman, 'In Journeyings Oft', second draft, 13.
110. BSA/F2/3/1/6/2, W. J. Wiseman to J. S. St Clair, 14 May 1925.
111. BSA/F2/3/1/1/6/2, St Clair to Wiseman, 13 June 1925.
112. BSA/F2/3/1/1/5, W. J. Wiseman to J. H. Ritson, 14 May 1925.
113. BSA/F2/3/1/3/2, W. J. Wiseman to F. Anderson, 18 Sept. 1928.
114. BSA/F2/3/1/6/2, W. J. Wiseman to J. S. St Clair, 21 July 1925.

pastors and evangelists. He continued: 'May God mightily bless these young men and women, and may Estonia ring with the glad tidings of the Gospel from their lips.'[115] As well as work with students and churches, Podin introduced Wiseman to another area of ministry: in the four leper colonies in Estonia.[116] Wiseman went with Podin to a leper colony in Saaremaa and wrote: 'Quite a number have recently professed conversion, and the main avenue through which the blessing came to them was undoubtedly the reading of the Scriptures in the quietude and loneliness of their little rooms.'[117] Not all Wiseman's dealings with evangelical leaders were positive. In 1926 there were frustratingly prolonged efforts by the Society to have money paid that was owed by Russians.[118] A year later Ritson wrote to Wiseman to say that William Fetler, an evangelical pastor in Riga, had raised sums for Bibles for Russia but had instead spent the money on church buildings.[119] Ritson accepted Wiseman's advice not to quarrel with Fetler, who was a significant church leader.[120]

Along with his encouragement of local church work among evangelicals, Wiseman also invested in building relationships with leaders who represented 'majority' Churches—Orthodox, Lutheran, and Anglican. During his investigation of the needs of the Belarusians, Wiseman spoke to Orthodox Church leaders. He also undertook research, in which he discovered that the Belarusians 'had been one of the first nations to have the Scripture printed in their own language', in 1517. Wiseman enclosed with a report to Ritson 'some notes concerning Dr. Franciscus [Francis] Skaryna, the White Russian translator of the early 16th century'.[121] In signalling assent to the provision of Bibles in Belarusian, Ritson said the Orthodox Synod was going to indicate its backing, 'and this would prevent prohibitions or misunderstandings locally'.[122] In 1930 Wiseman reported on conversations with Lutheran Church leaders in Finland, such as Matti Tarkkanen, head of the Finnish Lutheran Missionary Society. Wiseman was also cooperating with Lutheran leaders elsewhere: Bishop Irbe in Riga and Bishop Jakob Kukk in Estonia. Within Orthodox circles, the Archbishop of Finland, Herman Aav, who was an Estonian and was affiliated with the Patriarchate of Constantinople (not with the Russia Patriarchate), was supportive of the Society. The same was true of the Orthodox leadership in Lithuania.[123] Another helpful friend of Wiseman's was C. H. Jones, the Anglican chaplain in Helsinki.[124] Later, in Africa, Wiseman spoke at meetings such as one arranged by the Anglican Bishop of Sierra Leone for ministers of all denominations. Wiseman reported with typical enthusiasm that it was said there had not been such an inter-church event in living memory.[125]

---

115. BSA/F2/3/1/6/2, W. J. Wiseman to A. Podin, 18 Sept. 1925.
116. See Pilli, 'Podin', 110–12.
117. BSA/G1/1/82, 87, *BSAR*, 82 (1928), 87.
118. BSA/F2/3/1/1/6, C. H. K. Boughton to Wiseman, 1 Apr. 1926.
119. BSA/F2/3/1/1/7, J. H. Ritson to W. J. Wiseman, 12 July 1927.
120. BSA/F2/3/1/1/7, Ritson to Wiseman, 26 July 1927.
121. BSA/F2/3/1/1/8, Wiseman to Ritson, 24 Oct. 1928.
122. BSA/F2/3/1/1/8, Ritson to Wiseman, 30 Oct. 1928.
123. BSA/G1/1/84, *BSAR*, 74 (1930), 84; Wiseman, 'In Journeyings Oft', second draft, 34.
124. BSA/F2/3/3/, 1, C. H. Jones to W. J. Wiseman, 18 December 1930.
125. Wiseman, 'A Tour in West Africa', 136.

Conclusion

Wilfred Wiseman was described in his early period with the Bible Society as someone 'who has had considerable experience both in business and as a religious worker'.[126] When he later went to Burma, the BFBS commented: 'Mr Wiseman's experience and knowledge of the Bible Society's work in many other lands has been helpful in the advocacy of the Society's cause as well as in the work of administration.'[127] Wiseman found in the work of the Bible Society a ministry that fitted his personality and his spiritual aspirations, which had been shaped within the Brethren. He was strongly committed to the spread of the Bible, he was entrepreneurial in his approach, and he was eager to travel. Wiseman saw the effects of the circulation of the Bible in evangelistic terms. Evangelistic efforts won his admiration and support. He spoke of the impact of 'the simple, earnest preacher' who could speak of 'the sweetness and power he has found through the Bible'.[128] Wiseman admired those who travelled across countries taking the Christian faith, with Baedeker and Broadbent among his exemplars. Following the Second World War, until his retirement from the BFBS as he reached sixty, Wiseman continued his far-flung ministry. In 1947 he was the final speaker—taking as his subject Bible translation and distribution—at a major missionary conference in Leopoldville which drew together delegates from Western and African nations.[129] In his article 'The Bible Society and the Brethren', Wiseman concluded by quoting the Brethren traveller, A. N. Groves: 'Whatever I can do for the [Bible] Society, believe me, I will do it with all my heart.'[130] It was a sentiment Wilfred Wiseman echoed and implemented.

---

126. BSA/G1/3/54, *B in W*, 19 (July 1923), 100.
127. BSA/G1/1/78, *BSAR*, 78 (1934), 202.
128. Wiseman, 'In Journeyings Oft', second draft, 30–1.
129. BSA/G1/3/75, *B in W*, 43 (1947), 59–60.
130. Wiseman, 'Bible Society and the Brethren', 133.

Chapter 10

F. F. Bruce and the Bible

Tim Grass

It is my hope that you will not find this chapter[1] as dull as F. F. Bruce's audiences sometimes found his lectures. In the words of one of my informants:

> I remember him once saying that he was not a good public speaker, and preferred writing. He said he was to speak at Sydney Anglican Cathedral in Australia on one occasion, and as he was driven to the cathedral they found people lined up round the building waiting for entrance (such was his reputation). He said that he commented to his driver, 'My, these people will be disappointed', and then he paused, and added to me, 'And they were!'[2]

In considering the topic of 'F. F. Bruce and the Bible', we shall look at what the Bible was to him and how he approached the study of the Bible, setting him in the context of the biblical scholarship of his time and concluding with some lessons for today.

The Bible in Bruce's Life

Upbringing

It is nearly thirty years since F. F. Bruce died, and a new generation has arisen, so it will be helpful to begin by sketching out the life of Frederick Fyvie Bruce. Born in 1910 in Elgin, he retained a lifelong sense of his identity as a Scot from the north-east. This area was marked by a sense of intellectual independence and a refusal to defer to what people were thinking down south. This independence was fully reflected in the local communities of the Christian denomination to which his family belonged, the Open Brethren. Bruce's father Peter (1874–1955) was a full-time travelling evangelist among them. These Brethren were keen Bible students, but coming from where they did they saw no reason to adopt a particular approach to an issue or passage just because someone highly regarded among them did so. Bruce himself often said that his father taught him to think independently on the basis of the evidence, and never to accept any statement simply on the basis of someone else's say-so. Peter Bruce had himself come to some conclusions about aspects of eschatology which did not match the standard Brethren line at the time, and he may

---

1. This chapter was originally delivered as a lecture at Tilsley College, Motherwell, Lanarkshire, 1 Dec. 2015.
2. Charles Price to the author, 27 Jan. 2008.

have been frozen out of some local assemblies as a result.³ So Fred would have been aware that thinking for yourself can sometimes be costly.

We do not know precisely when Bruce came to a personal faith in Christ: his reserve means that he rarely cared to let slip many hints on the subject of his personal faith-journey.⁴ But he speaks of having absorbed the Christian faith with his mother's milk, and coming to a point as a late teenager at which he made that faith his own, apparently through the influence of a pharmacist and preacher named Kingsley Melling (1903–2004).⁵ Young Fred was evidently blessed with a questioning mind and took his father's advice: while still at school, he did some rethinking regarding the Brethren teaching under which he had been brought up—a process which would continue all his life.⁶ Just before going to university, Fred was baptized as a believer in the assembly at Lossiemouth.

Fred had a distinguished career as a classics student at Aberdeen and Cambridge, but as a student he seems to have had a crisis of faith, although he made little of it: 'At a time when I was as sceptical as an undergraduate ought to be, a paper of [W. R. Matthews] in the *Hibbert Journal* for January, 1930, on "The Destiny of the Soul" showed me how I might understand and continue to accept *ex animo* the Christian doctrine of the resurrection of the body.'⁷ It is worth noting that the crisis was about a big issue, not a minor aspect of assembly teaching.

Church life
In a previous generation, when Brethren had not produced many scholars who were recognized in the wider academic world, Bruce used to be seen as noteworthy for his lifelong membership of the Brethren; I get the feeling that sometimes people wondered either how he could stick them, or alternatively how they could stick him! But the fact is that he was fortunate enough to spend much of his life among open and outward-looking congregations which were at ease with things academic in general. He found the Brethren attractive because of their breadth of sympathy and their commitment to spiritual and intellectual freedom under Christ.⁸ He therefore found no difficulty in remaining not only a member of a Brethren congregation (or assembly), but also in serving them as a preacher and Bible teacher—and he saw no incompatibility between the approaches to biblical study adopted in the academy and the church.

Bruce was by no means the first member of the Brethren to write extensively in the field of biblical studies. In the nineteenth century J. N. Darby and William Kelly had both done so, followed in the early twentieth by W. E. Vine, for one—but Bruce *was* almost the

---

3. See Tim Grass, *F. F. Bruce: A Life* (Grand Rapids, MI, 2012), 9.
4. F. F. Bruce, *In Retrospect: The Remembrance of Things Past* (London, 1980), 306–7.
5. J. D. Douglas, 'A Man of Unchanging Faith', *Christianity Today*, 10 Oct. 1980, 16–17; Bruce, *In Retrospect*, 16. Melling always considered his two years in Lossiemouth to have been a mistake: S. Kent, *Faithful to the End: Biography of Kingsley Melling 1903–2004* (Horwich, 2005), 24–5.
6. Bruce, *In Retrospect*, 38–9.
7. *Journal of the Transactions of the Victoria Institute*, 84 (1952), 129, written response to a paper by W. R. Matthews, 'The Aims and Scope of the Philosophy of Religion'.
8. F. F. Bruce, 'Why I have Stayed with the Brethren', *Journal of the Christian Brethren Research Fellowship*, 10 (Dec. 1965), 5–6.

first to do so as part of the academic world. However, whilst Scottish Brethren may not have participated in the world of academic discourse, they relished solid Bible study, and they had their own approach to biblical interpretation supplied by a hermeneutic known as Dispensationalism. It was by no means uncommon for miners, joiners, and other skilled manual workers to spend their leisure hours learning biblical languages and poring over commentaries. Conversational Bible readings formed a significant part of assembly life, and the highlight of an assembly's year was its Saturday conference, a gathering which combined sessions of solid biblical exposition with socialization and romance over a brown bag tea. Neil Dickson's book *Brethren in Scotland 1838–2000* brings all this to life.[9]

The Bible in Bruce's career

What he did

He was a postgraduate student in Vienna when he cut short his studies to accept an appointment as Assistant in Greek at the University of Edinburgh in 1935. Three years later he became Lecturer in Greek at Leeds University. However, his interest in academic biblical studies was to lead to a change of course. He took a diploma in Hebrew at Leeds in 1943, and lectured in New Testament Greek to theological students. In addition, he was active in the formation and early development of an evangelical agency seeking to promote academic biblical study, Tyndale House at Cambridge, and the associated Tyndale Fellowship for Biblical and Theological Research. There was a scarcity of evangelical biblical scholars at that time, largely because of a combination of liberal exclusion of evangelicals and evangelical suspicion of things academic. The shortage was so severe that the Inter-Varsity Fellowship had turned to him to write for them on biblical topics because they had few if any biblical scholars to turn to, and he had offered to write a commentary on the Greek text of Acts for Tyndale Press, IVF's 'academic' imprint. Even more remarkably, in 1947 the University of Sheffield appointed Bruce as the first head of its new Department of Biblical History and Literature, even though he was not trained in biblical studies. This department came into being because the 1944 Education Act had given Religious Education or 'Scripture' the status of a compulsory subject, and people needed to be trained to teach it. For the first year at Sheffield he carried the department's teaching load single-handed, but gradually he built it up, developed the courses on offer, and began supervising postgraduates, and in 1955 he was promoted to a professorship. Bruce was very happy at Sheffield, but out of the blue he was approached regarding the Rylands Professorship of Biblical Criticism and Exegesis at the University of Manchester in 1959. He accepted the offer, remaining at Manchester until his retirement in 1978 after which his literary activity continued in full spate until his death in 1990.

Bruce achieved a range of academic distinctions. He was also a productive and versatile writer, with almost fifty books to his credit, of which about twenty-five remain in print, hundreds of articles, and over 2,000 book reviews. He also edited several journals[10] and

---

9. Neil T. R. Dickson, *Brethren in Scotland 1838–2000: A Social Study of an Evangelical Movement* (SEHT; Carlisle, 2002), 209–13.

10. *EQ* (1950–80); *Journal of the Transactions of the Victoria Institute* (1950–57); *Palestine Exploration Quarterly* (1957–71).

co-edited major reference works such as the *New Bible Dictionary* as well as serving as series editor for the *New International Commentary on the New Testament*—not bad for someone with no degree in biblical studies!

Where he did it
Bruce positively relished the opportunity to teach the Bible in a secular university. Quoting from his inaugural lecture as professor: 'To teach this subject above all subjects in the academic freedom which we value so highly . . . is the most rewarding and exhilarating work in the world.'[11] He had no problem with the stipulation that the teaching should be marked by scholarly objectivity and be 'non-doctrinal'; indeed, 'It would not have occurred to me that Biblical History and Literature could be taught otherwise in an academic context'.[12] But how did he justify the study of the Bible in this context, apart from the faith-communities among whom its constituent documents had been produced and interpreted?

Firstly, as he argued in his inaugural lecture as professor at Sheffield, the Bible formed a significant element of the matrix which had given rise to Western civilization, a good part of which was unintelligible apart from a sound grasp of the content of the Bible.[13] So everyone who wanted to understand their civilization—and where better to do that than a university?—needed to know the Bible. You only have to watch *University Challenge* and see the hash students sometimes make of answering questions about the Bible to see his point!

Secondly, he believed that all truth came from God, and therefore all valid insights could be welcomed from whatever quarter they came. And the conclusions need not be set in stone before starting. He explained his understanding of academic freedom as being that 'in the teaching and study of the Bible, as in the teaching and study of any other subject, one is not bound to follow any particular school of thought or promote any particular party line. It means that one's only commitment is to truth, that one is free to follow the evidence wherever it leads, in an atmosphere of free inquiry.'[14]

It is clear that he regarded this freedom as a particular delight, and one which resonated with his own approach to Christian spirituality. For him as a Christian, the concept of freedom was a key to the interpretation of Scripture, what we may call a hermeneutical principle: he argued at one point that where faced with a choice of equally plausible interpretations, the one which did more to promote Christian freedom was to be preferred.[15] And at the end of his time at Manchester, he could write, 'In a secular university I have had greater liberty to say and write exactly what I think than ever I should have had in most theological colleges.'[16] One reason why Bruce felt so much at home in the university

---

11. F. F. Bruce, *New Horizons in Biblical Studies* (Sheffield, 1957), 1.
12. Bruce, *In Retrospect*, 140.
13. Bruce, *New Horizons*, 1. One of his aims for the Tyndale Fellowship was 'to urge the claims of Biblical studies to a permanent and influential place in the national system of education'. T. A. Noble, *Tyndale House and Fellowship: The First Sixty Years* (Leicester, 2006), 318.
14. Bruce, *In Retrospect*, 143.
15. Bruce, 'Problem Texts, 12: The Call to Freedom', *H*, 66/12 (Dec. 1987), 21.
16. F. F. Bruce, 'Accountability in University Life', *Spectrum*, 12/1 (Sept. 1979), 10–11, at 11.

context was that he did not need to look over his shoulder for fear of upsetting someone.[17] This was no idle fear; several of his acquaintances experienced problems as a result of expressing opinions deemed to be at variance with their position as faculty members in evangelical and Adventist institutions.[18]

How he did it

What did it mean for Bruce to be a biblical scholar? Quite simply, biblical scholarship was about following the evidence wherever it might lead. He was deeply influenced by his father's insistence on doing that, and was therefore prepared on occasion to adopt views which would not have been accepted by his fellow evangelicals, because he believed that this was where the evidence led him. For instance, he considered that there were three Isaiahs,[19] and accepted a second-century date for the book of Daniel in its final form.[20] However, Bruce was always diplomatic about how and where he expressed himself, and so he was discreet about propounding his conclusions! But I suspect that he may have been allowed more latitude in his opinions by his fellow Brethren and other evangelicals because of his eminence in the academic world and the fact that he already had a reputation for soundness.

So how did Bruce set about Bible study? In a word, inductively. He tried to let each piece of evidence speak for itself before bringing them together in some kind of general framework. This was due in part to his upbringing and in part to his training in the classics. Apart from giving him a comprehensive acquaintance with Greek and Latin literature, this taught him to pay careful attention to archaeology and philology (the study of language). Looking back, Bruce argued that there was 'no better foundation than a classical education for the professional cultivation of biblical studies'.[21] In his presidential address to the Society for New Testament Studies in 1975 he argued that classicists were particularly well placed to study the New Testament because it was part of the same world.[22] As a result, his written work is marked by extensive engagement with the ancient texts, what historians call the 'primary sources'. Indeed, his emphasis on studying the texts themselves rather than the writings of others about them meant that when he was revising some of his commentaries it seems that he took little account of developments in scholarly debate

---

17. Ward and Laurel Gasque, 'F. F. Bruce: A Mind for What Matters', *Christianity Today*, 7 Apr. 1989, 22–5, at 25.

18. The most notable was a fellow member of the Brethren, H. L. Ellison (1903–83), who in 1955 was forced to resign from London Bible College after writing an article on biblical inspiration which was condemned as 'Barthian'; see Anon., 'Towards Barthianism: Is "The Evangelical Quarterly" Softening the Ground?', *Monthly Record of the Free Church of Scotland*, Feb. 1955, 29–31, at 29. Bruce expressed himself unusually strongly in print regarding the way Ellison had been treated, and the incident remained at the back of his mind for the rest of his life; see further, Grass, *A Life*, 88–91.

19. Personal recollection of one who worked with Bruce during the early 1950s.

20. Douglas, 'A Man of Unchanging Faith', 17.

21. Bruce, *In Retrospect*, 145; see Grass, *A Life*, 190.

22. F. F. Bruce, 'The New Testament and Classical Studies: Society for New Testament Studies Presidential Address, 1975', *New Testament Studies*, 22 (1975–76), 229–42; repr. in id., *A Mind for What Matters: Collected Essays of F. F. Bruce* (Grand Rapids, MI, [*c*.1990]), 3–16.

since their first editions.²³ Mind you, it also means that his writings have tended to wear rather well because they have not given too much attention to changing scholarly fashions!

The entry in the *ODNB* by his friend and fellow evangelical, Howard Marshall of Aberdeen, argues that Bruce's classical background 'tended to liberate him from the theological bias and even prejudice that can interfere with objective biblical study'.²⁴ And whilst Bruce usually came to conservative conclusions (as did several other contemporary classicists who studied the New Testament),²⁵ he did so on the basis of a methodology which his academic colleagues accepted; thus some evangelicals joined with James Barr in regarding him as a conservative liberal.²⁶

So how did this inductive approach shape Bruce's academic writings? Well, he would bring together a wide range of evidence, sometimes in narrative form, including comments on scholarly interpretation along the way. There is an emphasis on what the primary sources say. Often a conclusion is lacking, perhaps because he was not usually trying to build an argument but to present the evidence. And often he did so as a historian, telling the story, rather than as a systematizer. His major work on Paul, for example, was seen by some as offering a narrative approach of how Paul's thought developed rather than a systematic presentation of its major themes.²⁷ It was a case of 'here's the evidence; now you must make up your own mind', an approach which he also adopted with his children. But his work is always undergirded by a belief that at the centre of the Scriptures is their witness to Christ's saving work.

There is another point we must make about this inductive approach. The decision by Sheffield to set up a Department of Biblical Studies in isolation from any corresponding department of theology matched the confidence of many Brethren in advocating study of the Bible apart (as they thought) from the constraints of human traditions. Several Brethren therefore chose to study at Sheffield during a period when many assemblies were particularly aware of the value of academic study. But for Bruce, as for other Brethren, a major reason for giving priority to inductive study of the Bible over adherence to particular doctrinal formulations was that it was the Bible through which, uniquely, the Holy Spirit spoke to the human heart.

Now it would be possible to adopt an inductive approach to studying the Bible and yet to keep this rigidly separated from one's devotional life or ministry. Evangelical theological students used to be notorious for doing that, and I remember being warned about it when I began theological study in 1978. But Bruce saw no need to keep them separate; in his work each interpenetrated the other. And this sense of integration is also evident in his emphasis on mediating the fruits of academic study to a wider audience. He did so not only in churches, where he was a frequent conference speaker, but also through what used

---

23. Annotated copies of some of them in my possession show that he was aware of new work, but the lack of revision in the published versions may indicate that he saw no reason to alter what he had written in the light of it.

24. I. Howard Marshall, 'Bruce, Frederick Fyvie (1910–1990)', *ODNB*, <www.oxforddnb.com>, accessed 14 Apr. 2008.

25. E.g. G. B. Caird, C. H. Dodd, Bruce Metzger and E. V. Rieu.

26. See Grass, *A Life*, 149, 219, and the references cited there.

27. See Grass, *A Life*, 162–3.

to be called 'extra-mural' lectures and courses for the general public. He saw no tension between his lecturing and his preaching; the audiences might have been different, and the language used might have been different, but the basic approach was not.

> Naturally, when I discharge a teaching ministry in church I avoid the technicalities of academic discourse and I apply the message of Scripture in a more practical way. But there is no conflict between my critical or exegetical activity in a university context and my Bible exposition in church; the former makes a substantial contribution to the latter. At the same time, membership in a local church, involvement in the activities of a worshipping community, helps the academic theologian to remember what his subject is all about, and keeps his studies properly 'earthed'.[28]

And the same thing is true of his writings, especially his commentaries on books of the New Testament. Those which began life as series of articles in *The Witness* or *Believer's Magazine* do not take a fundamentally different approach from those written for an academic readership.

Bruce and others sought to facilitate the integration of Christian faith and critical scholarship through the work of Tyndale House and the Tyndale Fellowship. In an important article for the *Evangelical Quarterly*, which appeared in 1947, Bruce argued that commitment to the fellowship's evangelical doctrinal basis in no way precluded what he called 'unfettered study' of Scripture.[29] In his view, acceptance of the Bible as God-breathed, and its study in a spirit of loyalty to the historic Christian creeds and confessions, did not predetermine either the answers to questions about biblical interpretation or the methods of study to be used. He argued that such an outlook was itself scriptural: 'The biblical message inculcates, among other things, a love of truth for its own sake and a willingness to follow the evidence wherever it may lead.'[30]

Nowadays eyebrows might be raised at the ease with which he felt able to switch between the academy and the church. But if we look at the historical context, the 1950s was the heyday of the 'Biblical Theology' movement.[31] This sought to rediscover the essential message of Scripture without returning to older fundamentalist ways of treating it. Bruce found himself in considerable sympathy with the biblical theologians in their efforts to derive a unified theology from Scripture taken as a whole.[32] The 1950s were also a relatively conservative decade culturally; churches prospered, and religious stories

---

28. Bruce, *In Retrospect*, 143–4.
29. F. F. Bruce, 'The Tyndale Fellowship for Biblical Research', *EQ*, 19 (1947), 52–61; repr. in Noble, *Tyndale House and Fellowship*, 314–25.
30. F. F. Bruce, 'My View: Faith vs Scientific Study of the Bible', *Bible Review*, 3 (Summer 1987), 4–5, at 4.
31. Leading lights included John Bright, Alan Richardson, and Brevard Childs: Grass, *A Life*, 85.
32. In 1955, for example, he saw one of the most important developments in biblical interpretation as being the increasing recognition of the unity of the biblical message and the looking to Scripture for a word from God in the present situation: F. F. Bruce, 'Trends in New Testament Interpretation', *Journal of the Transactions of the Victoria Institute*, 87 (1955), 37–48, esp. 41–8.

were big news; to some extent it is fair to say that Bruce surfed these waves, as, perhaps, did his department at Sheffield.

But if Bruce's approach was the same whether in church or in academic life, and if all truth is to be welcomed whatever its source, we might well ask what the Christian brings to the task of reading and interpreting the Bible that the non-Christian does not? Bruce did not think the believer starts with a particular understanding of the inspiration of Scripture. This is something to be established on an inductive basis from careful study of the text.[33] Nor does the believer come to Scripture with a particular and predetermined set of conclusions about its interpretation.

What the believer brings to the study of Scripture, according to Bruce, is a distinctive motivation for such study. Bible study involves the same disciplines as the study of other literature of the period: philology, archaeology, textual criticism, and so on. And Bruce would insist that we should try to be objective in these, because all truth comes from God. To understand the biblical documents, it was necessary to ask questions about their date, authorship, provenance, and so on, the answers to which could only be found by a study of the evidence and could not be laid down by any external authority. But the Christian has an added incentive to engage in such critical study,[34] rather than a reason for not doing so, which is what some evangelicals have asserted. Faith involves sharpening, not suspension, of the critical faculty, and it is the man of faith who is best able to pass judgement (1 Cor. 2.15). Ultimately, then, he saw no tension between critical study and personal faith.[35] So his appreciation of Scottish 'believing critics' such as William Robertson Smith (1846–94) comes as no surprise.[36] One book to which he confessed himself indebted was by the Primitive Methodist scholar A. S. Peake, who sought to combine critical study and evangelical faith: *The Bible: Its Origin, its Significance, and its abiding Worth*. Peake too acknowledged that he had earlier benefited greatly from the work of Robertson Smith, but that in writing his book he had sought to look at the evidence afresh and come to his own conclusions—as Bruce had been taught to do.[37]

Secondly, although the believer does not approach Scripture with a particular set of ideas about what it teaches, he or she does bring a particular conviction about its overall message. Bruce argued that according to John 5:39, the primary purpose of the Scriptures is to bear witness to Christ; without faith we are in the same position as the Pharisees, who searched the Scriptures and missed the point of their message. As he commented on John 5:37–38, '[i]t was possible to have a minute knowledge of the letter of those writings which enshrined the former revelation and foreshadowed the final revelation, and yet not have the divine word which those writings recorded dwelling in their hearts.'[38] It is the work of the Holy Spirit to enable us to grasp this overall message of Scripture, this witness to Christ which it bears. As Bruce asked, 'who is so well qualified to interpret the

---

33. Bruce, *In Retrospect*, 311.
34. Bruce, *In Retrospect*, 144.
35. F. F. Bruce, 'Criticism and Faith', *Christianity Today*, 21 Nov. 1960, 9–12.
36. F. F. Bruce, *The Canon of Scripture* (Glasgow, 1988), 273; see Grass, *A Life*, 19.
37. Bruce, *In Retrospect*, 59; Bruce, *Canon of Scripture*, 317; A. S. Peake, *The Bible: Its Origin, its Significance, and its abiding Worth* (4th edn., London, 1913), x–xi.
38. F. F. Bruce, *The Gospel of John* (Basingstoke, 1983), 136.

sacred volume as the primary and perpetual Author?' But 'the wisdom which the Spirit imparts can be acquired only by diligent study, with humble and receptive minds'.[39] And the Spirit uses the aids to biblical interpretation, rather than bypassing them, to bring us to fuller knowledge of Christ.[40]

So, for Bruce, what the believer brings to the study of the Bible is not something *different* so much as something *additional*: an expectation of hearing God speak which springs from acquaintance with the divine author and involves openness to the illumination of the mind by the Holy Spirit and willingness to be obedient. A non-Christian can understand the text, and their scholarship may be helpful to us, but it is the work of the Spirit to convince readers that this is the Word of God and to enable them to submit to it; here we are not far from the teaching of his beloved Westminster Confession.

Bruce's belief in the illumination of the Spirit, coupled with the commitment to freedom that we noted earlier, meant that he opposed anything which smacked of a legalistic approach to Scripture. He could not sympathize with what he saw as a reduction of the Christian life to the observance of certain rules and patterns—even when it was Brethren who were doing it. That comes out in the 'Answers to Questions' column which he wrote for the Brethren monthly *The Harvester* from 1952 to 1975; correspondents would write in requesting his opinions about everything from tithing to miniskirts.[41] He always avoided giving them the legal ruling they wanted![42] For him, the Christian life was about being led by the Spirit, and, in the words of one of his favourite verses, 'where the Spirit of the Lord is, there the heart is free'.[43] This was not freedom to do whatever one wanted, but freedom to glorify Christ. As for church life, he thought it was wrong-headed to look for a detailed pattern for it in the New Testament and then to try to replicate it today. He pointed to the Brethren writer Henry Craik, whose *New Testament Church Order* (published in 1863) argued that the New Testament can be understood as providing support for several different patterns of church life. The only discernible pattern in Scripture was one of flexibility, following the guidance of the Spirit as new situations arise. What mattered was principles, not patterns.[44]

---

39. F. F. Bruce, *1 and 2 Corinthians*, New Century Bible (London, 1971), 39–40 (on 1 Cor. 2: 11–12).

40. F. F. Bruce, 'Divine Interpretation', *H*, 47/1 (Jan. 1968), 2. Incidentally, Bruce believed that it was this quality of apostolic witness to Christ, recognized by the whole church—not, significantly, their recognition as divinely inspired—which ensured that certain documents came to be recognized as forming part of the canon of Scripture. F. F. Bruce, 'The Bible and the Faith', *Free Church Chronicle*, 31/4 (Winter 1976), 8–16, repr. in *A Mind for What Matters*, 269–79; id., *Canon of Scripture*; see Grass, *A Life*, 205–6.

41. *H*, 31/9 (Sept. 1952), 104; 47/2 (Feb. 1968), 26.

42. See his comments in the Foreword to *Answers to Questions* (Exeter, 1972).

43. 2 Cor. 3: 17, Basic English Version; quoted on the title page of *Paul.*

44. See 'The Local Church in the New Testament', in P. O. Ruoff (ed.), *The New Testament Church in the Present Day* (n.pl., 1954), 24–41; 'Lessons from the Early Church', in David J. Ellis and W. Ward Gasque (eds.), *In God's Community: Essays on the Church and its Ministry* (London, 1978), 153–68, esp. 157, 159.

Bruce's doctrine of Scripture

Given what was said earlier about not starting with predetermined conclusions, readers will not be surprised that I have left discussing Bruce's doctrine of Scripture until the end!

Bruce's doctrine of Scripture was something which he drew out inductively from the evidence rather than an *a priori* commitment with which he approached the evidence.[45] In other words, he looked to see what the Scriptures said about themselves and worked from that. He respected other authorities, notably his beloved and oft-quoted Westminster Confession and Shorter Catechism; indeed, he learned the latter by heart at primary school.[46] In 1951 he ended a chapter on 'The Scriptures' in a symposium by Brethren on key Christian doctrines by quoting the relevant chapter of the Westminster Confession as the best available summary of Christian teaching about the Bible and its interpretation.[47] Thirty years later, he expressed the opinion that the confession began with 'the finest statement on the doctrine of Scripture ever published'.[48] Nevertheless, he insisted that theologians and the confessions of faith which they produced were all subject to correction in the light of the teaching of Scripture.[49] So for Bruce, Scripture was the supreme authority.

But some wanted a more precise understanding, and in the 1970s the word 'inerrancy' became for some evangelicals a defining mark of a sound doctrine of Scripture. There was what the American writer Harold Lindsell called *The Battle for the Bible*. In certain quarters there were moves to tighten up doctrinal statements and flush out individuals whose views were seen as unsound. Bruce resisted this and resisted attempts to impose the new term; he was happy simply with the word 'truth', which of course he could have defended as representing what Scripture says about itself. But for him it was not enough simply to say that Scripture was truth because it was God-breathed or 'inspired'. His doctrine of Scripture was closely linked with his understanding of the work of the Holy Spirit:

> Biblical inspiration is not an activity which took place once for all, when the words were spoken or written; it is an on-going quality of the Scriptures, as the Spirit continues to impart and maintain life through them, and it includes the work of the Spirit in the reader or hearer of the Scriptures, empowering him to respond to the prophetic invitation: 'Hear, and your soul shall live.'[50]

We might say then, that inspiration and illumination were inseparable in his thinking.

It is appropriate to sum up Bruce's beliefs about Scripture in his own words, written in a tribute to W. E. Vine: 'The Scriptures' chief function is to bear witness of Christ, and the chief end of their study and exegesis is to increase our inward knowledge of him, under the illumination of the Spirit of God'.[51]

---

45. See further Bruce, *In Retrospect*, 311; Grass, *A Life*, 94–5.
46. Ward and Laurel Gasque, 'F. F. Bruce – the Apostle Paul and the Evangelical Heritage', *H*, 68/7 (July 1989), 10–12, at 10.
47. In F. A. Tatford (ed.), *The Faith: A Symposium* (London, 1951), 13–26.
48. Douglas, 'A Man of Unchanging Faith', 17.
49. F. F. Bruce to the editor, *H*, 54/7 (July 1975), 198.
50. CBA, Box 11(11g), Bruce to Ian S. Davidson, 28 July 1987.
51. 'W. E. Vine—The Theologian', in Percy O. Ruoff, *W. E. Vine: His Life and Ministry* (London, 1951), 69–85, at 85.

So how might we learn from Bruce today?

There are areas where even those who approach biblical study as committed Christians would want to tackle things differently. Things have moved on somewhat since the 1950s, and historians are often rather more critical than was the case then. Bruce has been criticized as overly sanguine in his positive estimate of the historicity of the New Testament documents, failing to give due weight to the concerns of those who found matters less straightforward than he did.[52] His acceptance of a unified narrative into which the various parts of the Bible can be fitted is also likely to come under fire from various directions in our postmodern climate with its suspicion of the 'big picture'. However, Bruce gave confidence to many Christians regarding the foundations of their faith, and he blazed a trail for evangelicals to pursue a career in academic biblical scholarship. His influence upon the evangelical world was epochal, in that his example, and his willingness to supervise research students, drew numbers of evangelicals of all shades into the realm of academic biblical studies. So one thing we can draw from Bruce is that we need not be afraid of critical study, properly undertaken. If all truth is indeed God's truth, then we may look to increase our understanding of truth in this way; we need not be afraid of where our search for truth will lead. In consequence, we need not fall into the practice of compartmentalizing the way we study the Bible in the academic sphere (for examinations and so on) and the way we study the Bible 'devotionally'. These go better together.

Secondly, commitment to truth is more important than loyalty to a particular standpoint, although we should have the humility to acknowledge that our understanding is imperfect. When Bruce was differing from some standard Brethren view, perhaps in the field of biblical prophecy, he sometimes added the rider that this was how he saw it, and others might see things differently. That was not only him being diplomatic, but also an honest recognition that his understanding was subject to correction in the light of Scripture.

Thirdly, such a commitment to truth should make us, as it made him, thorough and careful in our study of the material. If we believe that the Bible rightly understood brings us a message from God, we dare not be slapdash in the way we read and teach it. It will not do to offer, as in the caricature of Brethren ministry at the morning meeting, 'a few scattered thoughts'. That challenges me as a preacher: preparation is not firstly about finding a catchy outline for our sermon with alliterating headings, but about wrestling with the text and working out what it actually says and how its argument develops. We must not rely on the Holy Spirit to give us a clear word for our hearers if we refuse to work at developing this for ourselves.

Another point concerns the whole question of 'freedom', and the underlying question of how we read the Scriptures. Whatever we may think about the concept of freedom as a key to interpreting Scripture, Bruce is certainly onto something when he criticizes the approach which treats the New Testament as a rule-book, whether in individual life or in church life. For Bruce, the New Testament presents principles rather than patterns. To read the Bible in this way helps us to avoid reducing Christian living and church life to following the rules. This does not lead to a 'do what you like' attitude because the Holy Spirit who is given to individuals and the church helps us to live out the unchanging principles by which God relates to us in a constantly-changing world.

---

52. See Grass, *A Life*, 160–1.

Perhaps a final point to learn from Bruce is, quite simply, to delight in the study of Scripture as he so obviously did. There is a responsibility lying upon those of us who teach and preach it to present it in such a way that our audiences can catch that sense of delight. As I read Bruce, I sense that he delighted in studying Scripture, in living scripturally, and in sharing it with others. It is small wonder, then, that his ministry was so widely influential.

CHAPTER 11

Use of the Bible among the New Brethren in Flanders

T. J. Marinello

Few would argue that the Bible has held a central place in the beliefs and practices of the Brethren since their commonly accorded beginnings in the early nineteenth century.[1] In fact, Rowdon has posited that the 'Bible reading' or Bible study was the 'most *characteristic* religious activity,' in the early history of the movement.[2] Given this emphasis among the early Brethren, and given the Brethren's place within evangelicalism with its 'biblicism',[3] this emphasis on the centrality of the Bible for beliefs and practices was, unsurprisingly, also an emphasis in the origins and development of the Evangelische Christengemeenten Vlaanderen (ECV), the name of the new assemblies planted primarily in Flanders at the end of the twentieth century by Brethren missionaries from Canada.[4] In particular, the Bible was used in at least two ways in this almost exclusively Roman Catholic setting: evangelistically and centrally.

---

1. The time and circumstances of the beginnings of the Brethren, however, is a debated point within the Brethren and ranges from the descent of the Holy Spirit as recorded in Acts 2 in an apostolic succession of ideas and ideals, to groups in Dublin and perhaps simultaneously in Plymouth, Bristol, and Barnstaple as well. For a rehearsal of the Brethren as part of an apostolic succession of ideas and ideals, see E. H. Broadbent, *The Pilgrim Church: Being Some Account of the Continuance through the Succeeding Centuries of Churches Practising the Principles Taught and Exemplified in the New Testament* (London, 1931), 44. For a Dublin origin in the mid- to-late1820s, see Tim Grass, *Gathering to His Name: The Story of the Open Brethren in Britain and Ireland* (Milton Keyes, 2006), 12–29; W. J. Ouweneel, *Het Verhaal van de 'Broeders': 150 jaar falen en genade*[*The Story of the 'Brethren': 150 Years of Failure and Mercy*], i, *1826–1889*. For a more or less simultaneous '[recognition of] truths in the New Testament' in several locations, see Robert H. Baylis, *My People: A History of those Christians Sometimes Called Plymouth Brethren* (Wheaton, IL, 1995), 7–13.
2. Harold H. Rowdon, *Who are the Brethren and Does It Matter?* (Exeter, 1986), 33. Italics in original.
3. David Bebbington, *Evangelicalism in Modern Britain: A History from the 1730s to the 1980s* (Grand Rapids, MI, 1992), 12–13.
4. 'The *Evangelische Christengemeenten Vlaanderen* (ECV) began in the early 1970s as a result of evangelistic church-planting efforts led by a group of Canadian, Christian Brethren missionaries. What began in Flanders as a series of evangelistic home Bible studies grew into a fully recognized denomination within a few decades of the first study.' Thomas J. Marinello, *New Brethren in Flanders: A History of the Origins and Development of the* Evangelische Christengemeenten Vlaanderen, *1971–2008* (Eugene, OR, 2014), ix.

Using the Bible evangelistically

The founders of the ECV were at their heart, evangelists. Their purpose in ministry was the proclamation of the gospel of Jesus Christ in the hope that the Spirit of God would create evangelical converts with a goal of then planting local churches all over Flanders.[5] Accordingly, the Bible was used apologetically—quite pointedly at times—in order to attract people to a series of evangelistic home Bible studies. The apologetic aspect dealt with raising an interest in a biblical, conservative, evangelical faith in contradistinction to the beliefs of the almost exclusively Roman Catholic listeners.

For example, one of the founders in particular, Richard Haverkamp, used pointed, unexpected questions to garner the attention of whomever it was he was having a conversation. The answers to his questions, then, were found in the Bible. Haverkamp's questions to his Roman Catholic listeners included, 'Do you know that Jesus had brothers and sisters?' He then would show them the answer from the Bible. Haverkamp followed this question with, 'Did you know that your first pope, Peter, was married?' He notes that 'fifty percent of the time the reaction was, "What else is in the Bible?"'[6] Even topics as potentially sensitive as the pope or the listener's relationship with and admiration of Mary, the mother of Jesus, were not off limits to Haverkamp's apologetic use of the Bible. Johan Lukasse—a long-term Dutch missionary to Belgium serving with the Belgische Evangelische Zending—said,

> He would talk with people, and they would say, 'I believe in the pope', or 'I believe in Mary' or something just to get rid of him. He'd say, 'That is wonderful. Where is the pope in the Bible?' He would open his Bible and turn the pages in a salesman style to demonstrate that he has gone through it many times with all his lines and exclamation points and colours and everything. 'Where is the pope? Where is the pope? I read this so many times and never have found him. Can you show me where the pope is?'[7]

In one of his more memorable confrontations, Haverkamp asked a very devout Roman Catholic man what he thought after this listener had attended his first night of an evangelistic Bible study. This man came from a family of many priests and nuns among his parents' generation and his own generation as well. This 'quiet Belgian' responded that he believed in 'our dear Lady'. Haverkamp responded, 'That is an abomination', opened his Bible to Deuteronomy 18 and said, 'Here, you pray to the dead. That is an abomination to God'![8]

The founders and early leaders of the ECV also used the Bible apologetically and evangelistically in a series of home Bible studies, the 'startstudies'. This was a ten-lesson Bible study from the first three chapters of the Gospel of John which was held in the home of a willing contact. After finding a contact, the Bible study leader would tell the person in whose home the study would be held to invite family and friends. Upon arriving,

---

5. See Richard Haverkamp, interview by author, St. Martens Latem, BE, 25 Apr. 2003.

6. Richard Haverkamp, 'Wie der Herr Jesus Christus Gemeinden baut', CD-ROM, eight lectures and one question and answer period (Deutsche Gemeinde-Mission, KfG Ostdeutschland, 2002), session 2. The sessions on this CD are numbered in order of occurrence: Seven lectures, one question and answer period, and one lecture.

7. Johan Lukasse, interview by author, Badhoevedorp, NL, 5 Dec. 2003.

8. Henk Gelling, interview by author, Houthalen, BE, 11 Sept. 2002. See Deut. 18: 9–12.

the Bible teacher would begin by giving everyone present a free copy of the Bible. The reasoning was that by having all use the exact same Bible edition and text, listeners would not be embarrassed when verses were sought out since the many Bible passages in any night's study would be referenced not merely as chapter and verse, but according to the page numbers. The lessons were a methodical, biblical presentation of the claims of the evangelical faith. They were 1) the existence of God and the veracity of the Bible; 2) the person of Christ; 3) the three kinds of life and death; 4) how to become a child of God; 5) sin; 6) the Lamb of God; 7) the Holy Spirit; 8) four testimonies confirming Jesus as the Christ; 9) the lessons of the wedding miracle at Canaan and the cleansing of the temple; and 10) the new birth.[9] The tone of these studies had a definite apologetic edge to them, and the presentations took the listener from one end of the Bible to the other. The teacher was told to expect that the Holy Spirit would use the Bible in the lives of the listeners. As Haverkamp often would say, 'God's Word is a hammer, a fire, and a sword; learn to use it'.[10] One careful observer—a long-term Dutch missionary to Belgium serving with another mission—said,

> The home Bible study was [Haverkamp's] strength. . . . Once he has a little group in the home, he would explain the gospel to them in different ways and challenge them to bring others along. . . . And so in the home, challenging people, and just going back and forth through the Bible . . . He was like a locomotive going through.[11]

Because of the apologetic tone of the studies, a careful progression was followed; the central tenets of Roman Catholicism were not challenged directly until the leader of the studies was sure the attendees were committed to coming and listening.[12] For example, challenges to the traditional Roman Catholic teachings on the role of Mary were not put forward until the ninth lesson.[13] This would have been after at least sixteen hours of teaching plus times of question and answer over the eight previous sessions. The ECV Bible teachers used this time both to teach the tenets of evangelical belief as well as to develop a relationship with those who attended. Over time, startstudies were led by the Brethren missionaries from North America as well as the Flemish and Dutch workers associated with the ECV.

Coming forward to the second decade of the twenty-first century, the startstudies are not used as frequently by the assemblies of the ECV. Whereas the 1970s and 1980s in Flanders were times of genuine revival, the twenty-first century has not seen a comparable

---

9. Richard Haverkamp, 'Startstudies: 10 Evangelische Bibjbelstudies vanuit Johannes 1–3' (1979?). While Haverkamp was the sole author, this series of Bible studies later was published as the book, Yvan Thomas and Richard Haverkamp, *10 startstudies, handleiding voor het doorgeven van geloofsprincipes* (Ieper, BE, 1995). See Richard Haverkamp, 'RE: *Startstudies*', e-mail to author, 31 July 2008.

10. Haverkamp, 'Startstudies', Enkele praktische opmerkingen, 2.

11. Lukasse, 5 Dec. 2003.

12. Haverkamp, 'Wie der Herr Jesus Christus Gemeinden baut', session 6.

13. Haverkamp, 'Startstudies', lesson 9.

in-gathering of evangelical converts to date.[14] The Flemish listeners are not anxious to consider the claims of the evangelical faith, so evangelistic Bible studies are far less frequent and far less well attended when they do occur.[15] This decline in attendees, however, was seen even in late-twentieth-century Flanders, and the decline only has increased. Looking back after what was then two decades in Belgium, Peter Gifford—one of the Canadian Brethren missionaries in Flanders who works with the ECV—noted a lack of interest and a change in attitudes. He observed,

> Where there was an openness for the Gospel twenty years ago, there is an overwhelming apathy today. Belgium, a formerly Catholic country, has thrown religion overboard and lives in the illusion of self-sufficiency—'I have everything I need. I don't need God'.[16]

Henk Medema, another prominent figure and observer of the Brethren in the Netherlands and Flanders, said in the early twenty-first century,

> What I am hearing from [Haverkamp and Gelling] and also from other brothers from the Christengemeente is that times are changing. It used to be a lot easier to get people into a room, and get them to listen to Bible teaching, and have a nice time together. Factually, this was kind of an Alpha Course [evening]. They followed the principles of an Alpha Course—having a good meal, talking to people in a very Flemish style—and people were able to identify with this. . . . Now [Haverkamp and Gelling] are saying, and I also observe, the open doors are closing. I also see this in Belgium at large.[17]

This mention of the Alpha Course style, then, brings up other questions. Why is it that the ECV did not use the Alpha Course in the late twentieth century, especially when the numbers of the ECV's new evangelical converts dropped precipitously, and why is it not being used in this second decade of the twenty-first century?[18] The answer is that the ECV did not and does not use the Alpha Course due both to the content and to the emphases in this well-known study.

First, the initial setting of the two studies is different. The Alpha Course began as a Bible study in an already established local church, Holy Trinity, an Anglican church in Brompton, London. The startstudies began as a home Bible study as a way to introduce the listeners to an evangelical faith with the goal that the ensuing converts would be formed into a new local church. Second, the purpose of the two studies is different. As sociologist

---

14. The working definition of revival for this essay is best described as 'not the employment of unusual or special means but rather the extraordinary degree of blessing attending the normal means of grace'. See Iain H. Murray, *Revival and Revivalism: The Making and Marring of American Evangelicalism 1750–1858* (Carlisle, 1994), 129.

15. Peter Gifford, SKYPE interview by author, 22 June 2015; Henk Gelling, SKYPE interview by author, 21 June 2015.

16. Peter and Joanna Gifford, letter to supporters, May 2005.

17. Henk Medema, interview by author, Vaassen, NL, 18 Sept. 2003. Medema was the head of the main Brethren publishing group in the Dutch-speaking world and one of the five 'leading brothers' among the Kelly-Continental Brethren in the Netherlands before the break-up of the early 1990s. See Marinello, *New Brethren in Flanders*, 208–11.

18. The author thanks Neil Dickson for raising this line of questioning.

Stephen Hunt noted in his 2005 study, while 'the working philosophy [of the Alpha Course] is to advance the principles and "basics" of the faith in an informal environment to the unchurched "seeker" in an exploratory and non-threatening way', it also was 'a refresher course for those who are already committed Christians'.[19] In fact, the Alpha Course started in 1977 as a means to educate 'new converts into the foundations of the faith and only later extended to non-converts'.[20] In contrast, the *Startstudies* content is aimed solely at the person who is not yet converted, and these ten lessons were designed for the Roman Catholic, Dutch-speaking people of Flanders in particular. This was not a translated, imported study even though its primary initiator was a Dutch-born, Canadian missionary—Richard Haverkamp.[21] Third, the Alpha Course's strong charismatic emphases culminating in a weekend away after which the participants were treated as converts, were not in line with the emphases put forward by the founders and later leaders of the ECV (or the emphases of historic, evangelical Christianity, for that matter). Additionally, the ECV held a stronger stance against charismatic-type beliefs and practices when the Alpha Course was becoming popular than was held later on in the first decade of the twenty-first century.[22]

One factor which caused the ECV to be wary of the Alpha Course was the damage to ECV assemblies caused by people who championed the views and practices of what commonly was called 'the Toronto-blessing',[23] a movement concurrent with the coming of the Alpha Course and a movement which many say shaped the Alpha Course.[24] More important than this unfortunate experience and others like it, however, was the actual content of the course. When Alpha first came to the fore, Henk Gelling—another of the founders of the ECV—and others went to a presentation in the Netherlands to see if it was a suitable tool. After hearing the presentation, they concluded it was not.[25] Gifford commented that the heavy charismatic emphasis and the de-emphasis on sin made the course not something the ECV could use in its standard form. He also noted presently that 'Some [ECV] churches are using [the Alpha course], but they've made it like a "Beta Course" adjusting it to a more biblical take on what sin is and what sin has caused'.[26] Further, the weekend away is not part of the ECV's version of Alpha.

---

19. Stephen Hunt, 'The Alpha Course and its Critics: An Overview of the Debates', *PentecoStudies*, 4 (2005), 1, <https://www.glopent.net/pentecostudies/online-back-issues/2005/hunt2005.pdf/download>, accessed 23 June 2015.

20. Hunt, 'The Alpha Course and its Critics', 5.

21. See Marinello, *New Brethren in Flanders*, 64.

22. For example, when the Verbond van Vlaamse Pinkstergemeenten (VVP) became part of the Evangelische Alliantie Vlaanderen in 2002, representatives of the ECV then had regular contact with the Pentecostal churches. Together they tried to further the cause of evangelical Christianity in Flanders. 'VVP—Gemeenten sluiten zich aan bij EAV', in *EAV-nieuws*, (ed.) Don Zeeman, Mar.–Apr. 2002, 4.

23. For example, thirty to forty of the practitioners of this more radical part of the charismatic movement left one assembly in West-Vlaanderen as well as caused damage among those who remained. Henk Gelling, telephone interview by author, 15 Dec. 2008. Henk Gelling, interview by author, Houthalen, BE, 1 May 2001.

24. Hunt, 'The Alpha Course and its Critics', 4–5.

25. Gelling, 21 June 2015.

26. Gifford, 22 June 2015.

Using the Bible centrally

Just as their Brethren forbears kept the Bible central in their thinking, so, too, did the Brethren founders of the ECV reflected a similar emphasis in their thought and practices: the Bible was central in their thinking and work.

First, the Bible was central in the personal lives of the founders of the ECV. Haverkamp's somewhat dramatic conversion, for example, came largely through his own reading of the Bible in private.[27] He recalled, 'I started reading and sure didn't understand much, but it was funny, the more I read, the more I wanted to read. There is some mysterious power in that book! Not only did it seem to draw me to read it more and more, it started doing something in my heart.'[28] Also, Haverkamp's initial decision to leave Canada for Flanders was associated with a vision from God or a really strong impression in 1971 during one of his daily times of personal prayer and Bible reading, his 'quiet time'.[29] Thus, while meditating on the word of God in the presence of God, Haverkamp understood he was called to southern Holland or Flanders.

Similarly, another of the founders of the ECV, Henk Gelling, also received his call to Flanders during a time of personal Bible reading and prayer. While he was willing to go to Flanders, he wanted an assurance that this was the Lord's will for his life, especially given his active role in the local assembly in Clinton, Ontario, and his successful milk transport business and very successful chicken farm. One Sunday night as he wrestled with what he thought was the Lord's call to go to Flanders, Gelling got on his knees instead of sleeping, opened a Bible, and sought the Lord's will. Interestingly, he said he avoided Acts as he was sure reading there would make him leave Canada and go to Belgium. Instead of reading in Acts, he decided to read in Mark. The passage that made the difference was Mark 1:36–38 (KJV): '[36] And Simon and they that were with him followed after him. [37] And when they had found him, they said unto him, All men seek for thee. [38] And he said unto them, Let us go into the next towns, that I may preach there also: for therefore came I forth.' Gelling realized that this was completely out of context. 'Somebody theologically would say, "This is crazy." But it was just like the Lord said, "I want you to go."'[30] Gelling both understood and was thankful that the Lord gave him an answer early in his time of reading and prayer as he had to work the next day! Gelling agreed with 'what the Lord told him' and never again looked back at his decision in doubt.[31]

In fact, Gelling's commitment to get his understanding from the Bible even had been central to his becoming part of the Brethren after his conversion. Gelling was raised in the Netherlands in the Christelijke Gereformeerde Kerk, he was educated at a Christian school as a child and he had committed evangelicals within his extended family, and so

---

27. Richard Haverkamp, 'Musings of an "Older" Man', *richardandmarina: Our experiences with God over more than 50 years*, nrs. 3 and 4, (posted 30 Dec. 2013) <http://richardandmarina.net/category/musings/?order=asc>, accessed 25 June 2015; also, Marinello, *New Brethren in Flanders*, 64–5.

28. Haverkamp, 'Musings of an "Older" Man', nr. 3.

29. Haverkamp, 'Wie der Herr Jesus Christus Gemeinden baut,' session 8, 'Fragen und Antworten'.

30. Gelling, 25 Apr. 2003.

31. Koen Schelstraete, 'Handelingen (3)', *De Werkerskrant: nieuws-en gebedsbrief van het binnenlands zendingsteam van de ECV*, (ed.) Rosario Anastasi, May 2000, 3.

he was familiar with the claims of Christianity even before his conversion.[32] Nonetheless, he questioned one of the core beliefs both of his upbringing and the local Canadian church where he was a member after his evangelical conversion as an adult—his own infant baptism. After his evangelical conversion, his desire to undergo believer's baptism garnered him a warning that he would be dismissed from the local Christian Reformed Church in Canada where he and his wife were members. Though he met with the minister and elders of his local Christian Reformed Church, he remembers none were willing to show him from the Bible their reasoning for infant baptism. Much to Gelling's surprise, they would not even open the Bible with him.[33] Convinced that the Bible taught believer's baptism by immersion, Gelling and his wife were baptized at the local Brethren assembly and subsequently dismissed from their local Christian Reformed Church. Gelling says he learned an important lesson from this encounter, and one which would be central to his work in Flanders. Simply, when he began to plant churches in Belgium, he tried to find biblical justification for the practices and beliefs of these churches.[34] One need only review his personal journals over the years and talk with him as was done during the writing of this essay to see that this commitment to a biblically-based reason for belief and action both personally and among the assemblies of the ECV remained important to him. In fact, even ECV statements of belief constructed in the later years of the group as it formalized as an organization made Gelling uneasy.[35] He said that he liked it before the formal statement of faith was adopted since when people asked what the ECV believed, he could just hold up his Bible.[36] Still, the ECV's formal statement of faith and practice over the years has remained a document visibly based upon and supported by the Bible.[37]

Second, the Bible was central in the evangelistic work of the ECV. At this juncture some might note that most if not all evangelical groups have the Bible at the centre of their evangelical message, and this would be true. For the ECV, however, the Bible's centrality was not just in the content of the message, but also in the preparation of the messenger and even in many of the techniques presented in a book by one of the leaders of a local ECV assembly, Yvan Thomas, entitled *Evangelisatie: wat doen u eraan?* [*Evangelism: how do you do it?*][38] This 215-page book contains a wide variety of practical techniques and methods for evangelism including suggested door-to-door surveys, a suggested order in which the content of the evangelical gospel can be presented, and even suggested publicity materials in appendices running to some thirty-three pages.[39] Nonetheless, the

---

32. Gelling, 25 Apr. 2003.
33. Gelling, 25 Apr. 2003.
34. Gelling, 25 Apr. 2003.
35. See 'Identiteit en Werking van de Evangelische Christengemeenten', *Evangelische Christengemeenten Vlaanderen* <http://web.archive.org/web/20020414172605/http://home2.pi.be/pin21516/onze_geloofsbelijdenis.htm >, accessed 31 July 2018.
36. Gelling, 25 Apr. 2003.
37. In the latest 'Proposed Policy Plan', for example, each of this document's five sections is based upon a 'core text' (kerntekst). See 'Om U te dienen: Voorstel Beleidsplan 2014–17', 16 Nov. 2013.
38. Yvan Thomas, *Evangelisatie: wat doen u eraan?* (Ieper, BE, 1993). NB: Unless noted otherwise, all translations are by the present writer.
39. Thomas, *Evangelisatie*, 183–213.

reader regularly encounters a conscious appeal to the authority of Scripture for most types of the suggested evangelistic outreaches, and certainly for the general justification for evangelism as well as the preparation of the one who would present the evangelical gospel. For example, the justification for personal evangelism is based upon principles drawn from an extended exposition of John 4: 1–32.[40] Open-air evangelism is based upon principles drawn from the work of Paul and the apostles generally, and specifically from the example of Jesus Christ in Matthew 13: 1–8.[41] In contrast, most of the information under the section entitled open-air evangelism is of a quite practical nature after a thin biblical justification. Even door-to-door evangelism has a few verses scattered among the techniques described, techniques to include a summary of those used by Evangelism Explosion, the American organization that provides materials to aid Christians in evangelism.[42] The last section of the book describes how to form a home Bible study which will use the startstudies, and then assures the reader, 'In a short time a new local church will form using this method'.[43] While hindsight might consider this promise is a bit overstated, the twenty years just prior to when Thomas was writing in 1993 had shown the startstudies to be a very successful method of presenting the evangelical faith and seeing the participants converted, and then, indeed, being able to form a new ECV assembly from the newly converted.

Third, the centrality of the Bible was evident in the identity of the assemblies of the ECV. Reviewing the ECV newsletters and other literature from the rapid growth years of the ECV clearly demonstrates that the founders' vision of a Bible-centred movement had come to pass. In addition to the usual Sunday morning meetings, each assembly had several Bible studies each week, and all were well attended. Further, the founders and leaders of the ECV established early on a regular time for a more in-depth Bible study or Bible conference. These times were called by various names over the years such as the 'one-day-a-month Bible school' established in the fall of 1977[44] and the men's Bible conference established in 1979.[45] In addition, more formal programs such as the Saturday classes in Limburg known as the Limburgse Studiedag Toerusting was established in 1989[46] and a national programme known as the Toerustingscentrum Christengemeenten Vlaanderen, established in 1990.[47] This had a notable effect in the atmosphere for guest preachers as

---

40. Thomas, *Evangelisatie*, 85–91.
41. Thomas, *Evangelisatie*, 91–3.
42. Thomas, *Evangelisatie*, 98–104.
43. Thomas, *Evangelisatie*, 105.
44. 'The "one day a month" Bible school has been going for two months now. About 100 are taking part, 85 are following the classes, while another 15 are following the lessons at home, using the stencils. It means an awful lot of extra work for us, but we believe it is worth it. Already it is bearing fruit.' Richard and Marina Haverkamp, letter to supporters, Nov. 1977.
45. 'About ninety brothers came from the nine assemblies. It was great to be together and Ps 133 really fitted the occasion. The Flemish brethren ministered plus Richard and I. The theme was God's purpose with the church and its members.' Henk Gelling, letter to MSC, 11 June 1979. MSC is the Canadian Open Brethren mission service agency with which Gelling was associated.
46. Henk Gelling, telephone interview by author, 8 Dec. 2008.
47. 'Eindelijk wat ik zocht!', *Nieuwsbrief van de christengemeentes*, (ed.) Eric Rutten, 2 (1989), 7; 'Nieuw initiatief voor de christengemeentes', *Nieuwsbrief van de christengemeentes*, (ed.) Eric Rutten, 1 (1990), 6.

referenced by a prominent Flemish professor of systematic theology who later would become the rector of the Evangelische Theologische Faculteit. He said of the ECV, 'Even as a theologian you had to be careful as the scriptural knowledge was above average.'[48]

While the centrality of the Bible has remained an identifying mark of the ECV until at least the second decade of the twenty-first century, the commitment to consistent, serious Bible study has diminished. Just as the unbelievers in Flanders developed a diminished interest in the claims of Scripture, so too did the believers in the mature churches of the ECV seem to have a diminished interest in Bible study, especially studying the Bible for its own sake. The studies linked more directly to a felt, practical need became those which were attended by noticeably higher numbers. Additionally, conversational Bible studies were more appealing and, hence, better attended than gatherings characterized by a time of teaching by a studied leader.[49] As Gelling observed when asked about weekly Bible studies sponsored by the local assemblies,

> Some do very well, and others—there are fewer people coming. We are finding that in a number of assemblies where they have a cell group, where there is more interaction . . . more people come to that.[50]

He then went one to cite specific examples of this practice at two nearby assemblies. Gifford provided further insight on this trend.

> There are still Bible studies organized, but it doesn't interest young people to come to Bible studies. If you want to give an evening on something very practical, then they'll come to that . . . I gave a study last week on Jacob, and the influences of self-pity on his life, and it was very practical so there were a lot of people there. But I did a study on Nehemiah chapter 5 the week before that, and I had half the people there.[51]

Conclusion

While the ECV has remained a remarkably Bible-centred movement from its beginnings until well into the second decade of the twenty-first century, this biblicism cannot be considered a given going forward. First, the retirement of the founders and, gradually, the early leaders of the ECV presents an opportunity for a change in vision in the not too distant future. For example, one careful observer notes that the commitment to the truth of the biblical text in context is even now not a given as evidenced by some of the preaching one can witness on a given Sunday morning.[52] Second, the culture in which the ECV finds itself and to which it ministers is more notably uninterested in the study of the Bible as rehearsed above. This has and will continue to affect especially the next generation of believers in the assembly as well as any whom may be added to their numbers through conversion. Third, the biblicism of the ECV is in many ways tied to the Evangelische

---

48. Patrick Nullens, interview by author, Heverlee-Leuven, BE, 10 Sept. 2003.
49. Gifford, 22 June 2015.
50. Gelling, 21 June 2015.
51. Gifford, 22 June 2015.
52. Anonymous observer.

Theologische Faculteit since an increasing number of the fulltime workers of the ECV receive their training there. While some observers view the ECV as a quite conservative, evangelical institution both in its beliefs and practices, others detect a subtle shift in outlook toward a more expansive view of Christianity. If the latter observers' estimation of this subtle shift is correct, the consequences of this change will be reflected in the view and use of the Bible within the ECV.[53]

---

53. Anonymous observers.

PART 3

Theology and the Brethren

CHAPTER 12

The Brethren and Systematic Theology: Outspoken Objectors; Unconscious Practitioners[1]

Mark R. Stevenson

It is widely acknowledged that the Brethren have made a significant contribution to biblical studies from the early days of the movement. Whether it be in the field of exegesis, translation, textual criticism, or lexicography, the movement has produced individuals whose works have been valued beyond the confines of Brethrenism.[2] The same cannot be said, however, in the field of theology. Tim Grass comments, 'With such an impressive line-up of textual scholars and commentators, it is significant that Brethren have not produced systematic theologians'.[3] David Bebbington makes a similar observation, stating, 'Brethren did not set out their beliefs in structured form . . . [They] were concerned not with systematic theology but with how to be saved'.[4]

The thesis of this chapter is that not only were Brethren unconcerned with systematic theology, they vigorously opposed it in favour of a radical biblicism. And yet, in the end, for all of their antagonism toward systematic theology, they could not avoid practising it themselves. Our focus here is limited to nineteenth-century perspectives. Some of those perspectives have changed in more recent history, but for some Brethren, the early outlook lives on.

---

1. The present chapter develops and expands themes discussed in Mark R. Stevenson, *The Doctrines of Grace in an Unexpected Place: Calvinistic Soteriology in Nineteenth-Century Brethren Thought* (Eugene, OR, 2017). A version of this essay also appears in Franklin S. Jabini, Raju D. Kunjummen, and Mark R. Stevenson (eds.), *Reflections from the Emmaus Road: Essays in Honor of John H. Fish III, David A. Glock, and David J. MacLeod* (Dubuque, IA, 2018), 112–31.

2. Some examples include J. N. Darby, S. P. Tregelles, G. V. Wigram, L. C. L. Brenton, W. Kelly, W. E. Vine, F. F. Bruce, and D. J. Wiseman. For more on twentieth-century Brethren scholarship, see Alan Millard, 'Brethren Biblical Scholarship in Britain in the Twentieth Century', *intra*, Chap. 7.

3. Tim Grass, *Gathering to His Name: The Story of Open Brethren in Britain and Ireland* (Milton Keynes, 2006), 171. See also the comments on Bruce vis-à-vis systematic theology in Tim Grass, *F. F. Bruce: A Life* (Milton Keynes, 2011), 46–7; 220–1.

4. D. W. Bebbington, 'The Place of the Brethren Movement in International Evangelicalism', in Neil T. R. Dickson and Tim Grass (eds.), *The Growth of the Brethren Movement: National and International Experiences* (SEHT: Milton Keynes, 2006), 249. See Oliver Barclay, *Evangelicalism in Britain, 1935–95: A Personal Sketch* (Leicester, 1997), 24–5.

A brief description of systematic theology

To clarify, we begin with a brief description of systematic theology. The discipline, in one form or another, goes back to the patristic period, and has been known by a variety of titles.[5] Origen spoke of *First Principles*. Calvin wrote *Institutes of the Christian Religion*, and Barth produced *Church Dogmatics*. Sometimes it is simply dubbed *theology*, *divinity*, or Christian *doctrine*. If theology is the study of God, *systematic* theology is concerned with setting forth a coherent and comprehensive presentation of Christian teaching rooted in biblical revelation. Wayne Grudem offers the following definition: 'Systematic theology is any study that answers the question, "What does the whole Bible teach us today?" about any given topic.'[6]

The work of systematic theology was often described in the nineteenth century as a science. For example, Lindsay Alexander, professor of theology at Edinburgh University in 1854–81, stated that systematic theology was commonly understood to be 'a scientific arrangement and presentation of the religious truths taught in the word of God'.[7] Theologians of this era were concerned to demonstrate that their work was objective and credible because they too employed the scientific method. The Methodist, William Pope (1822–1903), asserted, 'The methods of theology are scientific. It observes, tests, and arranges facts and makes generalisations'.[8] For the Princeton theologian, Charles Hodge (1797–1878), systematic theology was a science not simply because it dealt with facts or truths, but because it was the theologian's task 'to collect, authenticate, arrange, and exhibit [those truths] in their internal relation to each other'.[9]

It is, perhaps, not surprising, then, that the Brethren movement, which so valued a kind of mystical leading of the Holy Spirit, would bristle under the inhibiting structures of a scientific approach to Scripture.

---

5. J. I. Packer, 'Is Systematic Theology a Mirage? An Introductory Discussion' in John D. Woodbridge and Thomas Edward McComiskey (eds.), *Doing Theology in Today's World: Essays in Honor of Kenneth S. Kantzer*, (Grand Rapids, MI), 17. Bartholomäus Keckermann (c.1572–1608) is usually considered the first to use the term *theologia systematic*: John Webster, 'Introduction: Systematic Theology', in John Webster, Kathryn Tanner, and Iain Torrance (eds.), *The Oxford Handbook of Systematic Theology*, (Oxford, 2007), 5.

6. See Wayne Grudem, *Systematic Theology: An Introduction to Biblical Theology* (Grand Rapids, MI, 1994), 21.

7. W. Lindsay Alexander, *A System of Biblical Theology*, 2 vols. (Edinburgh, 1888), 1:2. See B. B. Warfield, 'The Idea of Systematic Theology', *The Presbyterian and Reformed Review*, 7 (1896), 243–71, and the extended discussion of the 'Nature and Definition of Theological Science' in William G. T. Shedd, *Dogmatic Theology*, (ed.) Alan W. Gomes (3rd edn., 1888–94; repr., Phillipsburg, NJ, 2003), 51–75.

8. William Burt Pope, *A Compendium of Christian Theology*, 2nd edn. (London, 1879), 25. Pope argued that like every science, theology 'obeys the law of the human mind, which demands that the materials of its knowledge should be inductively generalized and systematically arranged; and, in common with every science, it arranges its materials for use and practical application'.

9. Charles Hodge, *Systematic Theology*, 3 vols. (1871; repr., Grand Rapids, MI, 1946), 1:1.

Brethren attitudes towards systematic theology

We begin with Sir Charles Brenton (c.1807–62), who seceded from the Church of England in 1831 and soon afterward associated with the Brethren.[10] Brenton is best known for his English translation of the Septuagint, which was first published in 1844 and is still available today.[11] In a brief article entitled 'Thoughts on System in Religion', which appeared in the first volume of the *Christian Witness* in 1834, Brenton argued that the impulse to systematize theological views is 'deeply rooted in the human heart'. But this universal impulse is one that ought to be resisted because, he maintained, it is an 'error, dishonourable to God.'[12] Systematizing the doctrines of the Bible tends 'to limit that which God has not limited' and produces only opinions which 'awkwardly and artificially' refer to the Bible, but are not truly based upon it.[13] Developing systematic notions of the church, for example, ends up claiming to unite believers around something that lacks 'the sanction of God's word, or the presence of God's Spirit'. For Brenton, as for all the early Brethren, the unbiblical character of such an enterprise manifests itself 'by the adoption of a *name*' such as Baptist or Presbyterian.[14]

The depth of Scripture and its divine content meant that any attempt to harmonize theological tensions was unnecessary and wrongheaded. 'A disposition to reconcile every thing, to systematize every thing', Brenton asserted, 'must lead to failure'. He confessed, 'There are things to be joined, but God must join them; there are difficulties to be reconciled, but *we* cannot solve the problem.'[15]

C. H. Mackintosh frequently expressed what he perceived as the futility of systematic theology. He wrote, for example,

> Men might as well attempt to confine the ocean in buckets of their own formation as to confine the vast range of divine revelation within the miserable enclosures of human systems of doctrine. It cannot be done, and it ought not to be attempted. Better far to fling aside all systems of theology and schools of divinity, and come like a little child to the eternal fountain of holy scripture, and there drink in the living teachings of God's Spirit.[16]

---

10. For more on Brenton see *BDEB*, s.v.; Peter L. Embley, 'The Origins and Early Development of the Plymouth Brethren', University of Cambridge, Ph.D. thesis, 1966, 19–21; and Timothy C. F. Stunt, *From Awakening to Secession: Radical Evangelicals in Switzerland and Britain 1815–35* (Edinburgh, 2000), 296–8. A most unflattering account of Brenton's time at Oxford may be found in T. Mozley, *Reminiscences Chiefly of Oriel College and the Oxford Movement* (London, 1882), 2: 114–20. Francis Newman strongly objected to Mozley's account 'of my friend Charles Brenton'. See Stunt, *From Awakening to Secession*, 209 n.105.

11. This first edition did not include the Apocrypha or a Greek text. In 1851, an edition that included the Apocrypha was released. Evidently, the first diglot edition (Greek Septuagint with Brenton's English translation) appeared in 1870. See <http://ccat.sas.upenn.edu/ioscs/brenton>, accessed 5 June 2015.

12. [L. C. L. Brenton], 'Thoughts on System in Religion', *CWit* 1 (1834), 310.

13. [Brenton], 'Thoughts on System in Religion', 310.

14. [Brenton], 'Thoughts on System in Religion', 311. Emphasis original.

15. [Brenton], 'Thoughts on System in Religion', 311–12. Emphasis original.

16. [C. H. Mackintosh], 'One-Sided Theology', *Things New and Old*, 19 (1876), 12. In another place he wrote, 'We can no more systematize God's word than we can systematize God Himself. His word, His heart and His nature, are quite too deep and comprehensive to be

For Mackintosh, systematic theology was not only impossible, it was dangerous. He warned that if earnest souls 'are turned from Jesus to theology—from the heart of a loving, pardoning God to the cold and withering dogmas of systematic divinity, it is impossible to say where they may end; they may take refuge either in superstition on the one hand, or in infidelity on the other'.[17] Early in the twentieth century, a contributor to *The Bible Treasury* suggested that 'those who are entangled in human systematic theology' have 'unwittingly forsaken the ways of the Lord for the arrangements of men'.[18]

In 1843 John Eliot Howard, featured in a recent monograph in the *Studies in Brethren History* series,[19] expressed his desire 'only to drink water with joy out of the pure wellsprings of Scripture, and to cast systematic theology to the owls and to the bats'.[20] Similarly, although Donald Ross had once been known as 'the walking Shorter Catechism',[21] such human standards meant little to him after he associated with the Brethren. On one occasion, Ross likened searching for the way of salvation in the Reformed catechisms and confessions to looking for gold in a common sewer. Such human products are 'muddy streams' and 'nauseous' compared with the pure fountain of the Word of God.[22] After Ross's death, his friend, Donald Munro, wrote, 'We have heard him say that in his earlier days he read and studied not a few standard works on theology. But as he went on with God and His work, these lost their attraction for him. The Word in its majesty, grandeur, and perfection commanded his whole attention'.[23] At the close of the nineteenth century, John Ritchie reflected the same attitude when he urged young believers to 'make your Bible your daily companion . . . It is the sufficiency of the man of God . . . Draw your doctrines from *it* and not from a human compilation, whether "catechism" or "confession"'.[24]

The reason for Brethren aversion to systematic theology

Clearly the radical biblicism of the movement is the central explanation for Brethren aversion to systematic theology. Brethren writers claimed that systematic theology often imposed foreign ideas on the Word of God. In a discussion of ministry and ecclesiastical hierarchy, Darby wrote, 'The moment one searches the word, it comes out that theology and theologians are worth nothing at all.' A few lines later he added, 'It is impossible

---

included within the limits of the very broadest and best constructed human system of theology that was ever framed. We shall, ever and anon, be discovering passages of Scripture which will not fall in with our system.' C. H. Mackintosh, 'The Three Appearings', in *Miscellaneous Writings of C. H. Mackintosh*, 6: *Life and Times of David:* (New York, 1898), 7. The article originally appeared as a series in *Things New and Old*, 11 (1868).

17. [C. H. Mackintosh], 'Glad Tidings', *Things New and Old*, 10 (1867), 48.
18. G. S. M. 'The Test of Love', *Bible Treasury*, 9 n.s. (1912), 171.
19. Gerald T. West, *From Friends to Brethren: The Howards of Tottenham—Quakers, Brethren, and Evangelicals*, (ed.) Tim Grass (SBH: *Subsidia*: Troon, 2016).
20. I. E. Howard, *'New Views' Compared with the Word of God* (2nd edn. London, 1843), 24.
21. C. W. R[oss]. (ed.), *Donald Ross: Pioneer Evangelist of the North of Scotland and United States of America* (Kilmarnock, [1903]), 130.
22. [Donald Ross], 'Salvation, How Attained', *Northern Evangelistic Intelligencer*, 2 (1872), 44.
23. R[oss]. (ed.), *Donald Ross*, 103.
24. [John Ritchie], 'A Word to Young Converts', *Believer's Magazine*, 9 (1899), 65.

to read the word and to follow, even one moment, the system of theologians'.[25] William Kelly criticized both Calvinism and Arminianism because 'like other systems they are in part true and in part false—true in what they believe of scripture, false in yielding to human thoughts outside scripture'. He then declared, 'Happy those, who are content as Christians with the truth of God and refuse to be partisans on either side of men! Our wisdom is to have our minds open to all scripture, refusing to go a hair-breath farther'.[26] In the Brethren outlook, being party to a system meant that one could not be true to the whole of Scripture.

It was commonly expressed that systematic theology and especially creeds and confessions were merely human products that inevitably supplant the authority of Scripture. F. W. Grant complained, 'As authoritative expositions of doctrine, [creeds] substitute human authority for divine.' The problem for Grant was that 'the confession, with all its admitted liability to error, [stands] in place of the unfailing, infallible Word, by which the Holy Spirit . . . works in the hearts and consciences of men.'[27] Brenton expressed his hope that the recognition of error in the systems held by even 'the most honoured servants of the Lord' would wean people from human authority and teach them to constantly search the Scriptures, wherein lies the authority of God.[28]

The Brethren did not exhibit any sense of dependence on theologians or theological traditions; their stated loyalty was always to Scripture. Darby could express appreciation for reformers such as Luther and Calvin, but he refused to tie himself to them. If they were presented as a standard of truth, he would reject them 'with indignation'. 'They were not inspired', Darby explained. 'Their teachings are not the word of God'. He respected 'the gifted men', but they 'would become a horror to me if they were in any way substituted for, or made to compete with, the word of God'. He exclaimed, 'Do not bring their doctors or

---

25. J. N. Darby, *CW* (1844), 3:243. Nevertheless, many have recognized Darby was a theologian. John Goddard acknowledged that 'Darby never failed to speak disparagingly of theology as a science and would doubtless have issued a vehement demurrer if anyone had ever called him a theologian'. Goddard, however, insisted that Darby was 'a theologian in the best sense of the term': John Howard Goddard, 'The Contribution of John Nelson Darby to Soteriology, Ecclesiology, and Eschatology', Dallas Theological Seminary, ThD dissertation, 1948, 2. See Berthold Schwarz, 'J. N. Darby as Theologian, with Special Reference to his Understanding of the Relation of Law and Grace', in Tim Grass (ed.), *Witness in Many Lands: Leadership and Outreach among the Brethren* (SBH: Troon, 2013), 46–47. Neatby was not as convinced, however. He stated, 'It is impossible to consider Darby a very precise divine. Though he had undoubted power, it was rather as the mystic than as the systematic theologian'. William Blair Neatby, *A History of the Plymouth Brethren* (2nd edn., London, 1902), 171.

26. William Kelly, *Notes on the Epistle of Paul, the Apostle, to the Romans, with a New Translation* (London, 1873), 220. In a recent analysis of Kelly's thought, Critchlow observes, 'Kelly did not produce books which might be appropriate for a systematic or dogmatic theologian . . . he generally wrote works in which he concentrated on teaching one particular biblical book': Anne-Louise Critchlow, *Against the Trend: The Spirituality of William Kelly 1821–1906* (Eugene, OR, 2016), 6.

27. F. W. Grant, *Atonement: In Type, Prophecy, and Accomplishment* (New York, n.d.), 11. See Presbus, 'The "Record"', *Bible Treasury*, 4 (1863), 204–5.

28. [Brenton], 'Thoughts on System in Religion', 312.

their systems to me as authority. You are trenching on the authority of the word of God'.[29] On another occasion he declared:

> A system takes the place of godly subjection to the word. And alas! this is suited to a decline of spirituality. As [subjection to the word] becomes feeble, the exercise of mind, and the play of the mere natural feelings, become a necessary ailment. But to the soul, fresh in its spirituality, the word of God (and oh! how can it be otherwise?) has more sweetness in its least statements (for they come from God) than any indulgence whatever of the mental powers.[30]

This opposition to formal theology and creeds also reflected the influence of Romanticism on the Brethren movement. In reaction to the rationalism of the Enlightenment, Romanticism stressed imagination, mystery, emotion, and intuition.[31] By the 1830s, the evangelical movement was appropriating some of the values of Romanticism. Among other things, this led to exalting faith over reason, with a keen sense of God's hand in human affairs. It also involved elevating the simplicity of the Word of God over rational systems of theology.[32] Brenton worried that human systems undermined 'the searching of the scriptures' and 'the hope of the spirit for our guide, nay, the very fulfilment of the promise that He shall guide us'.[33]

The Brethren were not the only evangelicals to display these ideals,[34] but the impulse to exalt Scripture over every other source and authority tended to be stronger among them than other evangelicals. Thus Bebbington labelled the Brethren as 'extremists' in their devotion to the Bible. Yet this extreme commitment to Scripture is what preserved their fundamental orthodoxy when others who absorbed the spirituality of Romanticism drifted into 'doctrinal vagueness'.[35]

---

29. J. N. Darby, *CW*, 7: 205–6 (1858–59; 2nd edn., 1867).
30. *CW*, 11: 38 (1845).
31. See Bebbington, 'The Place of the Brethren Movement in International Evangelicalism'. On pages 248–60, Bebbington illustrates the ways in which Romanticism was evident in Brethren thought and practice. He argues that 'Brethren approximated to the ideal type of Romantic evangelicals—radical, intense, quixotic'. See also Grass, *Gathering to His Name*, 10–12. For this section, see Stevenson, *The Doctrines of Grace in an Unexpected Place*, 259.
32. However, Bebbington argues that aversion to metaphysical systems of theology was also part of the Enlightenment reaction to scholasticism. D. W. Bebbington, *Evangelicalism in Modern Britain: A History from the 1730s to the 1980s* (1989; repr., New York: Routledge, 1993), 57–8.
33. [Brenton], 'Thoughts on System in Religion', 312.
34. For example, the Anglican evangelical, Charles Simeon (1759–1836) wrote in the preface to his homiletical commentary on the Bible: 'The Author is no friend to systematizers in Theology. He has endeavoured to derive from the Scriptures alone *his* views of religion; and to them it is his wish to adhere, with scrupulous fidelity; never wresting any portion of the word of God to favour a particular opinion, but giving to every part of it that sense, which it seems to him to have been designed by its great Author to convey': Charles Simeon, *Horae Homileticae*, 21 vols. (London, 1832), 1: xxiii.
35. Bebbington, 'The Place of the Brethren Movement in International Evangelicalism', 252–3.

To illustrate this appropriation of Romanticism, we turn to an essay by Henry Borlase (1806–35) entitled 'Separation from Apostasy Not Schism', also from the first volume of the *Christian Witness* in 1834. At one point in his essay, Borlase took up the issue of creeds. He conceded that often the early creeds and confessions did articulate orthodox statements of Christian doctrine. He found the Athanasian Creed accurate and profound. 'But', he argued, 'all which is there stated in metaphysical language and exactness of position, an unlearned believer in the gospel apprehends as to its vital truth, by the *intuition* of faith'.[36] This is a remarkable statement suggesting that a challenging doctrine such as the Trinity may be absorbed by a genuine believer through the 'intuition of faith' rather than theological inquiry and reflection. Furthermore, Borlase objected to the requirement of signing a creed as altogether unscriptural. He explained, 'The real evil is, that the principle of union becomes *merely* one of *knowledge*, an assent of the understanding to certain propositions, which may be utterly unconnected with vital godliness, and which requirement therefore is unscriptural, and tends only to divide the true body of Christ.'[37]

So then, creeds were perceived as unnecessary, unbiblical, and dangerous in the sense of promoting merely an intellectual apprehension of doctrine rather than that which is borne out in the heart and life of the believer.[38] Furthermore, they do not prevent unconverted men from pressing into the ministry. Indeed, for 'a false teacher or idle shepherd' the Articles of the Church of England 'are but the shelter for formality and worldliness.[39]

Radical biblicism and the ethos of Romanticism thus merged to make Brethren wary of systematic theology. No doubt, they would have resonated with these lines from Tennyson:

> Our little systems have their day;
> They have their day and cease to be:
> They are but broken lights of thee,
> And thou, O Lord, art more than they.
>
> ('In Memoriam A. H. H.')

In the first substantial history of the movement, Blair Neatby described the Brethren attitude pointedly, if somewhat hyperbolically when he wrote, 'They did not master the truths of salvation in a logical concatenation; they saw them. Inference was nothing; immediate perception everything ... Where logical Puritan divinity was anxious to explain, Darby only cared to feel'.[40]

---

36. Henry Borlase, 'Separation from Apostasy Not Schism', *Christian Witness*, 1 (1834; 2nd edn., 1837), 348. Emphasis original.

37. Borlase, 'Separation from Apostasy Not Schism', 349.

38. Harold H. Rowdon, *The Origins of the Brethren, 1825–1850* (London, 1967), 271.

39. [Borlase], 'Separation from Apostasy Not Schism', 349. Darby likewise complained that the Thirty-Nine Articles and the Westminster Confession 'are elastic enough to admit many novel doctrines and all manner of evil ones.' Darby, *CW* (1862), 10: 32.

40. Neatby, *A History of the Plymouth Brethren*, 331.

The consequences of neglecting systematic theology

In Neatby's assessment, 'The abjuration of "system" was the special boast of the Brethren, and it has proved their ruin'.[41] Brethren were particularly opposed to ecclesiastical 'systems', and protested their formalism, hierarchy, and extra biblical tradition. But part of the 'ruin' Neatby seemed to have in mind was the several Christological controversies that produced such bitter division in the movement. It is beyond the scope of this paper to review all the debates on this score, but perhaps most germane to our study was the tendency to diminish the human nature of Jesus Christ. F. F. Bruce could say, 'A weakness on the doctrine of our Lord's humanity, verging at times on Docetism, has been endemic in certain phases of the Brethren movement'.[42] Neatby spoke of the 'quasi-Gnostic tendencies' that 'haunted the outworks of the theology of Darbyism' from the time of the Newton controversies.[43]

A few examples will serve to illustrate this tendency. B. W. Newton had described Christ's body as 'mortal', in the orthodox sense of 'capable of dying'. Yet the word 'mortal' was judged to be part of Newton's heresy and quickly became taboo among scrupulous Brethren.[44] As Bruce points out, although Isaac Watts had used the word 'mortal' to describe Christ's flesh, nevertheless, the Brethren hymn writer, James G. Deck, felt compelled to revise one of his own hymns that employed the offending word. Deck originally wrote the hymn in 1837 and acknowledged that it had been 'long used by godly brethren without consciousness of evil'. By 1850, however, he issued a retraction entitled *Confession of a Verbal Error in a Hymn*.[45]

S. P. Tregelles claimed to have direct knowledge that some Exclusive Brethren described Christ's human nature in the following terms: 'His humanity was *something divine* . . . it was a *spiritual humanity*.' Or again, 'He did not become man *by birth*, but in some other way . . . *made of a woman* (Gal. 4), does not mean born of a woman'. Tregelles added, 'It has been *repeatedly* denied that our Lord was *mortal,* and when this word was explained

---

41. Neatby, *A History of the Plymouth Brethren*, 331.

42. F. F. Bruce, 'The Humanity of Jesus Christ', *Journal of the Christian Brethren Research Fellowship*, 24 (1973), 5.

43. Neatby, *A History of the Plymouth Brethren*, 146. David Anderson-Berry, writing in the *Witness* in 1908, said of Darbyism, 'A docetic air characterizes many of the writings of that school leading to much sorrow and shame': David Anderson-Berry, 'The Lord of Glory—Had He a True Body?', *W*, 38 (1908), 122.

44. Neatby, *A History of the Plymouth Brethren*, 142–6; Bruce, 'The Humanity of Jesus Christ', 7–8.

45. Bruce, 'The Humanity of Jesus Christ', 8. The original version read:
Such was Thy grace that, for our sake,
Thou didst from heaven come down;
Our mortal flesh and blood partake,
In all our misery one.
The revised stanza became:
Such was Thy grace, that for our sake
Thou didst from heaven come down;
With us of flesh and blood partake,
And make our woes Thine own.

as meaning *capable of dying* (not *compelled to die*), it has been said that He had no more capacity for dying than he had for sin.'[46]

George V. Wigram accused Henry Craik of making statements that were 'blasphemous and heretical'[47] in regard to the human nature of Christ.[48] Wigram's concerns were ill-founded; if anything they raise questions about his own position on Christ's humanity. Craik expressed concern that if his entirely orthodox position was denied, then 'it seems to me that the faith of the Catholic Church (in all ages) is repudiated; and the necessary inference would be, that the Blessed One did not take our flesh, but flesh and blood essentially different from ours'.[49] Bruce insightfully comments on the exchange:

> Darby knew very well that there was nothing heretical in what Craik had written, and is reported to have said that, when he received Wigram's criticisms of Craik, he put them at the back of the fire. He must have seen, moreover, the docetic direction in which Wigram's arguments tended. But for purposes of ecclesiastical politics Wigram was too useful a henchman to be disowned.[50]

One case that drew widespread attention was a comment made by C. H. Mackintosh in the first edition of his *Notes on Leviticus* published in 1860. There he stated, 'The first Adam, even in his unfallen condition, was "of the earth;" but the second Man was, as to His manhood, "the Lord from heaven"'. Later in the same volume Mackintosh asserted that 'the precious truth of Christ's heavenly humanity' must be guarded 'with holy jealousy'.[51] Critics collectively raised their eyebrows and sharpened their swords, and charged Mackintosh with teaching a kind of Valentinian Gnosticism.[52] A second edition was released the following year with the flawed expressions removed. Darby sprang to his friend's defence, demonstrating that even in the *Notes on Leviticus*, Mackintosh clearly affirmed the true humanity of Christ. Darby conceded that although Mackintosh's orthodoxy was unquestionable, he had used unguarded language, and his statements were both mistaken and objectionable.[53]

A firestorm of controversy among Exclusive ranks arose toward the close of the nineteenth century over several doctrinal errors advanced by F. E. Raven, including notions about Christ's human nature. On one occasion, Raven complained a critic failed

---

46. Cited in Neatby, *A History of the Plymouth Brethren*, 143. Emphasis original.
47. G. V. Wigram, 'An Appeal to Saints that Remain Still in Bethesda and Salem, as to Certain Bad Doctrine' (London, 1848), online version <www.stempublishing.com/authors/wigram/appeal.html>, accessed 24 June 2015.
48. The statements from Craik's *Pastoral Letters* are cited in Neatby, *History*, 166.
49. As cited in G. V. Wigram, *An Answer of G. V. Wigram to 'Mr. H. Craik's Letter, Dated 15th November, 1848'* (London, 1848), 6. See Neatby, *History*, 168–9.
50. Bruce, 'The Humanity of Jesus Christ', 8.
51. As quoted in James C. L. Carson, *The Heresies of the Plymouth Brethren* (London, 1883), 9.
52. See *The Quarterly Journal of Prophecy* 13 (1861), 295. For more on the controversy see Edwin Cross, *The Life and Times of Charles Henry Mackintosh: A Biography* (London, 2011), 143–6.
53. J. N. Darby, 'The "Notes on Leviticus" and the "Quarterly Journal of Prophecy"', *CW* [1862], 10:31–5; J. N. Darby, 'Brethren and Their Reviewers', *CW* [1862], 10:43–53.

to understand the 'real heavenly humanity' of Christ. He explained that while Christ took 'man's form', the moral character of Christ's humanity was derived from his deity.[54] On another occasion, he stated of Christ: 'In Person He is God; in condition He is Man', and again, 'He is a divine person in manhood'.[55] Raven also taught a kind of Nestorianism in resolutely denying the unity of the divine and human natures in the person of Christ,[56] for which William Kelly and others charged him with heterodoxy.[57]

Notably, Raven himself stated, 'I earnestly entreat saints to come prayerfully and patiently to Scripture to get their thoughts of Christ formed by the word of God; and not to adopt the creeds or moulds into which men, often with pious intent, have cast the truth in the vain effort to guard against error'.[58] Ironically, however, in ignoring the creeds and going only to the word of God—with pious intent, to be sure—Raven fell into error.

Although these examples have focused largely on Exclusive teachers, Open Brethren have, occasionally, fallen prey to similar pitfalls. Neatby claims to have heard an address at the close of the nineteenth century from an Open brother, 'who actually taught that Christ did not die from crucifixion, but by a mere miraculous act'.[59]

The point here is that the Brethren might have avoided some of the pitfalls into which they fell if they had not assumed such an adversarial stance against theology. Granted, there were plenty of examples of bad theology which they were right to reject. Yet the centuries of Church history also yield a great deal of theological wisdom that many Brethren chose to ignore at their own peril. Neatby observed, 'The Brethren sought to effect a fresh start without authority, precedent, or guidance beyond the letter of Holy Scripture. For them, essentially, the garnered experience of eighteen Christian centuries was as though it were not'.[60]

In later years, some Brethren recognized these dangers and appealed to the theological insights of the past. In 1908, David Anderson-Berry (1862–1926),[61] wrote a series of articles on Christology in *The Witness* highlighting the Christological heresies condemned in the early centuries of the Church. He demonstrated that some Brethren had developed a docetic inclination that the early theologians had clearly rejected. Anderson-Berry rightly suggested that had these Brethren 'known the history of the Church they might never have been guilty of repeating mistakes, errors, heresies, that the Early Church condemned as not according to the Word of God'. Yet even in making this statement, Anderson-Berry

---

54. Neatby, *A History of the Plymouth Brethren*, 317.
55. Cited in Bruce, 'The Humanity of Jesus Christ', 8–9. See F. E. Raven, 'The Person of the Christ', in *Ministry,* 20 vols. (Kingston-on-Thames, n.d.), 3:268–73.
56. Raven, 'The Person of the Christ', 268–73. Noel quotes Raven as saying, 'Where the unity of the Person is got from, I know not. It seems to me perfect nonsense'. Napoleon Noel, *The History of the Brethren*, 2 vols., (ed.), William F. Knapp (Denver, CO, 1936), 511.
57. W. Kelly, *F. E. R. on Life Eternal, Other Divine Truths, and Above All Christ's Person* (London, 1902), 121–7. See R. A. Huebner, *F. E. Raven's Evil Doctrines on the Person of Christ and Their Present Bearing* (Morganville, NJ, 1980).
58. Raven, 'The Person of the Christ', 3:273.
59. Neatby, *A History of the Plymouth Brethren*, 170.
60. Neatby, *A History of the Plymouth Brethren*, 3.
61. On Anderson-Berry, who was a medical physician, see Henry Pickering (ed.), *Chief Men Among the Brethren* (1918; repr., Neptune, NJ, 1996), 16–19.

felt compelled to qualify that by the 'Early Church' he did not mean 'the fathers, or the theologians, or Church doctors, but the concourse of Christian men and women on earth at any one time'. For Anderson-Berry, the agreed opinion of ordinary Christians 'has been far more powerful in the rejection of error and the destruction of heresy than the most able dissertation of the most eminent theologian or father'. This is a peculiar statement, since the author clearly knew that it was the collective work of the theologians of the Church that formally condemned the heresies and defined Christian orthodoxy. Perhaps it demonstrates that the ethos created by the radical biblicism of the movement made it difficult even for informed individuals to grant any kind of positive status to theology and the work of theologians.

The practice of systematic theology among the Brethren

Professor Carl Trueman opens his book, *The Creedal Imperative*, with the following anecdote:

> A colleague of mine loves to tell the following story about a church he used to visit. The pastor there had a habit of standing in the pulpit, seizing his Bible in his right hand, raising it above his head, and pointing to it with his left. 'This,' he declared in a booming voice, 'is our only creed and our only confession.' Ironically, the church was marked by teaching that included the five points of Calvinism, dispensationalism, and a form of polity that reflected in broad terms its origins as a Plymouth Brethren assembly . . . Clearly, the church did have a creed, a summary view of what the Bible taught on grace, eschatology, and ecclesiology; it was just that nobody ever wrote it down and set it out in public.[62]

Some might surmise that in disavowing creeds and shunning systematic theology the Brethren were content 'to let sleeping dogmas lie'.[63] This, however, was not the case. They were more than eager to take on difficult doctrinal questions and often developed their own systematic approach.

The most obvious example, perhaps, is their development of dispensationalism. This was a theological approach to understanding the grand scheme of redemption, particularly in regard to the place of Israel and the Church in salvation history. What is not always appreciated is the fact that Darby's dispensationalism had strong theological underpinnings.[64] Each dispensation was a divine test which people inevitably failed, thus demonstrating their ruin and total inability to obey God.[65] Darby's view, argues Grass, that 'each dispensation was doomed to failure may be seen as an application of radical

---

62. Carl R. Trueman, *The Creedal Imperative* (Wheaton, IL, 2012), 12.
63. Credit for this expression goes to Perry Miller, *Jonathan Edwards* (New York, 1949), 80.
64. See Stevenson, *The Doctrines of Grace in an Unexpected Place*, 79–80.
65. Darby, 'The Apostasy of the Successive Dispensations', *CW* (1836), 1: 124–30. This theme also appears in other Brethren, e.g. William Kelly, *Lectures Introductory to the Study of the Minor Prophets* (5th edn., London, n. d.), vii; W. Kelly, *Lectures on the Church of God* (London, n.d.), 8; [William Trotter], 'No Man Becomes a Child of God by an Act of His Own Will', *Present Testimony*, 8 (1856), 308–17. See R. A. Huebner, *God's Sovereignty and Glory in the Election and Salvation of Lost Men* (Jackson, NJ, 2003), 15.

Calvinist soteriology, and in particular of the doctrines of divine sovereignty, original sin and human inability, to the realms of salvation-history and ecclesiology'.[66]

Closely related to dispensationalism is the elaborate scheme of eschatology they pioneered—often complete with detailed charts. Their version of premillennialism, with its division of the second coming of Christ into the secret rapture of the church and the subsequent return in power and glory, was a favourite theme of Brethren teaching. Brethren eschatology was not the product of mere biblicism. It was a theological approach, in which many texts were read through the lens of a systematic framework. That the Brethren were engaged in systematic theological work is demonstrated by the fact that dispensational premillennialism is regularly discussed in contemporary theologies and theological handbooks.[67]

Other examples of Brethren systematic thinking could be cited, but a particularly intriguing one involves the question of the extent of the atonement (or, for whom did Christ die?)—an issue which has exercised theologians for centuries.[68] Arminians advocated universal atonement, while Calvinists argued for various forms of particular redemption in which Christ died in a unique way for the elect. The Brethren advanced a nuanced position.[69] On the one hand, Christ's work of propitiation was universal and Godward; it vindicated God's righteousness and enabled him to offer mercy to all sinners. On the other hand, substitution was particular; Christ bore only the sins of believers. Their position could be neatly summarized as follows: 'Christ is a *propitiation* for the whole world. He was the *substitute* for His people'.[70]

The distinction between universal propitiation and particular substitution enabled the preacher to offer the gospel to all while affirming redemption was effective for all those for whom Christ died. Furthermore, it gave the Brethren a way of handling biblical texts that were either universal (e.g. 1 John 2:2) or particular (e.g. Eph. 5:25) in scope without diminishing the force of either, which is what they believed both Calvinist and Arminian interpretations did. Although they would never admit it, the Brethren approach was a creative exercise in systematic theology. From their perspective, they believed they had

---

66. Timothy George Grass, 'The Church's Ruin and Restoration: The Development of Ecclesiology in the Plymouth Brethren and the Catholic Apostolic Church, *c.*1825–*c.*1866', King's College, London, Ph.D. thesis, 1997, 96. See Matthew Austin Clarke, 'A Critical Examination of the Ecclesiology of John Nelson Darby', University of Gloucestershire, Ph.D. thesis, 2009, 260.

67. E.g. Michael F. Bird, *Evangelical Theology: A Biblical and Systematic Introduction* (Grand Rapids, MI, 2013), 274–300; Grudem, *Systematic Theology*, 1091–1139; Michael Horton, *The Christian Faith: A Systematic Theology for Pilgrims on the Way* (Grand Rapids, MI, 2011), 928–9; Alister E. McGrath, *Christian Theology: An Introduction* (Oxford, 1994), 472–3.

68. See, for example, David Gibson and Jonathan Gibson (eds.), *From Heaven He Came and Sought Her: Definite Atonement in Historical, Biblical, Theological, and Pastoral Perspective* (Wheaton, IL, 2013), 57–223.

69. For a thorough discussion of the Brethren approach, see Stevenson, *The Doctrines of Grace in an Unexpected Place*, Chap. 6 'The Extent of the Atonement: Universal and Particular', 165–200.

70. Mackintosh, 'One-Sided Theology', 16.

solved the Calvinism/Arminianism divide on this issue by simply adhering to Scripture and, thus, rising above 'the systems of men'.

Conclusion

In some ways, early Brethrenism was an experiment of sorts in radical biblicism. Could a Christian group, ignoring centuries of Church history and theology, claim the Bible alone as its creed, and live, teach, and worship solely on that basis? Could that same Christian group avoid theologizing altogether and adhere strictly to the plain sense of the biblical text? That was certainly the Brethren ideal.

In the end, however, it was a failed experiment in at least two ways. First, as we have seen, in ignoring the theological wisdom of the past, heresy seemed to be always lying at the door, and some Brethren were not always able to rule over it (to borrow the language of Genesis 4:7). Secondly, for all the objections they raised against theology, they inevitably, though perhaps unwittingly, engaged in the practice themselves. Surely here they made important contributions to theological discourse, but one is left with the nagging sense that their efforts might have been enhanced had they not taken such an antagonistic view of systematic theology.

Neatby captured something of the sentiment of nineteenth-century Brethrenism when he wrote, 'In systematic divinity they were weak, and their history shows the perilous character of the weakness. But the Bible, in a wonderful way, was a living book to them'.[71] In our age of biblical illiteracy, one is bound to appreciate Brethren devotion to the Bible. But, ironically, one also learns from the Brethren to value the theological wisdom of the centuries.

---

71. Neatby, *A History of the Plymouth Brethren*, 331–2.

CHAPTER 13

The Theology of George Müller

Neil Summerton

George Müller was not a theologian in the modern sense of the word. He did not hold a university position. He did not teach students. He did not write books of theology or commentaries. It is unlikely that his contemporaries would have thought of him as a great thinker, though they undoubtedly saw him as a great church leader and philanthropist. In these ways, he is in contrast with his colleague at Bethesda Chapel, Bristol, Henry Craik; and even more so with his protagonist, J. N. Darby, and his other scholarly contemporaries among the founders of the Brethren who found their way mainly into the Exclusive wing of the Brethren after 1848.

Müller did not, however, lack education, including in theology, biblical studies, and biblical languages. As he noted in public on a number of occasions, from the age of 11 he was being prepared in the German system, in the gymnasium and at the University of Halle, for entry into the Lutheran ministry. He continued at Halle for a further three years after his conversion in November 1825, and it was for further education and preparation for outreach to Jews that he came to England in March 1829, to study for a further six months at the Mission to Jews college of the London Society for Promoting Christianity among the Jews. At school, he had studied Classics, French, German, Greek, Hebrew, and Mathematics. (He referred on one occasion to his having written an oration in Latin while a student.) In London, he continued in Hebrew, and added to them some learning in Chaldean and Yiddish. At Halle, then 'at the pinnacle of theological training in Germany',[1] he studied theology, until he went to England. There, after his conversion, his particular mentor and friend was August Tholuck (1799–1877), 'Nowadays . . . described as the greatest theologian of the German revival movement.'[2] Consistent with his character, he studied hard, to the point that he made himself ill in his early months in London, the circumstance which led to decisive further spiritual experience in the South West of England.[3]

So, given that German education, particularly theological education, is probably to be regarded as ahead of its British, and certainly its English, counterparts in the period, Müller's theological credentials, and even more so his biblical linguistic credentials, should not be denigrated. His own later references to them tended somewhat to do so.

---

1. So, Stephan Holthaus, 'Georg Müller (1805–1898): His Life and Work', in Tim Grass (ed.), *Witness in Many Lands: Leadership and Outreach among the Brethren* (SBH; Troon, 2013), 7. Holthaus gives more details of Müller's educational experience.
2. Holthaus, 'Georg Müller', 8.
3. Holthaus, 'Georg Müller', 9.

But his object was to enjoin his hearers to understand that neither education nor facility in languages were any credential at all for acceptance by God, and that pride in them was positively dangerous.[4] That is not to say that he was not quietly proud of his education, and of the fact that conversation at his table could switch between German, French, and English if needed.[5] He enjoined the young to make the most of their 'time, talents, strength' and apply themselves 'in the cultivation of the mind and in becoming acquainted with the affairs of this life, all of which may afterwards be used, not only with regard to this life, but in the service of the Lord, and for the glory of God.'[6] And he may have been both a little wistful and a little guilty when he said of Craik after his death that 'his natural tendency was to aim after the cultivation of his mind with too great an earnestness and natural fondness, which, but for his weak constitution, might have become a great snare for his inner man.'[7]

The fact is that Müller was rare among those who remained in, or who were attracted to, the Open Brethren in the second half of the nineteenth century, in being both highly intelligent and educated in theology and ancient languages. How far he kept up his knowledge of theology once he came to England is open to question, however. Certainly, he rarely if ever mentioned scholarly works nor the increasingly liberal German theological scholarship of the nineteenth century. Nevertheless, he had a personal theology, and there are grounds for thinking that it was influential through his prominence in British evangelicalism, his prominence in the Open Brethren as their *de facto* founder along with Craik, and his startlingly-successful national and international preaching tours between 1875 and 1892. The structure and character of his theology must be discerned, however, from his journal entries, from the successive editions of his *A Narrative of some of the Lord's Dealings, with George Müller* first published in 1837,[8] and from his sermons and

---

4. See, e.g., 'Address to Young Men, Delivered Bethesda Chapel, Great George Street, Bristol, on Sunday, October 12th, 1873 Eccles. xxi. 9, 10 & xii. 1', in *Jehovah Magnified: Addresses by George Müller* (Bristol: The Bible and Tract Depôt of the Scriptural Knowledge Institution [1876]) [hereafter cited as *Jeh. Mag.*], 228–9: 'You speak about the pleasures of reading: I know them too; for when I was only thirteen years old I had my books by the month out of the library, and I devoured them with all eagerness—volume after volume. And you speak about learning, and the enjoyment in this: I was at school from the time that I was five years old, to the time that I was nineteen and a half, when I went to the university with honourable testimonials, and was there for four years; and then studying was not over, for when I came to England I went on with Hebrew, Chaldee, etc. And what did I find: That learning by itself gives no happiness,—real true happiness. I know seven languages; and with all this I should have gone to hell, if it had not been that I know Christ, Christ, Christ.'

5. 'Address to Young Men', 233.

6. 'Address to Young Men', 234. In the funeral address of his first wife, he lauded the fact that her education had been both liberal and practical ('Address on Psalm 119 v. 68 "The Lord is good and doeth good." A Sermon preached Bethesda Chapel, Great George Street, Bristol by Mr George Müller, founder of the Orphan Asylum, Horfield, upon the recent death of his wife, Thursday evening, March 3rd, 1870', Müller House transcripts [for these, see n.9 below]).

7. Müller, 'On the late Mr. Henry Craik. An Address printed as an Introduction to the volume entitled "Passages from the Diary and Letters of Henry Craik"', in *Jeh. Mag.*, 18.

8. Many passages from the *Narrative* are conveniently available a single volume, G. Fred Bergin (ed.), *Autobiography of George Müller or a Million and a Half in Answer to Prayer*

tracts (more than sixty of which are now available spanning the period 1860–98[9]). Based mainly on the last, this paper summarizes the main components of his theological thought.

Soteriology

It is as well to begin with Müller's understanding and communication of the doctrine of salvation. In 1825, as a student of 20, he had an undemonstrative but decisive evangelical conversion. For him, this was the first and most important decisive event in his life—a second, which will be discussed later, was almost as important, if not more so. He gave an extended account of his conversion in the *Autobiography*[10] and frequently referred to it as he preached. It was not unlike John Wesley's conversion: a meeting for prayer and reading of Scripture, at which a printed sermon was read because anything more was illegal in Prussia in the absence of an ordained clergyman. In the first place, he had felt inexplicably drawn to the Saturday evening meeting in the house of an illiterate tradesperson (who nevertheless impressed him by his kindness of spirit), and he left it happy though he did not know why. 'I lay peaceful and happy in my bed. . . . I have not the least doubt that on that evening He began a work of grace in me, though I obtained joy without any deep sorrow of heart, and with scarcely any knowledge. That evening was the turning point of my life.' Later he said that 'I never heard the gospel till I was twenty years and five or six weeks old; I never met with a Christian till I was twenty years and five or six weeks old',[11] and it appeared that up to that point none of his teachers had been Christians in the sense that he later understood: he said that only three of his 1260 or so contemporaries in the university were believers.[12]

The experience brought Müller spiritual peace, joy and happiness, as he affirmed on many occasions, in terms such as: 'I entered the house of this tradesman as dead in trespasses and sins, and as utterly reckless and careless of divine things as any person

---

(1905; facsimile, Denton, TX: Westminster Literature Resources, 2003) [hereafter cited as *Autobiography*].

9. These are available electronically at the George Muller Charitable Trust in Bristol at 'George Müller's Sermons', <https://www.mullers.org/mullerssermons>, accessed 13 Feb. 2018 [hereafter 'Müller House Transcripts']. They are available as a free PDF download which can be found by entering into an Internet search engine: "PDF The Writing and Teachings of George Müller of Bristol". Thirty-four were printed in *Jeh. Mag.* in 1876. It is certain that many more of Müller's sermons during his preaching tours begun in 1875 were printed, or summarized, in local newspapers particularly in North America and Australasia, as was customary. This is borne out by digitized Australian newspapers from the time of his visits to Australia in the period 1886–88 (see <https://trove.nla.gov.au/newspaper/>).

10. *Autobiography*, 9 & 10.

11. 'Address to Young Men', *Jeh. Mag.*, 224. There was perhaps an element of hyperbole here, because his friend, Beta, had come under conviction of sin following their roistering vacation in Switzerland in August and September 1825 and had come into contact with a Halle University teacher named Richter who was a believer and who provided Beta with a letter of invitation to Johan Veit Wagner in whose house the meetings were held (*Autobiography*, 9 and Holthaus, 'Georg Müller', 7). See also the sermon cited in n. 12.

12. 'Christ the Refuge of Sinners. A sermon preached by George Müller at Kensington Baptist Chapel, Stapleton Road, Bristol, on Sunday morning, March 28th 1897, on the occasion of the Chapel anniversary', Müller House transcripts.

in existence. I came away from that little prayer meeting a happy young man—a happy believer in Christ!'[13] This formulation of 1897 may have benefitted somewhat from the lapse of seventy-two years since the event. As he said when the relevant passage of the *Narrative* was first formulated, it was a decisive turning point, but he lacked both a sense of deep repentance and knowledge. So, it was as if his later presentations of the gospel were designed to prevent others from beginning their Christian lives with such ignorance, and to ensure that the young Christian's understanding was quickly enhanced. It did not matter that the probability was that, often, his audience was mainly believing Christians already: it weighed on him that some might not be, and needed to have the chance to hear the gospel. But, however brief the reference, soteriologically, it was a full gospel that he declared. The following is an extended example from the year 1876 (three other examples are given in an appendix):

> Let me affectionately ask,—Have we all obtained the forgiveness of our sins? That is the point! that is the point! Are we all pardoned sinners? We are all sinners, without exception. Are we all pardoned sinners? Have we all obtained the forgiveness of our sins? That is the point! I have no doubt many hundreds here have; but at the same time I cannot help feeling that there are many who have not. Now this is the momentous point,—To which of the two classes do we belong? Pardoned sinners,—sinners with a load of guilt removed; or unpardoned sinners, unable to look up to God peacefully, calmly,—through the atonement of the Lord Jesus Christ? Ask yourselves before God,—To which class do I belong? If I am not pardoned, I am without peace, I cannot look peacefully and calmly forward to eternity, and do not know what will be the end of my course. It is a fearful thing to go on day by day unpardoned.
>
> This leads to the question,—How can we obtain the forgiveness of our sins? Simply through laying hold by faith on the atonement of the Lord Jesus Christ. God, in the riches of His grace, instead of sending us to the place of perdition, as we deserved, laid all the punishment due to our numberless transgressions on His Son the Lord Jesus Christ. Him He sent into the world, that in our room and stead He might work out a righteousness for us in fulfilling the whole law of God; so that poor guilty sinners who trust in Him shall be looked on by God as if they had lived the holy and spotless life of the Lord Jesus Christ. The believing sinner, standing before God in the righteousness of Christ, hiding himself—as he does—in the righteousness of the Lord Jesus Christ wrought out for the poor sinner who trusts in Him, is accepted of Him. In our stead the Lord Jesus Christ bore every particle of the punishment we wicked, guilty sinners ought to have endured. Now God looks to us not to do something to complete the work of salvation, but to accept what He so graciously provides for the sinner in the person of His Son, whose righteousness He accepts for the sinner.
>
> But when the sinner believes in the Lord Jesus Christ, a different life begins; he seeks to please Christ, he seeks to adorn His doctrine, he seeks to walk according to His mind. He does this not to be saved thereby, or to add to the work of the Lord Jesus Christ. But having through faith been saved, having obtained forgiveness, and having been accepted in the righteousness of the Lord Jesus Christ wrought out for sinners, he seeks to please

---

13. 'Christ the Refuge'.

God. This is the way to obtain forgiveness—simply trusting in Jesus, thus believing in Jesus. Whosoever does this obtains forgiveness.

Another important point is the knowledge of our forgiveness. We are not to wait for this knowledge till we die, far less are we to wait for it for the judgment-day. The blessing is to be had now, is to be known now, is something to be enjoyed now.[14]

This, and the examples in the appendix, speak for themselves. But it is worth noting certain points about his gospel understanding and proclamation. First, his insistence that it was essential that, in coming to Christ, the individual had to recognize their sin and its seriousness. Secondly, that in Christ that serious circumstance was wholly dealt with without the saved sinner being able to contribute anything to the process on their own account. And, thirdly, his insistence on the atoning, substitutionary nature of Christ's death.

Müller had been converted without, initially, deep sorrow for his sin. As his life evolved he became more and more conscious of his own sin (even if the observer would have questioned whether Müller was a great sinner so much as the reverse). He regularly referred to his numberless sins and to his being the greatest sinner. He believed that those who were not Christians needed to see, first, that they were sinners in need of salvation: 'We must be brought to see', he told his hearers at Salem Chapel in February 1872, 'that we need a Saviour, that we are wicked persons who deserve nothing but punishment. As long as we have a good opinion about ourselves, and will do our best to please God, and make up for any little thing that might be wanting, we are altogether mistaken, we know nothing yet about the way to heaven. We must first see that we are sinners: that is, that we are wicked'.[15]

The same sermon also stressed the second and third points, those relating to the grace of absolute forgiveness and the means of atonement:

> But there is hope, hope for such wicked sinners as you and I are, but hope alone in God's appointed way. Hope in Jesus, but in no other way. Hope through the shedding of the blood of Jesus, but in no other way. Hope by God not sparing His only begotten Son, wounding Him, bruising Him, laying upon Him the punishment due to us. That blessed Holy One stands, and He has transferred to and laid on Him all our sins and all our iniquities. . . . So the Lord Jesus Christ became a substitute in the room both of such as you and I [*sic*]. We ought to be punished for our iniquities, for all our wicked deeds and wicked thoughts, for our pride and high-mindedness, for our self-will, and for our temper, and for all those things; but the blessed Lord Jesus has the punishment for all our sins laid on Him, he stood instead of us, and in our stead endured the torment, anguish, and punishment we ought to have borne throughout eternity. . . . all the woe, the misery, and anguish which ought to have come upon us throughout eternity was concentrated in that time when the Lord Jesus hung upon the cross. He came into the world to save sinners, to deliver them from hell, from the power of sin, to translate them into His own kingdom. . . . now you see what the sinner has to do—to depend upon Jesus for salvation. . . . here, in this very place, in this

---

14. 'The Forgiving God. A Sermon preached the Tabernacle, Penn Street, Bristol, on Sunday Morning, August 13th, 1876', in *Jeh. Mag.*, 308–10.

15. 'A Faithful Saying. Notes of a Sermon preached at the Opening of Salem Chapel, North Common, near Bristol, Feb. 27, 1872', in *Jeh. Mag.*, 162.

very hour it is to be had. No money to be paid for it, but only to accept what God in His wondrous grace and mercy has provided in His dear Son. If we do this we shall obtain forgiveness of sins, shall be accepted by God, shall be justified, shall be heirs of God and joint heirs with Christ, and have heaven at the last.[16]

From this, and indeed the whole extant corpus of his preaching, we can see that Müller's description of the means of salvation was classically evangelical. I have argued elsewhere, as have others, that the Open Brethren were substantially established by the evangelical revivals of 1859–62 and the succeeding revival campaigns, especially those of Moody and Sankey. In his national and international preaching tours from 1875 onwards, Müller saw himself as having the explicit task of deepening that work, including among both Christian ministers and the young.[17] In Britain in the 1870s, his itinerary was deliberately in the footsteps of Moody for that reason:

My purpose had been to go now to Liverpool, to follow up Mr. Moody's work there. I had corresponded with a beloved brother who particularly advised me to seek to lend a helping hand to the young converts. . . . What chiefly induced me to go to Newcastle was the desire to follow up Mr. Moody's work, and to seek to benefit young converts by seeking to instruct them in the things of God. Mr. Moody began his labours in England at Sunderland. From Sunderland he went to Newcastle; and I desired to follow in his track.[18]

So, his own exposition of the gospel rarely if ever failed to give a thorough account of why and how anyone could be saved, to ensure that people understood why they could reasonably consider themselves saved. And those of us who are familiar with Brethren gospel preaching over a long period of years can see how that cerebral style of proclamation has been widely replicated. This is so even perhaps in terms of language—many have heard the expression, 'room and stead', endlessly used in both the morning and gospel meetings. Whether consciously or not, Müller was adopting a usage which was familiar among Puritans and early evangelicals, and had legal pedigree in the later medieval term for military substitution for feudal obligations. But the question can still be asked whether Müller was in considerable part responsible for disseminating it to the Open Brethren more widely. What we can say is that it was a matter of normal practice for him to use it himself.

Implicit, too, in his soteriology was a strong doctrine of assurance—that the believer could be confident now that his or her sins are forgiven and rejoice in the sure and certain hope of eternal life. It can be discerned in the passages already cited. It remained explicit less than a year before he died:

I have not the shadow of a doubt that there are a vast number here present who do know and enjoy the knowledge of the forgiveness of their sins. But do you all? I have enjoyed the knowledge of the forgiveness of my sins. I have not the least doubt. I am as certain that

---

16. 'A Faithful Saying', 164–6.
17. The modern accusation that evangelicals have virtually always neglected what would now be termed 'discipling' or 'making disciples' is not justified in the case of Müller or the Open Brethren for most of their history.
18. 'Account of a Preaching Tour', 12 Jul.1875, in *Jeh. Mag.*, 282 & 285.

I shall go to heaven as if I were there already.... Therefore I know that my sins will be forgiven through faith in Christ; and that I shall go to heaven if I trust in the Lord Jesus!

Then, again, we may know that our sins are forgiven even whilst we are here.... there is no real state of enjoyment in God without knowing that we are accepted in Him—that our sins are blotted out by the atonement which the Lord Jesus has made for us![19]

'... it is a matter of deep moment that we be assured our sins are forgiven,' he told a conference in Bristol in November 1865, 'and habitually assured of it. Because it is just this which makes heaven certain to us—that we know that God has nothing against us.'[20] In the matter of assurance, too, Müller was classically evangelical.

Though he did not, so far as I can see, use the terms, Calvinism and Arminianism, his stance on this aspect of soteriology is interesting. While he referred to conversion as decisive for him, he acknowledged that, in July 1829 in Exmouth, Devon, there was a second experience that also shaped his life—he described it as being 'like a second conversion' because 'as to my soul, the change was so great'.[21] He wrote of its entailing 'an entire and full surrender of heart. I gave myself fully to the Lord. Honour, pleasure, money, my physical powers, my mental powers, all was laid down at the feet of Jesus'.[22]

Nearly sixty years earlier, he had described the experience in characteristically analytical terms, though he acknowledged that 'the Lord bestowed a great blessing upon me, for which I shall have cause to thank Him throughout eternity.'[23] Müller did not say who particularly influenced him, but, whoever he was,[24] he was connected with a group who had been associated with Norris Groves, who had left England on 12 June 1829 en route to Baghdad. Müller referred particularly to four insights: a new understanding of Scripture as 'alone our standard of judgment in spiritual things'; new understanding with respect to the return of Christ; the need for 'a higher standard of devotedness' (Groves's characteristic term); and, fourthly, new understanding of 'the doctrines of election, particular redemption, and final persevering grace.'[25] These last, following the new experience, he made a particular study of in Scripture: 'To my great astonishment I found that the passages which speak decidedly for election and persevering grace, were about four times as many as those which speak apparently against these truths; and even those few, shortly after,

---

19. 'Christ, the Refuge', Müller House transcripts.

20. 'A few words on "Crucified, Dead and Risen with Jesus." An Address delivered at a Conference of Christians held at the Victoria Rooms, Bristol, on the 7th of November, 1865', in *Jeh. Mag.*, 3.

21. *Autobiography*, 34.

22. Müller to J. Gordon Logan, 17 Jul. 1895, printed in G. H. Lang, *Anthony Norris Groves: Saint and Pioneer* (London, 1949), 39. Lang said that he transcribed the letter from the original while staying with Logan in Egypt in 1910.

23. *Autobiography*, 33.

24. In her short biographical account of Müller in 1883, his second wife referred to the key individual as 'a minister from London': Mrs Müller, *A Brief Account of the Life and Labours of George Müller (of Bristol)* (2nd edn., London, 1887), 11.

25. Mrs Müller, *A Brief Account*, 33–4.

when I had examined and understood them, served to confirm me in the above doctrines.'[26] He went on the state that these truths particularly resulted for him in a more devoted, holy and consistent Christian life.[27]

Unsurprisingly, his convictions did not change with time. In October 1871, he told his interdenominational audience at the Clifton Conference (which may have included not a few Calvinists),

> How then may we be "of God?" First, we have to trace it all up to the councils and purposes of God from eternity. He did choose us in Christ. He did apprehend us in Christ. He predestinated us to be conformed to the image of His dear Son. He arranged from eternity for our salvation in the Lord Jesus Christ.[28]

This was by no means the only time that he referred to predestination. But he was not deterministic in his understanding of it. It was, he went on to tell his hearers at Clifton, effective through faith and that depended on human choice:

> . . . we have to believe the testimony of God regarding the Lord Jesus Christ, we have to submit to the Gospel, we have to receive the atonement, and to rest on it alone as the ground of our acceptance. . . . the enjoyment, the blessedness, the realization of our having been predestinated of God and chosen in Christ comes through faith. . . . I have therefore to believe that the despised, the rejected, the crucified Jesus of Nazareth is the promised Messiah, the Saviour, and I have to depend on Him as such. And this settles the matter.[29]

He continued:

> But one peradventure says, "You have been telling us that believers are 'of God' primarily as regards election and predestination, and I can do nothing to save myself, but must wait until God does it for me." This is Satan's trap for the poor sinner. It is quite true that you cannot predestinate yourself; it is quite true that you cannot save yourself. Quite true! But what God expects is, that you should receive, as a poor lost sinner, the Lord Jesus Christ. If you say, "Oh, I wish I could believe!" well, I grant it, you cannot if left to yourself. But you can groan out to God, "Lord, help me to believe." If you say, "My heart is full of sin, and I cannot cleanse it,"—I grant it. But you can groan out, "Help me, O Lord; look on me, a poor, wretched, guilty sinner, through the Lord Jesus Christ;" and as truly as you desire anything from God, you will find Him more than ready to bestow the blessing than you are to receive it. Look at the whole life of our adorable Lord Jesus Christ. Did any ever come to Him really desiring blessing, and be denied? Assuredly not![30]

---

26. As Mark Stevenson has shown in depth, Müller was not alone among early Brethren in his Calvinistic soteriology: see Mark R. Stevenson, *The Doctrines of Grace in an Unexpected Place: Calvinistic Soteriology in Nineteenth-Century Brethren Thought* (Eugene, OR, 2017).

27. Mrs Müller, *A Brief Account*, 34.

28. '"Of God." An Address delivered at the Conference of Christians at Clifton, October 3rd, 1871', in *Jeh. Mag.*, 141–3.

29. '"Of God."', 142–3.

30. '"Of God."', 147.

No doubt, for some Calvinists, this is sufficient for them to conclude that he was not a Calvinist![31]

Finally, under the heading of soteriology, it is worth touching briefly on his approach as a gospel preacher. We have already noted that he missed no occasion to make the gospel plain and call his hearers to decision about it, even when there were likely to be few unbelievers present. Further, while he did not threaten his hearers into the kingdom with graphic descriptions of the fires of hell, in addition to stressing the extreme wickedness of the natural man or woman, he did underline that, naturally, they were in the grip of the enemy,[32] that they deserved eternal punishment, woe, misery, and anguish,[33] that eternal punishment was to be contrasted with the prospect of eternal joy and happiness,[34] that even orphans could expect 'the place of torment' if they did not trust Christ (and orphans sharing the same bed might find themselves separated in eternity).[35] Also, he did not shrink from reminding adults and children alike of the precariousness of life—all in the effort to press the gospel successfully upon his hearers.[36] He did so with restraint, but, given the common background knowledge of his audiences, perhaps it was not necessary to do more.

Sanctification and discipleship

It is fashionable in evangelical circles today to be dismissive of former generations of evangelicals on the alleged grounds that they focussed only on dramatic conversion and neglected the importance of the Christian life, of personal holiness, and of practical compassion for the world—in a word that they were antinomian. How this dismissal is achieved in the face of the widespread holiness movements of the last 200 years, the extensive works of compassion of evangelicalism, and Müller's own concern for the better instruction of the converts of revival meetings as already noted, is hard to comprehend.

Given Müller's own dual initial experiences, with a second set of events leading by his own account to a much deeper Christian life and commitment, it would have been surprising if he had neglected the need for life worthy of forgiveness and salvation through the gospel. It is true however that his understanding of the need for holiness was so intimately linked to his soteriology that it is perhaps easy to overlook it. For in his gospel

---

31. Mark Stevenson has questioned this assertion (*The Doctrines of Grace*, 133, n.120), but does so by arguing that such are hyper-Calvinists and therefore not Calvinists. The difference between us seems to be one of classification.

32. '... serving him, being led about by him according to his will, and our hearts naturally being in sympathy with the evil one, obeying him, and acting according to his bidding.' ('"Of God."', 141.)

33. '"A Faithful Saying" Notes of a Sermon preached at the Opening of Salem Chapel, North Common, near Bristol, Feb. 27, 1872 1 Timothy 1, 15, 16', in *Jeh. Mag.*, 163 & 165.

34. 'Address to Young Men', in *Jeh. Mag.*, 222.

35. 'The Rich Man and Lazarus, Portion of an Address delivered to the Orphans of the Ashley Down Orphan Houses, April 3rd, 1874', in *Jeh. Mag.*, 264–9.

36. 'How do you know that you will ever get to your death-bed? The next time you travel—rush! and in an instant you are carried away in a railway accident; the next time you ride in a carriage, off the horse goes, and in an instant you are thrown out, and in eternity; the next time you go out, a tile falls on your head from the roof, and in an instant you are in eternity.' 'Address to Young Men', in *Jeh. Mag.*, 239.

challenges he rarely failed to spell out the practical implications and expectations for the life of those who believed.

He habitually emphasized that salvation meant that the believer had become a child of God, a joint-heir with Christ and an heir of God: 'Throughout eternity we shall be unspeakably happy, and love one another perfectly and habitually. But we are to glorify God by manifesting this love now, while on earth, in weakness and exposed to conflict, while the struggle is going on'.[37] 'The two great objects of our salvation are—first, primarily and especially, that God may be glorified, and secondly, at the same time, that His children may be conformed to the image of His dear Son, in order to insure their eternal happiness.'[38]

> Such to whom God has been gracious . . . what becomes us to do? To show forth our gratitude to God who has done so much for us! That is our one great business of life, if we have believed in the Lord Jesus Christ, to be grateful to God for all He has done for us in Jesus, . . . How may I show forth gratitude? Evidently, by seeking to do those things which please God, according to His mind revealed to us in the Holy Scriptures . . . therefore . . . seeking to abstain from those things which contrary to the mind of God . . . we are to seek also to please God in doing those things which are according to His mind.[39]

In 1887, he was clearer still and gave an interesting example of what he meant by the Christian's duty to glorify God and be conformed to the image of his Son:

> Now this is being done, the question is—what next our hands find to do with our might. If the matter of our salvation is settled, the most deeply important point is to glorify God whilst life is continued to us. That is our great business whereby we shew our love and gratitude to God, for all His great love and wondrous grace in the gift of His only Son. To live for Him, to glorify Him we should make the great, sole business of our whole life, in comparison with which all other business is trifling. . . . thus it should be . . . with every true believer in the Lord Jesus Christ, after the matter of salvation is settled, there should be this **one** thing, to live for God, to glorify God. Now this implies a great deal and in order that the subject, to the utmost of my ability, may be of a practical character, I will hint at a few things, as illustrating how we may glorify God.
>
> For instance, we are surrounded by poor believers—do we care for these? Do we seek to minister to them with supplies from our own means? Are we really interested in their temporal concerns? Do we realise that this is the will of God concerning us—that if there are poor believers surrounding us that it is His mind that we should care for them? There are sick ones—do we care for their comfort, aid them, minister to their necessities, provide things to ease their pain and comfort them on their bed of languishing? Do we care for

---

37. 'A few words on "Crucified, Dead and Risen with Jesus": An Address delivered at a Conference of Christians held at the Victoria Rooms, Bristol on the 7th of November, 1865', in *Jeh. Mag.*, 4.

38. 'Love one another. Notes of Two Addresses delivered at a Conference of Christians at Clifton, October, 1863', in *Jeh. Mag.*, 34–5.

39. '"The Whole World lieth in Wickedness." An Address delivered at the Conference of Christians at Clifton, October 4th, 1871. 1 John v. 10', in *Jeh. Mag.*, 152–3.

them with our "might", not in a trifling, careless way, but with our "might", as the Lord Himself says in His own Word? Are we doing it?[40]

He went on to give a number of other practical examples of ways in which the believer was to glorify God, very much in the vein of activist evangelicalism. 'Works', he had said thirteen years earlier, 'have their right and proper place, and we cannot make too much of works in their right and proper place. But the right place of works is this: we must have the forgiveness of our sins, we must have peace with God, be at one with God, before there can be found in us one single good work in which God can be well pleased. . . . not working for life, but from life, . . . then we cannot work too much for God, cannot be too much dead to the world, cannot make it too much manifest that we are dead to the world and alive to God.'[41] That he felt it necessary to speak in these terms suggests that there were, as in all generations, shallow evangelical Christians who needed to grasp the implications of discipleship.

For Müller the practical manifestations of the Christian life were a natural consequence of understanding the spiritual standing which the Christian enjoyed. So he was as interested in the emotional state of the Christian as in his or her praxis. For him to be a believer was above all to be happy. This was a theme virtually throughout his ministry and reflected his own experience immediately on becoming a believer, as already noted. Joy and happiness were initiated by conversion: 'It is just this very reception of the Lord Jesus Christ which gives real joy, real happiness, real gladness of heart', he told young men and evidently many young women at Bethesda Chapel in 1873. 'The other is a mere fancy, a dream-like joy; there is no reality in it; it brings nothing but an aching heart afterwards, whatever the apparent joy for the time being may be.'[42] But this state was equally continued by the full surrender of discipleship; as was clear in both Testaments, holiness and happiness were intimately linked:[43] 'Are we occupied?', he asked the Clifton Conference in 1870:

> Are we living for the Lord: Are we labouring for the Lord? Is it our one great business in life to live for Him? How many objects have we set before us, on account of which we desire to live on earth? To please our God and Father, and to seek to imitate the blessed Lord Jesus Christ, this is the one business of life—the only one business of life. The one in a profession, or in any occupation of life, seeking to live, to labour, to bear fruit for the Lord! . . . Is my one great business of life to be a fruit-bearer, to live to the praise of Him who purchased us with His precious blood? Remember, these hands and feet and ears and eyes are not ours, they belong to Jesus—He bought them. Our tongue is his, and our brain is His; our time is His, all our talents are His. All He has given us belongs to Him, and at His feet we have to lay it down. And what will be the result of this? Ah! we shall have true wealth; we shall have true joy. I do not mean by this, that as soon as you get money

---

40. 'Address on Ecclesiastes 9 v. 10. A sermon preached at Alma Road, Bristol, on Sunday evening, July 24th, 1887', Müller House transcripts.

41. 'Holding Fast the Gospel. Notes of a Sermon delivered in Bethesda Chapel, Bristol, March 1st, 1874. 1 Cor. xv.1, 2', in *Jeh. Mag.*, 246.

42. 'Address to Young Men', in *Jeh. Mag.*, 224.

43. 'Part of an Address on Isaiah 3: 10–11. A sermon preached at Alma Road, Bristol, on Sunday evening, 26th June 1887', Müller House transcripts.

you are to throw it out of the window; or when God gives a business, to put it all aside and say you have nothing to do with the world. The very reverse of this. We are to do all to the honour and glory of the Lord Jesus, . . . This is true liberty, true joy, and true happiness.[44]

In this, Müller certainly anticipated the Keswick Convention's message of full surrender. The goal was 'out and out' Christians: '"out and out" we are His, and not our own ... for ... all the days of our life, we and all we have and are, belong to the Lord.'[45]

The joy and happiness of the believer who was surrendered to God did not however preclude asceticism in the disciple's conduct. However shallow may have been Müller's conversion in his own estimation, he said he immediately gave up his wicked companions and 'the habit of going to taverns was entirely discontinued'.[46] He also gave up his former passion for French and German novels,[47] and regretted that he had contracted himself to complete a translation of a French novel. He claimed to have known of the happiness of the billiard table, the theatre (of which he said that he was 'passionately fond'), and the ball-room, but had given them up as resulting in '[w]retchedness and misery' on becoming a Christian.[48] Elsewhere, I have written of his encouragement of Christian women to give up jewellery, fine clothing and other adornment and to make the resulting financial benefits over to the Lord's work.[49] Those who had sympathy for 'balls, theatres and some extraordinary parties and the prospect of joining them; . . . about becoming rich in this world, . . . [about] getting a great name in this world were either not true believers or were Christians who were 'not alive to the things of God, and if a spiritual thermometer were applied to your heart, it would be seen that you are all but lifeless.'[50] George Müller was a happy ascetic, and thought other Christians should be too.

Though Müller set high standards for himself and expected other Christians to achieve them too, he did not subscribe to perfectionism. While Christians had the means to overcome sin in a way that the unbeliever did not, they could nevertheless expect to struggle with sin in this life. As he said in 1889, his preaching tours were to encourage 'more real separation from the world, . . . to promote heavenly-mindedness . . . according to the Scriptures. At the same time, however, I warn them against *extravagances* (such as

---

44. 'Waiting for Christ. An Address delivered at the Annual Conference of Christians at Clifton, October 5th, 1870', in *Jeh. Mag.*, 120–1.

45. '"A Garden Inclosed." An Address delivered at a Conference of Christians of various denominations held at Clifton, on Tuesday, September 30th, 1873. Song of Solomon iv.12–16', in *Jeh. Mag.*, 196.

46. *Autobiography*, 10.

47. *Autobiography*.20.

48. 'Address to Young Men', in *Jeh. Mag.*, 227–8. Müller said that after his conversion in 1825 he went only twice to the theatre and once to a concert, 'when I likewise felt that it was unbecoming of me as a child of God, to be in such a place': *Autobiography*, 27.

49. Neil Summerton, 'The Spirituality of George Müller', in Neil T. R. Dickson and T. J. Marinello (eds.), *Culture, Spirituality, and the Brethren* (SBH: Troon, 2014), 259–76, spec. 274.

50. 'The Redeemed in the Wilderness. An Address delivered at a Conference of Christians of various denominations, held at Clifton on Wednesday, October 1st, 1873', in *Jeh. Mag.*, 211.

sinless perfection in the flesh), which are not taught in the Word of God.'[51] He enlarged on the point in one of his last sermons:

> ... we have now the spiritual conflict, our natural evil tendencies still are in us, though we are regenerated. The old nature is not removed; the old nature remains in us, just as it was before our faith in the Lord Jesus Christ. It is true we are regenerated, we are born again; it is true we have spiritual life—but it is also true that the old nature is not dead; the old nature still is in us, and can only be kept down by prayer and meditation and pondering the Word of God, and exercising faith continually. And therefore when trials come with regard to the old, evil, corrupt nature in us, we should spread the matter in all simplicity before God, ...
>
> ... On account of the evil habits that I had contracted as an unconverted young man, the ungodly way in which I had been living up to the end of the twentieth year of my life, I found it extremely difficult, though really a child of God and though hating sin and loving holiness, to overcome those evil tendencies which I had contracted.
>
> The appearance was, "O it will never be different, and my prayer will never be answered." But by the grace of God I have rolled my burden on Him, and come to Him again and again. Thus by little and little it came about—and it was by little and little only; it took some time—that these natural tendencies were overcome, and God helped me. ...
>
> We do not attain to it to the full while we are in the body; yet this will be our aim more and more, more and more, more and more to be like Christ.[52]

This chimed with what became a standard Open Brethren position on the Christian life, the struggle between the old and new natures, and the possibility of victory in Christ.[53]

Living by faith

The fourth particular of Müller's special spiritual experience in July 1829 at Exmouth was

> that it pleased the Lord to lead me to see a higher standard of devotedness than I had seen before. He led me, in a measure, to see what is my true glory in this world, even to be despised, and to be poor and mean with Christ. I saw, then, in a measure, though I have seen it more fully since, that it ill becomes the servant to seek to be rich, and great, and honoured in that world, where his Lord was poor and despised.[54]

Müller did not explain precisely how he came to this realization, apart from through the unknown mentor who was of the company at Exmouth in July 1829, and it was another fifteen months before he and his new wife, Mary Groves, chose to give up his stated

---

51. *Fiftieth Report of the SKI, 26 May 1888 – 26 May 1889*, 7.

52. 'Behold! what manner of love. A sermon preached by George Müller at Bethesda Chapel, Great George Street, Bristol, on Sunday evening, April 11th, 1897', Müller House transcripts.

53. I remember Montague Goodman speaking in similar terms in response to a question at Hildenborough Hall, Frinton, at the end of the 1950s, underpinned by an interpretation of *Romans* 6–8. There was an alternative, more perfectionist position deriving from Darby: see Neil T. R .Dickson, *Brethren in Scotland 1838–2000: A Social Study of an Evangelical Movement* (SEHT; Carlisle, 2002), 266–70.

54. *Autobiography*, 34.

salary as pastor of Ebenezer Chapel, Teignmouth. But the group that Müller was in touch with were certainly influenced by Norris Groves, who had, just as he was leaving for Baghdad, published the second edition of *Christian Devotedness, or The Consideration of Our Saviour's Precept, "Lay not up for yourselves treasures upon earth"*. The preface to this second edition referred not only to wealth per se but to 'the brassy admixture of earthly influence—the titles, honours, rank, wealth, learning and secular power of this world.'[55] And *Christian Devotedness* set out a very thorough-going, challenging, and practical application of Christian discipleship, one which Müller developed and enjoined throughout his ministry from 1830 onwards. It seems reasonable to suppose that *Christian Devotedness* played a part in the development of Müller's thinking in this period.

Müller's practice, and teaching, of living by faith are discussed extensively in my two earlier essays on the Scripture Knowledge Institution and his spirituality.[56] In the Annual Reports of the Scriptural Knowledge Institutions, which circulated in their thousands in the Christian community at home and abroad, he encouraged extravagant generosity in Christian giving; and held up his practice of living by faith as both remarkable evidence of the dependability of God and of a peaceful and joyful way of living the Christian life. There he clearly implied that it was the best way for a Christian worker's needs to be supplied, though he never regarded 'living by faith' as mandatory for believers, whether Christian workers or others, while he himself gave extensively, in effect from his own resources and from monies given to the SKI, to support those at home and abroad who were 'living by faith' ('labourers in the word and doctrine in the position of simple dependence on the Lord for their temporal supplies', as he termed it). But it is of interest that in his extant sermons, he rarely referred to living by faith, in the sense of the Christian worker's eschewing a salary and relying on God to supply temporal needs by way of others.

Ecclesiology

From more or less its very beginnings, Müller was at the heart of a new church movement within evangelicalism that we term 'Brethren'. Before and after the split of 1848, he was closely involved in shaping many of the key characteristics of what became the Open wing of the movement. This was not simply a question of reaction to the fact that Müller, Craik and Bethesda Chapel became the target of J. N. Darby's particular interpretation of the doctrine of separation after 1848.

A well-known feature of the aspirations and thought of the early Brethren was non-denominationalism, expressed in willingness to fellowship with all who were believers, including at the Lord's table, irrespective of current denominational connexion or lack

---

55. The second edition of the pamphlet was reprinted in its entirety in Lang, *Anthony Norris Groves*, 69–99. It can also be seen with Sentinel Kelp's reprint of *Memoir of the Late Anthony Norris Groves containing Extracts from His Letters and Journals Compiled by His Widow* (Sumneytown, PA, 2002). The sentence quoted appears on p.70 of Lang's volume. The preface to the second edition was dated 16 May 1829.

56. Neil Summerton, 'George Müller and the Financing of the Scriptural Knowledge Association', in Neil T. R. Dickson and Tim Grass (eds.), *The Growth of the Brethren Movement: National and International Experiences* (SEHT: Milton Keynes, 2006), 47–79; and id., 'The Spirituality of George Müller', in Dickson and Marinello (eds.), *Culture, Spirituality, and the Brethren*, 259–76.

of it. This noble aspiration itself became a source of doctrinal stress within the wider movement as it became a distinct, recognizable, and recognized church grouping (with its own sectarian wing) as the nineteenth century wore on. Müller himself retained the non- or inter-denominational aspiration, and if anything his commitment to it grew as the century and the character of his own ministry evolved. This was reinforced by the fact that the Bethesda group of churches had some characteristics, partly deriving from Müller's own de facto role in it, which were not classically Open Brethren, especially the linking of congregations planted from Bethesda.

The references to his soteriology earlier in this essay are sufficient in themselves to underline that for Müller the key distinction was between those who were true believers and those who were not, those who had been forgiven on the basis of Christ's atoning work and those who had not, those who were therefore children of God and those who were not. The former comprised the people of God, while the latter did not. The former included those who were at different stages in their spiritual growth and discipleship, but, in respect of acceptance by God, all were radically different from others. Müller was willing to fellowship and work with all the former. Hence, his willingness to take the platform at interdenominational conferences from the late 1850s onwards, his willingness to preach in, for example, Congregational and Baptist churches in the Bristol area, and his willingness to accept invitations from interdenominational groups of church ministers to speak in particular places during his national and international preaching tours (and to address groups of ministers during them). This would have been anathema to those Brethren who regarded the other Protestant denominations as 'the sects'. In the work of SKI and the Orphanages, it was always his practice to draw his personnel from Christians of all denominations. As he told a Clifton Conference in 1863,

> we must ever remember, that it is not the degree of knowledge to which believers have attained which should unite them, but the common spiritual life they have in Jesus; that they are purchased by the blood of Jesus; members of the same family; going to the Father's house—soon to be all there: and by reason of the common life they have, brethren should dwell together in unity. It is the will of the Father, and of that blessed One who laid down His life for us, that we should love one another.
>
> But it may be asked, *Is it possible*, that differing in this and that, brethren can be united together? They can. In the three orphan houses and six schools under my direction there are sixty teachers and other helpers. These are found belonging to the Church of England, Presbyterians, Independents, Baptists of close communion and open communion, Wesleyans of the Conference and of the Free Church parties, and of the so-called "Brethren". All these, though from different bodies of saints, are united together in this one object of labour for Christ. During the many years we have been thus engaged, I have never known a jar to take place because of such difference. This does not arise from any latitudinarianism in myself, but because, while holding firmly my own convictions, I have not required uniformity in these labourers. In engaging my helpers, it is indispensable that they belong to the Head, that they hold fast to the blessed Son of God.[57]

---

57. 'Love One Another', in *Jeh. Mag.*, 32–3.

This illustrates Müller's stance well enough. (Whether his helpers never discussed denominational difference between themselves seems doubtful, though they would probably have feared their master's rebuke if it had led to jarring. Also, even in the earlier days when the work of the SKI was less developed, Müller would have been hard-pressed to find his workers only from the Brethren.) He went on to warn his Clifton hearers not to 'make the basis of union an agreement about particular points of truth', nor to say that a difference was of no moment, or that they would never change their minds on particular points. Rather, 'Let there be more prayer, more study of the Word, more humility, more acting out of what we already know; thus shall we be more united together, not only in love, but in one mind and one judgment. There will be no difference in heaven. There all are of one mind. Let us aim at the heavenly condition.'[58]

Müller maintained this position throughout the remainder of his life. As he said in 1893, in a Baptist chapel:

> All the believers in Christ should love one another. No distinction between rich and poor, learned and illiterate, whether they belong to us of the same church, or to another church— we are to love one another because we belong to Christ. . . . I love all who love the Lord Jesus Christ, and for seventeen years, in which I was almost always travelling about in all parts of the earth . . . I preached in the Church of England, amongst the Congregationalists, amongst the Baptists, amongst the Methodists, among all denominations, and I preached provided they loved the Lord Jesus Christ. . . . Wherever the foundation of our "most holy faith" was laid, there I preached.[59]

There were however limits. He would not preach in 'Socinian chapels' nor in Roman Catholic churches 'lest it should be supposed I was an admirer of the Pope'.[60] And he continued to scruple about biblical truth. He was guarded about what he said in Clifton in 1863. He confessed that in the 1830s 'having just received certain blessed truths—as the coming of the Lord, etc.—my natural tendency was to look down upon those who did not see them'.[61] He had changed his mind in about 1840. Nevertheless, he had not sacrificed 'one particle of those truths which I received in the year 1829', and,

> If it be truth, it is dear to the heart of Jesus—we are instructed in it by the blessed Spirit—it is found in God's book; it is therefore of great value, and must be esteemed worthy of being carefully and jealously guarded. We are therefore, not at liberty lightly to esteem, undervalue, keep in the background (much less to give up) the truth, even for the sake of union.[62]

---

58. 'Love One Another', in *Jeh. Mag.*, 34.
59. 'Spiritual Building. A sermon preached at Philip Street Baptist Chapel, Bedminster, Bristol on Sunday morning 12 November 1893', Müller House transcripts. It is interesting that whereas in a similar formulation in 1875, he had referred to 'the so-called Brethren', in 1893 he did not do so, though perhaps it was tact in a Baptist chapel that led him to refer instead to 'all denominations'.
60. 'Spiritual Building'.
61. 'Love One Another', in *Jeh. Mag.*, 30.
62. 'Love One Another', in *Jeh. Mag.*, 31.

Here, Müller was evidently wrestling to reconcile aspects of his thought and practice. But it is also evidence that he should not be regarded as going as far as those who left the Brethren for overt non-denominational independence, such as Grattan Guinness, Hudson Taylor, and Thomas Barnardo.[63] Throughout his life he maintained his support for manifestly Brethren missionaries and evangelists, and his connections with Brethren, as did Bethesda itself. Bethesda operated as an Open Brethren assembly, consistent with the principles that Müller and Craik enunciated in 1839 (see below),[64] though, perhaps for external consumption, Müller identified himself as its pastor.[65] On his preaching tours, he broke bread with Brethren when opportunity arose, while preaching wherever he was given invitation—his preaching tours were mainly to places, including the USA, where there were few assemblies at the time.[66] Müller's consistent references to the 'so-called "Brethren"' as a group at once signifies his identification with the non-denominationalism of the early years and with the Open Brethren as a group. It is possible to wonder what, among other things, lay behind the purpose of his national preaching tours in the 1870s, for he spoke of a

> deep consciousness that I had learned truth in the school of Christ during the forty-nine years I had been a believer, which I felt responsibility was laid on me to seek to communicate to others. I felt I knew God in a way which was not generally known. I felt I had an acquaintance with Scripture, and was able to apply truths in a way in which truths are not generally applied.[67]

His later extensive explanations of the purposes of his preaching tours had a distinctly Brethren flavour.[68] The truths on which he focussed included what we have already been

---

63. Grattan Guinness was an elder of Merrion Hall, Dublin, for a few years in the 1860s, Hudson Taylor was nurtured among Brethren in the 1850s, and likewise Barnardo in the 1860s. They all later struck out independently of the Brethren, however, though they continued to be deeply influenced by their spirituality and ecclesiology.

64. This much is clear from Edward K. Groves's descriptions in *Conversations on Bethesda Family Matters* (London, 1885) and *George Müller and his Successors* (Bristol, 1906). Groves went so far as to say that Müller bestrode Bethesda to the extent that the elders would decide one thing in Müller's absence, only for it to be reversed when the matter was referred to Müller! See *George Müller and his Successors*, 24–5, 32.

65. In the 1880s, his second wife regarded him as *tout court* 'the pastor' of Bethesda Chapel, even if at the time he was absent from the church for all but a handful of weeks each year, and had been for over a decade: Mrs Müller, *A Brief Account*, 53. And in 1881, Müller himself asserted, 'I have now been a Pastor for more than *fifty-one years*': *The Second Coming of Christ*, March 1881, Müller House transcripts.

66. See, for example, Mrs Müller, *The Preaching Tours and Missionary Labours of George Müller (of Bristol)* (2nd edn., London, 1889), 89, 98, 116, 117, Florence, where T. P. Rossetti was his translator,122–3, 217, 224, 293, 295, 298.

67. 'Account of a Preaching Tour', in *Jeh. Mag.*, 279. His desire to reinforce revival was understandable in the light of the fact that he understood that it was reading of his *Narrative* which had inspired James McQuilkin and Jeremiah Meneely in their prayer for revival in 1857–8: Müller's 'Introduction' (May 1883) to Mrs Müller, *A Brief Account*, vi–x.

68. See his 'Introduction' to the first edition of Mrs Müller, *The Preaching Tours*, vi–vii; and *Fiftieth Report of the SKI, 1888–89*, 5–7.

considering, but they also included his ecclesiological commitments. Müller's approach is illuminated by what Samuel Smith, the Liverpool businessman and MP, wrote of him in 1902. Smith admired him and printed part of one of his sermons as an appendix to his own autobiography. But he noted that he 'could not now accept the excessive literalism with which Müller interpreted Scripture, nor his insistence upon entire agreement with his views.' Since Smith immediately went on to assert that 'true saints are found among all varieties of Christians' and referred to Thomas à Kempis, Luther, Bunyan, George Fox, Wesley, Whitfield, Spurgeon, and Keble, there is the suspicion that their disagreements centred on ecclesiology.[69]

Müller was certainly the author (with Henry Craik) and propagator of key ecclesiological insights which came to characterize the Open Brethren. Those insights go back to the key spiritual experience of July 1829. He very quickly concluded not only that he should give up a stated salary as a Christian minister (he had concluded already in 1829 that 'as long as I sought *"the kingdom of God and His righteousness,"* my temporal supplies would be added to me'[70]), but also that he should give up connection 'with *any* state church or national religious establishment'; that in his missionary labours he should henceforth be 'guided by the Spirit, and not by men, as to time and place';[71] 'that *believers* only are the proper subjects for baptism, and that *immersion* is the only true scriptural mode in which it ought to be attended to';[72] that the breaking of bread should be every Lord's day (not by commandment, but the example of the apostles);[73] and that

> it appeared to me to be scriptural, according to Eph. iv., Rom. xii., etc., that there should be given room for the Holy Ghost to work through any of the brethren whom He pleased to use; . . . Accordingly at certain meetings any of the brethren had an opportunity to exhort or teach the rest, if they considered that they had anything to say which might be beneficial to the hearers.[74]

He said that this last point he began to apply immediately at Teignmouth in 1830, though 'as the truth was but in part apprehended, there was much infirmity mixed with the manner of carrying it out.' Müller was however here claiming that he had personally received insights that were to shape the character of worship among the Brethren, though, as is the

---

69. Samuel Smith, *My Life-Work* (London: 1902), 40–1. 'My early life threw me much into contact with . . . the "Plymouth Brethren," . . . For a time I was fascinated by the wonderful power the Brethren had in extracting spiritual truth from the Old Testament and by their unworldly lives, . . . Yet longer experience taught me to distrust the extreme theories of verbal infallibility on which the Brethren proceeded; I refer to such men as John Darby, and in a much less degree to George Müller. I found they were defective in charity to their fellow-Christians and quarrelled among themselves to a surprising degree. They demanded absolute concurrence in their systems of interpretation, and, as human minds differ, this was found to be impossible'. He continued in the same vein and referred to Neatby's history (42).
70. *Autobiography*, 37.
71. *Autobiography*, 36.
72. *Autobiography*, 45.
73. *Autobiography*, 45–6.
74. *Autobiography*, 46.

way with such new insights, it is possible that others were coming to similar conclusions in the nascent movement at the same time.

Whatever the case, Müller went on to say that it was several years before 'the Lord was pleased to teach me about this point more perfectly':

> That the disciples of Jesus should meet together on the first day of the week for the breaking of bread, and that that should be their principal meeting, and that those, whether one or several, who are truly gifted by the Holy Spirit for service, be it for exhortation, or teaching, or rule, etc., are responsible to the Lord for the exercise of their gifts: these are to me no matters of uncertainty, but points on which my soul, by grace, is established, through the revealed will of God.[75]

This further teaching from the Lord was probably received in developing the life and affairs of Bethesda and Gideon Chapels in Bristol in the 1830s, in discussion with his colleague, Henry Craik, and, in the case of baptismal practice, in interacting with his friend, Robert Chapman of Barnstaple. He and Chapman discussed the latter when Chapman visited Bristol in August 1836. Chapman argued that if unbaptized believers were regarded as 'walking disorderly', then they should be withdrawn from completely, not simply excluded from the Lord's table. If, however, they were not walking disorderly, the implication was that they should be accorded full fellowship, including that of the Lord's table. (It should be recalled that a similar debate was going on among English Baptists at the time.[76]) Müller said that he (and Craik also—raised a Presbyterian before being briefly a Baptist) concluded '*that we ought to receive all whom Christ has received* (Rom. 15. 7), *irrespective of the measure of grace or knowledge which they have attained unto.*'[77] This was the conclusion that the great majority of the 180 members of Bethesda Chapels accepted at a meeting on 28 August 1837 (Gideon Chapel did not need to do so as it did not require believer's baptism for membership). It became the basis on which in the twentieth century the progressive wing, at least, of the Open Brethren admitted to the Lord's table and into fellowship.

Seminal as to the other matters of church order was a retreat by Müller and Craik at the end of February and beginning of March 1839 which was explicitly to discuss matters of order and discipline in Bethesda and Gideon Chapels. (There were tensions, for example, in Gideon Chapel—a longstanding fellowship—about what we would now call open

---

75. *Autobiography*, 46.
76. For debate on the matter among Suffolk and Norfolk Baptists (only one of the matters of dispute) between 1830 and 1870, see Ashley J. Klaiber, *The Story of the Suffolk Baptists* (London, [1931]), 108–52. At St Mary's Baptist Chapel, Norwich, the matter became the subject of litigation in Chancery and the Master of the Rolls judged on 28 May 1860 that strict communion was not a fundamental principle of the faith of Particular Baptists and 'it is established that each congregation was, from the earliest time, at liberty to regulate its practice, either to the Strict Communion or to the Free or Mixed Communion, as it might seem best to such congregation' and St Mary's was free to alter its practice 'if such should be the opinion of the majority of its full members.' (Ibid., 135–7).
77. *A Narrative of some of the Lord's Dealings, with George Müller*, 1:203, quoted in Harold H. Rowdon, *The Origins of the Brethren* (London, 1967), 123.

worship.[78]) They sought to adduce their conclusions carefully from Scripture and set them out carefully in writing; they were subsequently printed in the *Narrative*.[79] They referred to four matters which were evidently sources of contention in the Chapels, as well as of concern to them: should local churches be led by recognized elders and, if so, how should they be appointed? How, by whom and when should matters of church discipline (in effect, exclusion) be dealt with? And how frequently should the Lord's Supper take place, and what should be the character of the meeting?

On church leadership, they concluded that there was 'the office of rulers and teachers' and that 'this office (in spite of the fallen state of the Church [?*pace* Darby]) should be in being, even down to the close of the present dispensation.' They noted that as soon as churches were formed 'Elders were appointed to take the rule over them and to fulfil the office of under-shepherds.' Such elders were not however to be elected by the fellowship, but rather the fellowship should wait on God to 'raise up such as may be qualified for teaching and ruling in His church'. Appointment was by the Holy Ghost and made known to the individuals concerned 'By the secret call of the Spirit . . . confirmed by the possession of the requisite qualifications . . . and by the Lord's blessing resting upon their labours', the success of which was an outward confirmation of their calling. It was incumbent on members of the fellowship to acknowledge such people and submit to their pastoral authority.

On church discipline, they concluded that such matters were to be 'finally settled' (a significant qualification, no doubt) in the presence of the whole local church and as an act of the whole body. The whole was to be responsible for it: 'the act of exclusion was not the act of the elders only, but of the Church.' By contrast, reception into fellowship 'is an act of simple obedience to the Lord, both on the part of the Elders and the whole Church. We are bound and privileged to receive all those who make a credible confession of faith in Christ'. As to when acts of reception, restoration, and exclusion should be dealt with, there was no scriptural proof, but Müller and Craik favoured a change of practice in which they should be dealt with at the breaking of bread, mainly for reasons of avoiding delay, good communication to the whole church, and testimony to it. But a special weeknight meeting could be called if the circumstances demanded. While Bethesda and Gideon were linked, matters would have to be dealt with at both places.

On the Lord's supper, there was no explicit scriptural command but the practice of the apostles and the early church 'would lead us to observe this ordinance every Lord's day'. On the character of the meeting, they concluded:

> As in this ordinance we show forth our common participation in all the benefits of our Lord's death, and our union to him and each other . . . , opportunity ought to be given for the exercise of gifts of teaching or exhortation, and communion in prayer and praise . . . The manifestation of our common participation in each other's gifts cannot be fully given at such meetings if the whole meeting is, necessarily, conducted by one individual. This

---

78. Müller wrote, 'Before brother Craik and I left Bristol for the [retreat] . . . things wore a gloomy appearance. A separation in the church seemed unavoidable.' (*A Narrative*, 1:281)

79. *A Narrative*, 1, 276–81. The quotations in the following paragraphs are from this statement. It is summarized in Rowdon, *Origins*, 125–6.

mode of meeting does not, however, take off from those who have the gifts of teaching and exhortation, the *responsibility* of edifying the church, as opportunity may be offered.

On the question of whether the bread should be broken by one of the elders or by each individual present (the matter seems to refer to whether a president should break the bread in pieces or whether each person should tear a piece for themselves), they could not say that either way was 'positively unscriptural', but they leant towards each person breaking for himself or herself. This was because 1 Corinthians 10: 16–17 referred to 'The bread which *we* break', because it expressed the fact that each believer had by their sins broken the Lord's body, and that in so doing 'we manifest our freedom from the common error that the Lord's supper must be administered by some particular individual, possessed of what is called a ministerial character, instead of being an act of social worship and obedience.' (Müller and Craik had been insistent that they should not be termed pastors of the church to the exclusion of others.)

These are all matters which we can see as being subsequently reflected in Open Brethren practice across the board. Perhaps in part at least they reflected conclusions to which others in the nascent Brethren movement were also coming. But their inclusion in the *Narrative*, in its successive editions, must surely have assisted their dissemination across the growing movement.

An aspect that is worth dealing with finally under the heading of ecclesiology is Müller's understanding of the work of the Holy Spirit and spiritual gifts. The work and power of the Holy Spirit he saw as essential to efficacy in the life of the believer and the church. It is not clear what was the spiritual character of the second experience which he had in July 1829. He did not describe it as such, but from the perspective of the intervening years, we can suggest that it seems very much to have been a 'second blessing' or 'baptism in the Holy Spirit'. By his own account, it brought about a remarkable change, for example, in joy, in his enthusiasm for prayer, in his approach to the Scriptures, and in his preaching (both the way in which he approached it and in the results). Six months later, 'My heart was burning with desire to tell of the Lord's goodness to my soul, and to speak forth what I considered might not be known to most with whom I met.' His ministry now freed some Christians from bondage, as well as brought about conversions. He and it also divided believers in Teignmouth, and particularly the attenders at Ebenezer Chapel. When he and Craik moved to Bristol there was very significant blessing in Bethesda and Gideon Chapels, to the extent that there were in nine years of their arrival between 550 and 600 in fellowship. By the mid-1870s 2,500 people had been received into fellowship since 1832,[80] and there were 1,000 in fellowship at the linked churches of Bethesda and Salem. By 1897, in sixty-five years, some 6,000 had been received into fellowship, leaving aside

---

80. In 1870, Müller noted that, over the years, 90 had been excluded from fellowship, presumably according to the procedures that he and Craik had adduced in 1839. He did not enlarge on the grounds of exclusion: 'Address on Psalm 119 v. 68 "The Lord is good and doeth good." A Sermon preached at Bethesda Chapel, Great George Street, Bristol on Thursday evening, March 3rd, 1870', Müller House transcripts.

'the branch Churches that have sprung out of the Church at Bethesda', which would account for thousands more.[81]

Müller did not explain this in the same way as would a modern Pentecostal or Charismatic. But he recognized the role of the Spirit in making the word of God effective and in empowering the gospel and the Christian. To be sure, the first of the four elements of his experience in 1829 was 'That the Word of God alone is our standard of judgment in spiritual things; that it can be explained only by the Holy Spirit; and that in our day, as well as in former times, He is the teacher of His people.'[82] The result was a new attitude to Scripture and a new practice of prayer and meditation on it. But the role of the Holy Spirit was crucial in it, and he referred on a number of occasions to his first experience of it in similar terms. As he told an audience of young converts at the Mildmay Conference Hall in 1875:

> we should read the Scripture *prayerfully*, never supposing that we are clever enough or wise enough to understand God's Word by our own wisdom. In all our reading of the Scriptures let us seek carefully to have the help of the Holy Spirit; let us ask, for Jesus' sake, that He will enlighten us. He is willing to do it. I will tell you how it fared with me at the very first; it may be for your encouragement. It was in the year 1829, when I was living in Hackney. My attention had been called to the teaching of the Spirit by a dear brother of experience. "Well," I said, "I will try this plan; and will give myself, after prayer, to the careful reading of the Word of God, and to meditation, and I will see how much the Spirit is willing to teach me in this way."
>
> ... I went accordingly to my room, and locked my door, and putting the Bible on a chair, I went down on my knees at the chair. There I remained for several hours in prayer and meditation over the Word of God; and I can tell you that I learned more in those three hours which I spent in this way, than I had learned for many months previously. I thus obtained the teaching of the Divine Spirit, and I cannot tell you the blessedness which it was to my own soul. I was praying in the Spirit, and putting my trust in the power of the Spirit, as I had never done before.[83]

His teaching always dwelt more on the importance of Scripture than of the Spirit, and his position on the Spirit was pre-Pentecostal (and consistent with what became standard Open Brethren teaching). At a united prayer-meeting in 1870, *inter alia* to pray 'for the outpouring of the Holy Spirit in the conversion of souls', he cautioned:

---

81. '"Open thy mouth wide, and I will fill it." A sermon preached by George Müller at the Gospel Hall, St Nicholas Road, Bristol, on Sunday morning, January 10th, 1897', Müller House transcripts.

82. *Autobiography*, 33.

83. 'Address to young converts. A Sermon preached at Mildmay Conference Hall [1875]', Müller House transcripts. The sermon focussed on the importance of the Scriptures for growth in spiritual life. The reference to Hackney was probably a flourish to make connection with his audience, given their location near to it. *Autobiography* was clear that the event took place on the visit to Exmouth, when he was living at Hackney (33).

None of us suppose that by this is meant that we are to pray for the Spirit now to be given to the Church of God; for we know He was given on the day of Pentecost to the Church in her collective capacity, to abide with her for ever, and has not been taken away, notwithstanding our many failings. Just as the cloudy and fiery pillar was not taken from the Israelites, notwithstanding their many provocations, so the blessed Spirit of God has not been taken away from the Church. Moreover, God has given His Spirit to the individual believer,—to all who put their trust in the Lord Jesus Christ. But though the Spirit dwells in the Church of Christ as to her collective capacity, and in the individual believer, nevertheless it is fitting and suitable and right on the part of the children of God, that they should ask God again and again, and with great earnestness, that He would work mightily by His Spirit. We depend entirely on the power of the Holy Ghost for the conversion of sinners. There might be the most mighty preacher, as to the knowledge of the Scriptures and the clearness with which he sets forth the truth; yet if the Spirit of God is not pleased to bless the word, he may preach for months, and yet there will be no blessing.

The gospel had to come 'in spiritual energy, in spiritual power.' 'Only as the Holy Ghost works will the gospel be effectual. We should all therefore, above all seek by earnest, frequent prayer, the power of the Holy Spirit.' This power should be sought not only by preachers and church ministers, but by other Christian workers, teachers, parents, and 'by all classes of believers'. It was 'the result of a holy walk and a prayerful life.'[84]

We have seen that the conclusions of 1839 on church life at Bethesda and Gideon referred to 'the gifts of teaching or exhortation' and that, as early as 1830, Müller sought to give 'room for the Holy Ghost to work through any of the brethren' in teaching and exhortation. Though not expressed in such terms, this was the beginnings of a new recognition of the importance of charismatic gift in the life of the church. It was expressed in the 1860s and 1870s in the inter-denominational conferences like that held annually at Clifton, where the text for the evening was chosen by the organizers but the speakers did not know whether they would be called upon to speak to it. It was certainly expressed in the Brethren practice of the open platform at meetings for ministry, as well as at the Lord's table. But Müller did not go as far as to identify other gifts, and certainly not the gift of the apostle. He said on more than on occasion that the gift of the apostle was not now available, though the grace of the apostle was:[85]

The office of the apostle we can never have, but this spiritual state of heart which the apostle had *we* may have, yea, ought to have; and just in the degree in which we have it, will the gospel which we preach come in power and in the Holy Ghost. . . .

We may not expect to be able to perform miracles, nor to have the gift of tongues, nor the office of an apostle; but we can confidently look for this spiritual power, and we shall not be disappointed. . . . Let us pray that God, in the riches of His grace, would raise up, as pastors and teachers, as evangelists, as district visitors and tract distributors, as teachers

---

84. 'The Gospel in the Holy Ghost. Notes of an Address on 1 Thessalonians i. 5', in *Jeh. Mag.*, 59 & 60.

85. '. . . whilst we cannot be apostles, we may aim after the grace of apostles': 'The Mighty God. An Address delivered at the Annual Conference of Christians at Clifton, October 4th, 1870', in *Jeh. Mag.*, 107.

of schools, etc., holy men, who shall speak not in word only, but also in power, and in the Holy Ghost, and in much assurance; and who by their manner of life shall commend themselves to the consciences of men.[86]

Similarly, he asserted that he had the grace of faith, not the gift of faith: 'Think not, dear reader, that I have the *gift of faith* of which we read in 1st Cor. xii., 9, and which is mentioned along with 'the gifts of healing,' 'the working of miracles,' and 'prophecy;'... *It is true* that the faith which I am enabled to exercise is altogether God's own gift; ... but it is *not* true that my faith is the gift of faith [of 1 Corinthians].'[87]

For Müller the prime purpose of the power of the Holy Spirit was, unsurprisingly, power in the gospel.[88] In his understanding of the work of the Holy Spirit, as in his understanding of the need for full surrender in the Christian life, he can be seen as a type of bridge between early evangelicalism and the twentieth century.

Eschatology

The third key insight which Müller gained in his experience at Exmouth in July 1829 was about the return of Christ. Previously, he had

> thought that things were getting better and better, and that soon the whole world would be converted. But now I found in the Word, that we have not the least scriptural warrant to look for the conversion of the world before the return of our Lord. . . . I found in the Word that the return of Jesus, and not death, was the hope of the apostolic Christians; and that it became me, therefore, to look for his appearing.

He had gone down to Exmouth ill and expecting—if not looking for—death; he returned looking for the coming of the Lord.[89] By January, 1830, 'I had seen the leading truths connected with the second coming of our Lord Jesus; . . . [and] learned the heavenly calling of the Church of Christ, and the consequent position of the believer in this world.'[90] Given the prominence of thought on second coming among the early Brethren, it is not surprising therefore that there were frequent references to it in his preaching; promulgating it was one of the key purposes of his preaching tours; and he also produced a pamphlet on the subject.

---

86. 'The Gospel in the Holy Ghost. Notes of an Address on 1 Thessalonians i.5' in *Jeh. Mag.*, 61–63. Though Müller denied that he could be an apostle, very shortly after his death a book described him as such in its title: F. G. Warne, *George Müller: The Modern Apostle of Faith* (London, 1898).

87. *Narrative*, 1:451. See Mrs Müller, *A Brief Account*, 59, as evidence that Müller, who would certainly have vetted his wife's text, held to the view in 1887.

88. Also: 'The Holy Spirit is given to us for the very purpose that out of us may "flow rivers of living water" (John 7 v 38) and if we do not grieve or quench the Spirit it is impossible to say to what degree "rivers of living water" may flow from us as regards the conversion of our fellow-men, and the building up of our brethren and sisters in Christ. It is impossible to say to what degree the Holy Spirit is ready to use us, if we are desirous of being used and if we live in such a way as to be vessels "meet for the Master's use" (1 Timothy 2 v 21)': 'Address on Ecclesiastes 9 v. 10. A Sermon preached at Alma Road, Bristol, on July 24th, 1887', Müller House transcripts.

89. *Autobiography*, 34.

90. 'On the late Mr. Henry Craik', in *Jeh. Mag.*, 11.

By his own admission, he began as an enthusiast. In 1829, he had assumed that the Russo-Turkish war then in progress heralded the end.[91] He came to be more cautious on such details. But, from then on, expectation of the Return remained a spur to evangelism:

> ... the effect it produced upon me was this: From my *inmost soul* I was stirred up to feel compassion for the perishing sinners, and for the slumbering world around me lying in the Wicked One, and considered, "Ought I not to do what I can to win souls for the Lord Jesus, and to arouse a slumbering church?". I determined consequently to go from place to place, in order to preach the Gospel and arouse the Church to look and *wait* for the second coming of the Lord from heaven.[92]

In mature years, he remained a premillennial dispensationalist, he looked for the restoration of Israel as a key event in the last days, and he distinguished the first resurrection from a final one. But he was cautious about specifying future details and, above all, timing: 'If we attempt to say it will be next month, it will be next year, we should not stand on scriptural ground; for it is written, "Of that day and hour knoweth no man, not the angels of heaven."'[93] So,

> we should not be too hasty in at once forming a judgment, that because such and such an event has taken place, therefore in such and such a time it is certain that the Lord Jesus will return; lest, when such and such a time shall have passed, and after all our adorable Lord had not been revealed, unbelievers should turn round and say, "The time has passed, and the Lord Jesus, of whose return you talked so much, has not come; and after all, is there anything in the truth about His return?" We should be careful not to give a handle to those who speak evil of the truth; and not lay too much stress on certain events which may not be God's instruments in ushering in the return of the Lord.[94]

In his speaking and writing in his mature years, Müller for the most part sought to stress both what was certain from Scripture and what he judged practically profitable for unbeliever and believer alike. So the return of the Lord was certain, and the truth was neglected at practical peril for believer and unbeliever. 'We are to be living like men and women waiting for the return of their Lord.'[95] 'We should seek to have our hearts kept practically in such a state, that in any hour of the day or night we should be willing to give up everything; and when the last trump shall sound to [welcome the Lord]. . . . There should be no plans of ours regarding which we should not like to be interfered with by

---

91. 'Waiting for Christ. An Address delivered at the Annual Conference of Christians at Clifton, October 5th, 1870', in *Jeh. Mag.*, 113; & '"Watchman what of the Night?" An Address at the Clifton Conference of Christians, October, 1872. Is. xxi.11, 12', 175: 'many good, excellent Christians said, "Now is come the time that the Euphrates shall be dried up;" "now the Ottoman Empire will be destroyed, and Israel will be restored," and so on; and I, as a young disciple, very naturally took up the views and repeated words of my elder brethren.'
92. Müller, *Second Coming*, Müller House transcripts.
93. 'Waiting for Christ', 113.
94. 'Waiting for Christ', 114. He spoke in the same vein at the Clifton Conference two years later: *Jeh. Mag.*, 174–6.
95. 'Waiting for Christ', 118.

the coming of the Lord.' Otherwise, 'are we unfitted ourselves to be His instruments in promoting the glory of His name.'[96] Christians should 'love the very thought of being at last with Jesus, of being free from sin like Jesus'.[97] They should long for the return of Christ, rather than simply their own death, because death resulted only in the partial happiness of the believer while the return of Christ meant that believers would have redeemed bodies and 'the whole *family* [not just individual believers will be] brought into happiness and blessedness . . . [and] the *whole* elect family will receive their glorified bodies.'[98]

This did not at all mean that he abandoned the premillennial commitments that he had discovered in his youth. He had rejected post-millennial conviction of the conversion of the world and the improvement that it implied. Rather, he expected decline and that the establishment of the kingdom would depend on the return of the Lord:

> During the present dispensation, *before* the return of our Lord, Satan will not be bound; therefore sin and open wickedness will continue to the end of it; and instead of becoming better, things, according to Scripture, will *become worse and worse*. It is impossible to shut one's eyes to the fearful wickedness now around us everywhere; for murders of the most cruel character, and numerous other atrocious crimes, are, even in this enlightened nineteenth century, continually being committed. How certainly does all this prove that Satan is not yet bound, that he is *even now* the god of this world, and has power *still*; and because he *knows* that his time will be comparatively short, he manifests his hatred against God and against His people to the very utmost.[99]

---

96. 'Waiting for Christ', 114–5.
97. 'The Good Fight of Faith. 2 Timothy iv. 7, 8. Notes of an Address delivered in Bethesda Chapel, Lord's-day Evening, May 14, 1871', in *Jeh. Mag.*, 131.
98. '"Watchman what of the Night? "', 177.
99. *Second Coming*. He enlarged further on the point:
    we find passage after passage in the New Testament in which we are expressly told, either by Christ or by the apostles, that at the close of the present dispensation *wickedness will abound* both among professed believers and in the world at large, in proof of which I will refer to one single passage of Scripture only. In 2 Tim 3 v 1–5 we read, "This know also, that in the last days perilous times shall come. For men shall be lovers of their own selves, covetous, boasters, proud, blasphemers, disobedient to parents, unthankful, unholy, without natural affection, truce-breakers, false accusers, incontinent, fierce, despisers of those who are good, traitors, heady, high-minded, lovers of pleasures more than lovers of God; having *a form of godliness*, but denying the power thereof." Here we have particularly to keep before us that this is not a description of Pagans or Mahometans, but of the professed disciples of the Lord Jesus; for to such a state will Christendom, or the professing Church of Christ, be reduced at the end of the present dispensation.

Notice especially that of these persons it is said, they have a *form* of godliness. They wish to be considered Christians, they are not avowed infidels and atheists, but professed *believers*. Are we, then, to expect that things around us will gradually improve, or rather, that as we approach the end of the age the darker they will become? True it is that one day, "The earth will be filled with the knowledge of the Lord, as the waters cover the sea", but this will never be until Jesus Himself comes. In the meantime lawlessness will increase, and the socialism, the communism, the nihilism, etc., of which we now hear so much, will at last be headed up in the personal Antichrist, the man of sin.

This would be reversed only by the coming itself 'when Himself shall put aside war, Himself take the power and reign, and all the kingdoms of the world shall become the kingdoms of the Christ of God; . . . and subdue everything that is contrary to Himself.'[100]

Müller's pamphlet of 1881, *The Second Coming*, was on familiar premillennial lines. Space does not permit further analysis. But, certainly, he looked forward to glory. It is interesting, in particular, that he expected not rest there, but service, by which he meant work. More than once he spoke in terms such as these from 1897:

> And in this [resurrected] body, . . . we shall know nothing of weariness. At present, we may be able joyfully and gladly to work eight, ten, or twelve hours, sometimes fourteen, or even sixteen hours a day, but at last the weakness comes by reason of yet being in the body of humiliation, and not in the glorified body. But, then, there will be four and twenty hours' work hereafter, and the next day the same, and the next day the same; and thus seven times four and twenty hours every week the ability to work; and thirty days every month the whole day able to work. And thus it will go on, month after month, year after year, one hundred years after the other, one thousand years after the other, one million years after the other, and so throughout eternity. Work, work, work! Constant work to the glory of God in this our glorified body![101]

Heaven would be paradise for the workaholic too! God rested from his labour, but George Müller did not wish to, it seemed.

Müller also diverged from what were going to become standard Open Brethren views on the question of rapture and the tribulation. In answer to written questions put to him at an inter-denominational conference in Toronto on 10–12 December 1879, he stated:

> I know that on this subject there is great diversity of judgment, and I do not wish to force upon other persons the light I have received myself. . . . having been a careful, diligent student of the Bible for nearly fifty years, my mind has long been settled on this point, and I have not the shadow of a doubt about it. The Scriptures declare plainly, that the Lord Jesus will *not* come until the apostasy shall have taken place, and the man of sin, the "son of perdition" (or personal Antichrist), shall have been revealed, as seen in 2nd Thess. ii. Many other portions also of the Word of God distinctly teach, that certain *events* are to be fulfilled before the return of our Lord Jesus Christ.[102]

Preceding the Coming would be not only the apostasy or tribulation, but also 'The conversion and restoration of Israel nationally (who will have returned to their own land in *unbelief*); for in Scripture the glory and resurrection of the Church of the first born

---

100. 'The Mighty God', in *Jeh. Mag.*, 107–8.
101. '"Behold! What manner of Love"', Müller House transcripts.
102. Mrs Müller, *The Preaching Tours*, 140–141. Unusually for this work, Müller is quoted verbatim. It was suggested in correspondence in *Believer's Magazine* in the 1950s that Müller changed his mind on the timing and the rapture just before his death. G. H. Lang researched this and concluded that this was not so: *Believer's Magazine*, no. 783 (Dec. 1953), 218–9; and no. 788 (May 1954), 95; and F. Roy Coad, *Prophetic Developments*, CBRF Occasional Paper no. 2, 1966, 27i & n. 16, citing a paper said to be in G. H. Lang's papers—now in the Christian Brethren Archive.

ones is always connected with the time when Israel again "shall know the Lord." (Psalm 102 v 16).'[103]

Müller's view of the coming was however premillennial: it would be co-incident with the first resurrection (of believers only) who would then reign with Christ in a earthly millennium (Satan being bound in the bottomless pit), which would be followed by the second, general resurrection, judgment, the casting of Satan into the lake of fire, and the eternal reign in the new heaven and the new earth.[104]

There is a further point on which his eschatology was unusual for a premillennialist. Towards the end of his life, he believed that it was more than a 'little flock' that was going to be received by God in the last days:

> "I beheld, and lo, a great multitude, which no man could number." It is out of the power of any human being to count the vast number of the saved ones. "Which no man could number, of all nations, and kindreds, and people, and tongues stood before the throne." . . . all these saved ones, this innumerable multitude of all nations and tribes and peoples and languages were in the attitude of servants before Jehovah. . . .
>
> This is not a salvation for a few chosen ones, or a few hundreds, nor even a salvation of a few thousands; but of an innumerable multitude saved by the power of the blood of the Lord Jesus Christ.[105]

Perhaps his journeyings, and the company which he had kept, after 1875 had led him to see that the Church was less in ruins and the faithful company less small than had appeared in the early days of the Brethren.

Scripture

The first component that Müller noted of his experience at Exmouth in 1820 was 'That the Word of God alone is our standard of judgment in spiritual things.' He said that he 'now began to try by the test of the Scriptures the things which I had learned and seen, and found that only those principles which stood the test were really of value.'[106] Much of the early part of the *Narrative* demonstrates how he and Craik sought to give effect to the principle. It was not a question of Scripture alone in a mechanical sense, because he had come to see the need for the Holy Spirit to be explainer and teacher of the word. But at that stage and later the importance that he accorded to Scripture in determining thought and action is obvious, to the extent that in his extant sermons and pamphlets, for example, the word of Scripture figures much more prominently than does the Holy Spirit, notwithstanding the discussion earlier of his emphasis on the Spirit as the source of power in the gospel. It was Müller's analysis of and leading from the word which evidently determined his theology as it has been examined above. The priority which he gave to Scripture appeared to be the point which Samuel Smith seemed to find particularly unacceptable about the approach of the Brethren. Müller was by no means alone among the early Brethren in this

---

103. *Second Coming*.
104. *Second Coming*.
105. 'The Beloved of the Lamb. A Sermon preached at Bethesda Chapel, Great George Street, Bristol, on Sunday evening, June 6th, 1897', Müller House transcripts.
106. *Autobiography*, 33.

emphasis. But he was certainly typical, and one of the main purposes of his preaching tours after 1870 was to convey this point to his hearers. His purpose was always also to suggest *how* Christians should use the word in their lives so as to build them up spiritually and practically, but that belongs more to his spirituality than to his theology.[107] His approach to Scripture might be described as proto-fundamentalist; it seems that it was that which excited Samuel Smith more than anything else.

Conclusion

It is one thing to analyse Müller's theology and to note that his thinking came to be paralleled much more widely in the Open Brethren, particularly on what we would now describe as the more progressive wing of that body of churches. It is another to assert that Müller was to a considerable degree responsible for shaping their theology. That he was respected and admired among them cannot be doubted. He certainly had influence among evangelical Christians more widely. He at least asserted that that was so and that it was a reason for his initiating the preaching tours which between 1875 and 1892 took him to forty-two countries on journeys totalling 200,000 miles. Explaining in July 1875 his decision to begin touring, he said there had been blessing in Brighton and elsewhere, he had learned truth from Scripture which he had duty to pass on to others, and he could apply truths in a way not generally applied: 'But more: I felt I had a place in the Church of Christ which not every one has; that I was known to hundreds of thousands and millions, and that these hundreds of thousands and millions loved me and esteemed me; and that therefore if I came to a place I should get hearers.'[108]

There is no doubt that he was widely heard across the world. Many will have been Brethren. Many more perhaps may have been drawn to the Brethren because of the way he spoke and the subject matter that he covered—this was a period in which many from other denominations who had been converted in the evangelistic campaigns of the time identified themselves with the Open Brethren (and indeed some with the Exclusive Brethren). Müller no doubt reflected thinking in evangelicalism at the time, but there is reason to believe that he made his own substantial contribution to thought and practice, including among the Open Brethren. His wider influence as the exemplar of 'living by faith' is beyond dispute, both within the Brethren and elsewhere.[109] The tension in his thinking between the particular ecclesiology which he and others had developed in the 1830s and his late nineteenth-century tendency towards non-denominationalism has challenged the progressive wing of the Open Brethren down to this day.

David Bebbington has suggested that the Brethren had been evangelicals of the evangelicals.[110] It can be argued that George Müller was *par excellence* an, if not the, evangelical of the evangelicals.

---

107. See especially, 'Address to Young Converts', Müller House transcripts.
108. 'Account of a Preaching Tour', in *Jeh. Mag.*, 279–80.
109. See Klaus Fielder, *The Story of Faith Missions* (Oxford, 1994).
110. D. W. Bebbington, 'The Place of the Brethren Movement in International Evangelicalism', in Dickson and Grass (eds.), *Growth of the Brethren Movement*, 260.

Appendix

Other examples of George Müller's gospel presentation

The following are three further passages from Müller's extant sermons, from different stages in his life, which illustrate the manner in which he presented the gospel:

1865

How may we know that we are crucified with Christ, that we have died with Him, and that we are risen with Him? Possibly some believers may not know how to settle this point. It is of the deepest moment to have a clear understanding of it. It is not by a voice from heaven, not by some powerful impression made on us in a dream or otherwise, but simply by believing in the Lord Jesus Christ, trusting in Him for the salvation of our souls, that we settle the point that we are united to Him, that with Him we were crucified, that with Him we died, that with Him we are raised again, and with Him sit in heavenly places. We have simply to say to ourselves, Do I know I am a guilty, wicked sinner, deserving nothing but judgment; but do I trust, at the same time, in the Lord Jesus for the salvation of my soul? If so, then Jesus is my substitute; then Jesus died in my room and stead; then am I looked upon by God as one united with Christ; then have I been punished for my sins in the person of the Lord Jesus Christ; then was I hung, as it were, on the cross with Christ—God having accepted him as my substitute; then was I buried with Christ, and have been raised with Him; then, in my Forerunner, I am seated at the right hand of God in heaven; then, as assuredly as Christ is there, so shall I be.'[111]

1871

How then may we be "of God?" First, we have to trace it all up to the councils and purposes of God from eternity. He did choose us in Christ. He did apprehend us in Christ. He predestinated us to be conformed to the image of His dear Son. He arranged from eternity for our salvation in the Lord Jesus Christ. But all this, while true, would not give us the enjoyment of our being 'of God," the blessedness practically of our being "of God"; and, therefore, in order to this, we have to obey the Gospel, we have to believe the Gospel, we have to put our trust for the salvation of our souls in the atonement made by the Lord Jesus Christ. It is through faith in the Gospel, through faith in the Lord Jesus Christ, through receiving Jesus, through resting on Him alone, that the enjoyment comes of our being "of God," that the blessedness thereof comes to our souls. We are, through faith in the Lord Jesus Christ, "begotten again," . . . "As many as received Him, to them gave He power,"—the right, the title, the privilege, the blessing,— "to become the sons of

---

111. A few words on "Crucified, Dead and Risen with Jesus": An Address delivered at a Conference of Christians held at the Victoria Rooms, Bristol on the 7th of November, 1865', in *Jeh. Mag.*, 1–2. This may have been to one of the interdenominational Bristol conferences.

God, even to them that believe on His name." Thus we become the children of God, as to enjoyment, as to the power, as to the blessedness, as to the practical enjoyment, through faith in the Lord Jesus Christ. Therefore we have to believe the testimony of God regarding the Lord Jesus Christ, we have to submit to the Gospel, we have to receive the atonement, and to rest on it alone as the ground of our acceptance. Again, in Gal. iii.26, "Ye are all children of God by faith in Christ Jesus." That is, the enjoyment, the blessedness, the realization of our having been predestinated of God and chosen in Christ comes through faith. . . . I have therefore to believe that the despised, the rejected, the crucified Jesus of Nazareth is the promised Messiah, the Saviour, and I have to depend on Him as such. And this settles the matter . . .[112]

1897

If God had forgiven us, so that punishment had not come on us on account of our numberless transgressions, and had done no more, this would have been wondrous grace; but He has done far, *far*, FAR more than this. And therefore it is stated, "What manner of love." The greatness of it, that not only has the Lord passed by our numberless transgressions, and forgiven every one of them, so that we shall not be dealt with according to the thousandth part of the sins of which we have been guilty – nay, not concerning one single sin even, in action, in word, or in thought – but that He makes us His own children, takes us into the Heavenly Family. We, who are by nature rebels against Him, and despise His love, and care not in the least about Him, and manifest this entire dislike and disregard of God day by day by going our own way, doing the things which are hateful to Him – we are not only forgiven, not only shall not be punished for one single sin, out of the many ten thousands of sins of which we have been guilty, in action, or word, or thought, or feeling, or desire, or inclination, but are made His own children, taken into His family, and that not merely in name, but in reality. By the power of the Holy Spirit, through belief in the Gospel, He regenerates us, makes us a new creation in Christ, makes us His very own children. Not merely calls us so, but makes us His very own children. Gives us spiritual life, heavenly life, and thus makes us His very own children.[113]

---

112. "'Of God.'", in *Jeh. Mag.*, 141–3. Müller then, in mid-sermon, broke into a prayer of acceptance by which those who needed to, could become believers.

113. "'Behold! What manner of love.'", Müller House transcripts.

CHAPTER 14

William Kelly and his Mystic Spirituality

Anne-Louise Critchlow

William Kelly was born in County Down, Ireland, in 1821. He studied Classics and Hebrew at Trinity College, Dublin from 1836 till 1841 and he graduated with a first-class honours. As he was too young to realize his ambition of ordination into the Church of Ireland, he obtained a tutorial post in the Channel Islands for a year, where he experienced an evangelical conversion and joined the Christian Brethren movement. Kelly spent the years 1842 until 1871 in Guernsey, establishing his reputation as a Bible teacher and writer.[1] He did not take part in the early Brethren disagreements, and only moved to Blackheath, London in 1871 where he was a revered and published teacher and author. It was while staying here that he separated from Darby in 1879 over a disagreement about a disciplinary judgement , and those assemblies that followed his lead became the more moderate connexion within Exclusivism known as 'the Kelly Brethren'. He died in London in 1906.

Kelly's opus attracted a wide readership from the Victorian Christian world. As well as publishing exegeses on individual books of the Bible, Kelly edited and contributed many of the articles in *The Bible Treasury*, a monthly magazine that was published between 1856 and 1906. In it, as well as writing on varied Biblical and theological subjects, he reviewed nineteenth-century theological books written by clerics and laymen of every denomination. He also took up controversial topics of the day—for example on the Bible and science and philosophy, German higher criticism, and the varied theologies of the Church of England, Nonconformists, and Unitarians.

I have contended in my monograph on Kelly, *Against the Trend: The Spirituality of William Kelly* (2016), that he was much more than a follower of Darby or even merely just a teacher in the moderate Exclusive Brethren movement.[2] The Brethren of the nineteenth century are often easily labelled by religious historians as dispensationalists, precursors of the fundamentalist movement and theologically naive. They are rarely referred to in general books about church history, such as Owen Chadwick's *The Victorian Church*.[3] In the longer monograph, I examine Kelly's place as a textual exegete of distinction, and his place on the continuum of literalists and conservative intellectuals, but I also suggest

---

1. Tim Grass, *Gathering to His Name: The Story of Open Brethren in Britain and Ireland* (Milton Keynes, 2006), 18.
2. Chap. 6 of the present writer's *Against the Trend: The Spirituality of William Kelly* (Eugene, OR, 2016) has much more about Kelly's mystic theology, especially his understanding of the language of mysticism.
3. Owen Chadwick, *The Victorian Church*, 2 vols. (London, 1966–70).

that Kelly can be placed in the tradition of mystical teaching and in this paper I intend to justify this description by looking at one aspect of this mystic spirituality in more detail.

Can we justify calling Kelly 'a mystic'?

William James (1842–1910), a contemporary of Kelly, was a psychologist who was particularly interested in the variety of religious experience. In his seminal Gifford Lectures of 1901–2, James defined mysticism in the following ways: mysticism is a direct and ineffable experience; has a noetic quality; allows for significant experience and hence authority in the Christian community and leaves a legacy of written work; the mystic also has his own self in abeyance and is subject to a higher will.[4] All these definitions are relevant to Kelly's religious experience and the way in which he was a leading teacher in the Christian Brethren. It is interesting that James contested that evangelical Protestantism, within whose tradition we might normally place Kelly, had abandoned the methodical mystic discipline.[5] However, the Christian Brethren, while not using a set liturgy, nevertheless taught and demonstrated contemplative methods in their breaking of bread meetings, which formed clear patterns of worship and they taught personal meditation of Scripture at a deep level. There are many areas of Kelly's teaching that are relevant to his mysticism—his views on baptism, his promotion of the doctrine of the Trinity (especially his high Christology), his teaching on the experience of 'joy', his understanding of bridal imagery, his typology, his eschatology and his hymnology. But in this paper I will be concentrating on his teaching on the doctrine of the Ascension and the way Kelly expounded the Epistle to the Ephesians to highlight the significance of the Ascension and as being the high point in the canon of Scripture and his Christology.

The historians of the Brethren, Grass and Stunt, have shown that there were connections between the Brethren and the Quakers, and the Quakers had a mystic inheritance.[6] Moreover, when attempting to define the spirituality of the Brethren movement, Grass does more than point to the transfer of evangelical Quakers to the early Brethren.[7] He goes so far as to characterize the development of the Exclusive branch of the Brethren in the nineteenth century as showing 'increasing introversion and separation arising from the development of their assembly-orientated mysticism.'[8] Thus this suggests the possible mysticism of the Exclusive Brethren tradition and in this thesis I propose that Kelly contributed to this.

Before looking within Kelly's work at evidence for his own mystic theology, it is worth exploring what can be seen as his attitude to the corpus of mystical writings over the centuries. His extant library reveals 'the catholicity of the collection' and his careful

---

4. William James, *The Varieties of Religious Experience* (Edinburgh, 1902), 371–2.

5. James, *Religious Experience*, 397.

6. Timothy C. F. Stunt, 'Early Brethren and the Society of Friends', in id., *The Elusive Quest of the Spiritual Malcontent: Some Early Nineteenth-Century* Mavericks (Eugene OR, 2015), 32–58.

7. Grass, *Gathering to His Name*, 32, 38. Newton and Tregelles were examples of leading Brethren who had been Quakers.

8. Grass, *Gathering to His Name*, 199.

reading of the Church Fathers.[9] His library shows us his preoccupation with reading both the Greek mystics and those early Church Fathers who were also mystics. It also reveals his knowledge of German mysticism through the writings of Heinrich Suso (*c*.1295–1366) and Gerhard Tersteegen (1697–1769).[10]

Throughout his works of Biblical exegesis, Kelly was critical of the Greek tradition of philosophy which had such a vital effect on the work of the Church Fathers. In this he followed the example of St. Paul in his criticisms of the Gnostics in his letters.[11] Many of the later mystics also warned about that which was spurious spiritually and the dangers of ecstasy.[12] In warning of the theology of some of the Church Fathers, Kelly was clearly concerned about the influence of pagan philosophy on their Christianity. His library reveals his extensive reading of Plato, Plotinus, and Philo.[13] It is clear from other non-Brethren writers that Greek pagan philosophers, such as Plotinus, did have an enormous influence on the early mystics.[14] As far as Kelly was concerned, Plato, with his teaching about the soul being naturally divine and able to rise up to heaven after death, and Philo, with his mixture of Platonic and Jewish understandings of God, exercised too much influence on the theologians of the early Church.[15] Kelly also frequently mentioned the errors of Origen particularly with regard to his understanding of the incarnation, as a stage in the more Platonic unification with God.[16] In this we can see again Kelly's concern with an orthodox understanding of the incarnation and the way his high Christology separates him from other writers

---

9. Edwin Cross, *The Irish Saint and Scholar: A Biography of William Kelly 1821–1906* (London, 2004), 144. This quotation is from an extract of the librarian's report on William Kelly's library to the Free Library and Museum Committee, 11 October 1904, in the minutes of proceedings of the Middlesbrough Town Council 1903–4.

10. Suso was 'one of the chief German mystics and leaders of the Friends of God, a circle of devout ascetic Rhinelanders who opposed contemporary evils and aimed for a close association with God.' (*Britannica Online Encyclopaedia*). Tersteegen was a German Reformed religious writer who had a great influence on radical Pietism, and who translated the French mystics and Julian of Norwich: see, Neil Dickson, 'A Darbyite Mystic: Emma Frances Bevan (1827–1909)', *intra*, 225, 226. His influence led later to the founding of the Moravian Church by Count von Zinzendorf in 1727. The Moravians preached strongly in favour of the new birth and against worldly amusements. They had a strong influence on John Wesley and indirectly on the nineteenth-century Brethren movement.

11. The Gnostics' preoccupation with the soul, divorced from the body, and ecstatic utterances in the 'mystery religions' were always a source of danger to the early Church: e.g., Col. 2: 8, 18.

12. Evelyn Underhill, *The Mystics of the Church* (London, [1925]), 31.

13. In his library, he had all the major works of Plato and of Philo, including Philo's *In libros Mosis* (1552), and Plotinus's *Enneades*, (eds.) F. Creutzer, G. H. Moser and F. Dubner (1865).

14. Underhill, *Mystics of the Church*, 61.

15. W. Kelly, *The Gospel of John*, (1966 edn.; London, 1898), 16.

16. Andrew Louth, *The Origins of the Christian Mystical Tradition, from Plato to Denys* (Oxford, 1981), 65.

Mysticism and the doctrine of the ascension

For Kelly the word 'mystery' was primarily associated with the union of Christ in glory with believers on earth. He wrote, 'the mystical body is formed by the Holy Ghost, sent down after He rose from the dead.'[17] While the term 'the body of Christ', since Paul's writing of 1 Corinthians, has been regarded as a mystical association of believers attached to the 'headship' or leadership of Christ, Kelly's teachings stressed the 'union' of Christians with Christ in his position of glory 'at the right hand of God'.[18] The 'mystery' which was so important to Kelly was about the union of Christ and the Church, about the heavenly and the earthly being combined.[19] According to Kelly, Ephesians 3:18, referring to human inability to grasp Christ's love, was not about the incarnation or the passion of Christ but about the mystery of the Church being the body of Christ.[20] However, true mystic spirituality should not imply that the Christian is cut off from earthly life in some sort of esoteric experience. Such a false mysticism easily became, according to Kelly, 'the reverse of God's mysteries and the mere mist of men's fancies.'[21] The mystery was something that was kept secret in the Old Testament in order to be revealed in the New, not something that could not be understood.[22] He went on to explain that the mystery was about the absorption of Christ into the 'heavenly realms', rather than Christ taking over an earthly Kingdom, which was what the Jews had expected. Also Kelly taught that the whole earth would eventually be under Christ's authority—a position given by God the Father—but also leading Kelly to teach a theocentric mysticism for eternity in a new heaven and earth.[23] The position of the church was also to be important to the whole of society in the millennium. Christ would be over the Jews and the unbelieving Gentiles but he would be sharing his authority with the Church as equals. Therefore there is a strong sense of the Brethren saints looking to exercise authority in the future earthly kingdom and being given a sense of dignity and significance.

The importance of the affections

Kelly's language conveys high aspirations and an intense degree of intimacy, 'full of the richest comfort and the most exalted hope.'[24] Being one with Christ now should lead the Christian to long for the coming of Christ, and for the Christian, in contrast to the Jew, that longing would always be spiritual. For Kelly it was always important that the Son of God was coming for the Church in person—his understanding of 'the rapture'—and

---

17. W. Kelly, *Lectures on the Epistle of Paul the Apostle to the Philippians with a new translation* (London, n.d), 22.

18. This phrase occurs several times in the epistles, notably Eph. 1:20, Col. 3:2, and Heb.12:2.

19. W. Kelly, *Lectures on the Epistle of Paul, the Apostle, to the Ephesians with a new translation* (London, n.d.), 26.

20. Kelly, *Ephesians*, 138; Eph.3:18 (KJV), 'may be able to comprehend with all the saints what is the breadth and length and depth and height'.

21. Kelly, *Ephesians*, 75.
22. Kelly, *Ephesians*, 114.
23. Kelly, *Ephesians*, 114.
24. Kelly, *Ephesians*, 115.

so his eschatological view of union with Christ was also significant for his mysticism.[25] According to Kelly, his understanding of union with Christ both in a future event and in the present was beyond human intelligence and needed to be revealed by a higher power.[26] It was a greater blessing to have Christ in heaven than Christ on earth in incarnation.[27] To have God the Father revealed to them through the Son 'was wholly outside and above man.'[28] However, this deep spirituality was not about being a special type of person: it was about the integrity of Christian character, so there was in Kelly's teaching a special mixture of exclusivism and inclusivism.[29] This teaching based on John's Gospel and the epistles 'must be really entered into to be understood' and, if it were, Christians could 'rest in the Father's love.'[30] However, as with so much mystic teaching, there was a battle between good and evil, and the Devil was seen as the particular adversary of God the Son.[31] The Christian Brethren exhorted their followers to cling to the Ideal, personified in Christ. As in any reaching after the Ideal, there was always a straining after more, and inevitably a falling short, so that even if the Brethren rejected the idea of self-effort instead of grace in conversion, they always had aspirations for a greater spirituality. The theology of the Ascension had a huge effect on Brethren affections and 'affection' was the basis of Kelly's mystic spirituality.[32] His exegeses cannot be categorized as merely intellectual or theological analysis—their purpose was also to draw its audience into a mystic love relationship with Christ. Spiritual union was 'more real and permanent' than anything physical and it was with the risen Lord on high.[33] Kelly himself thought that Christians who emphasized the importance of the priesthood of Christ or even the atonement 'are apt to be a cold set of people, in danger of becoming formal and dry doctrinally, as well as deficient in sensitiveness of heart and conscience for the glory of God.'[34] Thus Kelly placed a premium on his own understanding of the affections which his spirituality drew out.

Such an inward looking experience was arguably always more important for Kelly than any concern with justice in society or Christian service.[35] This glorious preoccupation with 'the beloved' in a transcendent experience, gave his writings a different tone to any merely fundamentalist discourse. Kelly stressed that, while believers were looking for and obeying his commandments, they should also be feeling them deeply.[36] His use of language in his work on John's Gospel is particularly relevant to his mysticism. When writing about John 14:21, he explains the reason for the words 'hath the commandments' rather than 'keeps the commandments', which would imply a legalistic obedience. Kelly concluded, 'The desire to do His will finds and knows what it (i.e. the commandment)

---

25. Kelly, *Ephesians*, 284.
26. Kelly, *Ephesians*, 290 and 331.
27. Kelly, *Ephesians*, 338.
28. Kelly, *Ephesians*, 352.
29. Kelly, *Ephesians*, 287.
30. Kelly, *Ephesians*, 343.
31. Kelly, *Ephesians*, 287.
32. Kelly, *Ephesians*, 285. 363.
33. Kelly, *Ephesians*, 297, 355.
34. W. Kelly, *The Advocacy of Christ: A Lecture on 1 John 2: 1, 2* (London, 1897), 7.
35. Kelly, *John*, 316.
36. Kelly, *John*, 298.

is.'[37] His intellectualism and his mysticism are combined as his language soars above the ordinary, using interconnectedness, abstract vocabulary and Trinitarian register.[38] His writing revealed an expression of delicate understanding of the relationship of the persons of the Trinity, for example, 'loving Him (i.e. the Son) draws down his Father's love, who honours the Son and will not be exalted at His expense.' There is a use of moral and abstract language: 'Thus only does Christian practice flow from Christian principle and privilege; and all is of Christ by the Holy Ghost in us.' There is a terse use of paradox and exclamation: 'How comforting that our duty as Christians supposes our blessedness! How humbling that the gift of the Spirit makes our failure inexcusable!' There is a strong emotional aspiration in his language: 'And how cheering to the heart the abiding sense of the presence of the Father and the Son with us as thus walking! Would that we knew it better.'[39] There is a strong interconnectedness between different passages from the Bible in his teaching. He drew parallels between John's writing and Paul's in Colossians 1:9 and 10, thus linking revelation with practical holiness and stressed that, in the physical absence of Christ, obedience revealed the true state of the heart.[40] The cycle of obedience and affection would result in greater revelation. Kelly often explored metaphorical language to express the nuances of his mystical knowledge of God, for example his foregrounding of the word 'abode' in John 14.[41] The result would be that its followers would draw from an inexhaustible divine well of peace.[42] Here we see how individuals become part of the whole, but unlike Platonic and Eastern mysticism, where the individual no longer counts, the Brethren never lost their sense of the individual and this was partly the result of their strong belief in the humanity of Christ within the Ascension.

The importance of the epistles

An important characteristic of Christian Brethren life was a deep searching of the Scriptures. This made it much more of an intellectual movement than many other fundamentalist groups, and this ability to analyse sacred text was combined with mysticism in a powerful way. Kelly noted that none should be satisfied with what they already knew but should search more deeply to make spiritual progress.[43] Christian Brethren mystic worship was always informed by intellectual searching. For them Paul was a more important apostle than any other, because he, pre-eminently among the apostles, taught 'the mystery of the church' and completed the word of God.[44] This teaching of Paul took the Church forward

---

37. Kelly, *John*, 298.
38. Kelly, *John*, 298.
39. Kelly, *John*, 300.
40. Col. 1:9, 10 (KJV) 'For this cause we also, since the day we heard it, do not cease to pray for you, and to desire that ye might be filled with the knowledge of his will in all wisdom and spiritual understanding. That ye might walk worthy of the Lord unto all pleasing, being fruitful in every good work and increasing in the knowledge of God.'
41. Kelly, *John*, 300.
42. Kelly, *John*, 301.
43. Kelly, *Philippians*, 20.
44. Kelly, Philippians, 35, 36. This of course was not because it was thought that Paul wrote the final book of the New Testament chronologically, but because his teaching about the Church was considered by the Brethren to be its culminant teaching.

from the experience of the day of Pentecost, which was one of the reasons why the Brethren did not major on the Pentecostal gifts.[45] According to Kelly, if there was such a thing as apostolic succession, it should have been from Paul not Peter.[46] Prophetic Scripture in Romans 16: 25–6 referred to Paul because he was the one who revealed the mystery.[47]

Kelly saw the system of the epistles as a canon within the canon.[48] While Romans and Galatians were about justification, Colossians was about Christ in the heavens and why earthly systems were dangerous and should be rejected. Hebrews was about Christ pleading for humanity in the heavens, but Ephesians was the most important of all because it was about the Christian's privileges in the heavenly places in Christ now.[49] Therefore I suggest that Kelly's own translation and exegesis of Ephesians was particularly significant in his own opus and he saw the original text as the apex of Paul's teachings in his other epistles. Kelly's studies on the other Pauline epistles contributed to the teaching that culminated in his exegesis on Ephesians. His work on Philippians and Colossians was important because it did much to link the teaching of Galatians, Colossians, and Ephesians and to place this teaching in due perspective and order. Philippians stressed the joy of the Christian as he or she understood this teaching: 'He would thus make us more happy.'[50] Colossians was concerned with warning people about legalism, which Kelly associated with the Established Church.[51] Colossians, with much important teaching for his theology, was about 'the power of his glory' and showed the necessity of a deepening acquaintance with God as an important adjunct to obedience.[52] The Christian Brethren have often been accused of authoritarianism.[53] However, Kelly's teaching on the epistles shows that a particular understanding of Church leadership was only a small part of their collective worship experience—the experience of 'the glory of God' was far more significant.

Kelly's teaching about the book of Ephesians was in many ways the pinnacle of his insight and understanding of the Scriptures through the paradigm of Brethren understanding. The main theme was 'union with Christ and 'the privileges of the body'.[54] Ephesians was about Christ's likeness to God in his moral qualities and the ideal of what the Christian Church ought to be.[55] It concentrated on the Trinity and God's intentions before the world began, linking it with Genesis, which was very important as a foundational source for

---

45. Kelly, *Philippians*, 37.
46. Kelly, *Ephesians*, 118.
47. Kelly, *Ephesians*, 120.
48. Many strong adherents of the canon of Scripture have had their own canon within the canon—in other words, books of the Bible which they see as being particularly important. Thus Luther gave particular support to Romans as encapsulating his doctrine of 'justification by faith' and had little time for James, as being of practical rather than theological significance.
49. Kelly, *Lectures on the Epistle of Paul the Apostle to the Colossians, with a new translation* (London, n.d.), 54 –5.
50. Kelly, *Philippians*, 15.
51. Kelly, *Colossians*, 2.
52. Kelly, *Colossians*, 13.
53. T. C. F. Stunt, 'Two Nineteenth-Century Movements', *EQ*, 37 (1965), 229.
54. Kelly, *Ephesians*, 1.
55. Kelly, *Ephesians*, 88, 51.

Kelly's teaching.[56] Kelly's writing about Ephesians showed that understanding the nature of God, rather than theodicy or practical teaching, was what was important to Kelly, and how he made a significant contribution to nineteenth-century theological teaching.[57] His burning concern with understanding and teaching about the nature of God rather than apologetics per se, gave his work similarities with that of F. D. Maurice, whose profound grasp of the love of God so inspired the broader Anglican church, but whose theological stance as a 'Broad Church liberal' would normally set him far apart from Kelly.[58] Kelly's exegesis of Ephesians showed that for him the 'ideal' was brought into the present experience rather than merely a future hope.[59] This teaching was, interestingly, grounded in the belief in the ruin of humanity, not the Victorian Broad Church belief in the progress of humanity, and Kelly's insistence that there could be no spirituality without the experience of conversion.

Kelly's appreciation of the significance of Ephesians came to be part of the Christian Brethren paradigm, whereby typology of the Old Testament was fitted into the epistles. Elsewhere I have looked at the way his typology contributed to his mysticism,[60] but Kelly taught that, while Hebrews was about going through the desert, Ephesians was about being in Canaan with God.[61] While it is clear that Paul makes frequent allusions to the Old Testament in his epistles, the Brethren seemed to focus particularly on these allusions, and transfer all Old Testament typology to the New Testament, and fit their present spiritual experience into it. Their paradigm was all pervasive. Their confident assurance of the rightness of this method made them far more able to hold together the tensions of possible contradictions within the Scriptures than other Christian groups. Understanding the mystery of the Ascension and the spiritually dynamic position to which it gave Christians was about putting worshippers 'into another atmosphere as it were.[62] Kelly believed in the near coming of the Lord.[63]

Kelly's Christocentric mysticism

Kelly taught that individual and corporate worship were about enjoying the glory of Christ and having a daily, intimate relationship with Him. Appreciating the glory now and anticipating the Christian appearance in glory with Christ was part of the Christian experience.[64] The world, claimed Kelly, would see the glory of Christ when he came to reign, but would never understand his intimate love.[65] For the Brethren the experience must start with the individual before finding its corporate expression and that meant Kelly encouraged the individual believer to experience the fullest communication with God in

---

56. Kelly, *Ephesians*, 4.
57. Kelly, *Ephesians*, 5.
58. F. D. Maurice, 'Eternal Life and Eternal Death', in id., *Theological Essays* (2nd edn., Cambridge,1853), 450, 464.
59. Kelly, *Ephesians*, 21, 24.
60. Critchlow, *Against the Trend*, 172–98.
61. Kelly, *Ephesians*, 86.
62. Kelly, *Philippians,* 40.
63. W. Kelly, *Lectures on the Church of God* (7th edn., London,1897), 32.
64. Kelly, *Ephesians*, 51.
65. Kelly, *Ephesians*, 52.

the here-and-now as God had promised to dwell with his Church through all eternity.[66] Kelly also taught that, as the Holy Spirit always worked through individuals, it would be wrong to talk about the Church teaching particular doctrines.[67] This led to a very different spirituality than that held by the Tractarians. As the individual should be ruled by God, nearness to God in the affections was more important than obeying particular details of teaching.[68] This is interesting, as it has often been felt that the Brethren were a highly authoritarian church, who allowed no differences of opinion. The Darbyist form of Exclusive Brethren certainly followed a degree of ecclesiastical authoritarianism, but Kelly's teaching was free from such narrowness. It was his concentration on his intellectual analysis of Scripture and his encouragement of mystic joy which prevented this problem from arising amongst the moderate Exclusives. However, his teaching did promote an intense internality and necessity for concentration on spiritual matters. According to Kelly's teaching, other Christians should be valued only in so far as they sought Christ alone.[69] Christ had to be steadily adhered to in order to keep nature at bay, even after conversion.[70] Kelly warned about outward signs which could easily be 'vain and empty'.[71] Like many Christians who were leaders in the mystic tradition, Kelly encouraged his hearers and readers to aim only at the highest levels of spirituality. That he was successful in his aims is shown by the high regard in which his teachings and writings were held.

Kelly's contemplation of the Ascension and his high Christology had a transformative effect that went above and beyond contemporary evangelical teaching.[72] He called it 'the secret glory which none but His own are permitted to contemplate.'[73] There was a sense in which, according to him, most Victorian Christians thought they could only appreciate the enjoyment of the presence of Christ at death.[74] In contrast, the Christian Brethren claimed that enjoyment in their present, earthly experience and that is clearly demonstrated in their practice of collective worship. As far as Kelly was concerned, adherents of Christendom, like the Jews before them, had not been spiritual enough and had been 'too engrossed in earthly things.'[75] Brethren understanding of the 'mystery' was also rooted in their theology of man's ruin and incarnation. Since the Fall, humanity had always been the agent of dishonour for God, but when Jesus Christ was glorified as a human being in the Ascension, God the Father could once again delight in humanity. This drew the Brethren into the intimacy of the Trinity and idealized their humanity. Intense mystic spirituality was experienced by members of the Christian Brethren movement in general, but I claim that William Kelly had a particular place in explaining his theology lucidly, justifying it intellectually, and using language in such a way as to engage his readers' affections.

---

66. Kelly, *Ephesians*, 139, 141.
67. Kelly, *Ephesians*, 143.
68. Kelly, *Philippians*, 73, 21.
69. Kelly, *Colossians*, 84.
70. Kelly, *Colossians*, 84.
71. Kelly, *Ephesians*, 213.
72. Kelly, *Ephesians*, 363.
73. Kelly, *Ephesians*, 371.
74. Kelly, *Ephesians*, 9.
75. Kelly, *Lectures on the Church of God*, 43.

CHAPTER 15

A Darbyite Mystic: Frances Bevan (1827–1909)

Neil Dickson

> The hymns of Frances Bevan are chiefly translations from German Pietists (so called) of the Middle Ages. There is found in them, that mystical touch, that indefinable quality (also found in the hymns of J. N Darby) that reaches the inmost recesses of the soul, and calls forth the deepest longings of the spirit.
>
> E. E. Cornwall, *Songs of Pilgrimage and Glory: Part 2* ([1933]), 31.

Emma Frances Bevan was born in Oxford on 25 September 1827, the eldest of three surviving children. Although she rarely used her first name, 'Emma', but was known within the family by the diminutive 'Fanny', she was named after her mother, Emma Martha Welch, the daughter of a Lancashire squire.[1] Her father was Philip Nicholas Shuttleworth (1782–1842), who was the son of Lancashire vicar, and at the time of Frances's birth had been warden of New College, Oxford, since 1822. Shuttleworth was a Whig in politics and had tutored the son of the prominent Whig politician, Henry Richard Vassall-Fox, 3rd Lord Holland. While retaining his position as warden, Shuttleworth was presented in 1824 by Lord Holland to the living of Foxley in Wiltshire, and eventually in 1840, the Whig prime minister, Melbourne, reluctantly appointed him bishop of Chichester. Melbourne's reluctance was due to Shuttleworth's reputation for political trimming. Although he had supported the progressive causes of Catholic emancipation and the relaxation of the university tests that excluded Dissenters, he was one of the signatories to an address urging Peel to remain in office.[2] He had given great offence to the Tractarians in publishing

---

1. The title page of one work, *Trees Planted by the River*, gives her name as 'F. A. Bevan'. It is possible she had another given name beginning with 'A', but in her first two books she styled herself 'E. F. B.' and later ones 'Frances Bevan'. It is more probable that it is a printer's error unnoticed in the proofs by Bevan, an error that is made more likely by her sister-in-law, later Mrs Mortimer, initially publishing as F. A. Bevan. Frances was christened on 8 February 1828 in Oxford as Emma Frances Shuttleworth. There was an earlier child called Frances Emma Shuttleworth who was baptized on 10 May 1825 and who presumably died in infancy, although no burial record could be found. I am grateful to Dr Elisabeth Wilson for the notes on the baptismal and burial records.

2. *ODNB*, C. W. Sutton, s.v., 'Shuttleworth, Philip Nicholas (1782–1842)', rev. M. C. Curthoys.

in 1838 a work entitled *Not Tradition but Revelation* that had been warmly welcomed by the Evangelicals. When he died in 1842, Pusey thought, rather grimly, that his death was 'a token of God's presence with the Church of England'.[3] However, Shuttleworth's most significant act as bishop had been to appoint to an archdeaconry Henry Manning, the future Roman Catholic convert and cardinal.[4] He had done this against the opposition of his wife, a devout churchwoman. According to Henry Fox, the 4th Lord Holland and a hater of piety, Emma Shuttleworth was 'prim, precise and very dull'.[5] Shuttleworth, on the other hand, wrote some occasional verse, was known as a wit at New College who could '"set the table in roar"',[6] and had devised a railway in the senior common room to speed the circulation of port.[7]

Frances was academically precocious. When her father had enquired if she wished to take a story-book with her on a journey, she had replied, 'No thank you Papa, I have my book on pneumatics to take with me.'[8] She was also a gifted artist, and while still a child, John Ruskin reputedly went down on his knees to her in praise of her drawing.[9] She clearly enjoyed the association with Oxford, for in one passage of her later books she describes—in a rhapsodic passage that is Ruskinian in its particularity—'the sunny Oxfordshire meadows . . . gay in the spring days with yellow tulips, and cowslips and fritillaries . . . And there were no sounds that reached the ear but the song of larks and other birds, and the far-away bells of Oxford.'[10] New College gave her a wide circle of acquaintances, and according to Nesta, one of her daughters to whose not entirely reliable memoirs we are indebted for much of the detail of Bevan's life, she met the railway pioneer George Stephenson and the missionary David Livingstone.[11] She apparently was educated by private tutors, such as the German governess who inspired her love of Gothic

---

3. H. P. Liddon, *Life of Edward Bouverie Pusey* (London, 1893), 294, quoted in John S. Andrews, 'Shuttleworth, Philip Nicholas', *BDEB*, 2: 1012.

4. *ODNB*, s.v., 'Shuttleworth'.

5. N. H. Webster, *Spacious Days: An Autobiography* (London [1950]), 23.

6. Webster, *Spacious Days*, 22.

7. *ODNB*, s.v., 'Shuttleworth'.

8. Webster, *Spacious Days*, 25; probably this was a book on physics, such as Hugo Reid's *Natural Philosophy, Adapted for Self-instruction and Use in Schools. Book 1: Pneumatics* (not this actual volume, however, which was not published until 1841 when Frances was 14, as it would undermine the precocity implicit in the anecdote). Less likely is that it was a theological work in which the word 'pneumatology' is used, as in the title of the English translation of the work by the German Pietist, Johann Heinrich Jung-Stilling, published in 1834 as *Theory of Pneumatology: In Reply to the Question, what Ought to be Believed or Disbelieved Concerning Presentiments, Visions, and Apparitions, According to Nature, Reason, and Scripture*. Of course, Webster may have confused the two words.

9. Webster, *Spacious Days*, 25.

10. F. A. [sic] Bevan, *Trees Planted by the River* (London, [1894]), 82–3.

11. Webster, *Spacious Days*, 42. Nesta also claims her mother was friends with the mystic and utopian Laurence Oliphant, and the Roman Catholic priest and later cardinal, Edward Howard. However, both individuals were younger than Frances, who would leave Oxford in her teenage years, and so the exact degree of acquaintance with them is doubtful. I am grateful to Dr Timothy Stunt for pointing out this discrepancy.

art and medieval Christianity.[12] Her tutors would also have ensured she was proficient in Classical Greek and Latin, and as modern languages were characteristically seen as an essential accomplishment for middle-class young women,[13] she became fluent in French and German. According to Nesta she was 'tall, upright with regular features', but she had not been 'ever strictly beautiful'. At Oxford, however, she 'acquired a poise and *savoir faire* which, with her dignified appearance and talent for conversation, would have made her an admirable hostess . . . in a literary or artistic salon.'[14] Frances's early religious views were High Church.[15] In the Anglican Christ Church at Fosbury in Wiltshire she painted the reredos[16]—it is undoubtedly to acts such this to that she alludes when she later wrote of '[l]adies in our days who would seek to add to their store of sanctity by cleaning or decorating churches'.[17] She avoided the enthusiastic reaches of evangelicalism, for she would evade people who would speak to her of Christ, or be 'displeased' at being taken to hear the gospel preached rather than being 'left to go some church or chapel, where you could hear good music, or see beautiful painted windows', or feel 'dislike and contempt' for people 'always talking about the Bible', or sneer at the idea of conversion.[18] Her early religion appears to have been based on conventional Anglicanism, aesthetic religiosity, and—to judge by the frequency she later wrote against it—the efficacy of good works.

In 1854, when she was 27, she met the banker Robert Bevan (1809–90). Bevan came from a family that was descended from the Quaker apologist Robert Barclay (1648–90),[19] although his branch of the family was expelled from the Quakers in 1773 when his grandfather had made an exogamous marriage. Bevan's father ensured the Quaker past would be fully left behind his son by having him educated at Harrow and Oxford.[20] Robert Bevan had become the chairman of the Quaker banking foundation, Barclay, Bevan & Co., with which his family was associated and that increasingly was simply called Barclays. Under his stewardship, the bank's profits tripled, and while there were several richer contemporary bankers, Bevan became a millionaire.[21] In addition to Trent Park, the Bevan family estate in New Barnet, then in Hertfordshire, he inherited Fosbury House,

---

12. E. E. Cornwall, *Songs of Pilgrimage and Glory: Part 2. Notes on the Hymns of Certain Hymn-writers*. (London, [1933]), 34. Cornwall's work was published in 2 parts; the edition used here is a one-volume one which combines the two but keeps the original pagination in each.

13. Judith Johnston, *Victorian Women, and the Economics of Travel, Translation and Culture, 1830–1870* (Farnham, 2013), 20.

14. Webster, *Spacious Days*, 24, 42.

15. Cornwall, *Songs of Pilgrimage*, 2: 33–4.

16. Webster, *Spacious Days*, 37.

17. Bevan, *Trees Planted*, 94; see also her later disapproval of music, painting, and sculpture as worship in Frances Bevan, *William Farel* (2nd edn., London [1883]), 146.

18. Bevan, *Trees Planted*, 12.

19. John S. Andrews, 'The Recent History of the Bevan Family', *EQ*, 33/2 (1961), 81–92, spec. 82–3.

20. *ODNB*, s.v., Leslie Hannah, 'Bevan, Robert Cooper Lee (1809–1890)'.

21. His wealth at death, however, was just short of the million: £953, 382, 11s 11d.: *ODNB*, s.v., 'Bevan'. In 2017, this was equivalent to £116, 464, 278.41: 'Bank of England: Inflation Calculator', <http://www.bankofengland.co.uk/education/Pages/resources/inflationtools/calculator/>, accessed 10 Sept. 2018.

near Hungerford in Wiltshire, that had among its luxuries a melon yard.[22] In addition, he owned houses at Brighton and at Princes Gate, opposite Hyde Park in London, and eventually a villa in Cannes, where from 1880 onwards he would spend the winter due to his gout that gave him acute inflammatory arthritis. As a young man Bevan had been pleasure-loving. At six feet three inches, he was tall and handsome and was a source of fun and liveliness in company. He was a bold and confident horseman, and perhaps darker pleasures are hinted at in his later feeling about ones that had left a bitter taste.[23] One of Bevan's older sisters, Favell (1802–78), was to become famous in the Victorian era as the author of educational children's books, most notably the immensely popular evangelical reading-primer, *The Peep of Day* (1833).[24] It was she who first awakened her brother's conscience at Harrow in a letter that in later life he would carry with him.[25] She also corresponded with his closest school friend, the future cardinal, Henry Manning, and was in this period also influential in Manning's spiritual development.[26] In 1836 Bevan married Lady Agenta Yorke (d. 1851), the daughter of vice-admiral Sir Joseph Sydney Yorke. The couple were to have seven children, one of whom died in childhood.[27] About 1846 Bevan had an evangelical conversion. An early influence on his Christian development was the preaching of Baptist Noel, who was markedly Low Church and was about this time moving towards secession from Anglicanism to the Baptist ministry.[28] On the grounds of conscience, Bevan had given up dancing and his favourite sport of hunting, and he held daily prayer meetings at the bank's headquarters.[29] He became an adherent of the Evangelical Party in the Church of England, and as a friend of Lord Shaftesbury, dedicated himself to bettering the lives of the working classes. Bevan became a frequent preacher, to his employees and others, such as at the Calvinistic Methodist chapel at Botany Bay close to Trent Park.

A Tory in politics, in 1847 he had stood unsuccessfully for Parliament against Lord John Russell and Baron Lionel de Rothschild to oppose the removal of Jewish parliamentary disabilities, a position that Shaftesbury and other evangelicals also held.[30] Bevan had campaigned on the basis of retaining the Protestant character of Parliament.[31] Theologically, he was deeply conservative. When T. R. Birks, then the vicar of Holy Trinity

---

22. John Chandler, *Wiltshire: A History of its Landscape and People*, 1: *Marlborough and Eastern Wiltshire* (Salisbury, 2001), 230.

23. [Frances Bevan], *A Few Recollections of Robert Cooper Lee Bevan* (London, 1892), 16.

24. John S. Andrews, 'Mortimer, Favell Lee', in *BDEB*, 2: 798. It is tempting to speculate that Frances and Robert met through their mutual associations with Manning, but there is no evidence for this.

25. [Bevan], *Bevan*, 16–17; it was eventually stolen along with his wallet by a pickpocket.

26. Andrews, 'Mortimer', 798.

27. Charles E. G. Pease, 'The Descendants of Hopkin ap Davydd', 2–6, <http://www.pennyghael.org.uk/Bevan.pdf>, accessed 23 Jul. 2014.

28. [Bevan], *Bevan*, 18; David William Bebbington, 'Noel, Baptist Wriothseley', in *BDEB*, 2: 830.

29. *ODNB*, s.v., 'Bevan'.

30. Donald M. Lewis, *The Origins of Christian Zionism: Lord Shaftesbury and Evangelical Support for a Jewish Homeland* (Cambridge, 2010), 148–51.

31. Webster, *Spacious Days*, 18.

in Cambridge and the long-standing honorary secretary of the Evangelical Alliance (EA), published a revisionist account of hell in 1867 that envisaged its inhabitants eventually having a degree of joy in the redeemed cosmos, Bevan, who was the treasurer of the EA, wrote a letter in 1869 to the Alliance stating that he could not continue in it if Birks did. It sparked a protracted controversy as to whether Birks's views were consistent with the EA basis of faith. The council was obviously reluctant to dismiss him, but it led to Birks's eventual resignation. Bevan, however, and fifteen others also resigned in 1870 from the EA council, as in their view, Birks had not been denounced firmly enough.[32] This, then, was the Protestant evangelical conservatism with which Frances would come to identify.

When Frances first met Bevan, who was by then a widower, she was living in Wykeham Rise in Totteridge in Hertfordshire. She had been invited to stay at Trent Park for a short time, and in one of her first encounters with him he asked her what she had learnt from the Bible about the coming of the Lord Jesus. He proposed that they should read the Bible together in the evenings. Bevan's delight in his faith and its simplicity impressed Frances as much as the explanations he offered. She later claimed it was then she realized 'that faith necessarily includes a belief in the future as well as the past work of the Lord Jesus. I then saw that it was not possible to have full communion with God without looking forward, as Christ is looking forward, to the glorious and blessed future'.[33] Favell Bevan, by now the widowed Mrs Mortimer, who was staying with her brother, also impressed her by saying that people find the truth difficult to believe because they cannot accept 'anything so wonderful as the facts that are revealed.'[34] Bevan and Frances's mutual love for Bible readings led on to other things. As she later rather coyly noted: 'As time passed on, and I was no more a visitor but at home in his house, our readings became constant and regular.' On 30 April 1856, five months before her twenty-ninth birthday, Frances and Robert Bevan were married. Frances and he were to have nine children, one of whom died in childhood.[35] Three of them were to have entries in the *Oxford Dictionary of National Biography*: Anthony Ashley (1859–1933), an orientalist and biblical scholar; Edwyn Robert (1870–1943), an ancient historian and philosopher; and Nesta Helen, later Mrs Webster (1875–1960), whose historical writings led her to believe that there was a Judaeo-Masonic cabal controlling contemporary history.[36] Frances's move to evangelicalism

---

32. Ian Randall and David Hilborn, *One Body in Christ: The History and Significance of the Evangelical Alliance* (Carlisle, 2001), 122–32. When the 16 signatories to the letter of resignation were analysed, it was discovered that 2 of them, including one of Bevan's sons, were not members of the council.
33. [Bevan], *Recollections*, 6.
34. [Bevan], *Recollections*, 6.
35. Pease, 'Descendants of Hopkin ap Davydd', 6–7. Nesta gives 5 children from her father's first marriage and 8 from his second with 1 dying in infancy. For an account of Robert Bevan's children, see Andrews, 'Bevan Family', *EQ*, 86–90.
36. *ODNB*, s.v., S. A. Cook, 'Bevan, Anthony Ashley (1859–1933)', rev. John Gurney; Gilbert Murray and Clement C. J. Webb; s.v., 'Bevan, Edwyn Robert (1870–1943)', rev. Michael H. Crawford; s.v., Richard Griffiths, 'Webster, Nesta Helen (1875–1960)'. One of her step-sons is also included: *ODNB*, s.v., 'Bevan, Francis Augustus (1840–1919)'. Edwyn's family has a minor place in the history of photography, for they were identified in 2015 as being the subjects of some of the earliest colour photographs which are preserved in the Royal Photographic

was not immediate. It was evidently at some point not long after meeting Robert Bevan that Frances had painted the reredos in Fosbury, as it was during this period that he was having the church there built close to his house,[37] and according to Nesta, she was still High Church in her views when she married.[38] It is impossible to be dogmatic, but the illustrations of 1858 in her first book, which was verse translations from the German, were almost certainly by herself.[39] Most are of a variety of domestic settings in line drawings that are delicate and skilfully executed, but one of them is of the figure of Christ.[40] Whether the latter is from her own hand or not (and it is most probable that it is), its inclusion would be anathema to precise Protestants.

Her second book of hymns, published in 1859, had no illustrations. Her religious opinions were shifting, and she was now clearly dissatisfied with the Church of England. In the introduction she wrote:

> Whatever may be the advantages of an established Church, constituted and regulated as ours is, it is unfavourable to the growth of religious fervour. Spiritual joy is discouraged under the dread of enthusiasm, and a cold, calculating, unamiable caution is in ceaseless exercise, watching over and deadening the pulsations of heavenly life in the heart, which

---

Society collection, now in the Victoria and Albert Museum, London. Particularly striking are the images of his daughter, Christina Elizabeth Frances Bevan (1897–1981), taken at Lulworth Cove by Lt. Col. Mervyn O'Gorman in 1913. It would appear that Christina had a marked resemblance to her grandmother, Frances (which, if the case, belies Nesta's account of her mother's lack of beauty): <http://blog.nationalmediamuseum.org.uk/2015/06/12/solved-the-mystery-identity-of-our-social-media-starlet-christina/>, accessed 15 June 2015. I am grateful to Dr Samuel McBride for this last reference.

37. Bevan was lord of the manor at Fosbury and was the patron of 2 livings, one of which was Fosbury: Edward Walford, *The County Families of the United Kingdom* (London, 1869), 85. When the new ecclesiastical parish of Fosbury was created, the church and vicarage were erected in 1854–6 by Bevan. He employed the Gothic revivalist architect Samuel Teulon to design the church, which Teulon did in the Decorated style. The church, a Grade II listed building, was declared redundant in 1979: Nikolaus Pevsner, *The Buildings of England: Wiltshire* (2nd edn., rev. Bridget Cherry; New Haven, 1975), 250; Chandler, *Marlborough and Eastern Wiltshire*, 231.

38. Webster, *Spacious Days*, 37.

39. It is possible that she had begun translating before her marriage. Charles B. Snepp and Frances Ridley Havergal (eds.), *Songs of Grace and Glory: Hymnal and Musical Treasures of the Church of Christ* (London, 1875), state that hymn no. 732 is by Paul Gerhardt translated by Frances Shuttleworth in 1854; but the same book at no. 1011 also dates to 1854 a translation by her from the German of John Heerman under her married name of Frances Bevan. It is more likely that as both hymns appeared in her *Songs of Eternal Life*, which was undated, that this book was the source of both. That Miss Shuttleworth had become Mrs Bevan would be common knowledge in the Anglican circles that Snepp and Havergal moved in, the actual date less certain by 1875: cf. Cornwall, *Songs of Pilgrimage*, 2:50.

40. E. F. B[evan]., *Songs of Eternal Life* (London, [1858]), [between 72 and 73]. Nesta refers to her mother's 'exquisite drawings with which she illustrated her poems' (*Spacious Days*, 38). *Songs of Eternal Life* has seven full-page illustrations in a mid-Victorian style of line drawing. Each is decorated by a monogram that appears to be composed of Frances Bevan's intertwined initials. The book was printed by C. F. Hodgson & Son of Fleet St., London, which apparently specialized in educational publishing, especially in mathematics.

is seldom thrown open in the simplicity of confiding love to the influence of truth, as it is exhibited, recommended, and illustrated in the Holy Scriptures. There is little delight in the Lord . . .[41]

From the faint praise in her complaint, it would seem that she was still an Anglican at the time of writing, but was evidently seeking for something more. Institutional Christianity seemed moribund, while a more radical faith appeared attractive. Among the family friends in the late 1850s was Charles Hargrove, a former Church of Ireland clergyman who had seceded in 1835 to join the Brethren.[42] It was probably about this time that she also befriended an elderly member of the Exclusive Brethren in Barnet.[43] Although her husband was to remain an Anglican, she joined her new friend's assembly, probably sometime around 1860.[44] From then on, husband and wife would go their separate ways on Sundays. To extrapolate from what she later wrote about those who left an institutional church, this was not a step she took lightly, but was one in which she felt she was obeying Christ.[45] Significantly the first hymn in her second book is entitled 'Guidance'. It declares, with a clear echo of Brethren phraseology: 'It still remaineth true that blest are they / Who cleave unto Him only.'[46]

Nesta, who was the youngest of the sixteen children, thought that her mother's religious fervour took the form of a sort of mysticism that cut her off from family life, although temperamentally Bevan always had a 'superb disregard of mundane matters'.[47] Nesta maintains that her mother did not know how to hold a baby and always had the nurse standing by in case she dropped the child, and that she never visited her in the night nursery. Certainly, in the brief memoir Bevan wrote of her eldest child, Ada, who died aged 3, she only mentions going to the nursery in the morning to give her a kiss, but in the memoir

---

41. E. F. B[evan]., *Songs of Praise for Christian Pilgrims* (London, 1859), 6–7.

42. [Frances Bevan], *Reminiscences of Ada Frances Bevan. By her Mother* (London, privately printed, 1861), 39. Hargrove was Open Brethren and of the ecumenical persuasion: see *BDEB*, 1: 520; Timothy C. F. Stunt, *The Elusive Quest of the Spiritual Malcontents: Some Early Nineteenth-Century Mavericks* (Eugene, OR, 2015), 163–4.

43. According to the family historian, Richard Meredith, a descendant of the Reynolds family, Dr Edward Robert Bradley Reynolds (1835–*c*.1900), an Exclusive Brethren member in Barnet, lived near the Bevans in Barnet and was friendly with them. Members of the Reynolds family were to play a prominent role in Exclusive Brethren history.

44. Webster, *Spacious Days*, 37; 'Robert Cooper Lee Bevan', *The Times*, 24 July 1890, 9. Webster dates her move to the Brethren to 'after she came to live at Trent'. Andrews, 'the Bevan Family', *EQ*, 86, states 'in Barnet she soon became associated with the "Open" section of the so-called Plymouth Brethren' without citing a source for this claim. As he interviewed Nesta Webster, possibly this is an inference from what she told him. If so, as Nesta was clearly unaware of Brethren ecclesial politics (and was unreliable on other details in her mother's life), Andrews had been misled on this point. I am grateful to Andrew Poots for pointing me towards the sources that correctly identify her ecclesiastical affiliation.

45. See for example her comments on Jean de Labadie (1610–74) in Frances Bevan, *Sketches in the Quiet of the Land: or Lights in the Dark Ages of Protestant Germany* (London, [1887]), 141–2.

46. B[evan]., *Praise for Christian Pilgrims*, 10.

47. Webster, *Spacious Days*, 67.

she appears as an affectionate mother who talked with her children and sympathized with their concerns. It was their father who whipped the children when they were naughty.[48] Nesta's account also seems rather at odds with a passage in her writing in which Bevan asks if there is not, apart from the inner life, a legitimate one in 'an outer range where the level is the same as that of the world outside':

> A place where the relationships of the family and of ordinary intercourse exist, where earthly affairs occupy us, where we meet with friends and neighbours, and show ourselves interested in that which concerns them, where we play with the children, and share in the wholesome enjoyment of the beautiful and marvellous works of God; where, in fact, a great part of our daily life is spent on a ground common to men?[49]

Although Nesta stated it was not a factor, her claim about her mother's ineptitude with babies may be partly explained by her being the youngest with increasingly elderly parents. Bevan was a month short of her forty-eighth birthday when Nesta was born.[50] As a woman of middle-age, having been step-mother to several of the younger children from her husband's first marriage and borne a further nine herself, she might have been less energetic by the time of Nesta's childhood than she had been with the older ones.

The tone of her attitude to child rearing can be caught when she approves of Susannah Wesley's training of her son John: 'He was never allowed to eat or drink anything between his meals, unless he was ill, which was a very good rule.'[51] Nesta states that her mother did not give her children toys, but only useful presents, such as needlework or writing materials.[52] The only novels which were permitted were pious fictions from the early Victorian era, and she did not allow her children to read Scott, Thackeray, Dickens, or even the devout Charlotte Yonge.[53] As she later wrote, 'Those are very happy children who have all books kept out of their way, except such as are really good and wholesome.'[54] Approved early reading was *Peep of Day*.[55] The only fiction which Bevan refers to in her writing is *Pilgrim's Progress*, which she repeatedly cites, although she did apparently

---

48. [Bevan], *Reminiscences of Ada*, 9, 18–19. This book was later re-issued as the initial story in J[ohn]. L[eche]. K[raushaar]. [(ed.)], *Seven Little Girls in Heaven, and How They Came There* (London, n.d.), 5–58: e-text available at 'Brethren Archive', <https://www.brethrenarchive.org/media/360204/anon-seven-little-girls-in-heaven.pdf>, accessed 26 June 2018. The book has poems throughout and is illustrated, with p.160 appearing to be a portrait of Ada, but the illustrations have none of the delicacy of the drawings in B[evan]., *Songs of Praise*, and are clearly by a different hand.

49. Frances Bevan, *The Last Parable of Ezekiel* (London, 1900), 113–14.

50. Webster, *Spacious Days*, 38.

51. Frances Bevan, *John Wesley* (3rd edn., London, 1883), 2.

52. As is clear from [Bevan], *Reminiscences of Ada*, the children, however, were certainly not deprived of toys.

53. Webster, *Spacious Days*, 53.

54. Frances Bevan, *Wesley*, 150; for Brethren attitudes to literature, see Neil T. R. Dickson, '"Worldly and dangerous": Brethren and Culture in the Mid-Twentieth Century', in id. and T. J. Marinello (eds.), *Culture, Spirituality, and the Brethren* (SBH; Troon, 2015), 139–58, spec. 141–8.

55. [Bevan], *Reminiscences of Ada*, 46.

like *Alice's Adventures in Wonderland*.[56] The children, however, did not have an unhappy upbringing. Theirs was a highly privileged one, with private tutors, who were often foreign, and a variety of stimulating experiences at the different houses. Even in old age Robert Bevan had an overflow of gaiety and high spirits, and loved nothing better than a cricket match or a gallop over the Downs with the children.[57] It was he who would bring in children's dolls for his daughters. Frances, too, would fill sketch books with beautifully drawn children's heads, and she had a fondness for the cartoons of the French political satirist, Caran d'Ache.[58]

After her evangelical conversion, Bevan had probably engaged in evangelistic visitation, in the mode of Victorian Bible women.[59] She had taught herself Hebrew in the company of a friend who was a future missionary to Syria, so that they might read Psalms and Proverbs more carefully.[60] One can detect something of Bevan's practice in her approval of the early Methodist, Thomas Walsh, who, as described by her, 'would study the Bible for hours every day. For this purpose he got up at four o'clock, and taught himself Greek and Hebrew for the better understanding of the Scriptures.'[61] Certainly, even at the age of 70 Bevan would rise to read the Hebrew Bible at 8.30 in the morning. In the Bevan household, family Bible reading was held daily, although as Robert Bevan was only home twice a week at that time, presumably this was led by Frances or one of the older sons. After the children went to bed, Robert Bevan would hold Bible readings with friends from nine o'clock until 9.45 pm.[62] Sunday was very much a strictly observed Victorian Sabbath, given over to church and other religious activities.[63] His estates were centres for evangelical activity. In 1868 he facilitated (and probably financed) a 'Rustic Open-Air Tea-Meeting' held by William Carter, a London revivalist preacher, in a field near at St Michael's in Fosbury that attracted some 2000 locals.[64] Trent Park was a centre for an eclectic array of evangelicals from the upper and middle classes while Robert Bevan was alive,[65] although he was as happy talking to a labourer on his Wiltshire estate, 'Wullum' Mullens, who possessed a simple faith. According to Nesta, her mother frowned on social gaiety, and the only gatherings which were allowed were prayer meetings and Bible readings. Bevan's thinking in shunning frivolous entertainment can be seen when she reasons that since a church is but a building and the Christian is 'the true house of

---

56. Webster, *Spacious Days*, 25.
57. [Bevan], *Recollections*, 21.
58. Caran d'Ache was the nom-de-plume of Emmanuel Poiré (1858–1909).
59. This is an inference from the model of evangelical activity for women that is depicted in her book *Seven True Stories* (London, [1886]).
60. Frances Bevan, *Seven True Stories*, repr. as *Prayers and Promises: Timeless Gospel Stories* (Fearn, 2005), 89; the friend is named as 'Amy', who is possibly to be identified with the Amy F. Fullerton who corresponded with Elizabeth Copley regarding British Syrian Schools: see Durham University Library, Papers of Miss Elizabeth Mary Copley, GRE/G4/15/1 n.d.
61. Bevan, *Wesley*, 254.
62. [Bevan], *Recollections*, 7.
63. Webster, *Spacious Days*, 43.
64. Christina Evangelina Lawrence, 'Carter's Kitchen: "Extraordinary tea drinkings for the starving poor"', *BHR*, 13: 75–94, spec. 88–9.
65. Webster, *Spacious Days*, 40–1.

God', then those who would frequent a ballroom but would not dance in church are being 'more inconsistent to take the House of God to a ball-room than to make a ball-room of that which is but a house made with hands.'[66] As many activities are not appropriate in church, then her logic would exclude a number of otherwise innocuous pastimes. She remained a product of her social class. The Quaker practice of not removing hats in the presence of social superiors was queried by her.[67] Bevan did have a weakness for shops, especially those which sold oriental goods, in which Liberty's, the leading department store in London where she bought her clothes, also specialized. She travelled widely in Europe as is evident from the particularity of the description of places in her books. She was especially fond of Switzerland and would holiday on Lake Geneva every summer.

The central preoccupations of her time, however, were evangelism and philanthropy. In England she would arrange entertainments for shop or foundry girls, the Bus Drivers' Mission, or children from Jewish schools in Bethnal Green, while in France she visited the various asylums for the sick in the neighbourhood of Cannes and patronized the *Amis des Pauvres* and *Société protectrice des Animaux*,[68] the French arm of the Society for the Prevention of Cruelty to Animals, another good cause which in Britain owed its origin to evangelicals. After the death of her husband in 1890, Frances lived on in the Châlet Passiflora, the villa in Cannes,[69] which had been the only house she cared for. Summers were spent in Switzerland, and she visited England only twice in the last nineteen years of her life. Cannes was then a watering hole for the elite of European society, and Nesta notes the oddity of her mother preferring it to places such as Bournemouth or Bath where the religious atmosphere would have been more congenial.[70] The explanation possibly lies in the internal politics of the Exclusive Brethren. According to the Exclusive Brethren hymnologist, E. E. Cornwall,

> Saddened and perplexed by what transpired in England in 1885 among those believers with whom she was in fellowship, Mrs Bevan spent more and more of her time abroad . . . After her husband's decease, Mrs Bevan came no more to England, but spent her summers at Territet, midway between Montreux and the famous Castle of Chillon, on the shores of the Lake of Geneva.
> More or less isolated now at Cannes, yet occasionally she enjoyed fellowship with brethren who visited her house, and with whom she sometimes "broke bread."[71]

The Stuart (or Reading) schism of 1885 was concerned with the mystical teaching of the Exclusive Brethren, Hebrew scholar, C. E. Stuart, that Christ made propitiation after his death by presenting it in person in heaven.[72] Stuart was a member of the upper classes with

---

66. Bevan, *Ezekiel*, 122–3.
67. Bevan, *Quiet in the Land*, 195.
68. Webster, *Spacious Days*, 49.
69. Earlier, the family had owned the Villa Madeline at Cannes: Cornwall, *Songs of Pilgrimage*, 2:61, 62.
70. Webster, *Spacious Days*, 60.
71. Cornwall, *Songs of Pilgrimage*, 2:64–5.
72. Tim Grass, *Gathering to His Name: The Story of Open Brethren in Britain and Ireland* (Milton Keynes, 2006), 204.

aristocratic and royal connections, who, according to his entry in *Chief Men among the Brethren*, bore a marked similarity to his ancestor, Charles I.[73] The social class connection possibly gave her a degree of sympathy with him and made her uneasy at his treatment, which was by all accounts unpleasant, and his consequent expulsion. It is impossible, however, to attribute one single motive to her eventual residence in France. It was possibly due to her love of heat,[74] her retiring temperament, or indeed was a self-imposed exile from Exclusive Brethren disputes in Britain.[75] But neither Cornwall nor Roach, a later Exclusive Brethren hymnologist, distanced her from the connexion which, given its necessity for limits of fellowship, is conclusive evidence of her continuing attachment.[76] There was, in fact, an Exclusive assembly in the town for a while as is evident from a series of letters in 1879–81 from Edmund H. Peters to Darby which show that Cannes was not immune from Exclusive disputes.[77] One member of the Exclusives who continued to be a regular visitor was her long-term friend, Emilie ('Mimi') de Bunsen (1827–1911), the daughter of Baron von Bunsen, a former Prussian ambassador to Britain with whom the Bevans had been friendly and who had guided her early reading in German literature.[78] She frequently stayed with Bevan, and her presence brought royalty and aristocrats to the house in Cannes, although one grand duchess, who was known as an habitué of Monte Carlo, where there

---

73. 'E[dward]. E[lihu]. W[hitfield]., 'C. E. Stuart', in Hy Pickering (ed.), *Chief Men among the Brethren* (2nd edn., London, 1931), 128–31; Napoleon Noel, *The History of the Brethren*, (ed.), W. F. Knapp, 2 vols. (Denver, CO, 1936), 2:433–88.

74. Webster, *Spacious Days*, 57.

75. Between 1883 and 1887 she switched publishers from Exclusive Brethren ones to a general evangelical one. Perhaps the move has a wider significance and indicates her distancing from the Exclusive Brethren as it came after the Stuart schism of 1885. However, Exclusive Brethren publishers reprinted some of her later works. See below, n. 89.

76. Cornwall, *Songs of Pilgrimage*, 2:34; 'Mrs. Frances Bevan (1827–1909). Gathered to the Lord's Name', in Adrian Roach, *The Little Flock Hymn Book: Its History and Hymn Writers* (Jackson, NJ, [1974]), 13. Cornwall's chapters on Bevan and her translations appear to preserve authentic material on her life. He states that he first thought of compiling biographies of hymn writers in 1902, within Bevan's lifetime: E. E. Cornwall, *Songs of Pilgrimage and Glory, Part 1* (London, [1932]), [5]. The distance in time of Roach and his obvious dependence on Cornwall might be thought to count against him, but the need to preserve the knowledge of who took which side in the frequent Exclusive Brethren schisms means that oral tradition is very strong among them, which inclines the present writer to regard it as reliable.

77. The letters are concerned with charges of dishonesty made by Darby against Edmund Peters and his wife, Juliette Blanche du Thon, while at Cannes and how this impinged on Exclusive schisms in England: CBA, Edmund H[enry]. Peters to J. N. Darby, 31 May [1880?], JND/5/216; 12 Jan. 1881, JND/5/217; 20 Dec. 1879, JND/5/219; 6 Apr. 1880, JND/5/220, 18 Jan. 1879, JND/5/221. There is a letter from Darby about this dispute: J. N. Darby to 'My dear Brother' [?Samuel Peters], *c*.1880, 'Brethren Archive', <http://www.brethrenarchive.org/manuscripts/letters-of-jn-darby/letter/>, accessed 31 Jan. 2017. I am indebted to Dr Timothy Stunt for this reference. The attribution of the letter to Samuel Peters is his.

78. Cornwall, *Songs of Pilgrimage*, 2:34; 'Eine Große Familie: *Dr. theol. et jur.* Christian Karl Josias BUNSEN, later *Baron* VON BUNSEN, ♂, Prussian diplomat', <http://www.einegrossefamilie.de/egf/abfrage.pl?aktion=person_zeigen&person_id=9566&sprache=en>, accessed 29 July 2014.

had been a casino since 1862, was forced to speak to Fräulein de Bunsen in the garden.[79] In March 1905, Bevan's gardens were also the location for a meeting held by the French Calvinistic Baptist preacher, Ruben Saillens,[80] demonstrating that she did remain in contact with a wider evangelical scene. Bevan evidently retained her aesthetic sensibility in later years which found its outlet in perhaps surprising ways. Nesta notes of her mother:

> She herself was anything but "dowdy", the beads and bugles affected by other old ladies of her day were conspicuous by their absence from the long lines of her black, well-cut gowns, and she had always ordered charming frocks from Liberty's. She did not even disapprove of cosmetics, for although face powder at that date was considered somewhat daring, she used it freely.[81]

Nevertheless, it would appear that Bevan became increasingly isolated, and her final book, a commentary on Ezekiel published in 1900, is the work of someone out of sympathy with her times. She died in Cannes, aged 81, on 15 March 1909. Her body was returned to England, and she was interred in the Bevan family vault in the Anglican church near Trent Park in Cockfosters, London.[82]

Historiography

With seven collections of verse, eight prose works, and two brief memoirs of family members, Frances Bevan was the most prolific nineteenth-century female writer among the Brethren. In common with a number of other contemporary women, some of whom also translated from German hymns, it was her skill in modern languages which gave her entry to the world of publishing.[83] Julian's *Dictionary of Hymnology* (^{2}1907) notes of her first book, *Songs of Eternal Life* ([1858]), that it 'from its unusual size and comparative costliness has received less attention than it deserves, for the *tr*[anslation]*s*. are decidedly above the average in merit.'[84] Her next book, *Songs of Praise for Christian Pilgrims* (1859), mainly consisted of her own compositions, including a section for children, but there were also three further translations.[85] The publishing of both works had undoubtedly been encouraged by her husband, and a number of details of their production suggest his

---

79. Webster, *Spacious Days*, 91.
80. Jeanne Saillens to her children, 20 March 1905, cited by Sylvain Aharonian, *Les frères larges en France métropolitaine: Scoio-histoire d'un movement évangélique de 1850 á 2010* (Paris, 2017), 70 n.3. Aharonian is dependent on John Andrews's papers on Bevan, and so believed her presence in Cannes was evidence of an Open Brethren assembly there.
81. Webster, *Spacious Days*, 94.
82. 'Bevan', in Roach, *Little Flock*, 13.
83. Johnston, *Victorian Women*, 20; for a list of Bevan's contemporary women hymn translators from German, see: Cornwall, *Songs of Pilgrimage*, 2: 46–7; and Timothy C. F. Stunt, 'A Note Concerning Hannah Kilham Burlingham (1842–1901)', *BHR* (2018), 14: 47–54, spec. 54.
84. J. M., 'Bevan, Emma Frances, née Shuttleworth', in John Julian (ed.) *A Dictionary of Hymnology* (rev. ed. London, 1907), 139ii.
85. John S. Andrews, 'Frances Bevan: Translator of German Hymns', *EQ*, 34/4 (1962), 206–213, spec. 206.

financing of them.⁸⁶ Possibly, too, these collections came first partly because the demands of family life allowed her little time for anything else than working on the briefer texts of verse. In the final decades of her life, by which time her children were adults, she produced six historical works before her last work, the commentary on Ezekiel. The first of these later prose works were two biographies of figures to whom she was sympathetic, *John Wesley* ([1876]),⁸⁷ which was 'intended for the simple and unlearned',⁸⁸ and *William Farel* ([²1883]), a study of the French Reformer whom she particularly admired. Both were issued by the London Exclusive Brethren publisher, Alfred Holness, under the strapline 'True Stories of God's Servants'. These were followed by four works, which were issued by evangelical religious publishers.⁸⁹ They were largely of a biographical nature, but they also contained extensive translated extracts from their subjects' writings: *Three Friends of God* ([1887]); *Sketches in the Quiet of the Land* ([1891]); *Trees Planted by the River* ([1894]); and *Matelda and the Cloister of Hellfde* ([1896]).⁹⁰ The first of these works is a series of studies in the German Pietists of the seventeenth and eighteenth centuries with just over half the book devoted to Gerhard Tersteegen (1697–1769), whose hymns she also translated as epigraphs to the later chapters. The other three books are studies largely of German mystics of the thirteenth and fourteenth centuries: Mechthild of Magdeburg (*c*.1207–*c*.1282); Mechthild of Hackeborn (1240/1–1298); Gertrude the Great (1256–*c*.1302); Johannes Tauler (d. 1361); Nicholas of Basel (d. *c*.1395); and Henry Suso (*c*.1295–1366). However, *Trees Planted by the River* also includes the medieval English mystics Richard Rolle of Hampole (*c*.1300–49) and Julian of Norwich (*c*.1342–after 1416). Many of her verse translations from both these volumes were brought together in *Hymns of Ter Steegen* [sic] *Suso and Others* which appeared in two volumes in 1894 and 1897.⁹¹ According to Cornwall, she could no longer approve of her earlier hymns, but some survivors from the earlier collections were included in the new series. Her favourite poetic sources were Mechthild of Magdeburg and Henry Suso, with sixteen and

---

86. *Songs of Eternal Life* had a lavish cover with tooling, inset with gold lettering; it only gives a printer's name in the end pages and not a publishing company. The illustrations were produced by the lithographers to the Queen (whose services were presumably not cheap). B[evan]., *Praise for Christian Pilgrim*, 2, states it was 'published with the permission, though not under the direction, of the Author'. The most likely candidates for directing the publication are Robert Bevan or his sister, Lee Favell Mortimer, herself an author.

87. The dating of this work is based on the inference from her citing this year in the text when she calculates an equivalent contemporary sum for monetary value in 1743: Bevan, *Wesley*, 189.

88. Bevan, *Wesley*, iii.

89. Apart from *Sketches in the Quiet of the Land*, which was published by J. F. Shaw & Co., they were issued by James Nisbet & Co., which also published works by Frances Ridley Havergal and Hannah Pearsall Smith. However, *Trees Planted by the River* was reissued by the Exclusive Brethren publisher G. Morrish, and the Gospel Book Depot, which reprinted *Three Friends of God*, was probably the Exclusive Brethren publisher of the same name. *Sketches in the Quiet of the Land* was reprinted by the US Exclusive publisher, BibleTruthPublishers [sic] in the late 20th century.

90. Dates for these have been taken from the bibliographical data provided by the major UK and Irish libraries on Copac: <http://copac.ac.uk/>, accessed 25 June 2013.

91. Andrews, 'Frances Bevan', *EQ*, 34/4, 206–7.

twelve translations respectively, and Tersteegen with about fifty translations.[92] Tersteegen's melding of Reformed theology and divine immanence (which had, as will become apparent, a very specific meaning for him) she found especially congenial.[93]

Bevan was not alone in the Exclusive Brethren in translating German hymn writers, for her near contemporary, Hannah K. Burlingham (1842–1901), also translated German texts and published them in *The British Herald*.[94] Bevan worked from original sources in German or Middle English in the plentiful extracts that she translated and reproduced in her historical works. Some of the German individuals she examined were accessible to a wider monoglot British audience. Her contemporary, Susanna Winkworth, for example, had translated Tauler's sermons and prefaced them with a brief biography in 1857, and English readers had a plentiful supply of Tersteegen's writings, not least his hymns as translated by the elder Winkworth sister, Catherine. Bevan was aware of the latter's hymn translations, although not entirely approving of them, for she found them generally 'wanting in elevation and spirituality'.[95] But individuals such as Gertrude the Great and Mechthild of Hackeborn were not well represented in English, while Mechthild of Magdeburg, whose writings had been rediscovered in a Swiss library as recently as 1861, was not available at all in English.[96] Most nineteenth-century British Protestants would be put off the existing translations of Henry Suso which prefaced his name in their titles with 'Blessed', the designation of his papal beatification.[97] Bevan was, then, a pioneer in educating a more popular English readership in German religious history. Her secondary sources were also principally the writings of historians which were only available in German, and she frequently includes translated passages from their works. She was writing at a time when

---

92. In his analysis of Bevan's hymns translated from the German, John Andrews has shown that in addition to the medieval ones from Mechthild of Magdeburg and Henry Suso there were a further 6 from other medieval sources; in the Reformation and post-Reformation period she translated 7, including 2 by Paul Gerhardt (1607–76); from the Pietists of the late 17th and early 18th centuries (in addition to Tersteegen) there were 5 from lesser hymn writers; and there were only 7 from the later periods: Andrews, 'Frances Bevan', *EQ* 34/4 (1962), 206–213; id., 'Frances Bevan: Translator of German Hymns (Concluded)', *EQ*, 35/1 (1963), 30–8.

93. It may have been Tersteegen's writings that led her to some of her subjects, for although she was critical of it, his three-volume anthology of mystics, *Auserlesenen Lebensbeschreibungen Heiliger Seelen* [*Selected Lives of Holy Souls*] (1733–1753), included Gertrude von Hackeborn, Henry Suso, Julian of Norwich, and Mechthild of Hackeborn, whom he confused with Mechthild of Magdeburg. For her comments on Tersteegen's anthology, see Bevan, *Sketches*, 332–43.

94. Cornwall, *Songs of Pilgrimage*, 2: 14–81; and Stunt, 'Hannah Kilham Burlingham', 47–54. Her hymns and translations were collected and edited posthumously as Hannah K. Burlingham, *Wayside Songs: Poems and Hymns*, (ed.) T. Willey (London, [1901]).

95. B[evan]., *Praise for Christian Pilgrims*, 5.

96. Sara S. Poor, *Mechthild of Magdeburg and Her Book: Gender and the Making of Textual Authority* (Philadelphia, 2004), 2; see also Frances Bevan, *Matelda* [sic] *and the Cloister of Hellfde. Extracts from the book of Matilda* [sic] *of Magdeburg* (London, 1896), 41.

97. Suso is, however, included in the Protestant historian Karl Ullmann's *Die Reformatoren vor der Reformation* (1841) which was translated into English as *Reformers Before the Reformation*, 2 vols. (1854); cf. Frances Bevan, *Three Friends of God: Records from the Lives of John Tauler, Nicholas of Basle, Henry Suso* (London [1887]), xi.

the canon of texts by her medieval German subjects was still being established, a process of which she was aware,[98] but it leads her to dismiss Meister Eckhart as being 'more deserving of the name of heretic than many who ended their lives at the stake.'[99] Later historians would establish that some texts which passed as Eckhart's were not in fact his, and that some of his seemingly unguarded statements had been quoted out of context. She was probably also misled by the German Protestant historian, Wilhelm Preger, who in his enthusiasm to establish Eckhart as the father of German philosophy, succeeded in making him appear more unorthodox than he was. Preger was given to claiming too much—he was also the source of Bevan's identification of Mechthild of Magdeburg with the Matelda who is one of Dante's guides in the *Divina Comedia*.[100]

Bevan was also misled by her reliance on Karl Schmidt, the professor of history at Zürich University and subsequently at Jena. Schmidt was a pioneering German historian, but some of the positions he espoused would be later considerably modified by the scholarly Dominican friar Heinrich Denifle who showed that Schmidt was mistaken on a number of points, such as in the account of Tauler's conversion, and the identification of the mysterious *Gottesfreund im Oberland* with the obscure heretic Nicholas of Basel. The Friend of God from the Oberland was, Denifle convincingly argued, a fictitious creation of the Strasbourg lay-mystic Rulman Merswin (*c*.1307–1382).[101] This reassessment eliminated the one of Bevan's trio who plays a crucial linking-role in her narrative. Perhaps more serious was her reliance on the theories of Ludwig Keller, the state archivist of Münster, in his *Die Reformation und die älteren Reformparteien* [*The Reformation and the Older Reformed Parties*] (1885) with its binary opposition in medieval history between 'the Romish hierarchy' and the 'so-called Waldensian Brethren'.[102] Everything a Protestant might approve of in the convent at Helfta and the *Gottesfreunde*, Keller argued, was to be traced to the Waldensians. Another Protestant historian, Karl Ullmann, even claimed their influence on Richard Rolle made him a precursor of the Reformation, encouraging Bevan to speculate about Waldensian influence on Julian of Norwich.[103] The German historiography on which she was dependent has not worn well. The judgement of James Clark on Bevan's claim for the acceptability of the Waldensians to the *Gottesfruende* in his study of German mysticism might stand for much of her medieval history. Bevan, Clark writes, is 'quite incorrect'.[104]

---

98. Bevan, *Three Friends of God*, 91–2, 313–14.
99. Bevan, *Three Friends of God*, 321.
100. Wilhelm Preger, *Dante's Matelda, ein akademischer Vortrag von Wilhelm Preger* [*Dante's Matelda: An Academic Lecture by Wilhelm Preger*] (Munich, 1873), cited in Bevan, *Matelda*, vii, 38–44. Bevan refers to Mechthild under the Anglicized form 'Matilda' and Dante's guide under the Italian form 'Matelda'.
101. James M. Clark, *The Great German Mystics Eckhart, Tauler and Suso* (Oxford, 1949), 27–33, 53, 84–7; Bevan discusses Merswin in *Three Friends*, 199–201. Similarly misled by reliance on Schmidt was the Brethren missionary E. H. Broadbent in his *The Pilgrim Church* (London, 1931), 109–10.
102. Bevan, *Trees Planted*, 9; see also Bevan, *Three Friends*, vi–vii, 24–45.
103. Bevan, *Trees Planted*, 98–9, 100–2, 149–51, 234–5.
104. Clark, *German Mystics*, 93.

There are problems with Bevan's historiography of her own making other than that caused by the state of contemporary scholarship. Denifle's work was available by the time Bevan wrote, but she probably ignored it because she perceived him as a protagonist of Protestant historians. One of the books which she read to her children was a 552-page tome entitled *The Idolatry of the Church of Rome* (1844) by Algernon Thelwall, a radical Evangelical Anglican curate and a stalwart of the Protestant Association.[105] Her decided anti-Catholic bias, which this choice of educational reading shows, led her to select those sections of her medieval subjects' writings which fitted her sympathies, and to eliminate their Marian devotion and beliefs such as purgatory to make them presentable to Protestant eyes. Sometimes she was justified in claiming that there were interpolations in the writings of individuals such as Tauler which were markedly examples of Roman Catholic devotion. However, her bowdlerizing tendencies are frequently evident in the medieval period, such as when she writes of Richard Rolle's story that it is 'entangled and entwined in many wild and foolish legends, so we must content ourselves to know merely the facts which we can unearth from the encumbering rubbish.' She was delighted that the veneration of saints did not appear in Julian of Norwich's writings,[106] or when she has Gertrude say, 'The Lord has shown me that the most worthy relics which remain of Him are His Words.'[107] But Bevan's editing and translation of her sources make them more Protestant. For example, she reduces one passage from Julian of Norwich's *Revelations of Divine Love*, which has 868 words in Grace Warrack's almost contemporaneous translation of the so-called 'long text', to 175 words. She eliminates in the process statements such as 'he [Christ] fell full lowe in the maydns wombe', and summarizes Julian's graphic visualizing of Christ's physical suffering by the terse 'this work could not be finished short of his death'. The excisions reduce the medieval element in the piety. Her translation, too, moves Julian in a more Protestant direction. Julian's passage 'thus hath oure goode lorde Jhesu taken vppon hym all oure blame; and therefore oure fader may nor wyll no blame assign to vs than to hys owne derwurthy son Jhesu Cryst', is translated by Bevan as 'for Christ has suffered it, having taken upon Himself our guilt and our judgment. Therefore can God our Father no more impute guilt to us, than He can impute it to His dear worthy Son Jesus Christ'.[108] The language of sacrifice and the law has moved the passage decisively in the direction of penal substitutionary atonement. The choice of the Latinate 'impute' is unusual for Bevan, who generally preferred Anglo-Saxon coinages,[109] but it is also unwarranted for it makes Julian appear a precursor of Protestant theology.

---

105. Webster, *Spacious Days*, 69–70; Webster gives the author's name as 'Thirwall': see Ian S. Rennie, 'Thelwall, Algernon Sydney', in *BDEB*, 2: 1091–2.

106. Bevan, *Trees Planted*, 233.

107. Bevan, *Matelda*, 143.

108. Edmund Colledge and James Walsh (eds.), *A Book of Showings to the Anchoress Julian of Norwich*, Part 2 (Toronto, 1978), 535; Bevan, *Trees Planted*, 184–5; Grace Warrack translates the quotation as: 'And thus hath our good Lord Jesus taken upon Him all our blame, and therefore our Father nor may nor will more blame assign to us than to His own Son, dearworthy Christ.' Julian of Norwich, *Revelations of Divine Love*, ET Grace Warrack (Grand Rapids, MI, 1901), 115.

109. Webster, *Spacious Days*, 25. An interesting example of Bevan's adaptation of language for her own purposes can be seen in 'The Story of Cécile', in *Prayers and Promises*, 53–68,

History had a didactic function for Bevan. She makes frequent appeals to the reader to be converted, or to turn from a purely intellectual assent, such as in *Sketches of the Quiet in the Land* in which she hopes to show Protestantism can become a dead orthodoxy. The Pietists called their contemporaries to 'receive the Spirit that giveth life.'[110] She frequently critiques the theology of her subjects, such as when she laments the uncertainty of how far Tauler 'clung to any of the errors of his Church.'[111] Protestants, too, come in for their share of criticism. Her biography of Wesley, she bluntly tells the reader, will 'expose the defects and errors of this servant'.[112] Although she also uses the devotedness of the mystics to berate her contemporaries,[113] she distinctly felt that the nineteenth century was theologically superior, leading her to be sometimes condescending to the past with 'men in a dense fog of error and ignorance'.[114] Very occasionally the opposite, a delight in antiquarianism, shows in her writings, such as in her love of Gothic architecture, or in the chapters on medieval Oxford in *Trees Planted by the River*.[115] The attraction of medievalism for her is evident in the sentence which follows a description of the brutalities of the Thirty Years War (1618–48): 'Let us go back and consort with the men who went on crusades, and built abbeys and cathedrals and were knight-errants, and ascetics, and pilgrims and minne-singers, anything rather than those swine of history.'[116] Such romantic antiquarianism, which once launched her into archaeological excavations at Trent Park in the face of her husband's indifference,[117] is usually held in check in her prose, but is evident in her idealizing the putative proto-Protestantism of her chosen subjects. She did not produce historical works in the modern, technical sense, for although she occasionally contextualizes her subjects in their contemporary social and political circumstances, she fails to place them in the intellectual history of their time, of which she tends to be dismissive. Given it is the ideas of her subjects she is principally concerned with, this omission is a serious weakness. She believed that 'the similarity of the Divine teaching in ages far apart, amidst absolutely different mental surroundings, must be obvious to all who take the trouble to compare the writings of past and present times'.[118] This historical hermeneutic is an interesting application of that employed in contemporary evangelical

---

when compared with the original version of the same story in Alex. R. C. Dallas, *My Life &c.*, (the author, n.pl., [1870]), 179–94, reprinted as Anne B. Dallas, *Incidents in the Life and Ministry of the Rev. Alex. R. C. Dallas* (2nd edn., London: Nisbet, 1872). The story is about an incident in the life of Dallas (1791–1869), founder of the Irish Church Missions, and Bevan clearly had Dallas's autobiographical account before her when she wrote. She has simplified the language and made it less formal: e.g. 'Conceive what that was for me to hear from my mother's mouth', becomes: 'That encouraged me.' I am grateful to Dr Timothy Stunt for identifying Alexander Dallas as the subject of Bevan's story.

110. Bevan, *Sketches*, iii–iv.
111. Bevan, *Three Friends*, 90.
112. Bevan, *Wesley*, iii.
113. See for example Bevan, *Sketches*, 344–5.
114. Bevan, *Three Friends*, 74.
115. Bevan, *Trees Planted*, 57–79.
116. Bevan, *Quiet in the Land*, 62.
117. Webster, *Spacious Days*, 29–30.
118. Bevan, *Trees Planted*, 5.

scriptural interpretation which presented an undifferentiated doctrinal uniformity on the text. In her historical works her intention was to 'lead us to realise, as never before, the Presence on the earth, of Him who was sent down to "teach all things" to believing souls.'[119] Introducing Mechthild of Magdeburg's *Das fließende Licht der Gottheit* [*The Flowing Light of the Godhead*] she writes:

> The object in view in making the following extracts from Matilda's book is not to present it as a literary or historical study. Were it so, it would be needful to give extracts from the false as well as from the true teaching, so as to give a correct idea of Matilda and her times. But writing simply with a desire that the truth taught to Matilda by the Spirit of God should be made available for those in these later days who are glad of spiritual food, the false and the imaginary will be passed over, and the remainder given as much as possible in Matilda's own words.[120]

It is an enduring divine-human intercourse which is her true subject, and which she felt could not be relativized by the varieties of the individual mind or historical development.

There was one way, however, in which she relativized history. 'Let us cease to think of the Reformation as a bare protest against Catholic doctrine and practice,' she wrote, 'and ascribe to Protestantism all the light, and to Roman Catholicism all the darkness.'[121] For Bevan, the religious struggle was not between two opposing religious ideologies, but 'Christ and Belial', and both Protestants and Roman Catholics shared with all humanity in being 'ignorant and wicked'.[122] There was error on the Protestant side; but equally there was genuine devotion and belief within Catholicism. God, she maintains, 'will own and bless much love and little light'.[123] Human institutions were ambiguous being a mixture of good and bad and were, therefore, not as important as people's piety. She is in the tradition of evangelical historiography which began in the eighteenth century with Joseph Milner, who had promised to concentrate on '*real*, not merely *nominal* Christians' and had thought it unimportant in the early Christian era 'what EXTERNAL Church they belonged.'[124] This is a historiography that the Brethren, with the movement's instinctive anti-institutionalism, continued in the works on general church history by Andrew Miller, E. H. Broadbent, and F. F. Bruce.[125] However much Bevan edited the past for the religious susceptibilities of

---

119. Bevan, *Three Friends*, ix.
120. Bevan, *Matelda*, 50.
121. Bevan, *Trees Planted*, 53.
122. Bevan, *Farel*, iv, 11.
123. Bevan, *Trees Planted*, 35.
124. Joseph Milner, *The History of the Church of Christ . . . Continued after the same Plan by the Rev. Isaac Milner* (1794–1809; one-vol. edn. Edinburgh, 1839), iii.
125. Andrew Miller, *Short Papers on Church History*, 3 vols. (London, 1873–8): Miller (1873), 1: 4, states his intention to follow '*the silver line of God's grace in true Christians*'; Broadbent, *Pilgrim Church*, xi, notes, 'Her [i.e. the Church's] people are ever *pilgrims*, establishing no earthly institutions'; F. F. Bruce, 'Church History and its Lessons', in J. B. Watson (ed.), *The Church: A Symposium* (London, 1949), 178–95: Bruce makes much the same points by quoting (characteristically) the liberal churchman Dean Inge at the beginning of his essay. Roy Coad claims Bevan as the pioneer in Brethren writing about earlier Christian movements in his *A History of the Brethren Movement* (2nd edn., Exeter, 1976), 92, but Miller

nineteenth-century English Protestants or by her own stringent standards of theological truth, an enduring tradition of Christocentric devotion emerges from her writings.

Often, too, it is a spirituality in which women were involved. Quite apart from the major figures, such as Mechthild of Magdeburg and Julian, there are a host of other less celebrated women who wind in and out of her narratives. Her female readers are encouraged to be part of the religious elite who are marked by high achievement in the realm of Christian spirituality. The Brethren, too, are subsumed into this great tradition. Sometimes her historical descriptions might cause a knowing smile for the Brethren reader, such as when the Lord's supper in first-century Troas or its early celebration at Geneva is described in terms of a Brethren morning meeting.[126] But it is startling to find a sermon on the name of Jesus by Richard Rolle concluded with a quotation from J. N. Darby.[127] She found the mystical succession she had isolated within European Christianity continued within contemporary Brethren. However much she may have narrowed it, she shares Joseph Milner's conviction that 'a succession of pious men in all ages must therefore have existed'.[128] Bevan would undoubtedly have read such language generically to include women.

Theology

Neatby suggests that Bevan had perhaps turned to the study of German mysticism due to her disappointment in Brethrenism.[129] His speculation is not entirely plausible for her earliest translations from the German Pietists were in her first hymn collection of 1858, undoubtedly before she became Brethren. Even on Neatby's own terms, it is only partly acceptable if by 'Brethrenism' he means the operations of the system and not its dogma. However she may have found the reality of schism in the Exclusive Brethren, Darby remained her favourite theologian, and, with the single exception of a chapter in *Trees Planted by the River*, which consists of extracts from his loyal lieutenant G. V. Wigram,[130] the only one she quotes. She repeatedly gives extracts from a variety of Darby's writings in *Trees Planted by the River*, and he is quoted frequently, either in an epigraph or in the text, in her commentary in Ezekiel.[131] She had evidently read deeply in his *Collected Writings*.[132] Her unsuspecting reader would not realize this, though, for unlike her scrupulous attribution of quotations to contemporary historians, neither Darby nor his writings are credited. On

---

was slightly ahead of her in publishing. His first and second volumes, which dealt with AD 32–814 and AD 814–1529 respectively, appeared in 1873 and 1876, whereas Bevan's biography of John Wesley only appeared in this last year (Miller cites it as a source in vol. 3 (1878), 624), and the first of her earlier histories not until 1887.

126. Bevan, *Farel*, 2–3, 260.
127. Bevan, *Trees Planted*, 123–4.
128. Milner, *History*, v.
129. W. Blair Neatby, *A History of the Plymouth Brethren* (2nd edn., London [1902]), 333.
130. Bevan, *Trees Planted*, 238–45; the extract is from 'Gleanings 1', in *Gleanings from the Teaching of G. V. W*[igram]. (London, [n.d.]).
131. Bevan, *Trees Planted*, 35–7, 123–4, 152, 248–52; Bevan, *Ezekiel*, 22, 28, 85–6, 128, 129–31, 155, 184–5, 197.
132. The 34 volumes appeared between 1867 and 1883: E. N. Cross, *The Irish Saint and Scholar: A Biography of William Kelly 1821–1906* (London, 2004), 114.

specifically Darbyite points, however, such as the ruin of the church or the secret rapture,[133] she followed his teaching. Perhaps the *odium theologicum* in which he, and Brethrenism generally, was held by many, encouraged anonymity to make her writings acceptable to a wider public. Her Calvinism was more explicit. She held that humanity was incapable of doing works which please God for the race is dead in sin, and that God has elected some who will irresistibly be saved.[134] She repeatedly emphasizes that the blood of Christ as a substitutionary atonement for sin is the only ground of salvation. She was careful when writing about the gospel as it was presented to unbelievers not to say that Christ died specifically for the individual, a form of words that indicates her belief that his death was efficient for the elect only.[135] Her theology upheld the so-called 'five points' of scholastic Calvinism.[136] This is explicit in her biography of John Wesley whom she criticizes for not believing in the final perseverance of the saints. In the theological disputes between Wesley and Whitefield and Rowland Hill, she supports the last two, and she maintains that 'the Calvinistic Methodists, as they were called, showed far more faithfulness of heart to Christ on this occasion than did those who differed from them.'[137] Like other early Brethren, her soteriology was Calvinist.[138]

Despite her admiration for Calvin, she did not, however, follow him slavishly, and she made her differences explicit on three significant points. The first of these was Calvin's attitude to the state. Bevan contrasts epithets that had been applied to William Farel (1489–1565) and Calvin (1509–1564) in favour of the former: the itinerant Farel was 'the shabby preacher', but Calvin was 'the dictator of Geneva'.[139] She disapproved of Calvin's establishment of a theocracy with its imposition of the observance of the Ten Commandments on the civil population and the death sentence for heresy and blasphemy. Christ had foreseen the error of imposing civil punishment for religious offences, she asserted, and had taught that the tares and wheat should grow together—a parable Bevan applied, *pace* Augustine, not to the Church, but to society.[140] It was not that she believed in toleration of theological error in the Church or a mixed communion,[141] for she thought

---

133. Given the unexpected nature of the rapture as she presents it, it is clear she held to the specifically Darbyite secret rapture; see, for example, Frances Bevan, 'The Morning Star', in *Hymns of Ter Steegen* [*sic*] *and Others*, 2nd series (London [1897]), 128–9.

134. See, e.g., Bevan, *Farel*, 216, 269; *Three Friends*, 50.

135. See, e.g., Bevan, *Prayers and Promises*, 42–3, 77; and also, 'A True Story', in id., *Ter Steegen*, 2: 139–43. The latter is the more revealing as the indiscriminate statement 'Jesus washes our sins away' is put into the mouth of a child.

136. These are frequently denoted by the acronym TULIP: total depravity; unconditional election; limited atonement; irresistible grace; and the perseverance of the saints.

137. Bevan, *Wesley*, 322.

138. Mark R. Stevenson, 'Early Brethren Leaders and the Question of Calvinism', *BHR*, 6 (2010), 2–34; id., *The Doctrines of Grace in an Unexpected Place: Calvinistic Soteriology in Nineteenth-Century Brethren Thought* (Eugene, OR, 2017). For the discussion of Bevan in the latter work, which draws upon an unpublished draft of the present chapter, see 149–50.

139. Bevan, *Farel*, 391.

140. Bevan, *Farel*, 392–3; she also criticizes Calvin for applying to all Christians precepts in dress drawn from medieval asceticism: Bevan, *Sketches*, 69.

141. Bevan, *Wesley*, 138; Bevan, *Ezekiel*, 156.

the latter one of the shameful features of the modern ecclesiastical era, but believers were to separate from unbelief without invoking the arm of government. The second significant area in which she departed from Calvin was in ecclesiology. There was much she agreed with in Calvin's church doctrine and practice. She rejected an apostolic succession, and held the true succession was that of faithful believers.[142] She also agreed with the regulatory principle that only practices enjoined in Scripture should be adopted. She agreed, too, with Reformed iconoclasm and the abolition of feast days.[143] She even went as far as to speculate that the adoption of the eastward position by the celebrant at the Eucharist was foretold in Ezekiel when a pagan posture in that direction was condemned.[144]

But her major complaint against Calvin was that he tried to organize the Church. She felt that this was impossible for two reasons. On the one hand this was given to Christ to do, and he had already done it.[145] On the other hand, the Church cannot be reconstituted because it is—to use Darby's quasi-mystical phrase that she often employs—'the one body', which consists of all faithful believers, some of whom will in the nineteenth century be in pure communions, and some who will be mixed ones. The Christian, living in an era of different sects, she wrote (echoing Darby), had to accept, 'the sorrowful fact of the irretrievable ruin of that building, once so glorious and fair.'[146] She favoured a gathered church, rather than Calvin's acceptance of all who were within the visible Church, and approved of Tersteegen's resolution to participate in the Lord's supper with the converted only.[147] But she wanted to keep the ordering of the church to a minimum with, for example, a charismatic concept of ordination through which Christians might ordain each other.[148] This she saw as 'Christ's order', and anything else as 'inventions of men'.[149] Opposition between human order and God's order was an important one for Bevan. She saw it as exemplified in the two interpretations that were possible of Christ's parable of the pearl of great price. The human heart would rather consent to be the one who sells all to purchase it, but revolts at the notion that Christ is the merchant and the sinner 'the pearl of great price to His heart'.[150] As the latter exposition of the parable that she favoured shows, the conflict between human and divine orders is rooted in the doctrine of grace. Paradoxically, her distrust of anything that might be of human derivation, such as Calvin's ecclesiology, was a development, not only of the regulative principle in worship, but also from Reformed soteriology. Calvin, in trying to organize the body of Christ, had failed to see that 1500 years before it 'was done completely and for ever, by Him alone who could do it.'[151]

---

142. Bevan, *Three Friends*, 37.
143. Bevan, *Farel*, 200, 171, 214–15.
144. Bevan, *Ezekiel*, 92; the reference is to Ezek. 8:16.
145. Bevan, *Farel*, 383.
146. Bevan, *Sketches*, 178, 141–2.
147. Bevan, *Sketches*, 73–4, 301–3.
148. Bevan, *Farel*, 99.
149. Bevan, *Farel*, 232, 96.
150. Bevan, *Ezekiel*, 88; the parable is in Matt. 13:35–6; see Bevan, *Trees Planted*, 208–14, for her citing from Julian of Norwich a similar concept of the Lord seeking treasure on earth.
151. Bevan, *Farel*, 384.

The third area in which she was critical of Calvin was regarding the Old Testament law as a regulatory force for the believer and as applicable to unbelievers.[152] The Christian believer was free from a life of 'rigid rules'.[153] In this she followed Darby's version of antinomianism. This freedom from the law was not, however, a licence for immorality, and she did believe in 'the rules given in His word,' for 'the great society in which God has placed us'.[154] She followed Darby's version of the victorious Christian life. Wesley, she thought, was mistaken in teaching perfection was attainable through sin being rooted out of the believer. For Bevan, 'Christ was the only perfect man who was ever on this earth',[155] though, like Darby, she believed that the Christian was capable of overcoming sin. Christ indwells the Christian by the Holy Spirit, who enables the believer to bear the fruit of the holy life, and through Christ is given the power over sin.[156] Although Darby was an influence on the development of the higher-life teaching associated with the Keswick Convention, which held that complete consecration is the way to experiencing holiness by faith,[157] his position was distinct from it, and Bevan was critical of 'those well-meaning Christians who talk of consecrating themselves to God'.[158] Reformed thought saw salvation as complete in Christ, and sanctification as the process in which the Christian progressed in the practice of holiness. Darby's concept of positional sanctification went a stage further. The Christian was already consecrated to God having been 'set apart' at conversion.[159] The second longest of Bevan's quotations from Darby is to expound the point that the Christian was already sanctified.[160] Citing 2 Corinthians 3:18, 'we all with open face, beholding as in a glass the glory of the Lord', she held that practical or progressive sanctification came from the contemplation of Jesus, 'but it is the effect, not the cause, of our being set apart, separated to Himself by God.'[161]

Disagreement by the Brethren with Calvin on the place of the moral law in the believer's life, again paradoxically, was a theology derived from the movement's inheritance from early nineteenth-century hyper-Calvinism with its determination to minimize human effort and magnify divine grace.[162] Human moral effort was constantly downgraded in

---

152. Bevan, *Farel*, 385.
153. Bevan, *Sketches*, 69.
154. Bevan, *Wesley*, 89, 171.
155. Bevan, *Wesley*, 152. She exaggerates Wesley's position, however. She writes: 'He also believed, on the other hand, that a saved man could attain such complete victory over sin that it might at last be entirely rooted out of him, and nothing be left in him but what was perfect and holy. This he called attaining "perfection."'
156. Bevan, *Trees Planted*, 26; Bevan, *Wesley*, 317.
157. For this, see J. C. Pollock, *The Keswick Story* (London, 1964), 74–5; Charles Price and Ian Randall, *Transforming Keswick* (Carlisle, 2000), 228–44.
158. Bevan, *Ezekiel*, 126.
159. H. H. Rowdon, 'The Brethren Concept of Sainthood', *Vox Evangelica*, 20 (1990), 91–102.
160. Bevan, *Ezekiel*, 128, 129–131, quoting J. N. Darby, 'Sanctification, without which there is no Christianity', in *CW*, 16:190–206.
161. Bevan, *Ezekiel*, 128; see also Bevan, *Trees Planted*, 246–8, where in support of the same point she cites J. N. Darby, 'The Accepted Man: 2 Corinthians 3', *CW*, 12:336.
162. Neil T. R. Dickson, *Brethren in Scotland: A Social Study of an Evangelical Movement* (SEHT; Carlisle, 2002), 266–9; Ian S. Rennie, 'Aspects of Christian Brethren Spirituality', in J.

Bevan's writing, perhaps because she herself had been won from an ethical Christianity to evangelicalism. Probably this experience lies behind her dislike of Thomas à Kempis (c.1380–1471), as, according to her, his *Imitation of Christ* 'tells us we are to make ourselves pleasing to God by our doings; the gospel tells us we are made pleasing to God by the precious blood of Christ; that is to say, not by what we do for Him, but by what He has done for us.'[163] But there is a further theological point underlying her denigration of human works. The longest of all her quotations from Darby concerns 'the proper Christian state' which is the Spirit filling the believer when she abides in Christ 'so as to be the only source of thought in us'.[164] Bevan translates Mechthild of Magdeburg as writing:

> For all that shone forth from us was the light of the eternal Godhead. The good works we did were given to us through the holy Manhood of the Son of God, and we wrought them by the power of the Holy Ghost. Thus all our works, our love, our sufferings, flow back thither whence they came, from the Three in One, to His eternal praise.[165]

At the heart of her theology she asserts a quasi-mystical Christology. The Christian's life, Bevan wrote, 'is no longer an imitation of Christ, but we may rather say a continuation of Christ.'[166] If her soteriology followed that of Calvin, she departed from Calvin where he endorsed institutions, whether of the state, church government, or the moral law. Her theology went beyond him in holding that Christ acted directly on the sanctified spirit, uninterrupted by organizational or moral codes, but filled the believer as the unmediated source of the life of holiness. In this she was faithfully following Darby.

Spirituality

Christian spirituality has been defined as 'those elements in Christian belief and practice that concern the preparation for, the consciousness of, and the effects attendant upon a heightened awareness of God's immediate and transforming presence.'[167] Bevan's spirituality, with its emphasis on engrafting into Christ, horror of idolatry, and her practice of private devotion, also shows her debt to Calvin. It was, however, Calvinism as transmitted by evangelicalism.[168] David Gillett maintains that locating the 'creation point' is one of the surest ways by which to locate a particular spirituality, and he places

---

I. Packer and Loren Wilkinson (eds.), *Alive to God: Studies in Spirituality* (Downers Grove, IL, 1992), 205.

163. Bevan, *Wesley*, 24–5. Another Christian writer who comes in for similar criticism is William Law; see Bevan, *Wesley*, 51, 73, 84, and Bevan, *Ezekiel*, 79–80. It is very probable that she was familiar with the writings of both before her evangelical conversion.

164. Bevan, *Trees Planted*, 35–7, quoting J. N. Darby, 'In Christ', *CW*, 21:273.

165. Bevan, *Matelda*, 117.

166. Bevan, *Wesley*, 76.

167. Sandra M. Schneiders, 'Christian Spirituality: Definition, Methods and Types', in Philip Sheldrake (ed.), *The New SCM Dictionary of Christian Spirituality* (London, 2005), 1.

168. For a spirited defence of the position that Calvin was an evangelical in the modern Anglo-American sense, see Paul Helm, 'Calvin, A. M. Toplady and the Bebbington Thesis', in Michael A. G. Haykin and Kenneth J. Stewart, *The Emergence of Evangelicalism: Exploring Historical Continuities* (Nottingham, 2008), 197–220.

evangelical spirituality as being that of the twice-born.[169] It was because he felt that mysticism was a denial of the biblical revelation that the ex-Quaker, John Eliot Howard, who had joined the Brethren in 1838, was critical of the German mystics and of Mme Guyon, whom, he maintained, neglected redemption or the atoning blood.[170] But Bevan depicted the earlier historical figures whom she chose as her subjects as having had a conversion, and this included the medieval mystics. Even Dante is cautiously endorsed, and was approved reading for her children when learning Italian, as his *Divina Comedia* had been the means through which the Irish landowner and Brethren hymn-writer, Sir Edward Denny, 'learnt to know Christ as his Saviour'.[171] The Christian experience of God for Bevan began at conversion, and her Darbyite theology told her that everything that was necessary for the deepening of that encounter was contained within it.[172] Her spirituality rejected the practice of scholastic Calvinism in categorizing salvation history into doctrines. Historical facts were not doctrines: 'We believe the great and marvellous *facts*, and the soul passes from death to life, and we find ourselves no longer climbing up the toilsome ladder of our own feelings to reach to heaven, but already, in the person of Christ in the bosom of the Father, in the centre of that unspeakable love which flows from us to God.'[173] The sentence alludes to the classic mystical metaphor of 'ascent'. In all probability it was the robust assurance offered by Darby's theology that had given Bevan psychological resolution to her emotional struggles. It gave her an assured, confident spirituality. As a true Protestant, she would not follow the classical three-stage spiritual journey of the mystic.[174] There would be no dark night of the soul.

There is a strand of common-sense philosophy running through radical nineteenth-century evangelicalism with an emphasis on 'fact'.[175] It is present in both Favell Mortimer's comment to Bevan quoted above[176] and Darby's propositional assurance, which based assurance on the plain statements of Scripture, and alluded to his theology of 'in Christ'. The believer apprehends the direct, unmediated 'facts' of revelation. As in Denys Turner's characterisation of the writings of Julian of Norwich, Bevan did not claim union with

---

169. David K. Gillett, *Trust and Obey: Explorations in Evangelical Spirituality* (London, 1993), 22.

170. John Eliot Howard, *Seven Lectures on Science and Scripture* (London, 1865), 195–9. Both Darby and William Kelly were critical of classical mysticism: see Anne-Louise Critchlow, *Against the Trend: The Spirituality of William Kelly (1821–1906)* (Eugene, OR, 2016), 150–2.

171. Bevan, *Matelda*, 100–1; Bevan does not refer to Denny by name, but identifies him by a quotation of a verse from his hymn 'A pilgrim through this lonely world / The blessed Saviour passed'.

172. Belden C. Lane, 'Calvinist Spirituality', in Sheldrake (ed.), *Christian Spirituality*, 162i–2ii.

173. Bevan, *Sketches*, 281.

174. David Perrin, 'Purgative Way', in Sheldrake (ed.), *Christian Spirituality*, 517i; see also Carlos Eire, 'Redefining the Sacred and the Supernatural', in Thomas Albert Howard and Mark Noll (eds.), *Protestantism after 500 Years* (New York, 2016), 75–97, spec. 82–4.

175. Martin Spence, *Heaven on Earth: Reimagining Time and Eternity in Nineteenth-Century British Evangelicalism* (Cambridge, 2013), 107–12. For the relevance of the evangelicals Spence describes for Robert Bevan, see below at n. 202.

176. At n.34 above.

God through ineffable experiences, but thought the experiences of the Christian should be communicable.[177] This was a significant factor in her selection of the works from which she translated, such as those of Tauler or Tersteegen. In someone of such an intellectual nature, this strand in contemporary evangelicalism might suggest that she would have a rationalist bias. However, cultural Romanticism was reasserted in her feeling that 'in spiritual matters the head is no match for the heart', and when the head prevailed over the heart it led to a dead orthodoxy or to spiritual pride as had happened after the Reformation.[178] Additionally, her grasp of the multivalence of language gave the imagination a central place. She shared the contemporary assessment of the dangers more extreme forms of imagination might pose for women. As she noted, 'in our days the wholesome fear of being sent to a lunatic asylum serves as a check upon the wild imagination of undisciplined woman kind'.[179] Truth should have the effect, not of 'exciting' the mind, but 'controlling and calming' it.[180] In medieval times, however, visions were greatly to be desired. In places such as the influential convent at Helfta, where the two Mechthilds and Gertrude the Great lived, Bevan maintained there was an 'unwholesome excitement of the brain and nerves', that meant new revelations, 'which, if spiritual at all, and not wholly the result of disease, were the work of the evil one.'[181] It was a point in Tersteegen's favour that he did not have visions, though he, too, came in for his share of criticism for their indiscriminate inclusion in his *Heiliger Seelen* [*Holy Souls*].[182] Her spirituality was restrained, but despite this distaste for an unfettered imagination, she also believed that 'the servants of God have seen visions divinely shown to them, no one can doubt who believes the Bible'.[183] In an incident she describes in two different places in her writings, a Hertfordshire farmer is converted through a dream. He cannot understand the absolute sufficiency of Christ, until he dreams that he has vanished and only Christ exists.[184] Apart from her openness to accepting some visions on biblical and experiential grounds, she is also open to accepting them because of the nature of language. She writes of the descriptions of visions and dreams of 'really holy people':

> Occasionally, it was merely a form of writing in symbol, as when John Bunyan describes having seen in his dream Christian escaping from the City of Destruction . . . They spoke, therefore, largely in symbol, whether by word or by forms and devices of architecture. . . . In the second place, the want of adequate words to express spiritual truths must always be felt, and much can be said in symbol which could not be said at much greater length in plain speech. In how many words could that be taught us which we learn from the one expression, "The Lamb of God"?[185]

---

177. Denys Turner, *Julian of Norwich, Theologian* (New Haven, 2011), 28; for Bevan's similarity with Kelly in this respect, see Critchlow, *Against the Trend*, 152.
178. Bevan, *Matelda*, 130; Bevan, *Sketches*, 344.
179. Bevan, *Matelda*, 16.
180. [Bevan], *Reminiscences of Ada*, 4.
181. Bevan, *Matelda*, 18.
182. Bevan, *Sketches*, 343, 397, 431.
183. Bevan, *Matelda*, 16.
184. Bevan, 'The Man who Vanished', in *Prayers*, 30–8; Bevan, *Trees Planted*, 37.
185. Bevan, *Matelda*, 20.

Figurative language was not just a form of shorthand, but could encapsulate the meaning of spiritual truths which were beyond ratiocination. Bevan's writings abound in the quotation and use of symbolism, drawn from mystical sources that are rooted in the Bible, as signs for spiritual states: the wilderness, running water, the garden, summer fields, the temple, pilgrimage, the bride and bridegroom. A scriptural filter must always be present, but her spirituality could apprehend God's presence through the imagination.

More problematic, perhaps, is the social withdrawal which her spirituality enjoined. John Andrews feels that her hymn translations 'fostered the dangers of quietism: passivity and abandonment of the will.'[186] Undoubtedly a simple, ascetic life appealed to Bevan, and, despite her anti-Catholicism, she found much to admire in monasticism.[187] Her evangelicalism made her feel that 'though it is a daily necessity to meet on common ground, as regards our earthly life, those who have nothing in common with the children of God as regards the eternal life', a 'wall is always around the holy people of the Lord'.[188] She quotes with approval her subjects on the avoidance of 'empty amusements'.[189] Separation rather than integration was always her preferred option. However, her wealth is impossible to avoid, for the Bevans were among the richest people of their times. One disgruntled applicant for a handout from Robert Bevan had bitterly replied in verse to Bevan's refusal:

> Mr. Bevan, Mr. Bevan,
> Your name of earth doth rhyme with Heaven,
> But how, dear sir, about your acts
> Of hoarding wealth and giving tracts?
> Keep your tracts, Sir, to yourself,
> And spare a little of your pelf,
> And remember, Mr. Bevan,
> The rich man hardly ever enters Heaven.[190]

Immense wealth combined with evangelical piety left the individual open to the Dickensian charge of hypocrisy. In addition, Frances Bevan's writings give few examples of specific ethical actions the believer might undertake. She does translate Tauler to the effect that religious contemplation might legitimately be left to attend to the elderly or the sick.[191] Generally, however, in the manner of a high Calvinist, she is so keen to condemn good works as a route to salvation and to proclaim the worthlessness of even the best of human actions, that the casual reader might be left with the feeling that ethical action was of no importance to her. In one of her admonitions against works-righteousness, she feels it necessary to qualify her comments to stress the importance of 'rightmindedness and right

---

186. Andrews, 'Frances Bevan', 35/1 (1963), 37.
187. Bevan, *Trees Planted*, 255; see also her comments on the lifestyle of Elizabeth of the Palatinate in *Sketches*, 205.
188. Bevan, *Ezekiel*, 115.
189. See, for example, Bevan, *Three Friends*, 173; Bevan, *Sketches*, 154; cf. Bevan, *Ezekiel*, 157.
190. Webster, *Spacious Days*, 34.
191. Bevan, *Three Friends*, 119–22.

conduct'.[192] Startlingly, she notes that the two examples of divinely approved good works in the Epistle of James have no ethical merit: 'A man took a knife to slay his son, a woman betrayed her country to invaders.'[193] She was even critical of the twice-born believer being associated in philanthropy with others as it led the latter to believe they were Christians.[194]

However, she did practise a spirituality of the quotidian. She condemned those who, comparing themselves to Mary of Bethany, looked down on those cast in the role of Martha, such as the poor who must necessarily work to earn their living.[195] She translates at length a sermon of Tauler's in which he preaches that Christians should serve God in their daily work.[196] Tauler tells his hearers in another sermon God will meet them in 'whatever God has given you to do, from moment to moment'.[197] As was noted above, the contemplation of Jesus for her was intended to foster growth in holiness. It is clear, however, that along with her dismissal of Calvin's theocracy went the loss of Calvinism's socially transformative impulse. Through a quotation from the French Protestant politician, Comte Agénor Etienne de Gasparin (1810–71), she condemns the rise in the nineteenth century of more communitarian social orders as a development from the latent values of Roman Catholicism. Individualism was a product of Protestantism.[198] Her philanthropic individualism is implicit in her children's book, *Seven True Stories* ([1886]), which recounts contemporary incidents. Some of the stories are concerned with the life of the indigent, and it is divine intervention, of which sometimes Christians are the agents, that is seen to lighten their poverty. In one story a man is peremptorily dismissed by his employer and his family is left without blankets. Due to the mother's conversion at gospel meetings and her subsequent prayers, even better blankets are unexpectedly supplied to them than the ones of which they had been deprived, and through a sequence of other providences, the family is assisted.[199]

Bevan practised a form of benign paternalism. Her Whiggish father may have written a book entitled *The Consistency of the Whole Scheme of Revelation with itself, and with Human Reason* (1832), which was recommended to students as a useful supplement of Bishop Butler,[200] but his daughter would only have agreed with the first of the propositions in the title. Human reason was decisively not in accord with God's thoughts. She was pessimistic in her assessment of human nature, and, like other futurist premillennialists, she saw world history as being interrupted by a series of divine interventions which would culminate in imminent apocalyptic events. Robert Bevan had belonged to the circle

---

192. Bevan, *Ezekiel*, 122; cf. the criticisms of César Malan quoted in Boyd Hilton, *The Age of Atonement: The Influence of Evangelicalism on Social and Economic Thought 1785–1865* (Oxford, 1988), 17–18.

193. Bevan, *Ezekiel*, 46; the reference is to the actions of Abraham and Rahab, Jas. 2:21–5.

194. Bevan, *Ezekiel*, 136.

195. Bevan, *Three Friends*, 115–6.

196. Bevan, *Three Friends*, 116–21.

197. Bevan, *Three Friends*, 169.

198. Agénor Étienne, Comte de Gasparin, *La Vie d'Innocent III* (1873), quoted in Bevan, *Ezekiel*, 138–46.

199. Bevan, *Prayers*, 9–19.

200. Philip N. Shuttleworth, *The Consistency of the Whole Scheme of Revelation with itself and with Human Reason* (London, 1832); *ODNB*, s.v., 'Shuttleworth'.

of evangelicals described in Martin Spence's work, and exemplified in Bevan's friend, Lord Shaftesbury, after whom he and Frances had named their first son. They believed in a scheme of paternalism that was a system of mutually binding obligations on the rich and the poor.[201] Bevan was probably in the more conservative section of these historicist premillennial thinkers, for, although he evidently shared their optimistic future vision, he had rejected decisively the more extreme restitutionist optimism of T. R. Birks.[202] But Bevan believed in his duty to those whom he regarded as the deserving—as opposed to the idle—poor and practised tithing on his considerable income.[203] Frances, by adopting the futurist Darbyite version of premillennialism, possibly came closer to the social thought described by Boyd Hilton which modelled itself on divine intervention to practise a paternalistic correction of the evils of society.[204] Despite the decided down-playing in her writings of 'good works', whatever the precise relation of her eschatology to her social views, her spirituality led her to be philanthropically active at an individualistic level.

Although intercessory prayers, such as the ones which are operative in *Seven True Stories*, have a role in her writings, she is unusual among evangelicals in that it is contemplative prayer which is central to her spiritual practice. In a phrase of Richard Rolle's, used in a letter to a female ruler, Bevan's was 'the mingled life', which she explains as that of contemplation and action.[205] 'Prayer is the ascent of the heart to God', she translates Tauler as saying, and Julian as writing 'the highest prayer is that which is a complete trust in His perfect love'.[206] She was critical of the 'unbelieving mystic' who saw the soul as being united to God which, she wrote, 'meant nothing better than the dreams of a Buddhist'.[207] She was even wary of describing Tauler as a mystic.[208] She clarified Tersteegen's use of 'mysticism' as meaning 'the communion of the believing soul with God'.[209] Her selection of mystics were those who could be read in harmony with this rubric. The Holy Spirit dwells in the believing soul and, in her translation of Tauler,

---

201. Spence, *Heaven on Earth*, 211–28; see also Geoffrey B. A. M. Finlayson, *The Seventh Earl of Shaftesbury 1801–1885* (London, 1981), 74–6.

202. For Birks, see Spence, *Heaven on Earth*, 162–4. However, it is not certain that Robert Bevan was a historicist, and he may have been a futurist. The assumption made by the present writer is that he would have shared the thinking of his circle of friends rather than that of the Irvingites and the Brethren. It is, of course, possible that Frances won him for futurist premillennialism when she adopted Darbyite views.

203. Webster, *Spacious Days*, 35.

204. Hilton, *Age of Atonement*, 10–11, 13–19, 212–13; for a critique of Hilton's views as applying to Shaftesbury and other historicist premillennialists, see Spence, *Heaven on Earth*, 211–15. If Bevan were a historicist premillennialist, it is probable that he would mean his optimistic statement about the future (quoted at n. 33 above), when he first met Frances, to apply to earth as much as heaven. Any optimism Frances had about the future was for a heavenly post-Rapture one. She was decidedly pessimistic about any earthly future.

205. Bevan, *Trees Planted*, 131; the whole passage, 131–6, is suggestive of Bevan's own practice.

206. Bevan, *Three Friends*, 167; Bevan, *Trees Planted*, 163.

207. Bevan, *Matelda*, 93; see also Bevan, *Sketches*, 173.

208. Bevan, *Three Friends*, 192.

209. Bevan, *Sketches*, 388.

'lifts thy heart far into the heights of heaven'.[210] The 'intercourse between the soul and God in His secret place [is] to be a sacred communion, a joy with which the stranger may not intermeddle.'[211] This was heaven upon earth, 'a present possession, where the soul dwells in peace and rest,'[212] in which God is, as he was known to Tersteegen, 'Rest and Stillness of his soul.'[213] God could not come, as she translates Tauler, 'through any other creature, nor through any image or any symbol'. By this imageless apprehension of the divine Tauler meant something Christological, for after casting off everything that might come between the soul and God, Bevan cites him as stating there is the 'Image', that is Christ, in which 'as a mirror you reflect His glorious face, you will be changed into that blessed Image, in soul and spirit, and in all your being.'[214] Absorption in God becomes the central experience of the contemplative. The hymn for which Bevan is most widely known at present is 'My God', which is a translation of lines attributed to Tauler, and which give expression to this:

> As the bridegroom to his chosen,
> As the king unto his realm,
> As the keep unto the castle,
> As the pilot to the helm,
> So, Lord art Thou to me.
> . . .
> As the ruby in the setting,
> As the honey in the comb,
> As the light within the lantern,
> As the father in the home,
> So, Lord, art Thou to me.[215]

The relationship between the terms is organic, and the harmony of the relation is conveyed in the main by Kantian analytic statements: one term is contained within the other, as 'bridegroom' contains the concept of 'chosen bride'. They function as forceful similes of the connection of God to the believer. The encounter is one of love, and love, Bevan translates Tersteegen as defining, is 'to look upon the face of God, and to be looked upon

---

210. Bevan, *Three Friends*, 109.
211. Bevan, *Ezekiel*, 111.
212. Bevan, *Three Friends*, 179.
213. Bevan, *Sketches*, 273.
214. Bevan, *Three Friends*, 160.
215. Frances Bevan, *Hymns of Ter Steegen* [sic] *Suso and Others*, series 1 (London [1897]), 52–3; it is found as No. 340 in the Anglican collection, *Hymns Ancient & Modern: New Standard Edition* (Norwich, 1983), and No. 459 in *Seventh-day Adventist Hymnal* (Hagerstown, MD, 1985), 'As the bridegroom to his chosen': Hymnary.org', <http://www.hymnary.org/text/as_the_bridegroom_to_his_chosen>, accessed 2 July 2013; it is also popular for choirs of the Church of Jesus Christ of Latter Day Saints and has been given a modern choral setting by the English musician, John Rutter. Its popularity at present has much to do with its first line and the demand for appropriate music at increasingly elaborate contemporary wedding services, but also its lack of dogma means it can fit a variety of religious contexts.

by Him.'[216] The loving relationship was thus a mutual one, and the central metaphor which the mystics employed, and which Bevan endorsed, was that of bride and bridegroom. Her verse, as John Andrews notes, 'was steeped in the language of the Canticles.'[217] This was not union with the divine, but marriage to Christ as the second Adam.[218] As the Lord says to Mechthild of Magdeburg in Bevan's translation:

> "Before the worlds, O soul, I longed for thee;
> And still I long, and thou dost long for Me;
> And when two longings meet, for ever stilled,
> The cup of love is filled."[219]

True Quietism, Bevan felt, such as that of Teresa of Avila or Mme Guyon, was 'a desire to have no will but the will of God . . . and all that God should will and do be the delight of the heart.'[220] Contemplative practice and the experience of the mutuality of love between the believer and God were at the core of her spirituality.

Meditation on Scripture was also central to her contemplative practice. The evidence for this is in the prefacing her own verse with a biblical reference which evidently arose out of an imaginative engagement with the text of Scripture.[221] It is significant that Bevan regarded all her collections of verse as 'hymns', although for many of them this must be understood as a metaphor for a form of worship rather than something singable as the metre is often unsuitable for congregational music. Bevan was not musical, something which can be seen in the occasional loss of rhythm in her verse. She regarded music as the lowest of the arts, and Nesta claims her mother could only recognize three tunes.[222] John Andrews notes that her hymns were not fitted for 'extensive congregational praise' due to their nature as 'introspective ones of consecration',[223] and her translations certainly lacked the vigour and emotional depth of John Wesley's.[224] None of her hymns have as their subject the Lord's supper, pointing to a lacuna in her spirituality. Among Brethren the Lord's supper had a central place in spiritual practice, and it gave rise to a number of hymns unique to them.[225] Her radical evangelicalism and reaction against the Catholicism of the

---

216. Bevan, *Sketches*, 430.
217. Andrews, 'Frances Bevan', 35/1 (1963), 36.
218. Bevan, *Matelda*, 92–4.
219. Bevan, *Metelda*, 114.
220. Bevan, *Sketches*, 275.
221. I owe this point to Dr Beth Dickson.
222. Webster, *Spacious Days*, 38.
223. Andrews, 'Frances Bevan', *EQ*, 35/1 (1963), 37.
224. *ODNB*, s.v., Neil Dickson, 'Bevan [née Shuttleworth], (Emma) Frances (1827–1909)'. See also Cornwall's parallel translations of Bevan's and Wesley's translations of Gerhardt's 'Commit thou all thy ways'/'Commit thou all thy griefs': Cornwall, *Songs of Pilgrimage*, 2: 50–1.
225. See: Neil Dickson, '"Shut in with Thee": The Morning Meeting among Scottish Open Brethren, 1830s–1960s', in R. N. Swanston (ed.), *Continuity and Change in Christian Worship* (SCH 35; Woodbridge, 1999), 276–89; George Bristow, '"The Remembrance Meeting": Christian Brethren Theology Of The Lord's Supper', *Emmaus Journal*, 16 (2007), 182–220; Thomas J. Marinello, 'The Lord's Supper in Brethren Ecclesiology: The Mark of Identity, Unity,

High Church Movement was undoubtedly a factor here, for the other Protestant sacrament, baptism, received no attention at all from her.[226] Like William Kelly, with whose strand of mysticism she had much in common, she 'promoted an internal intimate spirituality rather than an external sacramental theology.'[227] The absence of sacramentalism from her spirituality can be seen in the contrasts she draws in her reimaginings of a first-century breaking of bread and a late medieval mass: the former is an austere remembrance, while the latter is an ornate transformation of a wafer into God.[228] Perhaps a further factor in this neglect was the personal rather than communal nature of her spirituality, doubtless reinforced by her exile in Cannes. Silence was undoubtedly one of her spiritual practices, which, combined with her lack of a community sense, means her bald statement about first-century worship should be read as representing no great hardship for her: 'The women keep silence.'[229]

Despite the lack of a developed communal sense, however, some of her hymns did pass into general use in congregational singing, in addition to 'My God', three in particular had a reasonably widespread use. Hymn-singing plays an important part in evangelicalism.[230] Like the popular fictional bestseller, the popularity of a hymn points to a coalescence of its writer's ideas and the spiritual *zeitgeist*.[231] They are a guide to which aspects of her spirituality coincided with that of others. One of her hymns that was widely anthologized in hymnals was 'The Welcome', which was a translation from the German Pietist, Erdmann Neumeister (1671–1756):

> Sinners Jesus will receive—
> Say this word of grace to all
> Who the heavenly pathway leave,
> All who linger, all who fall!—
> This can bring them back again,
> Christ receiveth sinful men.[232]

The 1888 edition of Sankey's *Sacred Songs & Solos* was the earliest hymnal to include it. Its permeation of popular revivalist evangelicalism had been ensured by the American composer, James McGranahan (1840–1907), supplying a bouncy tune and the inevitable

---

and for some, Purity', in id. and H. H. Drake Williams III (eds.), *My Brother's Keeper: Essays in Honor of Ellis R. Brotzman* (Eugene, OR, 2010), 122–39.

226. As a follower of Darby, and a former Anglican, she would undoubtedly be a paedobaptist.

227. Critchlow, *Against the Trend*, 168. For the discussion on Kelly's mysticism, see ibid., 150–71; see also chap. 14 *intra.*'

228. Bevan, *Farel*, 2–7.

229. Bevan, *Farel*, 2; cf. Bevan, 'The Secret of the Lord', in *Ter Steegen* 1: 104–6: 'I, in wonder and in silence, / Listen and adore'.

230. Ian M. Randall, 'Evangelical Spirituality', in Sheldrake (ed.), *Christian Spirituality*, 290i.

231. Cf. John Sutherland, *Bestsellers: A Very Short Introduction* (Oxford, 2007), 3, 29.

232. 'Song of Welcome', in B[evan]., in *Songs of Eternal Life*, 23–5; repr., 'The Welcome', in Bevan, *Ter Steegen*, 2: 87.

repetitious chorus was also added.[233] The second verse of another of Bevan's own hymns, 'The Gospel According to Paul', was widely quoted and sung among faith missionary societies:

> Christ, the Son of God, hath sent me
> Through the midnight lands;
> Mine the mighty ordination
> Of the pierced Hands.[234]

John Allan, while admitting the lines are not great poetry, sees them as an example of Bevan possessing 'some ability to combine a number of ideas in one memorable phrase.... "Midnight lands" manages to suggest the darkness of the world, the loneliness of the messenger, and the lateness of the hour.'[235] The Open Brethren missionary and itinerant Bible teacher, Harold St. John (1876–1957), offered them as the only explanation of why he felt impelled to resign his employment and become a full-time Christian worker.[236] Klaus Fiedler, the historian of faith missions, notes of the hymn: 'As faith missionaries usually appreciated mysticism, it can be assumed that they appreciated this poem too.'[237] It was included in *The Keswick Hymn-Book*, and it was sung at the funeral of the Canadian heroine of the China Inland Mission, Isobel Kuhn (1902–57).[238] 'This is the perfect expression of Brethrenism on its strongest side', writes Neatby. 'The soul has to do with Christ through no human or superhuman mediation. In direct communion with Him the commission must be received, the work executed, the account rendered.'[239] The lines encapsulate how both the Brethren and faith missionaries understood ordination as an action of God without any human intermediary.

A hymn which became a Brethren standard was 'The Bride', and its use was confined to the movement.[240] The opening lines reflect the mood of cultural pessimism which Darbyite premillennialism fostered:

---

233. John S. Andrews, ' 'Sinners Jesus will receive'—the British Reception of Neumeister's Hymn', *EQ*, 55/4 (1983), 223–30; Cornwall, *Songs of Pilgrimage*, 2:55, thinks the chorus was possibly composed by the evangelist and American gospel-song lyricist, D. W. Whittle (1840–1901), when he arranged it for *Sacred Songs & Solos*.

234. Bevan, *Ter Steegen*, 1:142.

235. John Allan, 'Brethren and the Arts', unpublished paper presented at Regent College, Vancouver, 1990, 219–26, spec. 224.

236. Patricia St John, *Harold St. John: A Portrait by His Daughter* (London, 1961), 31.

237. Klaus Fiedler, *The Story of Faith Missions: From Hudson Taylor to Present Day Africa* (Oxford, 1994), 187.

238. 'Isobel Kuhn—Funeral Service—March 22, 1957', <http://www2.wheaton.edu/bgc/archives/docs/Isobelkuhn08.htm>, accessed 3 July 2013; Lauren Pfister, 'Kuhn, Isobel', in A. Scott Moreau (gen. ed.), *Evangelical Dictionary of World Missions* (Grand Rapids, MI, 2000), 584ii.

239. Neatby, *Plymouth Brethren*, 334.

240. *The Believers Hymn Book* (London, [1885]) advised it be sung to Philip P. Bliss's tune for 'Hold the Fort', but it was frequently sung to a plangent tune by another American composer, Clara H. Scott.

> 'Midst the darkness, storm, and sorrow,
> One bright gleam I see;
> Well I know the blessed morrow
> Christ will come for me.

But Christ, too, has a lack: 'the Bride the Father gave Him / Yet is wanting there.'[241] The hymn combines a dramatic narrative with a mood of eager anticipation of marriage, picturing divine desire for the beloved as much as human. Both groom and bride remain unfulfilled, but their eventual union will be consummated in love. As an allegory of Christ coming for his Church, it uses the biblical story of Isaac going out into the fields to meditate while waiting for the arrival of Rebecca, his bride, and then, on seeing her camel train, going to meet her, although the point of view in the hymn is that of Rebecca.[242] The joy of the imagined meeting at the Rapture envisioned by Darbyite eschatology is followed in the hymn by the eternal mutual absorption of Christ and his bride in each other's company, an erotic quality that Mark Sweetnam finds 'almost Donneian in its intensity':[243]

> He and I, in that bright glory,
> One deep joy shall share—
> Mine, to be forever with Him;
> His, that I am there.

The original published location of the hymn was at the end of the chapters in *Trees Planted by the River* which contained the translations from Julian of Norwich. The bride and bridegroom imagery, which is itself derived from the Bible, is employed by Julian and is quoted by Bevan, but the hymn is immediately followed by a chapter which consists of a lengthy quotation from a passage by Wigram in which he invokes the analogy of Isaac and Rebecca, and makes extensive use of the same imagery as Julian.[244] Bevan's hymn, therefore, acts as a textual and conceptual bridge between medieval spirituality and that of the Brethren. She did not see that gap as a hard one to cross, and although those Brethren who enthusiastically sang it were entirely unaware of the post-biblical sources of the lines, they found it an expression of their piety. It sums up her spirituality

---

241. Bevan, *Ter Steegen*, 1:91–2. According to a note that F. F. Bruce appended to Andrews's study of Bevan, this hymn was translated into Gaelic by the Free Church of Scotland minister, John Macleod: 'Frances Bevan', *EQ*, 33/4 (1962), 208, n. 9. Bevan's habit of appending the initials of where her original compositions were written and the initials of German composers in translations led the editors of the Open Brethren *The Believers Hymn Book* to attribute this hymn to Paul Gerhardt. 'P.G.' appended to this hymn was, in fact, 'Park Gate', the family's London house: To add to the confusion, it is attributed to Tersteegen in another Open Brethren hymnal, *Hymns of Light and Love* (Bath, [1900]). Cornwall, *Songs of Pilgrimage*, 2:60, lists the abbreviations she uses for her various houses and identifies several of them.

242. The reference is to Gen. 24:62–5.

243. Mark S. Sweetnam, 'Raptured, Rewarded, and Reigning: The Hope of the Believer in *The Gospel Hymn Book*', in Dickson and Marinello (eds.), *Culture, Spirituality, and the Brethren*, 237-57, spec. 249–51; Sweetnam's allusion is, of course, to John Donne (1573–1631).

244. Bevan, *Trees Planted*, 187, 236–7, 243.

of a direct, interpersonal communion of love as symbolized by marriage between the individual believer and Christ.

Conclusion

We know more about Frances Bevan's clothes and shopping habits than we do about any other nineteenth-century Brethren figure. Reconstructing her biography means a scrutiny of her age, children, and biology. This is to say, she is a woman. She was a strong-minded and in many ways a formidable woman, in ways often typical of her social class, who was not afraid to edit her quotations from the imperious Darby.[245] Issues of gender, however, come to the fore in ways in which they usually remain unstated for men. Probably her choice of history and spirituality rather than sermons and theology, which were male preserves, were cultural effects of her times, as was her middle-class education for women which gave her the competence in European languages necessary for translation. Her hymns and verse translations were never widely popular, however, except among the Brethren, because, among other reasons, they generally lacked the literary quality of other contemporary and near contemporary translators.[246] Webster, too, notes the limited audience for her mother's books.[247] They would bring in regular publishing royalties, for, as with her hymns, this specific audience could identify with her spirituality.[248] But to a wider public, doubtless the hybridity of her spirituality counted against it.

Two of the dominant cultural forms of the age were expressed in Bevan. Her interest in medievalism was in step with the nineteenth century when the Middle Ages influenced everything from Pugin's architecture to William Morris's socialism. Her Protestant evangelicalism also aligned her with one of the dominant forces of the era. Hers was of a high Calvinist variety, and in common with other Brethren, her faith expressed a heightened sense of the supernatural, one which denigrated the institutional and earthly and prized the heavenly and immediate. Both this form of evangelicalism and her fascination with

---

245. For example, see J. N. Darby, 'The Accepted Man, 2 Corinthians 3', *CW*, 12:338, and the quotation in Bevan, *Trees Planted*, 248. Among the changes, the following has been edited out: 'Christ, that I admire; Christ, that I care for; Christ, whose flesh I eat, and whose blood I drink—what wonder if I am like Christ? The Christian thus becomes the epistle of Christ; he speaks for Christ, owns Christ, acts for Christ.' Possibly she was afraid that the phrasing might lead readers to think she had an affinity with transubstantiation in contemporary Anglo-Catholicism.

246. Andrews, 'Frances Bevan', 35/1 (1963), 37, suggests various other reasons for their lack of popularity: their subjective nature; their length; the price of the original editions; and their re-printing chiefly in hymnals that circulated among the Brethren. Cornwall writes of her hymns: 'The translations of Mrs. Bevan have exercised a deep influence upon the hearts of those to whom her poetry more particularly made its appeal, i.e. those with whom she was linked in assembly fellowship.' Cornwall, *Songs of Pilgrimage and Glory*, 2:32.

247. Webster, *Spacious Days*, 25. *Metelda*, however, was reviewed favourably in *Expository Times*, 7 (1896), 315. F. Elizabeth Gray, *Christian and Lyric Tradition in Victorian Women's Poetry* (New York, 2010), 6, describes Bevan as 'entirely obscure'.

248. Bevan's *Three Friends* went through three editions; *William Farel* was translated into French; and her 2-volume *Hymns of Ter Steegen* was republished in 1920. At present two of her books, *Sketches* and *True Stories* are in print, and most of her writings are available as e-texts on the Internet.

the faith of the Middle Ages and of Germany, were expressions of the Romantic mood of the age.[249] What was unusual was that both existed in the same person. Darby, for example, had decisively moved away from his earlier attraction to medieval Christianity as his radical evangelical views developed.[250] Ironically it was Darby's writings which provided the glue that enabled her to bond the two. His mystical theology of positional sanctification, which saw the believer as sitting in the heavenly places with Christ, and communing with God while Christ did his works through the believer on earth, allowed Bevan to view earlier Christian mystics through this lens. It is why she can move from Richard Rolle of Hampole to Darby between paragraphs, or from Julian of Norwich to Wigram with 'The Bride'—that most Brethren of hymns—bridging the chapters. The hymn is a perfect expression of, in Gary Nebecker's phrase, Darby's 'nuptial mysticism' with its 'synthesis of pre-existing bridal mysticism with an emerging futurist premillennial theology.'[251] Even her fascination with the cloistered life, her physical isolation, and her lack of sympathy with the twentieth century can find a parallel in the introversionism of the later Exclusive quest for holiness.[252] On this point Neatby is right. Bevan's historical works, he writes, contained 'a catena of quotations in which the Darbyite is startled by the clearness and intensity of the echo of tones that have become familiar to his ear in such different surroundings.'[253] There was a line of what Bevan called 'evangelical witnesses',[254] from the medieval past that reached into the nineteenth century, that her historiography and verse translations, despite their deficiencies, linked through her spirituality of divine-human communion.

---

249. For evangelicalism and Romanticism, see D. W. Bebbington, *Evangelicalism in Modern Britain: A History from the 1730s to the 1980s* (London, 1989), 74–104.

250. Donald Harman Akenson, *Discovering the End of Time: Irish Evangelicals in the Age of Daniel O'Connor* (Montreal, 2016), 203–7, 222–3.

251. Gary L. Nebeker, '"The Ecstasy of Perfected Love": The Eschatological Mysticism of J. N. Darby', in Crawford Gribben and Timothy C. F. Stunt (eds.), *Prisoners of Hope? Aspects of Evangelical Millennialism in Britain and Ireland, 1800–1880* (Carlisle, 2004), 69. My attention was drawn to the significance of this essay for Bevan through its citation by Mark Sweetnam, 'Raptured, Rewarded, Reigning', 245–6. Andrews, who thought Bevan was not a 'Darbyite', admits the justice of Neatby's assessment: Andrews, 'Frances Bevan', *EQ*, 35/1 (1963), 38.

252. Bryan Wilson, *Religion in Secular Society: A Sociological Comment* (1966; Pelican edn., Harmondsworth, 1969), 225.

253. Neatby, *Plymouth Brethren*, 333.

254. Bevan, *Ter Steegen*, 2: v.

Chapter 16

'I do not know that there is such a term in Scripture as eternal sonship': James Taylor and the Question of the Eternal Son

Roger N. Holden

The Brethren, meaning throughout this chapter the Taylorite Exclusive Brethren, considered that the Lord had uniquely made known to John Nelson Darby the truth as to the assembly, that is that there are two distinct peoples of God—Israel, whose hopes are earthly; and the Church, or assembly, whose hopes are heavenly, this truth having been lost since the time of the apostles. This was not considered to be some extra-Biblical revelation but truth that was present in Scripture. Darby was given almost apostolic status, James Taylor on one occasion asserting that:

> Mr. Darby stands by himself; spiritual instinct is not evidenced in linking him . . . with Athanasius, Augustine and Luther. The plane on which Mr. Darby served, as having judged as contrary to the mind of God the whole clerical system beginning with the early so-called fathers and extending to the present time, was altogether above that of those who preceded him since the apostles went to be with the Lord. Those who keep the Lord's commandments as loving Him, regard J.N.D. in this way, valuing his ministry as marked by the energy and wisdom of the Spirit; being without an equal since apostolic times.[1]

The very high view of Darby expressed here contrasts with a low view of the whole of Church history from the apostles until Darby. This strong view of apostasy after the apostles and the claim to have recovered the truth was of course not unique to the Brethren; it was held, for example, by some Anabaptist groups in the sixteenth century and by the Quakers of the seventeenth century. The Brethren considered that this unfolding of the truth by the Spirit was ongoing, continuing after Darby's death through the ministry of Frederick Edward Raven and then James Taylor, the object being to perfect the assembly for the rapture. This unfolding of truth continued in the face of conflict arising from the opposition of the devil. This was the view of Brethren history expressed in the volume *Recovery and Maintenance of the Truth*, compiled by Alfred J. Gardiner and first published in 1951 with a second edition in 1963.[2] After an initial chapter concerning the first recovery of the truth through J. N. Darby, subsequent chapters then consider particular conflicts and

---

1. [James Taylor], *Letters of James Taylor*, 2 vols. (Kingston-on-Thames, 1956), 1:388.
2. A. J. Gardiner, *Recovery and Maintenance of the Truth* (2nd edn., Kingston-on-Thames, 1963), 249–71.

the truth established by each. Each chapter consists of extracts from relevant documents, usually letters or notes of meetings, with a brief introduction written by the compiler. The chapters are not numbered as such, but the fourteenth is entitled 'The Sonship of Christ' and concerns events of 1929 when James Taylor explicitly denied the Eternal Sonship of Christ during meetings held at Barnet in England. Despite the opposition of some, this rapidly became established Brethren doctrine and in particular was incorporated in a new revision of the Brethren hymn book, *Hymns and Spiritual Songs for the Little Flock*, issued in 1932.[3] Taylor was, of course, not the first person to deny the Eternal Sonship of Christ, but his development of the subject perhaps had some novel features. In Brethren terms it was novel because this appears to be the first time that something was introduced that was clearly and admittedly contrary to what Darby believed and taught, Taylor claiming that if Darby were still alive he would accept the new teaching.

In contrast to Darby, Taylor wrote very little and the huge corpus of his ministry is transcripts of what was said by him during meetings, either the Brethren-style conversational Bible readings or addresses. This was, of course, before the days of sound recording and would have been taken down in shorthand, then normally checked over, and revised by Taylor himself before publication. Initial publication was somewhat haphazard, but when collected together and re-published in the 1960s it amounted to 100 volumes plus two volumes of letters. As Taylor's authority amongst the Brethren was established, virtually everything he said was written down and published. Thus there is no single exposition of a subject such as the Eternal Sonship, but what he said is diffusely spread through this published ministry. What are the key points are not necessarily obvious and what he says at different times is not necessarily consistent or clear. Thus adequately referencing statements has not always been easy and generally only one reference is given where it would be possible to provide a whole series of references. The most relevant items are listed in the bibliography below, but references will be found elsewhere in his ministry.

A disputed doctrine

The doctrine of Eternal Sonship is part of orthodox Trinitarianism, being explicitly affirmed by the Athanasian Creed—'The Father eternal, the Son eternal: and the Holy Spirit eternal'. Chalcedon affirms that the Son was 'begotten before all ages of the Father', while the Nicene Creed asserts that the Son was 'begotten of the Father before all worlds'. This is not the place for a full historical survey of those who have disputed the doctrine in one form or another over the centuries. For example, in the fourth century Marcellus of Ancyra held that the Son was generate at birth.[4] In the period since the Reformation some, such as Socinus and John Biddle, have denied it as part of their move towards Unitarianism. In eighteenth-century England, many Presbyterians, under the influence of Enlightenment rationalism, moved towards Arianism and eventually Unitarianism, claiming to appeal to Scripture alone over the creeds and confessions of men. Under these influences some were

---

3. Roger N. Holden, '*Hymns and Spiritual Songs for the Little Flock*: A Sectarian Hymn Book?', in Neil T. R. Dickson and T. J. Marinello (eds.), *Culture, Spirituality, and the Brethren* (SBH; Troon, 2014), 209–36, spec. 214–21.

4. H. R. Mackintosh, *The Doctrine of the Person of Jesus Christ* (2nd edn., Edinburgh, 1913), 189–91.

led to at least question the doctrine of the Eternal Son, including figures of apparently impeccable orthodoxy such as the hymn writer Isaac Watts and the Evangelical Anglican William Romaine, whose comments on the subject Taylor was pleased to discover.[5] More recently some American evangelicals have questioned the doctrine.[6] John MacArthur did so in a commentary on the book of Hebrews published in 1983 but subsequently revised his views in favour of the orthodox teaching.[7]

Closer to home for our present purposes, is the dispute on the issue that arose amongst the Strict Baptists in the nineteenth century.[8] In 1859 J. C. Philpot, as editor of the *Gospel Standard* magazine, published three articles in defence of the doctrine of Eternal Sonship.[9] This was followed up with two further articles in the June and July issues of 1860.[10] It is unclear who Philpot was aiming at originally, but things became acrimonious when John Andrew Jones of Shoreditch and James Wells of the Surrey Tabernacle wrote against Philpot in the *Earthen Vessel*, another Strict Baptist magazine. Other contributions to the *Earthen Vessel* supported the orthodox view, and the editor Charles Waters Banks made clear that he only published the contributions of Jones and Wells because he thought debate was healthy, not because they represented the views of the magazine. Subsequently Philpot gathered and edited his contributions into a book *The True Proper and Eternal Sonship of the Lord Jesus Christ*, published the following year and reprinted many times since.[11]

Now of course there was a connection between Philpot and Darby in that Philpot had been tutor to the children of Edward Pennefather, whose wife, Susan, was sister to Darby. Moreover, Darby claimed that he had been instrumental in the conversion of Philpot, although Philpot himself never mentions this and he did not follow Darby's dispensational views.[12] Like Darby, Philpot subsequently seceded from the Anglican Church and joined that section of the high-Calvinist Strict Baptists associated with William Gadsby, John Warburton, and John Kershaw, identified with the *Gospel Standard* magazine of which Philpot was editor from 1840 until his death in 1869. In the issue of March 1842 he published an article about the Plymouth Brethren, in the guise of a review of the magazine

---

5. [Taylor], *Letters*, 2:248. Probably what is being referred to here are comments in Romaine's 'Discourse upon the Self–Existence of Jesus Christ' in which he speaks of Christ covenanting to be the Son and that the names Father, Son, and Spirit do not describe them as they exist as divine Persons but the manner in which they have acted for our salvation: 'A Discourse upon the Self–Existence of Jesus Christ', *The Whole Works of the Late Reverend William Romaine*, vol. 6 (London, 1821), 210–34, 222–4.

6. 'What is the Doctrine of Eternal Sonship and is it Biblical?', <http://www.gotquestions.org/eternal–Sonship.html>, accessed 11 June 2013. 'The Eternal Sonship of Christ' <http://www.catholic.com/tracts/the–eternal–Sonship–of–Christ>, accessed 11 June 2013.

7. 'Re–examining the Eternal Sonship of Christ', <http://www.gty.org/resources/articles/A235>, accessed 11 June 2013.

8. Kenneth Dix, *Strict and Particular: English Strict and Particular Baptists in the Nineteenth Century* (Didcot, 2001), 93–6.

9. [J. C. Philpot], 'Review', *The Gospel Standard*, 25 (1859), 88–98, 121–31, 155–63.

10. [J. C. Philpot], 'Review', *The Gospel Standard*, 26 (1860), 186–95, 216–27.

11. J. C. Philpot, *The True Proper and Eternal Sonship of the Lord Jesus Christ* (London, 1926).

12. [J. N. Darby], *Letters of J. N. D.*, 3 vols., (Kingston-on-Thames, n.d.), 3:167.

The Christian Witness.[13] Whatever else he charged the Brethren with, he considered their views of the Trinity to be orthodox.

Darby and Raven

Taylor's denial of the Eternal Sonship during the Barnet meetings was clearly unexpected. At meetings in Birmingham in 1932 someone remarked 'I think it is the biggest readjustment of thought that many of us have had in the last few years'.[14] There are indeed references to people having being removed from fellowship for denying the doctrine of the Eternal Sonship, one writer asserting that in the past Taylor would himself have been removed from fellowship.[15] Darby maintained that the Trinity was one of the great foundational and distinctive truths of Christianity, but he added he would not go to the Fathers of the first four centuries to seek proof—this he found in Scripture.[16] He said he maintained no creed, but that as to doctrine he liked the Athanasian Creed best of all, although it is far too scholastic in form.[17] To give just one example from his writings where Darby speaks of the Eternal Son, in a passage that is clearly referring to John 1:18 he writes of the 'Eternal Son of the Father, enjoying the infinite love of Him in whose bosom He dwelt, it is He who reveals Him as He Himself has known Him.'[18] The fact that up until Taylor's time the Brethren, including leaders such as Darby, had held the orthodox view was undeniable and Taylor acknowledged this.[19] This, of course, presented something of a difficulty given the almost apostolic status granted to Darby. But, Taylor maintained, Darby's writings must not be made equal to Scripture, nor must any ministry be accepted as final as if the Holy Spirit has ceased to speak. Scripture was the final authority, but the Holy Spirit was still leading the Brethren into a greater understanding of it. Thus not only had Darby and Raven adjusted their ministry in accord with the leading of the Spirit, but if they were still alive they would have accepted what was being taught.[20] Although the argument does not seem to have been used at the time, it might have been argued that the truth specifically made known through Darby was that as to the assembly, while in other areas he simply accepted prevailing views that could be subject to further adjustment.

Nevertheless, Taylor evidently scoured Darby's writings for support and maintained that Darby 'seems to have had a remarkable subconsciousness that Scripture treats of sonship as applying to Him in the flesh as man only' and that in later life he became dissatisfied with the orthodox doctrine of the Eternal Sonship.[21] In support of this view, he repeatedly

---

13. [J. C. Philpot], 'Editor's Review—*The Christian Witness*', *The Gospel Standard*, 8 (1842), 77–84.

14. [James Taylor], *Ministry by J. Taylor*, (new series) 100 vols. (Kingston-on-Thames, n.d), 34:112.

15. A. J. Pollock, *An Open Letter to C. A. Coates* (London, n.d), 3; E. Middleton, *Reversal not "Adjustment": An Appeal to my Brethren* (Ayr, 1932), 10; Arthur Oglesby, *The Eternal Son* (York, n.d., [c.1930]).

16. [J. N. Darby], *CW* (repr. 1956; Kingston-on-Thames), 15:291.

17. [Darby], *CW*, 9:298.

18. [Darby], *CW*, 7:101.

19. [Taylor], *Letters*, 1:265–6; 2:181.

20. [Taylor], *Letters*, 1:393; 2:140–1.

21. [Taylor], *Letters*, 1:266; 2:141.

referred to a single passage in Volume 7 of Darby's *Notes and Comments on Scripture* on John 1: 14 where Darby states 'Nor do I see that in this character He is spoken of as Son save as known in the flesh. He is spoken of as the Word, etc.; now as Son'.[22] But there is a footnote to this evidently added later where in reading over his words he feared that they approached Sabellianism. Although not the clearest of passages, for *Notes and Comments* were after all Darby's own personal notebooks not intended for publication, it hardly supports Taylor's contention as Darby evidently added the note because he feared what he wrote earlier could lead in heretical directions. Elsewhere Taylor refers to some notes by Darby on 'The Son of Man' and to a letter of 1881, but it is difficult to see how either of these provides any support and we may concluded that Darby continued his belief in the Eternal Sonship until the end of his life.[23]

With F. E. Raven, Darby's successor, the situation may initially appear to be clear cut since he wrote in 1894 that 'if a man intended to deny the eternal sonship of Christ I certainly should not care to remain in fellowship with him'.[24] Similar statements can be found elsewhere in his ministry.[25] Again Taylor responded to this inconvenient fact by claiming not only that Raven had changed his views later, but that it was from Raven he had learnt the doctrine he was now teaching. It is well known that Raven had caused division amongst the Brethren for his teaching on eternal life and on the person of Christ. Clearly Raven had great influence on Taylor, who first came to notice amongst the Brethren as one who defended Raven's teaching on eternal life. On the person of Christ, Raven began to teach unorthodox views, which have been seen as akin to Apollinarianism, that in the incarnate Christ the divine Logos took the place of the human mind or soul; or to Docetism, that Jesus was not really a man but only seemed to be one. Raven stated that in person Christ was God, but in condition he is man. Therefore, Raven objected to the view that Christ's person consists in the union of God and man, as expressed in the formula from the Athanasian Creed: 'God and man one Christ'.[26] He considered that the wording of the Athanasian Creed is derogatory because it means that in becoming man a change has taken place as to his Person, whereas the truth is that the divine Person assumed human flesh, so was 'a Person in a condition in which he was not previously.' We can see the influence of Raven's views in Taylor's comment on the Athanasian Creed that:

> Here it is stated that our Lord was begotten of the Father before the worlds and begotten of His mother in the world; 'one, not by confusion of substance, but by unity of Person'. He is 'of a reasonable soul and human flesh subsisting'. God and man (dual personality) is 'one Christ'. The thought conveyed is that the Lord was personally a man with 'reasonable soul', as we are, and besides this is another 'substance', God, another Person, the unity

---

22. J. N. Darby, *Notes and Comments on Scripture*, 7 vols. (Kingston-on-Thames, n.d), 7: 4–5.

23. [Taylor], *Letters*, 1: 266 & 389; ibid., 2, 140; Darby, *Notes and Comments*, 2: 300–1 (p.423 in original Morrish edition quoted by Taylor); [Darby], *Letters*, 3: 142–3 (pp.468–9 in original Morrish edition quoted by Taylor).

24. [F. E. Raven], *Letters of F. E. Raven* (Kingston-on-Thames, n.d.), 101.

25. For example: [F. E. Raven], *Ministry of F. E. Raven*, (new series) 20 vols. (Kingston-on-Thames, n.d.), 3: 271.

26. [Raven], 'The Person of the Christ', *Ministry*, 3: 262, 268–73. This item is undated.

was not 'confusion of substance', but of Person. Thus Christ was a union of God and man, a dual Person, not a divine Person become flesh; the latter is the truth Scripture presents. There is no change in the Lord's Person, but in His condition.[27]

This contrasts with Darby's more positive view on the Athanasian Creed quoted above.

Whether or not Taylor was right that Raven changed his views, there are things in Raven's ministry which could point in the direction taken by Taylor. Having said that he should not care to remain in fellowship with someone who denied the Eternal Sonship of Christ, Raven immediately adds 'The eternal relations subsisting between the Father, the Son and the Holy Spirit are entirely beyond our knowledge'.[28] This was to be insisted on by Taylor, with the additional claim that we cannot apply the titles Father, Son, and Holy Spirit before the incarnation. At the Barnet meetings, 'F.H.B.' remarked that 'I remember F.E.R. saying that we have no testimony in Scripture of the relationship of divine persons in past eternity' to which Taylor responded by saying 'I was helped by remarks made by F.E.R. in America on this subject'.[29] In subsequent letters Taylor expanded on this, saying that Raven had expressed these views during readings on John's gospel when he visited in America in September to November 1902 but these remarks had been omitted in the published notes.[30] Taylor was indeed present at these meetings and contributed, but if he is correct that some remarks were edited out, it is not possible to identify where. However, there is a mystery here and it may have been Raven's previous visit to America exactly four years earlier in 1898 when Raven made the remarks that Taylor referred to. The editors of the published volume of Raven's letters have inserted a letter written from Chicago on 14 October 1898 by Mr Broomhead of Greenwich, who accompanied Raven on his visit. This letter refers to a reading held in upstate New York at Rochester on 11 October 1898, and says that:

> In the latter part of the meeting there was a very interesting digression as to the way in which divine Persons have been revealed. F.E.R. thought that 'the Son' is used in special reference to the Father and the name 'Son of God' in reference to man, but that none of these titles are applied to Him in Scripture until incarnation, and therefore we are not authorised to carry these titles back into eternity.[31]

Moreover, there follows a letter written by Raven on 23 November 1898, after his return home, to an unidentified person who was evidently questioning him on what had been said during the meetings in America. In it Raven states:

> As to what you refer to, my point was that it was permitted to us to know divine Persons as and when revealed and only so. In view of that revelation the Son has taken a new place relatively, that is, of inferiority to the Father, coming to do the will of God, though of course there would be no change morally or in affection. The names under which we

---

27. [Taylor], *Letters*, 1:325
28. [Raven], *Letters*, 101.
29. [Taylor], *Ministry*, 29:368–9. The identity of F. H. B. is unknown.
30. [Taylor], *Letters*, 1:260, 263, 343, 392, 394; 2:141. [Raven], *Ministry*, 17:7–96.
31. [Raven], *Letters*, 146–7.

know divine Persons, that is, Father, Son and Holy Spirit are, I judge, connected with this position, and I doubt if we are allowed to enter into the eternal relation of divine Persons apart from this revelation.[32]

Taylor was present at and contributed to these American meetings. The published notes are stated to have been edited by Raven but contain no remarks like those referred to.[33] Raven may indeed have made comments in 1898, and perhaps again in 1902, going beyond what he said in his letter of 1894, and questions raised may have suggested to him that it was best to edit them out. The Glanton brother, Algernon J. Pollock, later alleged that it had been admitted by one who was editor of the 1902 notes that extreme and novel statements were made and it was feared that if published they would lead to division.[34]

Whatever Raven said in 1902, it seems to have fallen on fertile soil in Taylor's mind, but the only evidence of Taylor's thought between then and 1929 is a letter he wrote on 25 February 1921 in reply to an English brother, Percy R. Morford. In this Taylor says:

> Your remarks as to the great and blessed subject of our Lord's sonship were most interesting. My mind has travelled on similar lines as yours has in regard of what F.E.R. said at different times. I was present at the reading to which you refer. My recollection is that our beloved brother hesitated to apply the title of "Son" to the Lord, before incarnation, but I do not think he was dogmatic on the point, and I remember him dwelling on John 17:5. "The glory which I had with thee before the world was". As far as I am able to say, my understanding of the subject has been governed by what I learned through F.E.R.[35]

The letter has a postscript saying 'I do not think it would be wise to publish my letter on this subject.' Unfortunately, we do not have Morford's letter, and so we cannot be exactly sure as to the direction in which his mind was travelling. But this letter does suggest that Raven's remarks were not as definite as Taylor later represented them when he asserted that it was 'well known' that Raven changed his mind on the subject of the eternal Son.[36]

On the other hand, while apparently the phrase 'Eternal Son' does not appear in any of Taylor's published ministry before 1929, he did make statements that implied acceptance of the doctrine. Some of these statements were redacted when Taylor's ministry was reprinted as the New Series after his death in 1953. One of these is in a passage quoted by Ernest Middleton dating from 1911:

> Now, as believing in the Son you have come to that which is permanent and immutable; but then it is also needful for us to see, and to be very clear about the fact that the Son became Man . . . Leaving out for the moment the eternal relationship that ever existed between the Father and the Son . . .[37]

---

32. [Raven], *Letters*, 147–8 (emphasis in original).
33. [Raven], *Ministry*, 12:110–21.
34. A. J. Pollock, *The Eternal Son* (London, n.d.), 45.
35. [Taylor], *Letters*, 1:189–91.
36. [Taylor], *Letters*, 1:394.
37. Middleton, *Reversal*, 5. Middleton quotes from volume 14 of the original series but this has not been seen by the present writer to check the possibility that he was misquoting. However, this is unlikely because Taylor would have pounced on this fact in his response to Middleton.

In the New Series, although the first sentence quoted above has been left as it is, in the second the phrase 'the Father and the Son' has been replaced by 'divine Persons'.[38]

The highly respected English brother, Charles A. Coates, supported Taylor's new teaching in 1929 and also claimed he had been considering the question for thirty years.[39] Nevertheless, his printed ministry does contain statements before 1929 in agreement with the doctrine of Eternal Sonship and at least one explicit use of the term. Again some of these statements were redacted when his works were later re-printed. Middleton quotes Coates as saying 'To accomplish this the Eternal Son must become a man in this world of sin, and must be lifted up upon the cross.' but when reprinted this was altered to 'To accomplish this His beloved Son must, as the Son of man, be lifted up upon the cross.'[40] Later Taylor did not deny the accuracy of these quotations by himself and Coates, but responded they now had clearer light on the matter and that he was not aware of making any statements that were inconsistent with what he now held.[41]

The road to Barnet

James Taylor was of Irish origin but emigrated as a teenager to North America. He first came to notice amongst the Brethren when in 1890, aged only 20, his name appears on a letter signed by six brothers from New York affirming F. E. Raven to be sound in doctrine when much of New York meeting was opposed to him.[42] On subsequent visits to America, in 1898 and 1902, Raven was evidently struck by Taylor's contributions in meetings, and following his death in 1903, it was Taylor who rapidly became the acknowledged leader of the Raven group of Brethren. Following the death of Darby, the Brethren developed an expectation that there would be a successor, one supreme leader, although this was probably not explicitly formulated until James Taylor Jr. was in that position. Raven initially had filled this place and Taylor was now slipping into it. Roger Shuff has described the growing acceptance of Taylor's authority, culminating in the concept of 'authoritative ministry' in the 1940s, although Taylor would have denied having apostolic or anything akin to papal authority.[43] Undoubtedly there was something striking about Taylor's speech and ministry, but, as Raven before him, Taylor courted controversy and there were questions raised about the notes of meetings held in Chicago over New Year, 1904–5.[44] Taylor denied an intention to be dogmatic but maintained that what he said was 'substantially the truth which the Lord has been calling our attention to for some years'.[45] Roger Shuff considers that Taylor may not have been personally power-seeking, but appears to have come to believe that the Spirit was working through him, a conviction

---

38. [Taylor], *Ministry*, 4:310.
39. [C. A. Coates], *Letters of C. A. Coates* (Kingston-upon-Thames, [c.1960]), 201.
40. Middleton, *Reversal*, 4; C. A. Coates, *A Sure Foundation*, (Kingston-upon-Thames, [c.1960]), 36–7. Again the original version has not been seen to check the quotation, but we can be sure that an inaccurate quotation would not have gone unnoticed.
41. [Taylor], *Letters*, 1:394.
42. [Taylor], *Letters*, 1:3–5.
43. Roger Shuff, *Searching for the True Church: Brethren and Evangelicals in Mid–Twentieth-Century England* (Milton Keynes, 2005), 113–121.
44. [Taylor], *Ministry*, 1:108–255. Gardiner, *Recovery and Maintenance*, 153–8.
45. [Taylor], *Letters*, 1:31–3.

perhaps endorsed by the position the Brethren accorded to him.[46] The Chicago notes issue suggests that this conviction was developing as early as 1904–5, less than two years after Raven's death. *Recovery and Maintenance of the Truth* has ten chapters dealing with conflicts in which Taylor was involved in between the death of Raven in 1903 and his own death fifty years later in 1953. This tendency of Brethren to dispute and divide amongst themselves was well established by 1903. Most of the disputes Taylor was involved in would be esoteric and largely incomprehensible to an outsider, even from another church. They often concerned Brethren views on the assembly, but the issue of the Eternal Son is a matter that related to the wider world of Christian doctrine.

From 1910 onwards James Taylor made regular trips across the Atlantic to Britain. These were in part business trips, first for his employers Mills and Gibb, who were linen importers, and after 1919, for his own company, the Taylor Linen Company, which he had set up with his son James Taylor Jr. His second wife, whom he married in 1913, came from Barnet, which explains why he always visited this otherwise insignificant town in London suburbia. After 1921 Taylor spent three or four months in the spring of each year visiting the British Isles, usually travelling to the continent of Europe as well.

In 1929 he had departed New York in early March on the White Star liner *S. S. Cedric*, scheduled to arrive in Liverpool on 12 March. He returned home in early July being back home by 15 July. During those four months he had twice crossed to the continent of Europe, the first crossing to Belgium being primarily for business purposes, while on the second he visited meetings in France and as far east as Leipzig in Germany. For the rest, he travelled extensively in Britain and Ireland, included visiting Belfast which was of course a centre of the linen trade, taking meetings in at least fifteen different places.[47] Some, but not all, of these meetings were the so-called conferences or three-day meetings, starting on a Friday and continuing over the following Saturday and Sunday. During this time he would be expected to lead six Bible readings and give at least one or two addresses. While all local Brethren would be free to attend, others would be by invitation. Some places he visited regularly and although his itinerary suggests a concentration on the large cities he also visited smaller places, perhaps in response to specific invitations. The Barnet meetings were three-day meetings and took place in June somewhere near the end of this punishing schedule, although the exact dates are not known.

The Barnet Meetings

Evidently considerable importance was attached to the meetings at Barnet and invitations had been sent to so-called 'leading Brothers', that is men who were considered to have a gift for the ministry and who would themselves be invited to take meetings, thus disseminating Taylor's thought. Taylor said later that he had 'no doubt that the spiritual intelligence in the meetings warranted attention' to the subject of the Eternal Sonship.[48] In opening the first reading he said: 'It was intimated that these meetings had those more or

---

46. Shuff, *Searching for the True Church*, 118.

47. These details of his itinerary in 1929 comes from Taylor's *Letters*, 1:258–9 and indexes to *Ministry*, vols. 29, 30, 31, 39, 77, 95, & 98. As will be appreciated from this, arrangement of items in Taylor's *Ministry* is not always chronological.

48. [Taylor], *Letters*, 1:263.

less engaged in the Lord's service especially in view, and it was thought that this epistle might be considered profitably from the standpoint of service as having special relation to the gospel of Mark.'[49] The epistle referred to was Paul's Second Epistle to the Corinthians and the six Bible readings based on this were subsequently published under the title 'The Divine Standard of Service'.[50] There is no indication in the opening reading that the question of Eternal Sonship was going to be considered, and indeed Taylor himself may not have intended doing so but for the apparently innocent question posed by Samuel J. B. Carter during the second reading. Carter (1858–1938), son of William and Hephzibah Carter, was a notable evangelist who had moved from Open to Exclusive Brethren and had lived for a long time in Australia before returning to England.[51] He published a number of tracts and pamphlets one of which had been on the subject of the Eternal Son. It has been suggested that this was written in 1925 when a brother in Melbourne was excluded from fellowship for denying the doctrine, an action moreover that Taylor had supported at the time.[52] In reference to 2 Corinthians 1:19 'For the Son of God, Jesus Christ, he who has been preached by us among you',[53] Carter asked: 'Referring to the Son of God, would it be the Son as begotten in time, or would it suggest resurrection? He was "marked out Son of God in power, according to the Spirit of holiness, by resurrection of the dead" (Romans 1:4), or would it be His eternal sonship?'[54] He did not really receive a reply to this question as Taylor only responded to that final phrase:

> I do not know that there is such a term in Scripture as eternal sonship. "Son of God" is a question of a Person. The Son of God is announced in Scripture after the Lord Jesus was here. In Luke 1:35 it says, "The holy thing also which shall be born shall be called Son of God". That is what Luke says, meaning that that should come out in Him in due course. Jesus asserts His relation as Son at the age of twelve in saying, "My Father's business", but the Father's voice announcing it is at His baptism.

Although it is clear that in meetings like this Taylor had a general idea of what was to be considered, the format provided for the leading of the Spirit and Taylor subsequently 'thought that it was of the Lord that Mr. Carter raised the question'.[55]

---

49. [Taylor], *Ministry*, 29:330.
50. [Taylor], *Ministry*, 29:330–489.
51. Christina Evangelina Lawrence, 'Carter's Kitchen: "Extraordinary tea drinkings for the starving poor."', *BHR*, 13 (2017), 75–94; 'Samuel James Boulter Carter', <https://www.brethrenarchive.org/people/samuel-james-boulter-carter/>, accessed 23 Feb. 2018.
52. Carter's pamphlet is referred to in Taylor *Letters* 1:263 but unfortunately it has not been possible to trace a copy of the pamphlet. Taylor says he was sent a copy by a Mr Ghinn of Melbourne. The further information comes from participants at the 6th IBHC. Taylor's *Letters* (1:208–13) show that he did visit Australia in 1925 spending a week in Melbourne, but they make no reference to this issue, nor do the notes of the meetings in Melbourne (*Ministry*, 23:1–164).
53. This and all other Scripture quotations are from J. N. Darby's New Translation.
54. [Taylor], *Ministry*, 29:361. As was the Brethren fashion, only initials of people taking part appear in the notes but 'S.J.B.C.' can be readily identified as Samuel James Boulter Carter from Taylor, *Letters*, 1:262.
55. [Taylor], *Letters*, 2:415.

Clearly Carter was somewhat taken aback by Taylor's response and sought clarification by asking 'You believe He was the Son in eternity?' to which Taylor further elaborated:

> What the Scriptures say is, "In the beginning was the Word". It does not say 'the Son'. "In the beginning was the Word, and the Word was with God, and the Word was God" (John 1:1), that is to say, His eternal personal existence is stated, He was there personally in the beginning. To go so far as to give Him a personal name or designation then, is going beyond Scripture it seems to me, but that the *Person was there* is the great point. To give Him a name is another matter, but the Person was there. It is the foundation of Scripture that He was a divine Person and so was there in the beginning.

After further remarks and questions by other persons, Carter returned to the point: 'I thought that in incarnation He took up in new conditions a relationship that had ever existed in eternity and that as the Son of God it was the relationship in a new condition.' This brought the rather sharp response from Taylor: 'I think you are asserting too much in saying the relationship 'had ever existed'. After that, Carter withdrew from the fray. But clearly Carter was not the only one surprised by what Taylor had said. In response to a later question Taylor says:

> You have to bear in mind that Scripture is dealing with a mediatorial system of things. Christ has come within the range of men to speak to men, but to attempt to give Him a name before He became Man is going beyond Scripture, it seems to me. Because of His taking up a mediatorial position as Son we can understand the references to subjection, obedience, etc.[56]

This is one of Taylor's essential points, that all three Persons in 'absolute Deity' are totally equal, without thought of subordination, so the term 'Son' which implies subordination can only apply after the incarnation. This statement prompted a question from 'W.R.P' regarding the title of Word: 'You would not carry the title "Word" into what he was in Deity?', to which Taylor simply replies 'No', adding enigmatically 'He acquired that name among the saints.' Later to make his point clear he says 'You cannot give names to, or define relations between divine Persons before incarnation. You have to go by Scripture.'[57]

While some were clearly troubled about what Taylor was saying, others appear more inclined to agree, notably Henry D'Arcy Champney and 'F.H.B.' whose remark that 'I remember F.E.R. saying that we have no testimony in Scripture of the relationship of divine Persons in the past eternity' elicited the response from Taylor that 'I was helped by remarks made by F.E.R. in America on this subject'.[58] Possibly Taylor had discussed these issues in private with people beforehand or perhaps others had come to similar conclusions from what F.E.R. had said. In concluding the reading Taylor reiterated his point that 'while it is said the Father sent the Son, we cannot fairly deduce from this that

---

56. [Taylor], *Ministry*, 29:365–6.
57. [Taylor], *Ministry*, 29:366 & 368. The contribution from 'W.R.P.' is not actually printed as a question but it reads like one.
58. [Taylor], *Ministry*, 29:368–9.

He was actually in that relation with God as "in the form of God".[59] In the remainder of the Barnet Meetings, four readings and two addresses by Taylor, the subject does not seem to have been alluded to again.

After Barnet

Although the main focus of the ministry at the Barnet meetings was elsewhere, what had been said on Eternal Sonship, although occupying just part of one of the readings, rapidly became the most important aspect. As it had been said by Taylor himself, it could not be lightly taken back or ignored. In accord with the fundamental premise of Exclusivism established over the 'Bethesda Question' in 1848, once an issue has been raised, all must judge it in order to remain in fellowship and preserve the unity of the body. Ultimately those who did not accept Taylor's teaching would have to leave. Earlier believers would not be judged for unknowingly holding erroneous views, but now the Lord had corrected his people, it represented a moral fault, a manifestation of unrighteousness, to refuse this teaching.[60] Some, after much heart-searching, left voluntarily as in all conscience they could not accept Taylor's teaching; others were forced to leave.[61] But it is not clear how many did leave at this time and it does not seem to have been a large number because no distinctive separate group of Exclusive Brethren resulted. As with later issues, many were undoubtedly perplexed and did not fully understand, but even though they may have thought something was wrong ultimately acquiesced. Brethren discipline could be harsh. V. W. J. H. Lawrence, who had suffered under it for the temerity of going into print against Taylor's views, used the term 'persecution':

> As regards persecution, the system has wrought a monumental work (perhaps never equalled outside the Church of Rome) to Miss A[nna]. M. S[toney]———., of F———, and all that has transpired as a consequence, to say nothing of the iniquity evidenced in connection with Bath and elsewhere, following upon the publication of the writer's book, "The Divine Sonship".[62]

Acceptance of the issue was forced with the publication of the 1932 hymn book revision which contained alterations to bring hymns into line with Taylor's new teaching. For example, the first line of Josiah Conder's hymn 'Thou art the Everlasting Word' was

---

59. [Taylor], *Ministry*, 29: 374.
60. [Taylor], *Ministry*, 13: 207.
61. Middleton, *Reversal*, 12–15.
62. V. W. J. H. Lawrence, *Elements of the Taylor Apostasy* (Newport, n.d.), 5–6. Anna Stoney (1839–1932) wrote hymns and devotional works and was the daughter of J. B. Stoney who had been the leading individual at Park Street assembly in London after the death of Darby (for J. B. Stoney, see Roger N. Holden "You have to go by Scripture': Taylorite Exclusive Brethren, the Bible, and The Holy Spirit', *intra*, 75–6). According to P. J. Jensen, Miss Stoney 'had looked with suspicion on Mr. Taylor' and seceded over the issue of Eternal Sonship: P. J. Jensen, 'History of the Work of God in America Especially that in Connection with the "Recovered Truth" Movement of Past Century [*sic*] sometimes called "Brethren" Beginning about 1827', unpublished typescript, Los Angeles, 1950, 23.

changed to 'Thou art the blest incarnate Word'. All meetings were expected to move over to using the new hymn book and any who refused were disciplined.[63]

Leading Brethren, including those who were present at Barnet, rapidly accepted Taylor's new teaching. This included Charles Coates, who had not been present at Barnet, but whose ministry was accorded a very high status, although not on the level of Taylor himself. His major contribution was a pamphlet *The Personal and Mediatorial Glory of the Son of God*, although the date of publication of this is not known.[64] He examines various passages of Scripture and essentially makes the same points as Taylor, opening with the statement that 'Scripture makes clear that the Son of God is a divine Person, and that His Person is eternal and changeless, whether as subsisting in the form of God, or as come in flesh, or as the subject Son when He gives up the kingdom that God may be all in all.' He proceeds to argue that the Son as being sent implies a subjection to the authority of the sender, whereas 'To think of our Lord as in Deity being in a place of subjection is derogatory to Him. It is assigning to Him an inferior or subordinate place in Deity, and this is not only contrary to Scripture, but it is inconceivable to any one who believes in His true and full Deity.' In conclusion he states that:

> I do not think that any scripture can be adduced that applies the title "Son", or "Son of God", to our Lord Jesus Christ as in Deity in the past eternity. Scripture teaches unquestionably that His *Person* is eternal, but it invariably attaches these *titles* to Him, whether prophetically or actually, as in manhood. This is, I believe, indisputable.

Taylor returned to the subject at meetings in Bristol in 1931 and Birmingham in 1932 and he evidently regarded the notes of meetings as also making important contributions to the subject, along with an address entitled 'Inscrutability' given in Edinburgh in 1932.[65] In 1933 he took the unusual step of writing a paper entitled *Names of Divine Persons*.[66] The objective of this was not stated, but it was evidently seeking to draw together some arguments and counter criticisms, the opening sentence stating a fundamental premise that runs through the whole that 'we must distinguish between God in absoluteness and in relativeness'.

However, not all were convinced and many people continued to more seriously question Taylor's new teaching. Some people wrote privately to him seeking clarification while others went into print with something of a pamphlet war developing, involving not only people from the Taylor fellowship but also people from other groups of Exclusive Brethren and the Open Brethren. The large amount of material produced, listed in the bibliography below, is impossible to consider in any detail, but it is evidence of the concern that Taylor's teaching raised. One writer reports that the Brethren were warned not to read any literature

---

63. Edward Cardoe, *"If any one love me, he will keep my word,"* John xiv., 23 (Newcastle-on-Tyne, 1940), 6.

64. This was re-printed in C. A. Coates, *An Outline of John's Gospel*, (Kingston-on-Thames, n.d), 254–82. Coates suffered from ill-health and this may be why he was not present at Barnet. In view of his response it is possible that Taylor had previously broached the matter with him.

65. [Taylor], *Letters*, 1:384; [Taylor], *Ministry*, 13:205–13.

66. James Taylor, *Names of Divine Persons* (London, n.d.). This was re-printed in: [Taylor], 'Names of Divine Persons', *Ministry*, 50:426–52.

that controverted Taylor's teaching, while another asserts that determined efforts were made to destroy copies of such literature.[67] Apart from the pamphlet *Names of Divine Persons*, Taylor did not respond publicly to any of these published tracts and pamphlets but only in private letters. Some people wrote sending him copies of pamphlets and asking him to comment. It is evident that some of the letters written in response circulated among the Brethren at the time, whether as printed or manuscript copies is not clear, and after his death they appeared in the published volumes of Taylor's letters. A historian needs to seek some sort of objectivity in viewing this material, remembering that it has 'political' dimensions. Some was written by people who left, or were forced to leave, the Taylor fellowship over this issue. Some was written by people from other branches of Exclusive Brethren, such as Kelly and Glanton, to whom the issue demonstrated the increasingly erroneous direction taken by the Raven-Taylor Brethren.[68] Some was written by Open Brethren to whom it would be a further demonstration of the errors of the Exclusive Brethren. Conversely, from the view point of Taylor Brethren all these were people who stood in positions that were morally wrong and therefore unable to accept new truth. Taylor does indeed seem to have only taken serious notice of critics from within the Taylor fellowship.

A number of Taylor's letters do show a certain amount of self-reflection on the matter after the Barnet meetings, but ultimately he asserted the rightness of what he had said at Barnet and his conviction that the Lord himself was behind this. Writing to Percy Lyon on 28 August 1929 he said 'I believe the Lord is helping in this great matter' and to an unidentified correspondent on 1 May 1931 he says 'I have weighed the matter much before the Lord since, especially in regard of what has been advanced in support of the expressions ['Eternal Son' and 'Eternal Word'], and I am confirmed in what I have held'.[69] Writing next month to Arthur J. H. Brown he says:

> As regards 'Eternal Sonship', I am assured the Lord is through the exercise asserting the authority of Scripture and that in due course its teaching as to His Person and revelation generally will be much more clearly understood. . . . Nothing has exercised me more than this matter, but as waiting on the Lord I am confirmed that what was said at Barnet is in accord with the teaching of Scripture and makes for a clearer and truer apprehension of Deity and of revelation. One is, however, greatly afraid of extremes and so cast on God as to this as to himself and others.[70]

It is not quite clear how this last comment should be taken but Roger Shuff has commented on Taylor's tendency to make bold assertions and then make apparently neutralizing statements.[71] Taylor could be gracious and patient in his dealing with those who were honestly troubled by what he had said. In his letter of 1 May 1931 he writes 'I am sorry

---

67. Russell Elliot, *A Few Words on John V.17–27 and Remarks on Recent Doctrine concerning The Trinity* (London, n.d. [c.1933]), 4; Lawrence, *Taylor Apostasy*, 6.
68. Edwin Cross, *The Irish Saint and Scholar: A Biography of William Kelly* (London, 2004), 90–1.
69. [Taylor], *Letters*, 1:268 & 321.
70. [Taylor], *Letters*, 1:326.
71. Shuff, *Searching for the True Church*, 118–9.

you are so seriously troubled over what has been said recently about our Lord's sonship. I am assured you will find in time that there is no real cause for this.'[72]

One of those who engaged in correspondence with Taylor on the issue was S. J. B. Carter.[73] This correspondence was amicable in tone, Taylor addresses him as 'My Dear Mr. Carter' and thanks him for his 'brotherly letters'. Taylor assures Carter that his remarks were not directed to him personally since he was unaware, or had forgotten, that Carter had himself written a pamphlet on the subject. Evidently Carter was persuaded and remained within the Taylor fellowship until his death in November 1938.[74] Perhaps he had persuaded himself by seeing this as part of the testimony moving forward. In an address in Edinburgh he had once said 'about one hundred years ago there was a wonderful movement, and the truth of the unity of the church of God came out. Since then the testimony has moved again and again. We must not be afraid of movement. The testimony may move again.'[75] But Carter may have remained under suspicion since his initials were replaced by '*Ques.*' or '*Rem.*' when the relevant sections of the Barnet notes were reprinted in *The Recovery and Maintenance of the Truth*.

Nevertheless, Taylor's graciousness and patience had its limits with people who offered more serious and persistent criticism. Mostly these are people who subsequently left the Taylor fellowship and so their full names are not given in the published volumes of Taylor's letters but some can be readily identified. One persistent critic, 'Mr. C———', first mentioned in a letter of 24 February 1933, was probably Edward Cardoe of Newcastle-on-Tyne who in 1940 was circulating a pamphlet in response to Taylor's *Names of Divine Persons*.[76] Later in 1933 Taylor refers to a 'pamphlet from Ayr' and a tract, *The Divine Sonship of the Lord Jesus Christ*.[77] The 'pamphlet from Ayr' is clearly Ernest Middleton's *Reversal not "Adjustment": An Appeal to My Brethren*, while the *The Divine Sonship of the Lord Jesus Christ* is the tract by V. W. J. H. Lawrence.

Taylor's letters refer to a number of items that were in circulation, including some of his own letters that cannot now be identified.[78] Although Taylor's response to his critics

---

72. [Taylor], *Letters*, 1:321. It is possible that this is the letter to Mr. Allen Oliver that he refers to in a letter to 'Mr. McB———' of 26 December 1931 (p.334).

73. [Taylor], *Letters*, 1:262–5 (18 July 1929). This is the only published letter to Carter, but there may have been others as elsewhere (p.268) he refers to correspondence with him. Carter evidently wrote more than once as Taylor's letter of 18 July 1929 thanks Carter for his letters to him but, as always, Carter's letters are not printed.

74. The initials 'S.J.B.C.' last appear in [Taylor], *Ministry*, 85:357. This is in notes of a reading in Bournemouth in April 1938.

75. Samuel J. B. Carter, *The Tabernacle of Testimony: An Address given in Buccleuch Hall, Edinburgh* (London, n.d), 21.

76. [Taylor], *Letters*, 1:388; 2:180–1. Edward Cardoe, *"If any one love me, he will keep my word," John xiv., 23* (Newcastle-on-Tyne, 1940).

77. [Taylor], *Letters*, 1:392–5 & 400–3.

78. Taylor lists a number of these items in a lengthy letter to an unnamed correspondent on 9 Feb. 1933, including 'a letter to Mr. A. Oliver'; 'a letter to Mr. Besley re W.H.W———'s printed letter'; and letters and papers from and to 'Mr. P———' (Taylor, *Letters*, 1:383–6). The letter to Oliver cannot be identified but may be that of 1 May 1931 (Taylor, *Letters*, 1:321–6). The 'printed letter' of W. H. W——— must be that by W. H. Westcott of Sutton Coldfield, who was a Glanton Brother, entitled *A Letter on Eternal Sonship with Notes* (Sutton Coldfield,

did treat some of the biblical passages used, ultimately, because he considered that what he had said had been of the Lord, these people were refusing to accept the truth and evil was implied in what they said, Satan himself being behind these attacks. This was the standard Exclusive way of dealing with criticism that goes back to Darby himself, for example, when challenged by Hall and Dorman over his views on the third class of Christ's suffering.[79] Ernest Middleton raised the question as to how earlier Brethren, whose adherence to Scripture is unquestioned, could have been so wrong, but Taylor dismisses this saying 'The Pamphlet from Ayr . . . advances the principle that the ministry of a previous generation is the test of a current one' and 'evil is implied in the manner in which the earlier ministry is used'.[80] He does not elaborate on the exact nature of this evil. The letter of Edward Cardoe evidently raised similar questions and was dealt with similarly:

> His letter reveals a mind moving in opposition, based mainly on orthodoxy, to a presentation of a certain feature of the truth. Almost the whole letter is taken up with what others have said, which shows that, like several that have taken part in the current controversy, his soul in regard of the truth in question is not buttressed in the word of God . . . .the writer's mind runs in the current of false accusation. The whole letter is of a sinister character; not only is there opposition to the truth but an evident effort to influence others against it. The Lord will surely have to say to all this, especially in one nominally (as I understand) in fellowship with us. May he recover himself from the snare of the devil.[81]

By 1940, Cardoe had left the Taylor fellowship, presumably over the issue of Eternal Sonship although Taylor says 'he is one of a group of brethren in Newcastle who got out of fellowship some years ago through association with certain ones who made false charges against a brother there'.[82]

While Taylor dismisses Lawrence because of his extensive use of the term 'Divine Nature' which is, Taylor says, a scriptural term being used unscripturally, his final argument is that the author is refusing the working of the Spirit amongst the Brethren:

> Much more could be pointed out as to the character of this pamphlet, but what I have written will show how unscriptural and misleading it is. It has a tinge of mysticism, and this very feature is calculated to deceive souls, especially when accompanied by apparently pious phrases. But its object is to discredit or deny the truth as to our Lord's sonship which, through some years of patient enquiry in dependence on the Holy Spirit, and of

---

1931). See also W. H. Westcott, *The Person of the Son* (Sutton Coldfield, n.d.). The letter to Mr Besley may be that of 15 Jan. 1932, the recipient of which is again unidentified (Taylor, *Letters*, 1:341-7.). This refers to a paper by 'Mr. W———— which has not been identified as it is clearly not Westcott. The letters and papers to and from Mr. P———— also cannot be identified, but A. J. Pollock of the Glanton Brethren can be ruled out.

79. Michael Schneider, ''The Extravagant side of Brethrenism': The Life of Percy Francis Hall (1801–84)', in Tim Grass (ed.), *Witness in Many Lands: Leadership and Outreach among the Brethren* (SBH; Troon, 2013), 40.

80. [Taylor], *Letters*, 1:392.

81. [Taylor], *Letters*, 1:388–90. Percy Lyon was a prominent English brother, a regular correspondent of Taylor's who had been present at the Barnet meetings in 1929.

82. [Taylor], *Letters*, 2:181.

conflict too, has been made plain to us, and is now "fully believed among us". There is in it thus a challenge as to whether the Spirit of truth has His place amongst the saints, and whether such scriptures as John 8:32 and 1 John 2:27 apply today. Besides this there is latitudinarianism in the publication of this paper, as the persons responsible continue (nominally) in fellowship.[83]

The publication of Lawrence's Divine Sonship evidently caused considerable concern and the Stow Hill Bible and Tract Depot published a short reply to Lawrence entitled *Is It Light?* by Dennis L. Higgins, who had been present at the Barnet meetings.[84] Basically this makes the same point as Taylor regarding use of the term 'Divine Nature' and that it is the Spirit who has drawn attention to the unscriptural nature of the term 'Eternal Son'. Whether the author's use of the term 'Divine Nature' is helpful or not, we can be fairly certain that he would have strongly refuted the implication that he had any intent to deceive. Not surprisingly Lawrence subsequently left the Brethren but continued to write and publish against Taylor's teaching, some of his writings dealing with the implications of the denial of Eternal Sonship for the doctrines of redemption and atonement.[85] Lawrence clearly had become seriously disaffected from the Brethren and indeed he felt he had been persecuted over the matter, ultimately charging Taylor with apostasy.[86] This accusation of apostasy turns the argument that the Brethren used against others back on themselves. He was not the only one to do this; Arthur Oglesby calls Taylor a deceiver and urges Brethren to separate from such evil.[87]

In some cases, public response, particularly to critics from outside the Taylor fellowship, was left to others, one assumes with Taylor's approval. It was left to C. A. Coates to respond to a booklet, *The Eternal Son*, written by the Glanton brother A. J. Pollock.[88] Pollock responded with an open letter to Coates which was in turn responded to, not by Coates himself but by D. L. Higgins.[89] Pollock also produced a pamphlet *John V.26 Clearly Teaches Eternal Sonship*.[90] Kelly Brethren also entered into the fray with two lengthy contributions from the English numismatist William J. Hocking and Roy A. Huebner from America, who traced the errors of the Raven-Taylor Brethren from Raven to Taylor's

---

83. [Taylor], *Letters*, 1:403.

84. D. L. H[iggins]., *Is It Light?—A Few Fundamental Remarks on the Paper "The Divine Sonship of The Lord Jesus Christ"* (London, n.d).

85. V. W. J. H. Lawrence, *Redemption and Eternal Sonship* (Bath, n.d); id., *The Sufferings of Christ and Atonement* (n.d., [c.1939]).

86. V. W. J. H. Lawrence, *Elements of the Taylor Apostasy* (Newport, [n.d.]).

87. Arthur Oglesby, *The Eternal Son* (York, [c.1930]). Arthur Oglesby, *"Inscrutability" by J. T.* (York, [c.1933]).

88. A. J. Pollock, *The Eternal Son* (London, n.d.). Although undated this is clearly after publication of the new edition of the *Little Flock* hymn book in 1932; C. A. Coates, *Remarks on a Pamphlet by A. J. Pollock entitled The Eternal Son* (London, n.d). Note that this duplicates some of the material in Coates *The Personal and Mediatorial Glory of the Son of God* although it is unclear which was written first.

89. A. J. Pollock, *An Open Letter to C. A. Coates* (London, n.d); D. L. H[iggins]., *Reply to "An Open Letter" by A.J.P.* (no publishing information).

90. A. J. Pollock, *John V.26 Clearly Teaches Eternal Sonship* (London, n.d.).

denial of the Eternal Sonship.[91] Publication of the new hymn book in 1932 resulted in a critical pamphlet from W. F. Knapp of the Kelly Brethren entitled *The Heretical Taylor Hymn Book*.[92]

News of Taylor's teaching also reached the Open Brethren, resulting in considerable comment in their periodicals and longer responses from William Hoste and W. E. Vine.[93] William Hoste, the editor of the *Believer's Magazine*, had previously written a pamphlet entitled *The Eternal Sonship of Christ* in 1924.[94] He now published a series of articles in the *Believer's Magazine* in 1932 entitled 'Divine Relations before the Incarnation'.[95] These articles were evidently brought to Taylor's attention but he dismisses Hoste as indulging in 'theological speculation'.[96]

As we have noted above, this was not the first time Taylor had expressed views that resulted in controversy amongst the Brethren, nor was it the last. Earlier controversial teaching could have been put under a heading of 'adjustment' but now he had overturned something that had been clearly held by Darby and earlier Brethren. Ernest Middleton therefore saw this more as 'reversal' than 'adjustment'. Subsequently Taylor overturned Darby's insistence that the Holy Spirit was not to be worshipped. This resulted in yet a further revision of the hymn book in 1951 to include hymns addressed to the Holy Spirit.[97] This was of course something of an eccentricity of Darby's rather than a generally accepted view amongst Christians. Roger Shuff has investigated this in more detail together with the more explicit enunciations of the concept of 'authoritative ministry' that Taylor was making at this time.[98] Ultimately, it was to be Taylor's son, James Taylor Jr., who was

---

91. William John Hocking, *The Son of his Love: Papers on the Eternal Sonship* (London, 1934); Roy A. Huebner, *The Eternal Relationships in the Godhead: Fundamental Truth Concerning the Trinity, the Incarnation, the Word, the Eternal Life, and the Eternal Sonship, with Reference to the Teachings of F. E. Coates, Raven, J. Taylor, Sr., and C. A. Coates* (Morganville, NJ, n.d).

92. W. F. Knapp, *The Heretical Taylor Hymn Book (1932)* (London, 1936). John R. Stephen from Aberdeen who wrote another pamphlet on the revised hymn book, *The New Hymn Book* (Aberdeen, n.d.), was in the Glanton connexion.

93. Tim Grass, *Gathering to His Name: The Story of Open Brethren in Britain and Ireland* (Milton Keynes, 2006), 294.

94. W. Hoste, *The Eternal Sonship of Christ* (London, [c.1924]). For a review of this see: 'The Eternal Sonship of Christ: Notice of a book by W. Hoste', *The Gospel Standard*, 90 (1924), 305–10. *The Gospel Standard* is a slightly surprising place to find a review of a booklet written by a member of the Open Brethren, but it should be noted that this was around the time when the issue of Eternal Sonship was being agitated as a means of forcing a formal separation between 'Gospel Standard' and 'Earthen Vessel' groupings of Strict Baptists, referring back to J. C. Philpot.

95. Subsequently published as a separate booklet and more recently reprinted in his collected writings: W. Hoste, *The Collected Writings of William Hoste*, (ed.) W. M. Banks, vol.1 (Kilmarnock, 1991), 53–93.

96. [Taylor], *Ministry*, 34: 435–7; Hoste, *Eternal Sonship*, 60.

97. Holden, '*Hymns and Spiritual Songs*', in Dickson and Marinello (eds.), *Culture, Spirituality, and the Brethren*, 217–18.

98. Shuff, *True Church*, 113–21.

to take these emphases in his father's ministry to establish his own authority and cause major divisions amongst the Brethren in 1959 and again in 1970, just before his death.

Those who remained loyal to James Taylor Jr., will have maintained Taylor's teaching on the Eternal Son, although we may ask whether or not 'new light' could change it again. Among those who have left the Taylor fellowship at that time, or indeed any time after 1929, the situation is less clear. Some of these will adhere to Taylor's teaching, for example the Kingston Bible Trust which publishes James Taylor's ministry. Certainly it has become an issue where former Taylor brethren have sought to join pre-1929 groups of Exclusives or Open Brethren, some saying that persons who still accept Taylor's teaching should not be accepted into fellowship.[99] James Taylor's teaching enhanced the distinctiveness of the Taylor brethren and isolated them further within the wider Brethren movement.

Assessment

J. C. Philpot distinguishes four different approaches to the denial of the Eternal Sonship: those who say he became Son at the incarnation; those who say he became Son at the resurrection; those who say he became Son by virtue of his exaltation to the right hand of God; and those who say he is Son by office, that is that the three persons agreed among themselves that one would be the Father, one the Son and one the Spirit for the purposes of redemption.[100] Probably the first of these has been the most common and this is the category Taylor fell into, asserting 'our Lord's sonship is contingent on His incarnation'.[101] But there are also hints of Philpot's fourth category, when for example, in reference to the Spirit, Taylor says 'The title is taken by one of the Persons in relation to the declaration of God'.[102] Philpot says the main prop of incarnational Sonship is Luke 1:35—'the holy thing also which shall be born shall be called Son of God'. Here Taylor is true to form since, as we have seen, he referred to this verse at Barnet in his initial response to Carter's question. Elsewhere he maintained that if Christ's Sonship extended back before the incarnation, then the angel would have said 'is called'.[103] Essentially, he then interprets the rest of Scripture in the light of this interpretation of Luke 1:35. But he did not neglect other Scriptures that have been used to support incarnational Sonship, in particular the phrase from Psalm 2:7—'this day have I begotten thee' that is quoted in Acts 13:33 and Hebrews 1:5. Commenting on Hebrews 1, Taylor said:

> Throughout that chapter it is the Son, it is a divine Person in that relationship which involves subjection. There are those who would seek to force back *that relationship* into absolute deity, thus making the Lord inferior to the other divine Persons in absolute deity. It is not the truth. The Lord Jesus is equal in deity. He never had a place of inferiority, relative or otherwise, in absolute deity. He was *in the form of God*.[104]

---

99. Grass, *Gathering to His Name*, 434–5.
100. Philpot, *Eternal Sonship*, 25, 36–8.
101. [Taylor], *Ministry*, 50:330, 441.
102. [Taylor], *Ministry*, 50:433 (emphasis in original).
103. [Taylor], *Ministry*, 5:330.
104. [Taylor], *Ministry*, 35:492 (emphasis in original).

But then Taylor went further than anticipated by Philpot who says 'As far as we can understand the views of those that at present we are combating, they hold that the Lord Jesus Christ, before His incarnation . . . was the eternal Word, but not the eternal Son'.[105] But Taylor even denied that the title 'Word' could be applied before the incarnation and in this respect that Taylor's thought does seem to have an element of novelty. He asserted that the Son came down from heaven and was not sent until he was actually here on earth, because to have been sent from heaven would imply a position of subordination.[106] With reference to Matthew 11:27, Taylor appealed to the concept of 'inscrutability', stating 'His part in the Deity, plainly told us in John 1, but which is nevertheless inscrutable, as He Himself declares, "No one knows the Son but the Father".'[107]

The names for divine Persons, Father, Son and Spirit, are relative, not absolute, terms.[108] Terms such as the Son, the Word or Wisdom apply to Him as man and not as in deity, 'We can see nothing of divine relations save in manhood'.[109] Taylor clearly thought he was maintaining the absolute equality of the three persons, thus avoiding the error of subordinationism. The orthodox view has rejected the subordinationism in the sense of assigning a status of inferior being to the Sons and the Spirit, affirming that they are equal in being while subordinate in role as they relate to creation.[110]

Taylor dismisses the terms 'eternal sonship' and 'eternal word' as originating in 'theology':

> Having looked into the matter of 'eternal sonship' and 'eternal word', I am persuaded they originate in theology. As creed-making began, there was a felt need of definitions, and theologians did not hesitate to attempt to define the relations existing among divine Persons as in absolute Deity. This resulted in much blasphemous error; but even orthodoxy is not free from this as is to be seen in the 'Creed of St. Athanasius'.[111]

On one occasion, when speaking in Germany, Taylor said that Luther did not learn Eternal Sonship from Scripture but from the creed of Athanasius, which begs the question as to where the writers of the creed got it from.[112]

His initial response to Carter suggests that he dismissed the term 'eternal sonship' on the basis that it did not appear in Scripture. Yet he readily recognized that one could not simply dismiss the term on this basis, as that would have meant a rejection of the term 'Trinity' and the terminology of 'Persons'. When a correspondent raised this point he responded: 'The answer is that the Trinity is formally stated in our Bibles to exist and so true Christians believe in it; eternal sonship is not. The absence of the term 'eternal Son' in Scripture, although important to notice, is not the determining factor, but the general

---

105. Philpot, *Eternal Sonship*, 28–9.
106. [Taylor], *Ministry*, 34:111; Coates, *Remarks on a Pamphlet by A. J. Pollock*, 6.
107. [Taylor,] *Ministry*, 13:213.
108. [Taylor], *Letters*, 1:390.
109. [Taylor], *Letters*, 1:280; [Taylor], *Ministry*, 97:20.
110. Wayne Grudem, *Systematic Theology* (Nottingham, 2007), 248–56.
111. [Taylor], *Letters*, 1:324–5.
112. [Taylor], *Ministry*, 77:221.

teaching of Scripture.'[113] He does not here give the Scriptures he had in mind when saying 'the Trinity is formally stated in our Bibles', but elsewhere he says the Trinity is formally presented in Matthew 3: 16–17, 'after the baptism of Christ, both the Father and the Spirit coming into view'.[114] But in passing it is however worth noting 'Trinity' was a word somewhat suspect among the Brethren because of its non-scriptural origin. F. E. Raven once said 'We have long been accustomed to the idea of the Trinity, which, though true, is a human expression. I very much prefer scriptural expressions'.[115] In Taylor's printed ministry the word appears only 121 times compared with 1369 occurrences of the word 'deity'.[116]

But 'theology' and 'definitions' could not be avoided, and Russell Elliott suggests that Taylor borrowed more than he admitted from the doctrine he was denying.[117] Terms such as 'Divine Persons' and 'Absolute Deity', arguably also non-scriptural, passed into common Brethren usage. More complex phrases arose to avoid naming the persons of the Trinity before the incarnation and one critic referred to the use of phrases such as 'The Lord in Deity'; 'The position and form of God in which our Lord was absolutely, before his incarnation'; or 'Our Lord as in the form of God' as being 'sinister'.[118] The term 'Persons' is of course credal and has indeed invoked theological controversy over the centuries, even being questioned by people of otherwise impeccable orthodoxy. John Calvin himself was at one time in difficulties over this question, in the debate with Pierre Caroli. The early Quakers did not use the terms 'Trinity' and 'persons' because they were not found in Scripture. The Westminster Confession says the 'in the unity of the Godhead there be three persons' but the derivative 1689 London Baptist Confession turns this into 'there are three subsistences'. More recently Karl Barth criticized the term 'Person' as misleading, suggesting instead the German term *Seinsweise*, normally translated into English as 'mode of being'.[119]

James Taylor never really tackles the issue of what his view means for the Father and the Spirit. If the Sonship of the Second Person is contingent upon the incarnation then by implication the Fatherhood of the First Person and the Spirithood of the Third Person are similarly contingent. On the question of the Father it is difficult to find any clear statements, but Coates states that 'Our knowledge of God as declared by the Son, and as known by the holy Name of Father, is dependent on the Incarnation'.[120] Moreover, he asserts that

---

113. [Taylor], *Letters*, 1:346 (emphasis in original).
114. [Taylor], *Ministry*, 42:247.
115. [Raven], *Ministry*, 11:364.
116. Similar low usage of the word 'Trinity' will be found amongst other Brethren ministry. C. A. Coates uses it only 14 times, and F. E. Raven uses it only 11 times, discounting two usages of the phrase 'trinity of evil'.
117. Elliot, *A Few Words on John V.17–27*, 21. Nothing is known about the author of the pamphlet, but he was clearly not a member of the Taylor Brethren at the time he wrote this.
118. Stephen, *The New Hymn Book*, 8.
119. Robert Letham, *The Holy Trinity: In Scripture, History, Theology and Worship* (Phillipsburg, NJ, 2004), 275–6; Karl Barth, *Church Dogmatics*, 4 vols., ET, G. W. Bromiley (Edinburgh, 1975), 1/1:355–61.
120. Coates, *John's Gospel*, 267; Coates, *Remarks on a Pamphlet by A. J. Pollock*, 23.

It is quite beside the mark to say that "the Father was the Father before the Lord Jesus was born into the world". Of course there is no change in God; what He is now He ever was and ever will be. But He was not known to any man as Father until the Man was here who was "called the Son of God". He was not known as such, nor could be. This is a question, not of what God is essentially in His inscrutable Being, but of how He is pleased to be known by men.[121]

Although the terms 'eternal Father' and 'eternal Son' may not appear in Scripture then 'eternal Spirit' certainly does, in Hebrews 9:14. Coates acknowledges this fact and accepts the Holy Spirit is indeed a title that applies before the incarnation: 'The Spirit is not a Name of relationship like Father or Son. The Holy Spirit has not been manifested like the Son, or revealed like the Father; He remains in His eternal character as an unseen Spirit, and can therefore be spoken of as "the eternal Spirit"'.[122]

Taylor, at least in his published ministry, does not seem to mention this, but he does admit, referring to Genesis 1:2, that the Spirit 'is seen as a distinct person from the outset'.[123] He adds, the Spirit 'cannot be regarded as a name of One only of the divine Persons viewed in the conditions of absolute Deity . . . the title is taken by one of the Persons in relation to the declaration of God'.[124] On Scripture referring to the Son and the Spirit as being active in creation he says 'The Persons we know as the Son and the Spirit were active in the creation'.[125] In reference to John 7:39, 'the Spirit was not yet, because Jesus had not yet been glorified', he says that this 'does not refer to the eternal personality of the Spirit, but to the form in which he is here now'.[126] Jesus quite clearly states that the Spirit will be sent by the Father in John 14:26 and 15:26 and Taylor acknowledges this without suggesting that it points to an inconsistency in his thought.[127] We may ask, if the Son is not sent from heaven because that would imply inferiority, then how can the Spirit be sent without also implying inferiority?

There was indeed much trading of Scripture between the participants in the debate, all equally claiming to be guided by it. Philpot was equally emphatic in his following of Scripture, saying, 'Our first rule must be that *the Scriptures* shall be our *only standard of appeal*'.[128] Much Scripture was brought forward as presenting difficulties to Taylor's views and passages from John's Gospel in particular were frequently referred to, several pamphlets dealing specifically with passages from this Gospel. We have seen how he simply denied that John 1:1 referred back before the incarnation, however much this may seem to be against the clear sense. We might of course play Taylor at his own game here and assert that if he is correct then the Spirit would have written 'In the beginning was the Person we know as the Word and the Person we know as the Word was with God, and the Person we know as the Word was God'. Scripture which speaks of the Son or Word as

---

121. Coates, *Remarks on a Pamphlet by A. J. Pollock*, 20.
122. Coates, *Remarks on a Pamphlet by A. J. Pollock*, 41.
123. [Taylor], *Ministry*, 50:432.
124. [Taylor], *Ministry*, 50:433 (emphasis in original).
125. [Taylor], *Ministry*, 34:86.
126. [Taylor], *Ministry*, 34:85.
127. [Taylor], *Ministry*, 34:111; 36:409; 70:144.
128. Philpot, *Eternal Sonship of the Lord Jesus Christ*, 18 (emphasis in original).

becoming or being sent is dealt with in a similar way. For example, John 1:14 'the Word became flesh and dwelt among us', he asserted does not refer back to eternity, despite the plain reading that the Word must have existed before becoming flesh.[129] Asked whether the reference to Christ being loved 'before the foundation of the world' in John 17:24 involves family relationship he simply replies 'I do not think so at all'.[130] But later, as we shall see, he was to contradict himself on this point.

Particular difficulties were presented by John 1:18, 'the only begotten Son who is in the bosom of the Father', with great efforts being expended to show that the Greek *eis*, translated 'in', implied a movement into, as if to say there was a time when the Son was not in the bosom of the Father.[131] Darby was again invoked to support this reading despite the fact that his translation uses 'in' and, as we have seen above, took this passage as referring to Eternal Sonship. Edward Cardoe's paper, *"If any one love me, he will keep my word," John xiv., 23*, dealt specifically with this point.[132] Although Taylor was willing to quote such authorities as Liddell and Scott's *Greek Lexicon*, Cardoe's reference to contemporary professors of Greek at Oxford, Cambridge, and Dublin universities was dismissed by saying 'in all probability these men are worldly, if not unconverted'.[133]

It is true of course that we do not know God as Father, Son, and Spirit until the New Testament, until the incarnation in other words. Also it has generally been maintained that some titles for the Son refer to him specifically as incarnate rather than as eternal. For example Calvin writes 'the designation Christ has a meaning that is appropriate to his human nature '.[134] But to say that the Son was not the Son before the incarnation raises the question as to what he was before it. To say that he only came into existence at the incarnation is Arianism. To say that he was the one God appearing in a different mode is Sabellianism, or modalism. From the orthodox viewpoint, both of these have been seen as heresies and Taylor denied being either on the basis of his affirmation that the Three Persons existed before the incarnation.[135] Sabellianism he said was a dreadful error that denied the distinct personality of the Persons. But Taylor was adamant that we can know nothing about the nature and relations of the Three Persons, and that the declaration of God in Christ tells us nothing about God as he exists; to think otherwise is contrary to John 1:18 and Colossians 1:15 which state that God is invisible.[136] The Trinity is seen as 'relative to creation' and 'While God remains in impenetrable absoluteness, yet in

---

129. [Taylor], *Ministry*, 33:209.
130. [Taylor], *Ministry*, 33:211.
131. [Taylor], *Ministry*, 34:9; 50:439–40; Taylor, *Letters*, 1:264 & 322.
132. Edward Cardoe, *"If any one love me, he will keep my word," John XIV., 23* (Newcastle-on-Tyne, 1940). The quotation of John 14:23 in the title is an exhortation, the pamphlet deals with John 1:18.
133. [Taylor], *Letters*, 2:180.
134. John Calvin, *Commentary on 1 Corinthians* (ed. & ET.), John W. Fraser, (Carlisle, 1996), 210.
135. [Taylor], *Letters*, 1:394; 2:181.
136. [Taylor], 'Names of Divine Persons', *Ministry*, 50:426. What is meant on this page is not totally clear and this sentence is an attempt to summarize the general drift as accurately as possible. The two Scriptures quoted are, of course, saying Christ has made the invisible God known.

the economy of grace the Trinity is seen serving men'.[137] Here Father, Son, and Spirit become simply names applied to the Persons of the Trinity which they adopted at the time of the incarnation for a specific purpose and by which they are now known to us. While perhaps not strictly Sabellian, this may be seen as a form of modalism as Father, Son, and Spirit become modes of the three Persons, or simply how we see the three from our relative position. Either way what Karl Barth noted of Sabellius and others of similar views applies here:

> [They] . . . did indeed assert the substantial equality of the trinitarian "persons" but only as manifestations behind which God's true being is concealed as something other and higher, so that one may well ask whether revelation can be believed if in the background there is always the thought that we are not dealing with God as He is but only with a God as He appears to us.[138]

Personal recollection of the present writer when he worshipped with the Brethren is that the term 'Divine Persons', all said to be equally God, when combined with the later Brethren emphasis that the Persons should only be addressed individually gave the impression of tritheism. Taylor does deal with the charge of tritheism in *Names of Divine Persons*. His response is unclear, but again he appeals to the unknowability of relations between divine Persons before the incarnation.[139]

The contrary question can also be asked. If the Father, Son, and Spirit only became such at the incarnation, do they remain as such or do they at some time cease to be in this form? In the fourth century Marcellus of Ancyra held that the Son would cease to be the Son at his second coming, the *parousia*.[140] No clear answer has been found to this question in Taylor's published ministry, but the phrase used amongst Brethren was that 'he was Son to eternity'.[141]

In perusing Taylor's ministry and the material produced during the 'pamphlet war', with its ostensibly detailed examination of Scripture, one often feels that the wood is being lost for the trees. Even the critics rarely seem to have a sufficiently wide view to ask the key questions. The question has to be asked how do we know there are three divine Persons in absolute Deity, apart from their being Father, Son, and Spirit? This consideration seems fatal to Taylor's thought and we would suggest that Taylor could not consistently maintain his position. The judgement of Russell Elliot was that he gets into a 'hopeless muddle'.[142] Although he asserted that he was not going beyond Scripture, he had to resort to phrases such as 'the Person we know as' that are hardly Scriptural, nor, it may be argued, in accord with the sense of Scripture. Moreover it is difficult to see how maintaining that there were eternally three Persons is consistent with the claim that God is ultimately inscrutable: if God's form and mode of existence are ultimately unknown then how can it be known that there are three Persons?

---

137. [Taylor], 'Names of Divine Persons', *Ministry*, 50: 428 (emphasis in original).
138. Barth, *Church Dogmatics*, 1/1, 353.
139. [Taylor], *Ministry*, 50: 429.
140. Mackintosh, *Person of Jesus Christ*, 189–91.
141. Information from participants at IBHC 6.
142. Elliot, *A Few words on John V.17–27*, 39.

Ultimately Taylor could not avoid the fact that Scripture does use the titles Father, Son, and Spirit to refer to the Persons of the Trinity before the incarnation. This is explained by saying that these relative names may be used to refer to the persons absolutely before the incarnation without suggesting that they actually applied to them then. Referring to Hebrews 13:8, 'Jesus Christ is the same yesterday, and today, and to the ages to come', Taylor says that this shows that 'names applying to our Lord in time may be employed to designate His Person in the past eternity without intimating that they applied to Him then'.[143] In his paper *Names of Divine Persons*, he even suggests that before the incarnation the Persons of the Trinity may have borne names, but we do not know what they were, before later admitting that 'There is really no means ... of distinguishing the Persons in absoluteness save as by employing the relative names furnished in Scripture'.[144] Coates makes a similar admission:

> now that God is made known as the Father we can speak of Him by that blessed Name, and Scripture speaks of Him thus, even when referring to the past eternity. Divine Names and titles, when known, are used in Scripture to identify the Persons without necessarily meaning that they were so known in the conditions referred to.[145]

This all sounds more like philosophical speculation than biblical exegesis, but an even graver admission follows. During an address given at Winnipeg in 1941, while still maintaining that you cannot call 'That Person who was there before the foundation of the World' the Son, in reference to John 17:24 Taylor says 'That Person was there before the foundation of the world. Love was there then, love between the Persons'.[146] So we can know something about relations between the Persons of the Trinity before the incarnation after all! And we can be grateful for that admission because the insistence on the absolute unknowability of God, that the revelation of God in Scripture as Father, Son, and Spirit tells us nothing about the ultimate nature of God, would surely undermine the whole of Christian doctrine which sees creation and the whole history of redemption as ultimately rooted in the character of God as Trinity, as three Persons in relation.

Conclusion: the people without history

Really it is not that the Brethren had no history, but that they rejected the vast majority of Church history. Although they admitted there had been some light, for example they acknowledged the recovery of the doctrine of justification by faith by Luther and the reformers, by and large all had been dark from the time of the apostles until Darby. In particular the creeds and confessions were rejected as representing man-made theology and rationalisation. Darby by contrast had gone back to the Scriptures.[147] But there was a

---

143. [Taylor], *Letters*, 1:335 (emphasis in original). He also used this argument to explain passages in his ministry before 1929 where he appears to be accepting Eternal Sonship.
144. [Taylor], *Ministry*, 50:429 & 431.
145. Coates, *Remarks on a Pamphlet by A. J. Pollock*, 23–4.
146. [Taylor], *Ministry*, 89:193.
147. However, as Timothy Stunt has shown in his 'John Nelson Darby: The Scholarly Enigma', *BAHNR*, 2/2 (2003), 70–4, Darby was familiar with the writings of the Church Fathers and drew upon them in his writings.

twist to this in that the Brethren saw themselves as being led into a fuller understanding of the Scriptures by the Lord himself, through the ministry of their leaders Darby, Raven, and Taylor. So in this case it was possible for one of the later leaders to overturn something that Darby himself had believed, but it would not have been acceptable for anybody else to do this. As this came from the leading of the Lord himself, this teaching was enforced in the interests of unity amongst the Brethren.

To somebody standing back and looking at Church history, particularly in this case the history of the doctrine of the Trinity, Brethren claims to being led into a recovery of truth are rather unconvincing. The denial of the Eternal Sonship was not new and Taylor was certainly not the first person to puzzle over the issue of subordination—that is, how to reconcile the equality of the Persons with the fact that that the Son and Spirit are presented as being subordinate to the Father, or the issue of how to relate God's invisible transcendence to his manifestation in revelation. Whether Taylor's views can be formally considered to be Sabellian, Apollinarian, or Arian could be debated at length, but either way his views do fall into a category that implies that the revelation of Father, Son, and Spirit does not tell us about God as he really is, which has far reaching implications for the whole of Christian doctrine. While he claimed to be not going beyond Scripture, others, including we might suggest the authors of the Athanasian Creed, have concluded that Scripture enables us to say rather more than this. Rather than being led by the Spirit into a recovery of the truth, the Brethren seem to have been acting out the old saying that the people without history are condemned to repeat their history.

Acknowledgements

Acknowledgements are due to Graham Johnson of the Christian Brethren Archive, the University of Manchester Library, and Simon Attwood of Chapter Two Bookshop in London, for making available copies of many of the items listed in section 3 of the Bibliography. Simon Attwood also made enquiries, sadly without success, to try to locate a copy of S. J. B. Carter's pamphlet on the Eternal Son. Gregory Morris and Crawford Gribben commented on an earlier draft of this paper. A summarized version was presented at the Sixth International Brethren History Conference, which generated some helpful discussion.

Bibliography

This bibliography is of material published in 1929 and after, although a few earlier items are included where relevant. It is split into three sections, items from the ministry of James Taylor, items from C. A. Coates and other published items.

1. Items from the Ministry and Letters of J. Taylor

The entries for the ministry refer to the New Series of James Taylor's ministry published by the Stow Hill Bible and Tract Depot, Kingston-upon-Thames, c.1960, 100 volumes. All these items had been published previously either in what became known as the 'Old Series' or as separate pamphlets. They are listed here in order of volume number as they appear in the New Series which is not chronological. Note that these are only major references to the subject; references will be found elsewhere in Taylor's ministry. The entries for the letters refer to *Letters of James Taylor*, 2 volumes. Both the ministry and the letters have been accessed using the electronic version available from the Kingston Bible Trust.

'The Divine Standard of Service (2)', *Ministry*, 29: 349–74. One of a series of 6 readings at Barnet, June 1929.
'Eternity to Eternity (1)', *Ministry*, 33: 198–213. One of a series of 6 readings at Bristol, 1931.
'The Glory of the Son of God', *Ministry*, 34: 1–125. Six readings at Birmingham, 1932.
'Inscrutability', *Ministry*, 13: 205–13. An address given at Edinburgh in 1932.
'Names of Divine Persons', *Ministry*, 50: 426–52. This originated as a specially written and separately published pamphlet, which can be dated to c.1933.
Letter to Arthur J. H. Brown, 16 June 1931, *Letters*, 1: 326–7.
Letter to C. A. Coates, 20 September 1929, *Letters*, 1: 271–2.
Letter to C. A. Coates, 9 September 1929, *Letters*, 1: 270–1.
Letter to Francis Willey, 31 October 1929, *Letters*, 1: 273–4.
Letter to Mr M———, 9 February 1933, *Letters*, 1: 383–6.
Letter to Mr McB———, 26 December 1931, *Letters*, 1: 333–5.
Letter to P. Lyon, 24 February 1933, *Letters*, 1: 388–91.
Letter to P. Lyon, 27 February 1933, *Letters*, 1: 391.
Letter to P. R. Morford, 25 February 1921, *Letters*, 1: 189–91.
Letter to S. J. B. Carter, 18 July 1929, *Letters*, 1: 262–5.
Letter to unidentified recipient, [day and month not stated] 1929, *Letters*, 1: 265–7.
Letter to unidentified recipient, 15 July 1929, *Letters*, 1: 259–62.
Letter to unidentified recipient, 7 August 1930, *Letters*, 1: 279–80.
Letter to unidentified recipient, 1 May 1931, *Letters*, 1: 321–6.
Letter to unidentified recipient, 9 January 1932, *Letters*, 1: 338–41.
Letter to unidentified recipient, 15 January 1932, *Letters*, 1: 341–7.
Letter to unidentified recipient, 25 March 1933, *Letters*, 1: 392–5.
Letter to unidentified recipient, 4 August 1933, *Letters*, 1: 400–3.
Letter to unidentified recipient, 3 December 1938, *Letters*, 2: 140–1.

Letter to unidentified recipient, 30 April 1940, *Letters*, 2: 180–1.

2. Items from the Ministry and Letters of C. A. Coates

The 34 volumes of Coates's ministry, including a volume of letters, had individual titles and volume numbers were only added in later printings, *c.*1960, by the Stow Hill Bible and Tract Depot, Kingston-upon-Thames. This material has been accessed using the electronic version available from the Kingston Bible Trust.

'The Personal and Mediatorial Glory of the Son of God', *An Outline of John's Gospel*, 254–82. This was originally published as a separate pamphlet.
'Remarks on a Pamphlet by A. J. Pollock entitled *The Eternal Son*'. This was a separate pamphlet.
Letter to unidentified recipient, 5 March 1931, *Letters*, 191–5.
Letter to unidentified recipient, 10 April 1931, *Letters*, 195–8.
Letter to unidentified recipient, 28 July 1931, *Letters*, 200–1.
Letter to unidentified recipient, 23 March 1934, *Letters*, 225–7.
Letter to unidentified recipient, 11 May 1934, *Letters*, 227–9.

3. Other published items

Many of the items listed here do not carry full bibliographic data, indeed some do not carry any, so if place of publication, publisher, or date are omitted below, it is because they are not given on the original. Sometimes there is sufficient internal evidence to suggest a date of publication.

Edward Cardoe, *"If any one love me, he will keep my word," John XIV., 23* (Newcastle-on-Tyne: the author, 1940).
Samuel J. B. Carter, *The Tabernacle of Testimony: An Address given in Buccleuch Hall, Edinburgh* (London: G. Morrish, n.d).
R[ussell]. E[lliot]., *The Eternal Son* (London: the author, n.d. [*c.*1930]).
———, *A Few Words on John V.17–27 and Remarks on Recent Doctrine concerning The Trinity* (London: the author, n.d. [*c.*1933]).
D[ennis]. L[ambert]. H[iggins]., *Is It Light?—A Few Fundamental Remarks on the Paper "The Divine Sonship of The Lord Jesus Christ"* (London: Stow Hill Bible and Tract Depot, n.d). Note: the author's name appears on the pamphlet simply as 'D.L.H.' but somebody has pencilled in the full name on the copy held by the Christian Brethren Archive.
———, *Reply to "An Open Letter" by A.J.P.* (no publishing information). 'A.J.P.' is A. J. Pollock.
William John Hocking, *The Son of His Love: Papers on the Eternal Sonship* (London: C.A. Hammond, 1934).
W. Hoste, *Divine Relations before the Incarnation* (London: Pickering & Inglis, n.d. [*c.*1933]). Originally published as a series of articles in *The Believer's Magazine*, 1932; more recently re-printed in his collected writings: id., *The Collected Writings of William Hoste*, (ed.) W. M. Banks, vol.1 (Kilmarnock: John Ritchie, 1991), 53–93.
———, *The Eternal Sonship of Christ* (London: Pickering & Inglis, n.d. [*c.*1924]).
Roy A. Huebner, *The Eternal Relationships in the Godhead: Fundamental Truth*

concerning the Trinity, the Incarnation, the Word, the Eternal Life, and the Eternal Sonship, with Reference to the Teachings of F. E. Coates. Raven, J. Taylor, Sr., and C. A. Coates (Morganville, NJ: Present Truth, n.d).

W. F. Knapp, *The Heretical Taylor Hymn Book* (1932; London: C. A. Hammond, 1936).

V. W. J. H. Lawrence The Divine Sonship of the Lord Jesus Christ (Birmingham: H. S. Pailthorpe, n.d.[*c*.1933]).

———, *Elements of the Taylor Apostasy* (Newport: Williams Press, n.d.).

———, *Eternal Sonship /Eternal Sonship. A Contrast.* [No publishing information].

———, *The Foundations Preserved* (Newport: Williams Press Ltd., [*c*.1935]).

———, *Redemption and Eternal Sonship* (Bath: H. Sharp, n.d).

———, *The Revelation of God in His Eternal Son* (London: Thynne, 1935).

———, *The Sufferings of Christ and Atonement* (n.pl., [*c*.1939]).

E[rnest]. Middleton, *Reversal not "Adjustment": An Appeal to my Brethren* (Ayr: the author, 1932). Two editions of this are known. One gives the author's name on the cover and title page simply as 'E.M.', although his name appears in full at the end and as publisher. The second gives the author's name on the cover and title page as E. Middleton. Apart from some typological differences, the only difference in the text is that p.3 of the second version has an additional quotation from James Taylor. Both carry a date of 24 October 1932.

Arthur Oglesby, *The Eternal Son* (York: The author, n.d. [*c*.1930]).

———, *"Inscrutability" by J. T.* (York: the author, n.d. [*c*.1933]).

A. J. Pollock, *The Eternal Son* (London: Central Bible Truth Depot, n.d.).

———, *An Open Letter to C. A. Coates* (London: Central Bible Truth Depot, n.d).

———, *John V.26 Clearly Teaches Eternal Sonship* (London: Central Bible Truth Depot, n.d.).

John R. Stephen, *The New Hymn Book* (Aberdeen: the author, n.d.).

William Edwy Vine, *Christ's Eternal Sonship* (London and Glasgow, [1933]).

W[illiam]. H[enry]. Westcott, *A Letter on Eternal Sonship with Notes* (Sutton Coldfield: the author, 1931).

———, *The Person of the Son* (Sutton Coldfield: the author, n.d.).